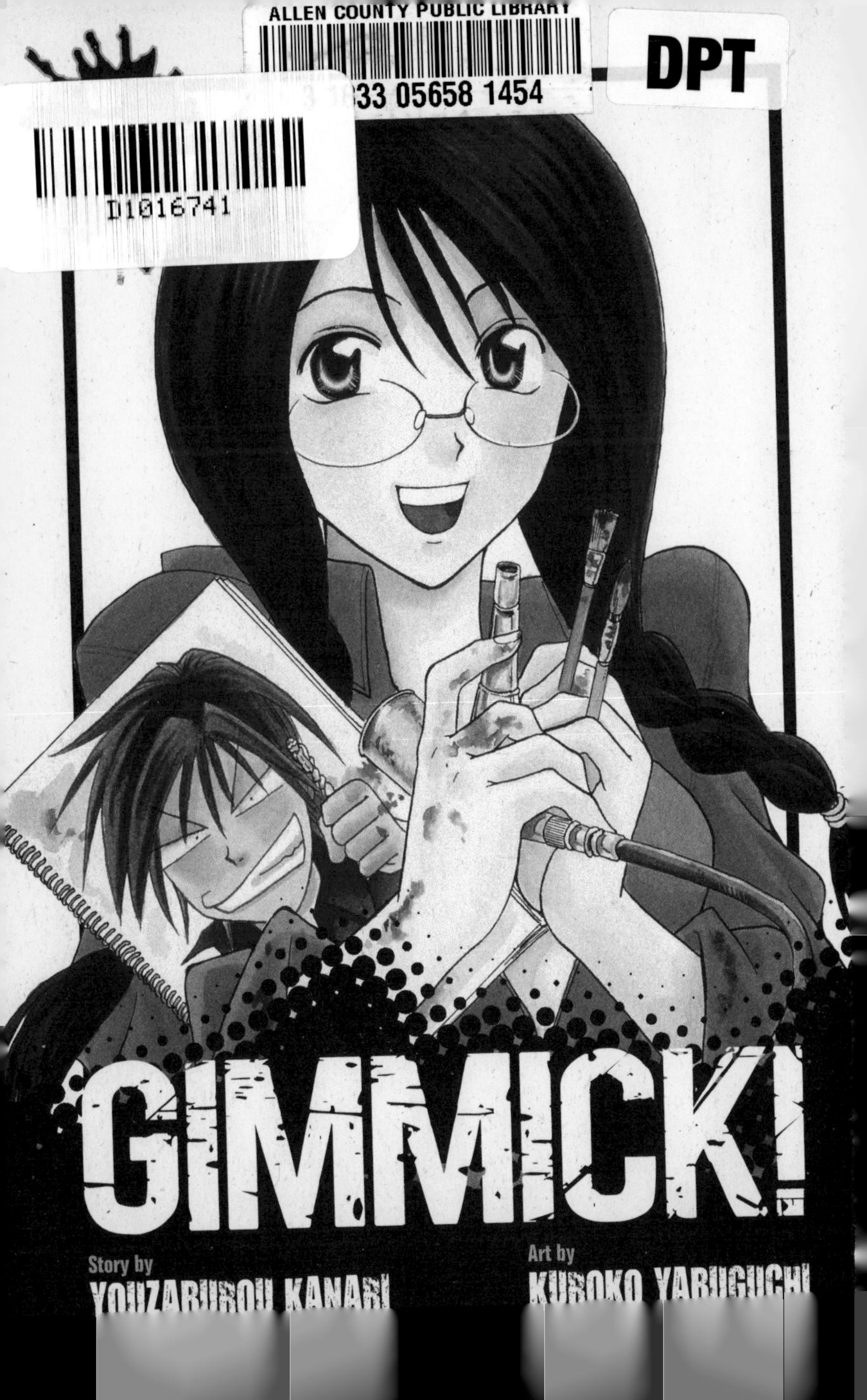

GIMMICK!

Story by
YOUZABUROU KANARI

Art by
KUROKO YABUGUCHI

GIMMICK!

CONTENTS

Scene 37	Snow Flower (Part 1)	3
Scene 38	Snow Flower (Part 2)	22
Scene 39	Field of Dreams (Part 1)	41
Scene 40	Field of Dreams (Part 2)	59
Scene 41	Field of Dreams (Part 3)	77
Scene 42	Field of Dreams (Part 4)	97
Scene 43	Field of Dreams (Part 5)	117
Scene 44	Field of Dreams (Part 6)	137
Scene EX	Old Lady Mach!!!	155
Scene 45	My Favorite Things (Part 1)	181
Scene 46	My Favorite Things (Part 2)	199

VOL 5

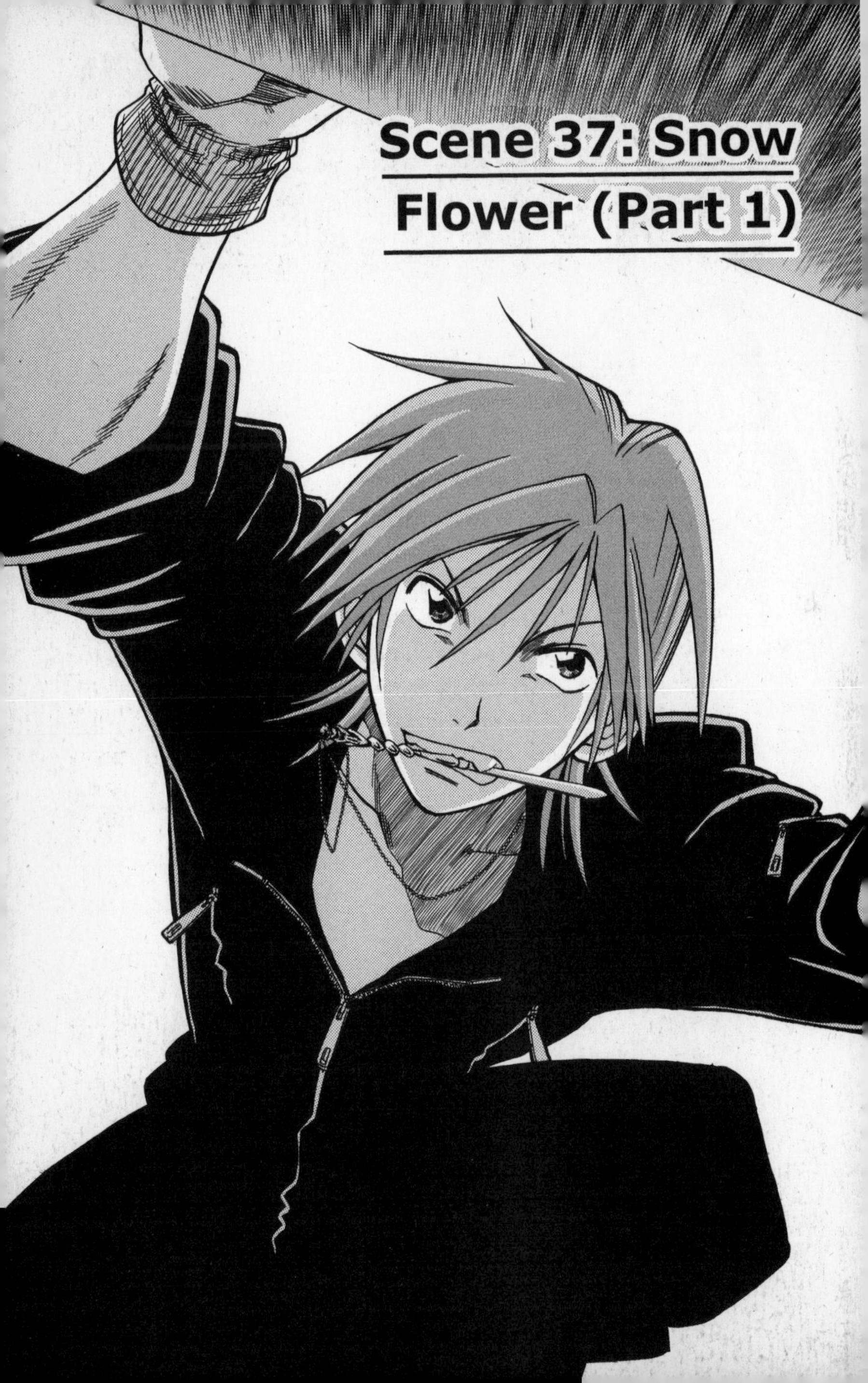
Scene 37: Snow Flower (Part 1)

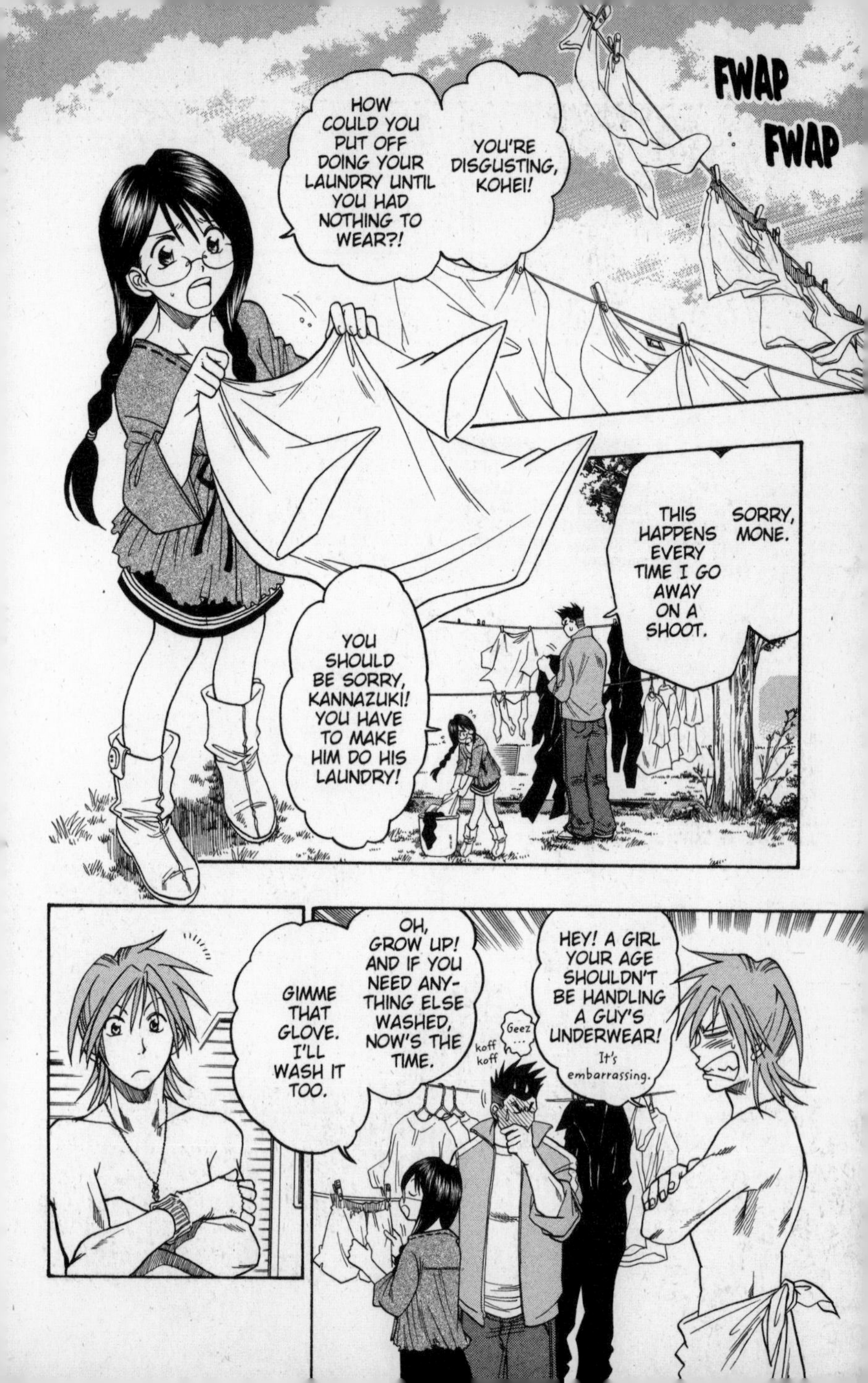
FWAP FWAP
YOU'RE DISGUSTING, KOHEI!
HOW COULD YOU PUT OFF DOING YOUR LAUNDRY UNTIL YOU HAD NOTHING TO WEAR?!
SORRY, MONE.
THIS HAPPENS EVERY TIME I GO AWAY ON A SHOOT.
YOU SHOULD BE SORRY, KANNAZUKI! YOU HAVE TO MAKE HIM DO HIS LAUNDRY!
HEY! A GIRL YOUR AGE SHOULDN'T BE HANDLING A GUY'S UNDERWEAR!
It's embarrassing.
Geez ...
koff koff
OH, GROW UP! AND IF YOU NEED ANY-THING ELSE WASHED, NOW'S THE TIME.
GIMME THAT GLOVE. I'LL WASH IT TOO.

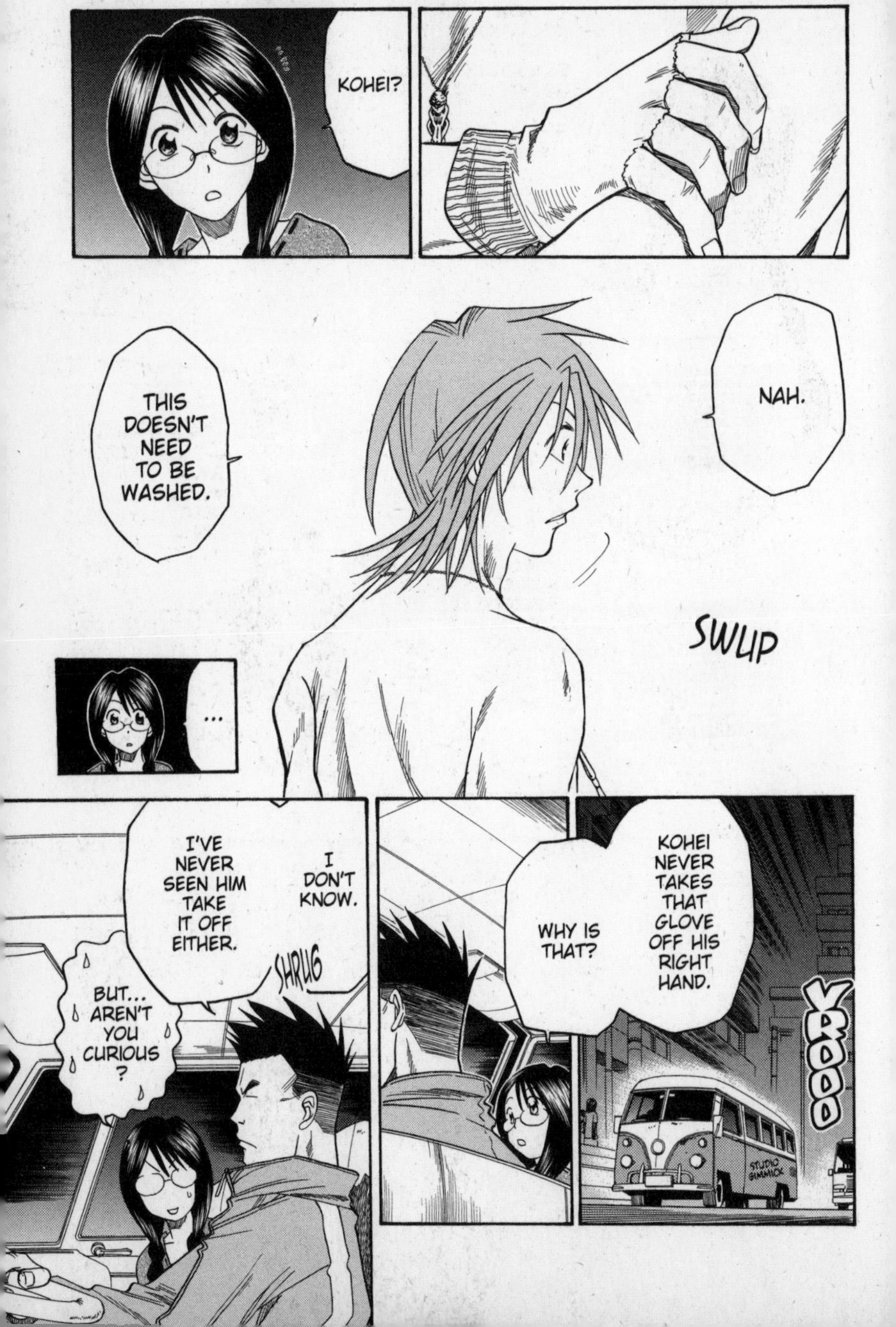
KOHEI?
NAH.
THIS DOESN'T NEED TO BE WASHED.
SWUP
...
VROOOO
STUDIO GIMMICK
KOHEI NEVER TAKES THAT GLOVE OFF HIS RIGHT HAND.
WHY IS THAT?
I DON'T KNOW.
I'VE NEVER SEEN HIM TAKE IT OFF EITHER.
SHRUG
BUT... AREN'T YOU CURIOUS?

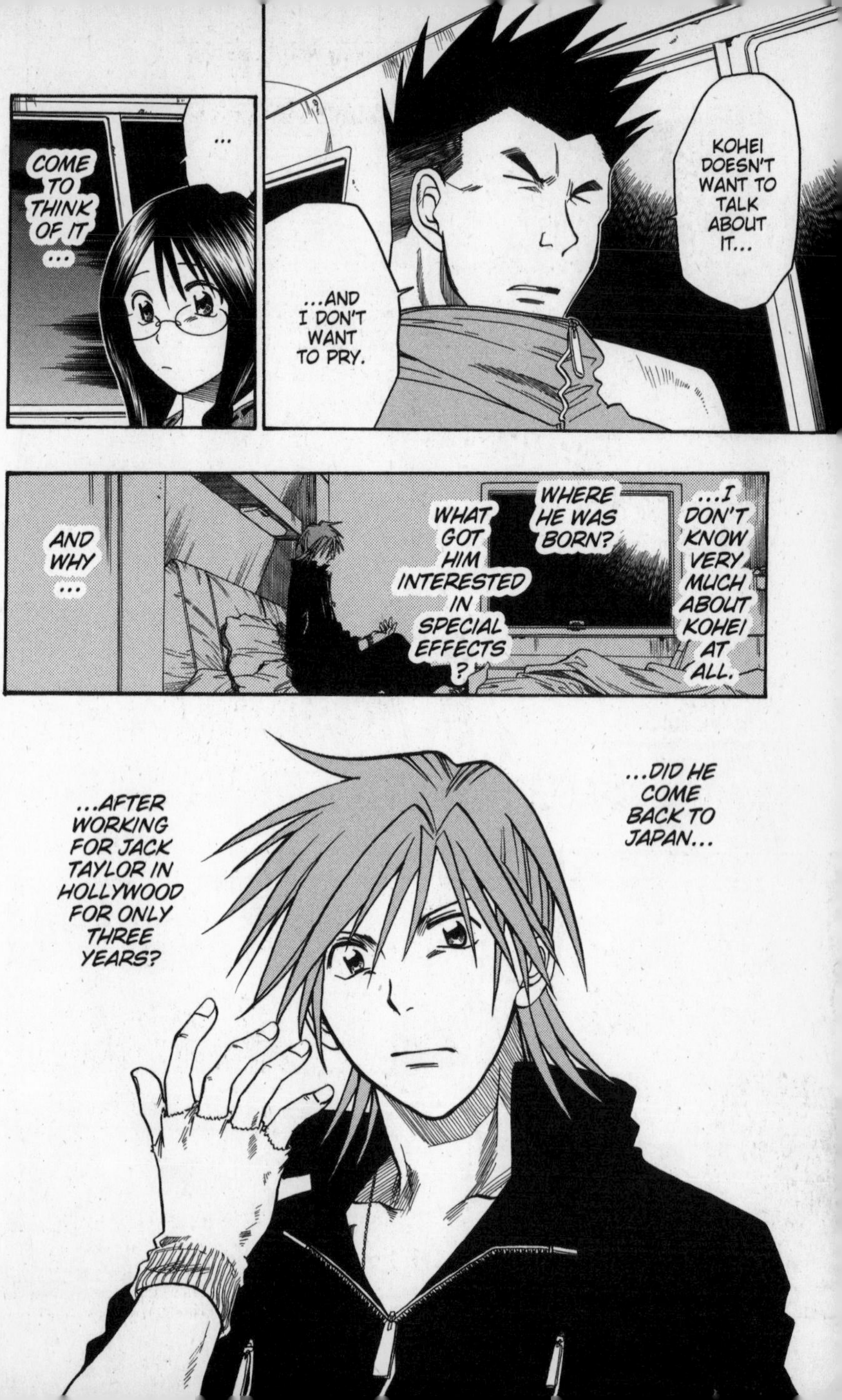
KOHEI DOESN'T WANT TO TALK ABOUT IT...
...AND I DON'T WANT TO PRY.
...
COME TO THINK OF IT...
...I DON'T KNOW VERY MUCH ABOUT KOHEI AT ALL.
WHERE HE WAS BORN?
WHAT GOT HIM INTERESTED IN SPECIAL EFFECTS?
AND WHY...
...DID HE COME BACK TO JAPAN...
...AFTER WORKING FOR JACK TAYLOR IN HOLLYWOOD FOR ONLY THREE YEARS?

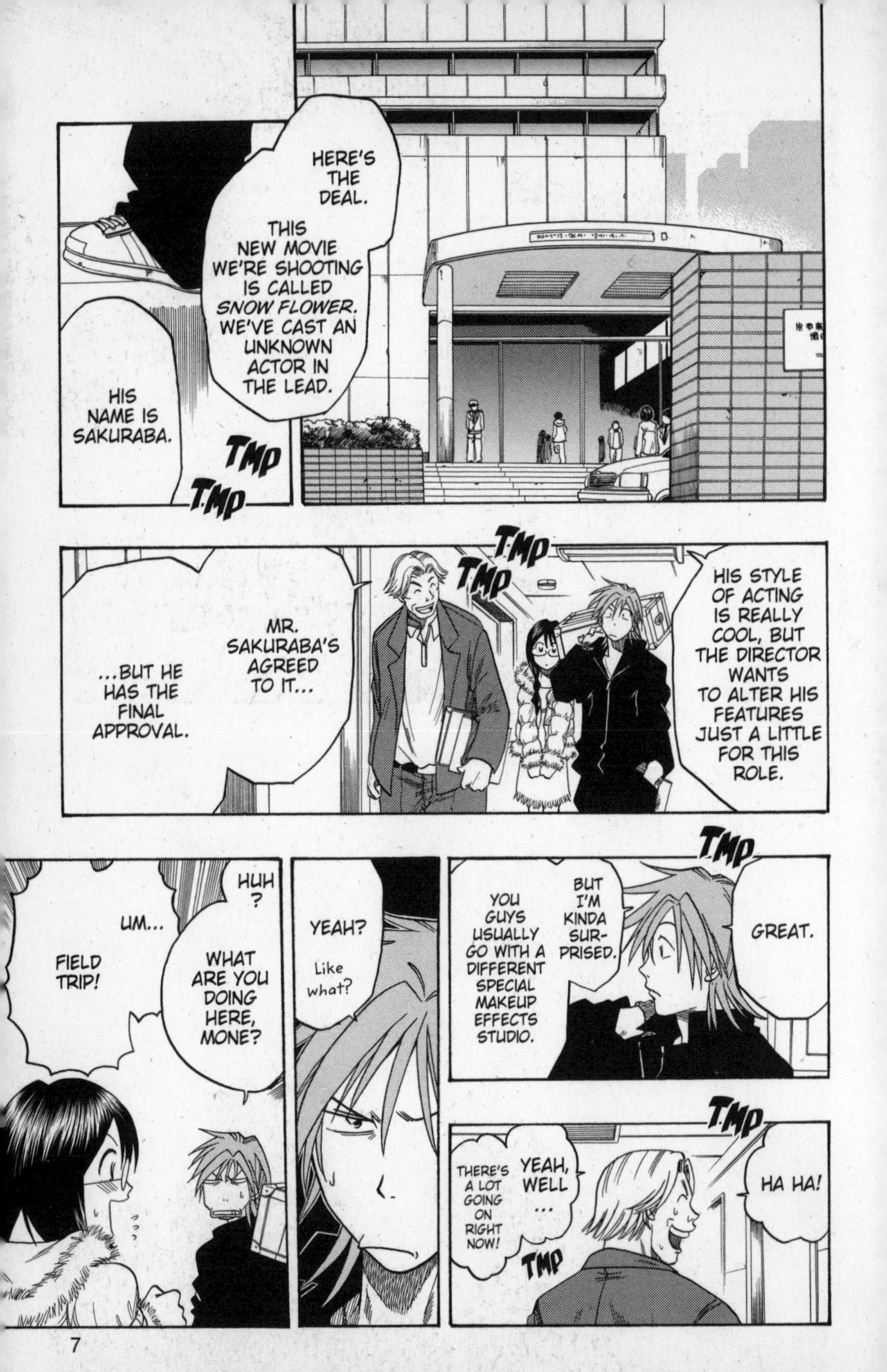
HERE'S THE DEAL.
THIS NEW MOVIE WE'RE SHOOTING IS CALLED SNOW FLOWER. WE'VE CAST AN UNKNOWN ACTOR IN THE LEAD.
HIS NAME IS SAKURABA.
TMP
TMP
TMP
TMP
HIS STYLE OF ACTING IS REALLY COOL, BUT THE DIRECTOR WANTS TO ALTER HIS FEATURES JUST A LITTLE FOR THIS ROLE.
MR. SAKURABA'S AGREED TO IT...
...BUT HE HAS THE FINAL APPROVAL.
TMP
GREAT.
BUT I'M KINDA SUR-PRISED.
YOU GUYS USUALLY GO WITH A DIFFERENT SPECIAL MAKEUP EFFECTS STUDIO.
TMP
HA HA!
YEAH, WELL ...
THERE'S A LOT GOING ON RIGHT NOW!
TMP
YEAH?
Like what?
HUH?
WHAT ARE YOU DOING HERE, MONE?
UM...
FIELD TRIP!

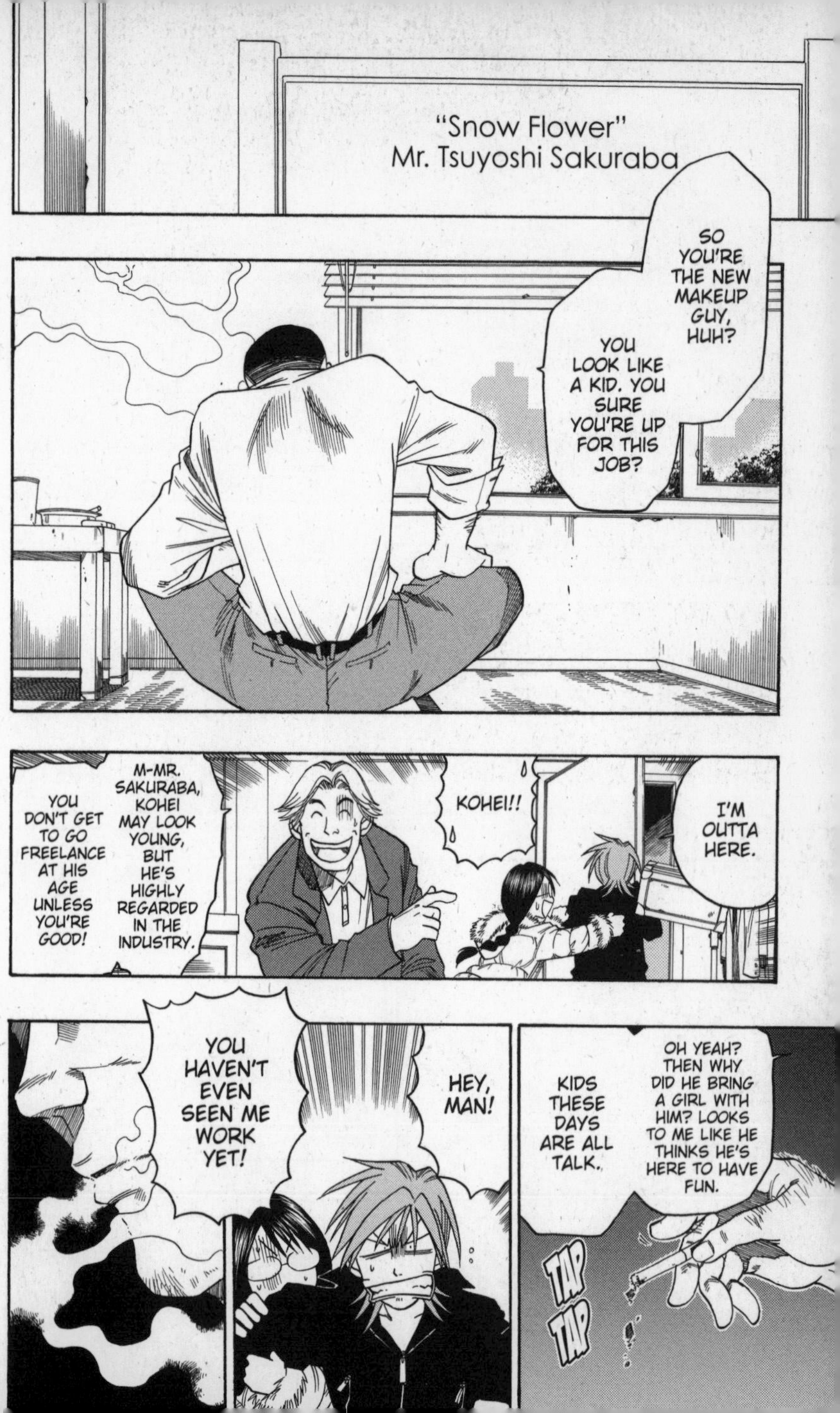

"Snow Flower"
Mr. Tsuyoshi Sakuraba
SO YOU'RE THE NEW MAKEUP GUY, HUH?
YOU LOOK LIKE A KID. YOU SURE YOU'RE UP FOR THIS JOB?
I'M OUTTA HERE.
KOHEI!!
M-MR. SAKURABA, KOHEI MAY LOOK YOUNG, BUT HE'S HIGHLY REGARDED IN THE INDUSTRY.
YOU DON'T GET TO GO FREELANCE AT HIS AGE UNLESS YOU'RE GOOD!
OH YEAH? THEN WHY DID HE BRING A GIRL WITH HIM? LOOKS TO ME LIKE HE THINKS HE'S HERE TO HAVE FUN.
KIDS THESE DAYS ARE ALL TALK.
TAP TAP
HEY, MAN!
YOU HAVEN'T EVEN SEEN ME WORK YET!

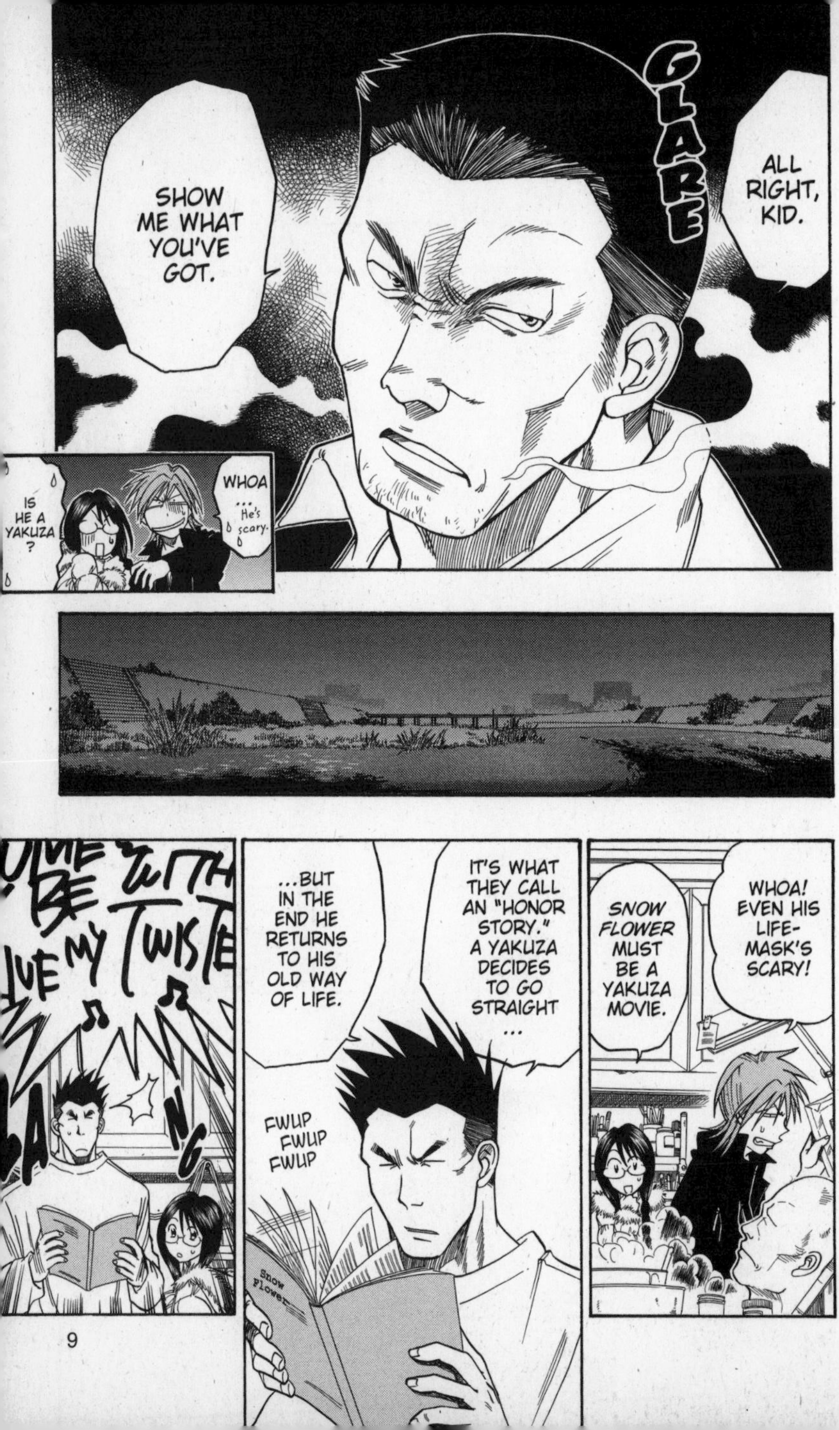
ALL RIGHT, KID.
GLARE
SHOW ME WHAT YOU'VE GOT.
WHOA... He's scary.
IS HE A YAKUZA?
WHOA! EVEN HIS LIFE-MASK'S SCARY!
SNOW FLOWER MUST BE A YAKUZA MOVIE.
IT'S WHAT THEY CALL AN "HONOR STORY." A YAKUZA DECIDES TO GO STRAIGHT...
...BUT IN THE END HE RETURNS TO HIS OLD WAY OF LIFE.
FWUP FWUP FWUP
Snow Flower

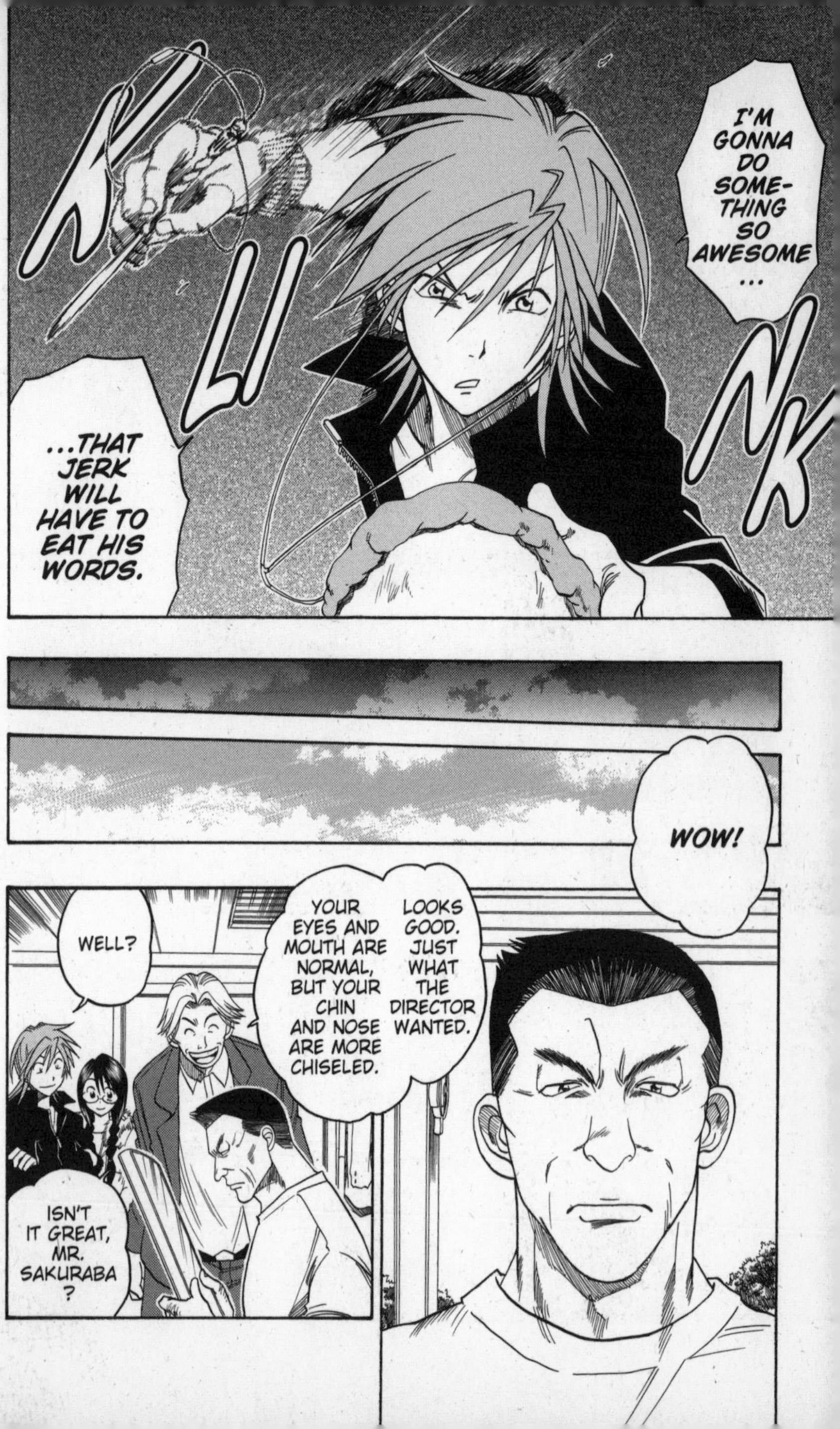
I'M GONNA DO SOMETHING SO AWESOME...
...THAT JERK WILL HAVE TO EAT HIS WORDS.
KLINK
WOW!
WELL?
YOUR EYES AND MOUTH ARE NORMAL, BUT YOUR CHIN AND NOSE ARE MORE CHISELED.
LOOKS GOOD. JUST WHAT THE DIRECTOR WANTED.
ISN'T IT GREAT, MR. SAKURABA?

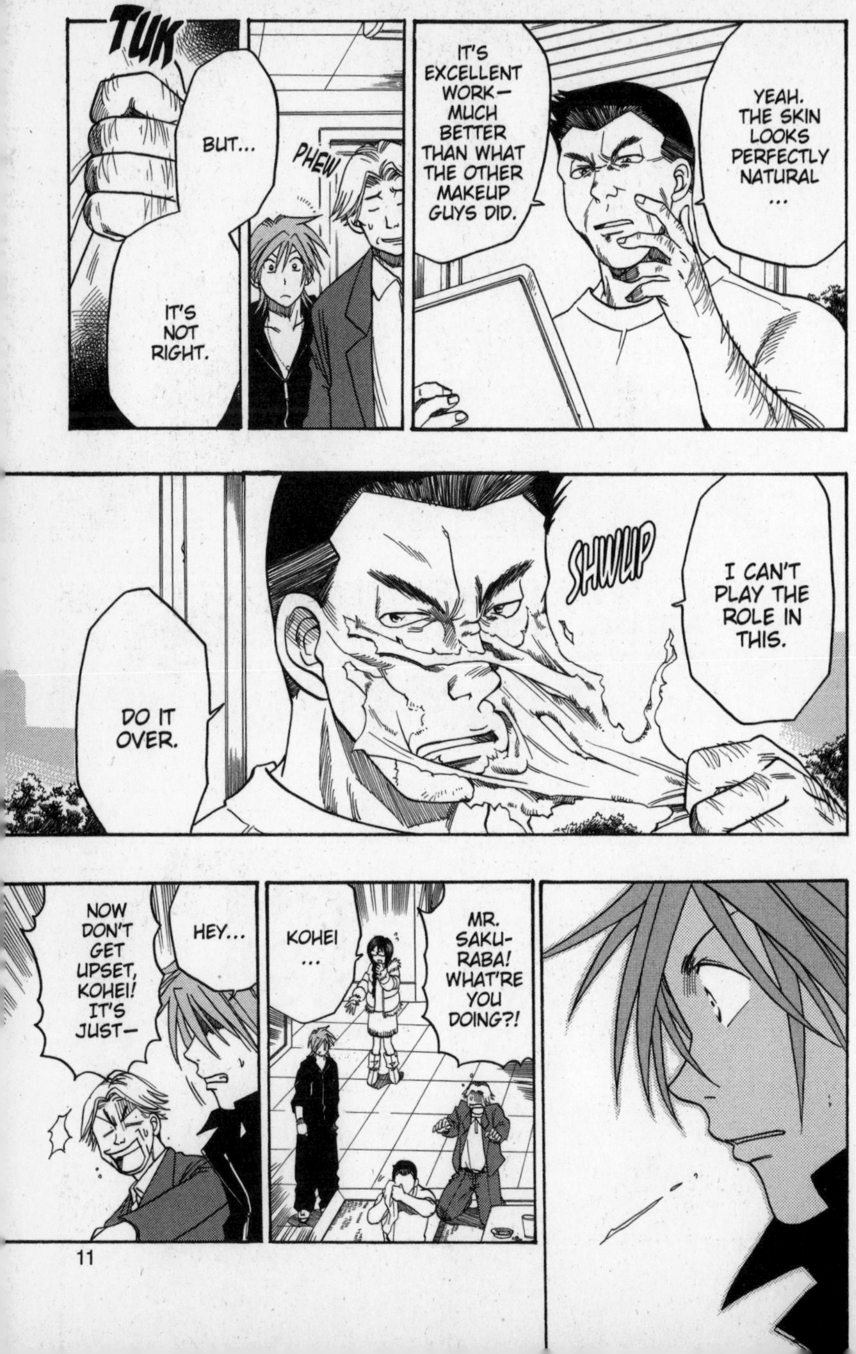
YEAH. THE SKIN LOOKS PERFECTLY NATURAL ...
IT'S EXCELLENT WORK— MUCH BETTER THAN WHAT THE OTHER MAKEUP GUYS DID.
PHEW
TUK
BUT...
IT'S NOT RIGHT.
I CAN'T PLAY THE ROLE IN THIS.
SHWLIP
DO IT OVER.
MR. SAKU-RABA! WHAT'RE YOU DOING?!
KOHEI ...
HEY...
NOW DON'T GET UPSET, KOHEI! IT'S JUST—

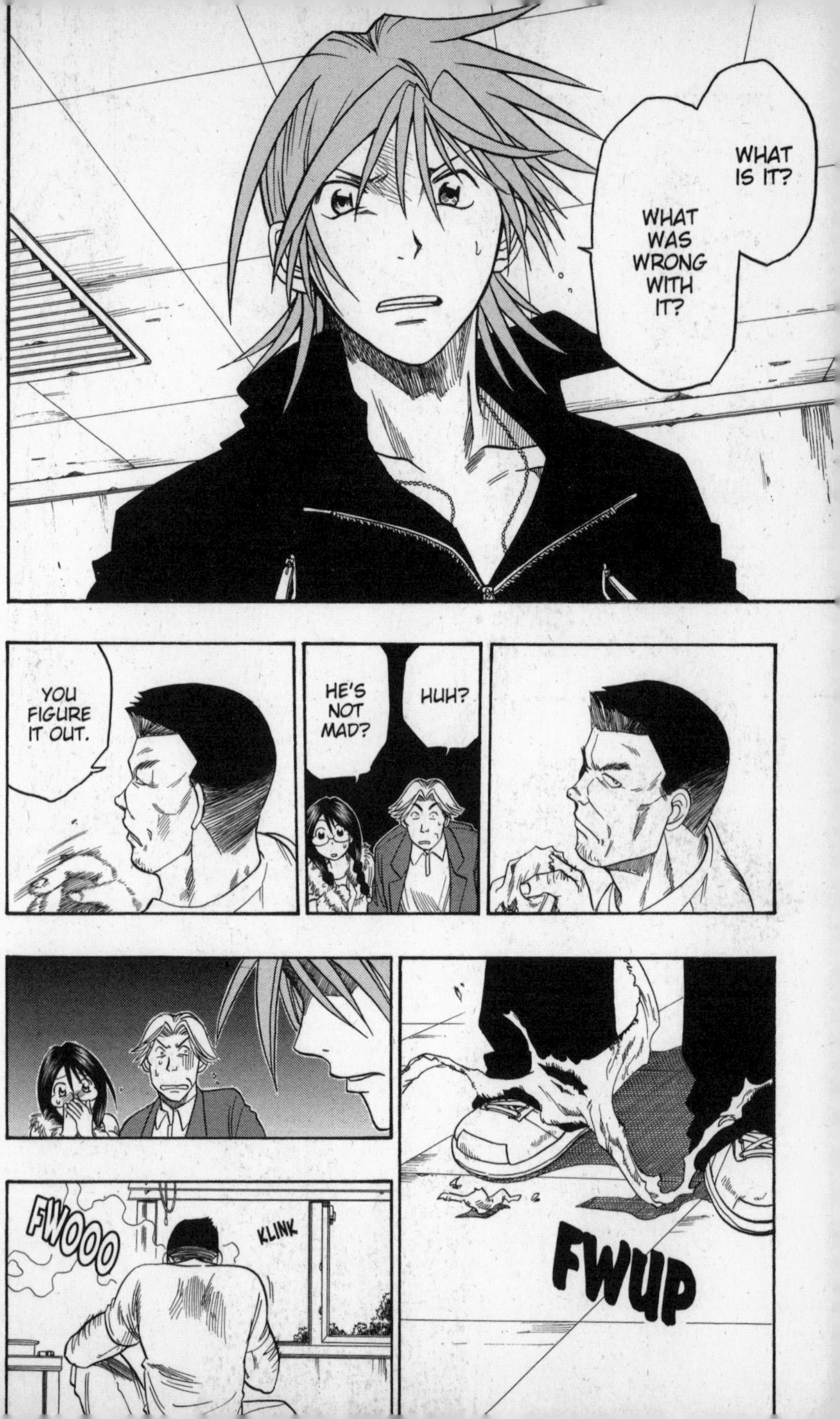
WHAT IS IT?
WHAT WAS WRONG WITH IT?
HUH?
HE'S NOT MAD?
YOU FIGURE IT OUT.
FWUP
KLINK
FWOOO

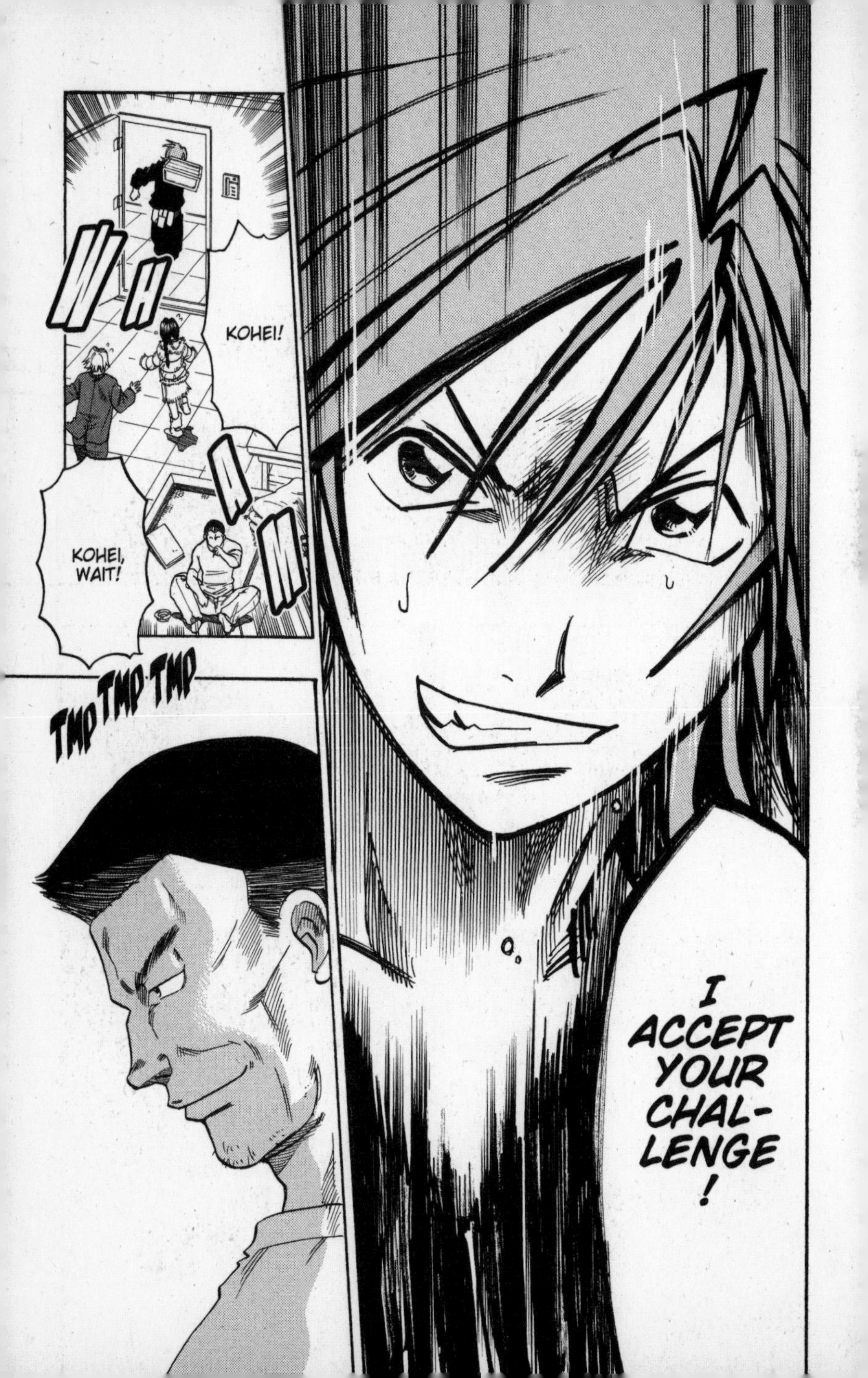
I ACCEPT YOUR CHAL-LENGE!
WHAM
KOHEI!
KOHEI, WAIT!
TMP TMP TMP

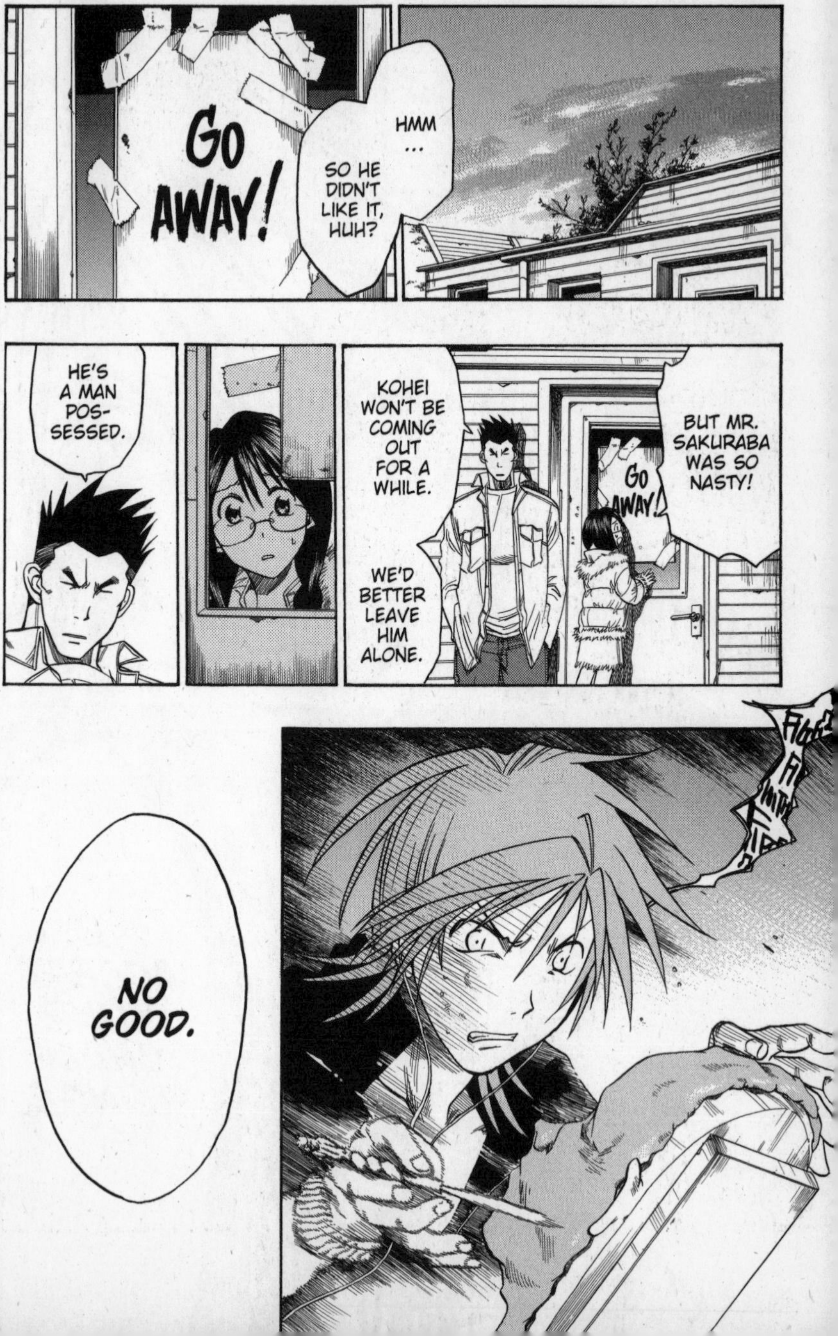
HMM... SO HE DIDN'T LIKE IT, HUH?
GO AWAY!
BUT MR. SAKURABA WAS SO NASTY!
GO AWAY!
KOHEI WON'T BE COMING OUT FOR A WHILE.
WE'D BETTER LEAVE HIM ALONE.
HE'S A MAN POS-SESSED.
NO GOOD.

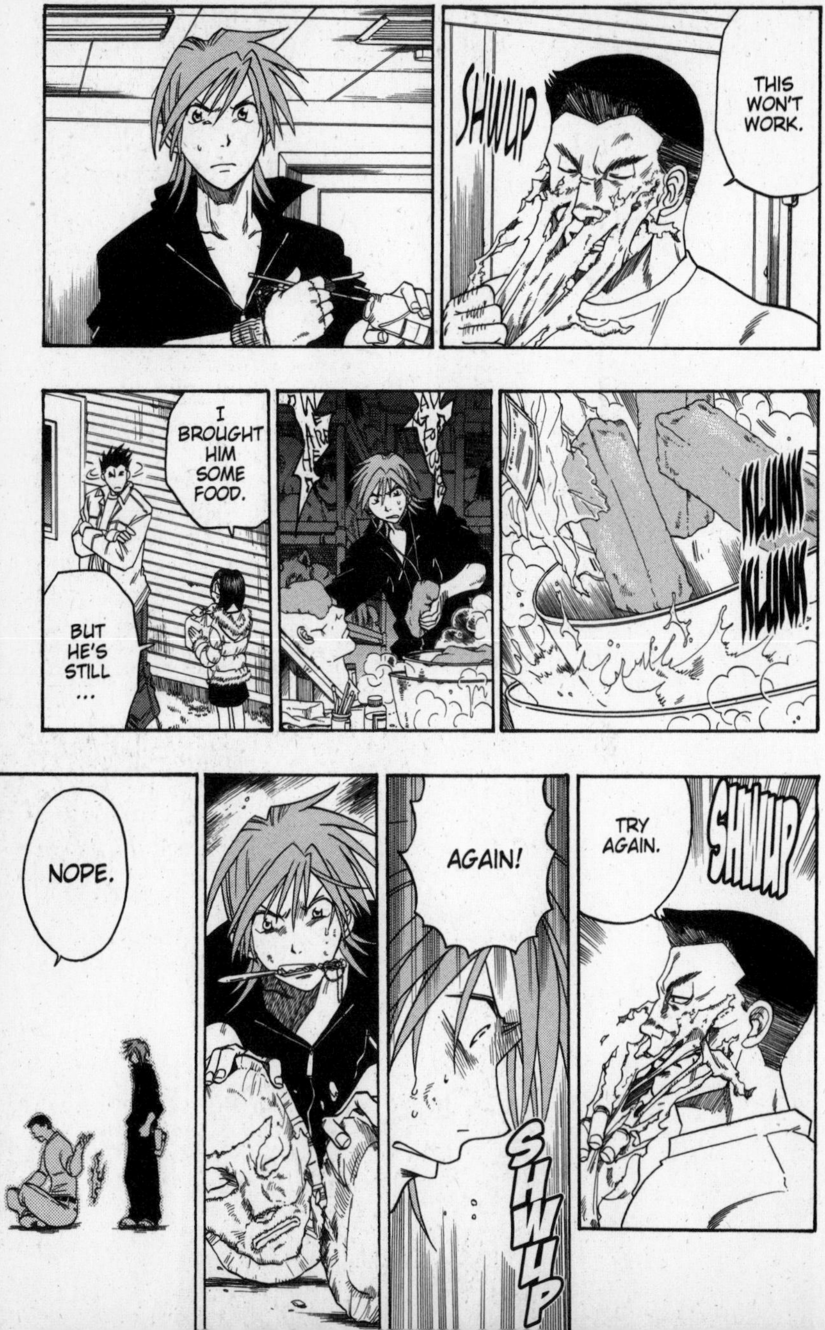
SHWUP
THIS WON'T WORK.
KLUNK KLUNK
I BROUGHT HIM SOME FOOD.
BUT HE'S STILL ...
SHWUP
TRY AGAIN.
AGAIN!
SHWUP
NOPE.

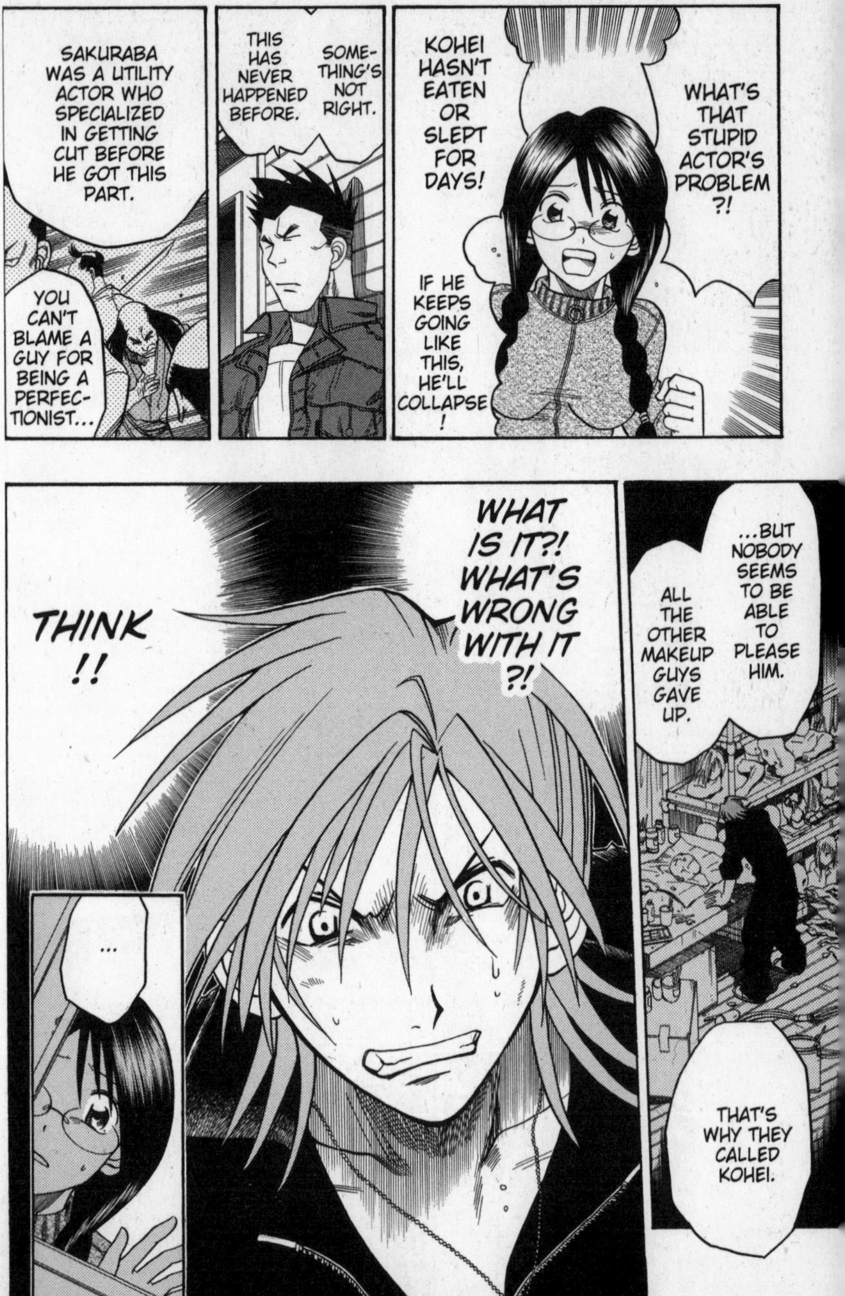
WHAT'S THAT STUPID ACTOR'S PROBLEM ?!
KOHEI HASN'T EATEN OR SLEPT FOR DAYS!
IF HE KEEPS GOING LIKE THIS, HE'LL COLLAPSE !
SOMETHING'S NOT RIGHT.
THIS HAS NEVER HAPPENED BEFORE.
SAKURABA WAS A UTILITY ACTOR WHO SPECIALIZED IN GETTING CUT BEFORE HE GOT THIS PART.
YOU CAN'T BLAME A GUY FOR BEING A PERFECTIONIST…
…BUT NOBODY SEEMS TO BE ABLE TO PLEASE HIM.
ALL THE OTHER MAKEUP GUYS GAVE UP.
THAT'S WHY THEY CALLED KOHEI.
WHAT IS IT?! WHAT'S WRONG WITH IT ?!
THINK !!
…

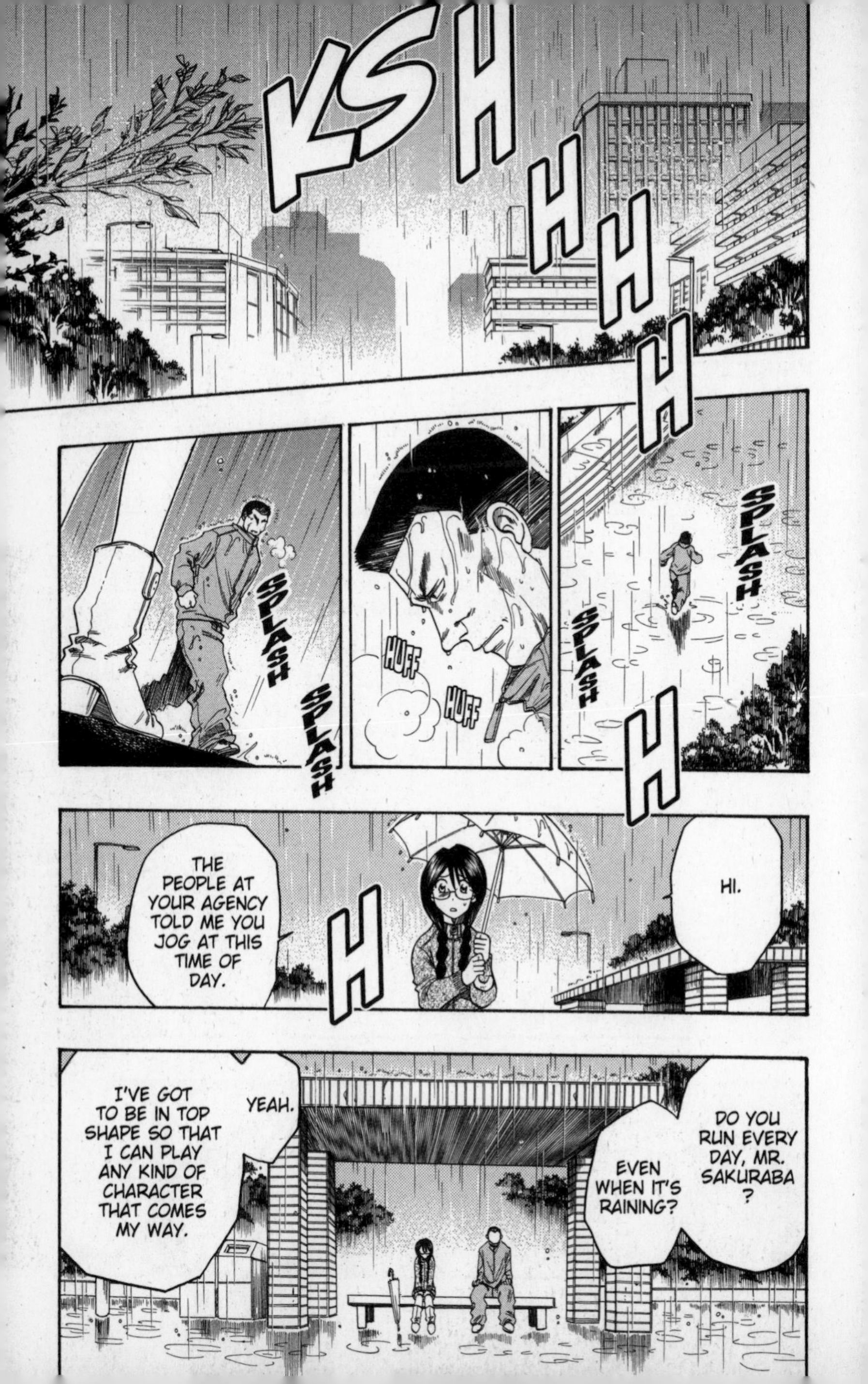
KSHHHHHHH
SPLASH
SPLASH
HUFF
HUFF
SPLASH
SPLASH
HI.
THE PEOPLE AT YOUR AGENCY TOLD ME YOU JOG AT THIS TIME OF DAY.
DO YOU RUN EVERY DAY, MR. SAKURABA?
EVEN WHEN IT'S RAINING?
YEAH.
I'VE GOT TO BE IN TOP SHAPE SO THAT I CAN PLAY ANY KIND OF CHARACTER THAT COMES MY WAY.

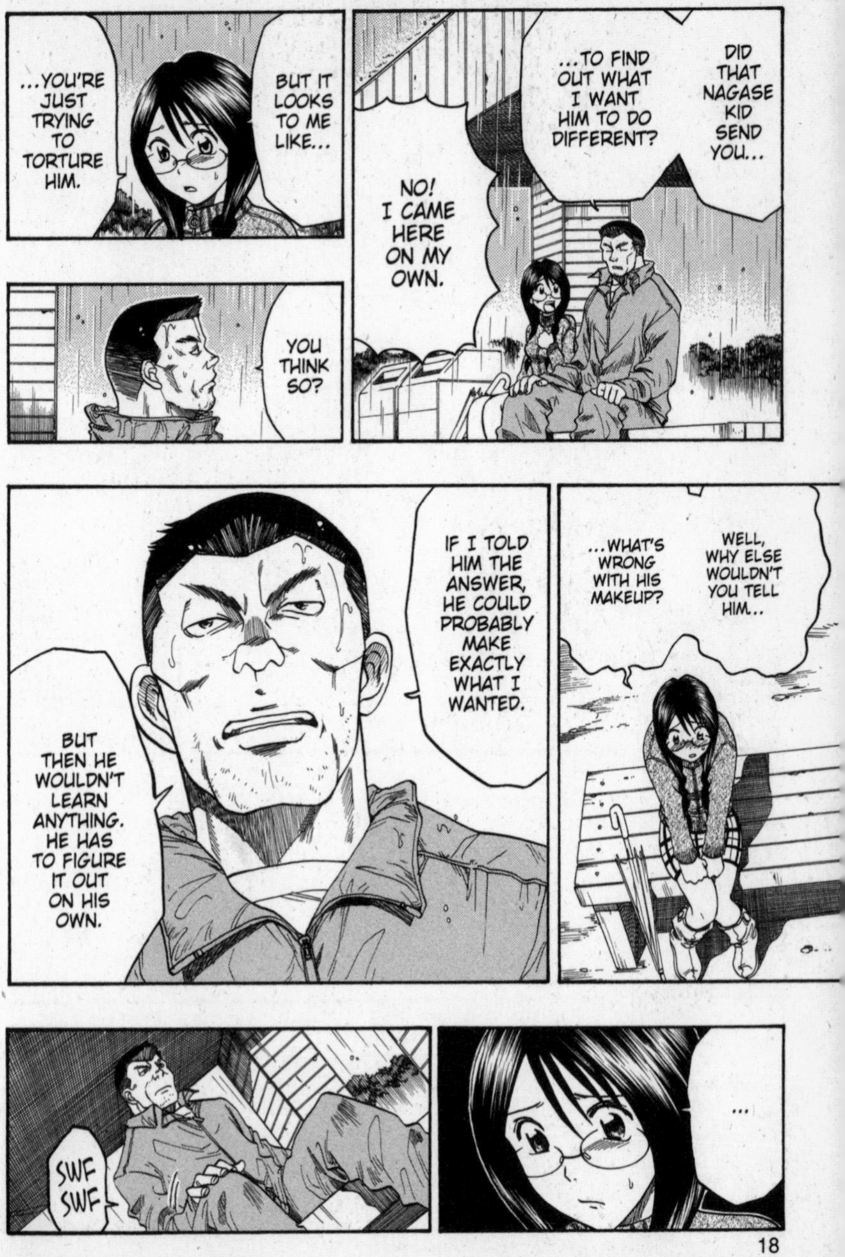
DID THAT NAGASE KID SEND YOU...
...TO FIND OUT WHAT I WANT HIM TO DO DIFFERENT?
NO! I CAME HERE ON MY OWN.
BUT IT LOOKS TO ME LIKE...
...YOU'RE JUST TRYING TO TORTURE HIM.
YOU THINK SO?
WELL, WHY ELSE WOULDN'T YOU TELL HIM..
...WHAT'S WRONG WITH HIS MAKEUP?
IF I TOLD HIM THE ANSWER, HE COULD PROBABLY MAKE EXACTLY WHAT I WANTED.
BUT THEN HE WOULDN'T LEARN ANYTHING. HE HAS TO FIGURE IT OUT ON HIS OWN.
...
SWF SWF

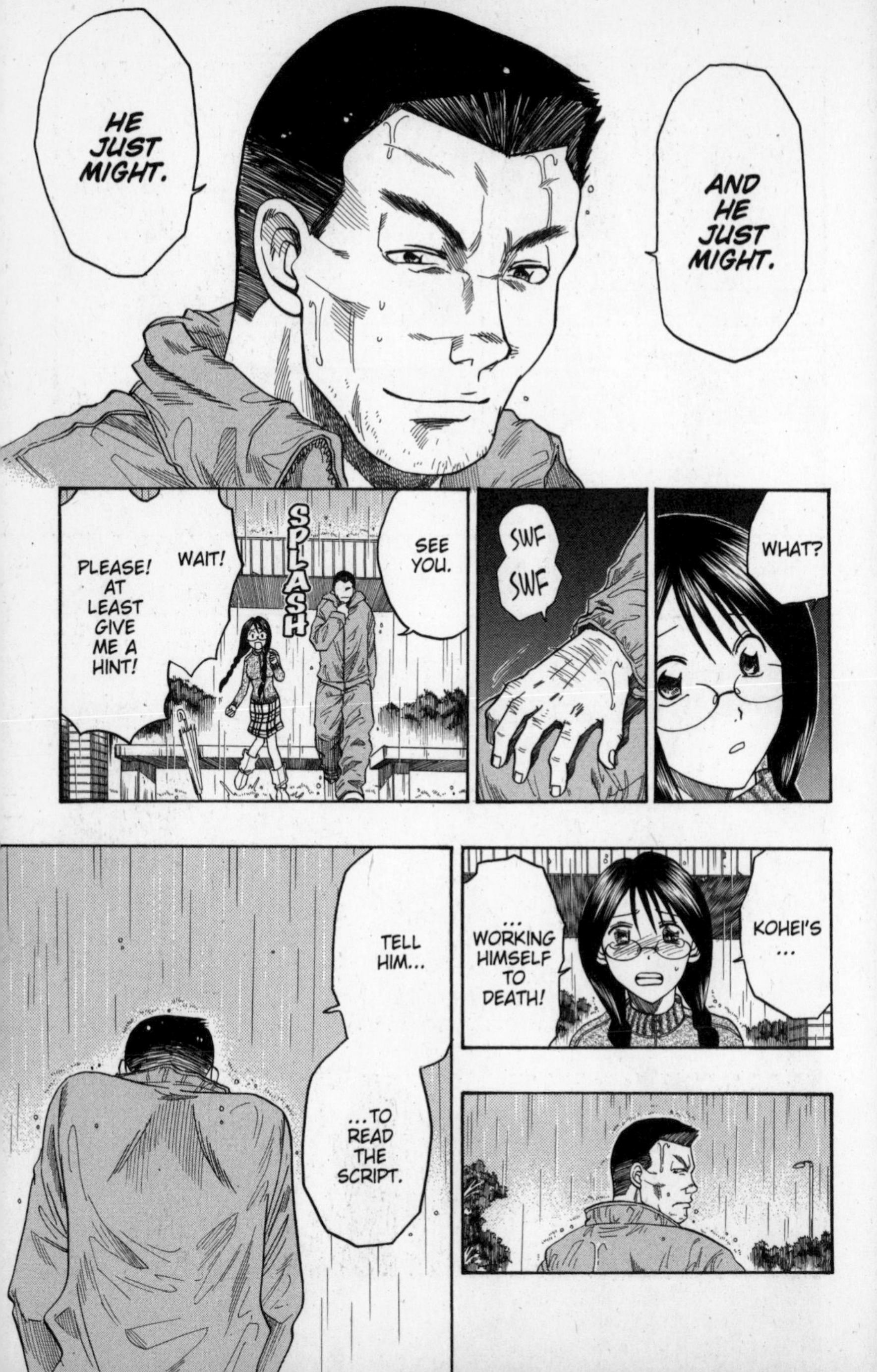
AND HE JUST MIGHT.
HE JUST MIGHT.
WHAT?
SWF SWF
SEE YOU.
SPLASH
WAIT!
PLEASE! AT LEAST GIVE ME A HINT!
KOHEI'S ...
... WORKING HIMSELF TO DEATH!
TELL HIM...
...TO READ THE SCRIPT.

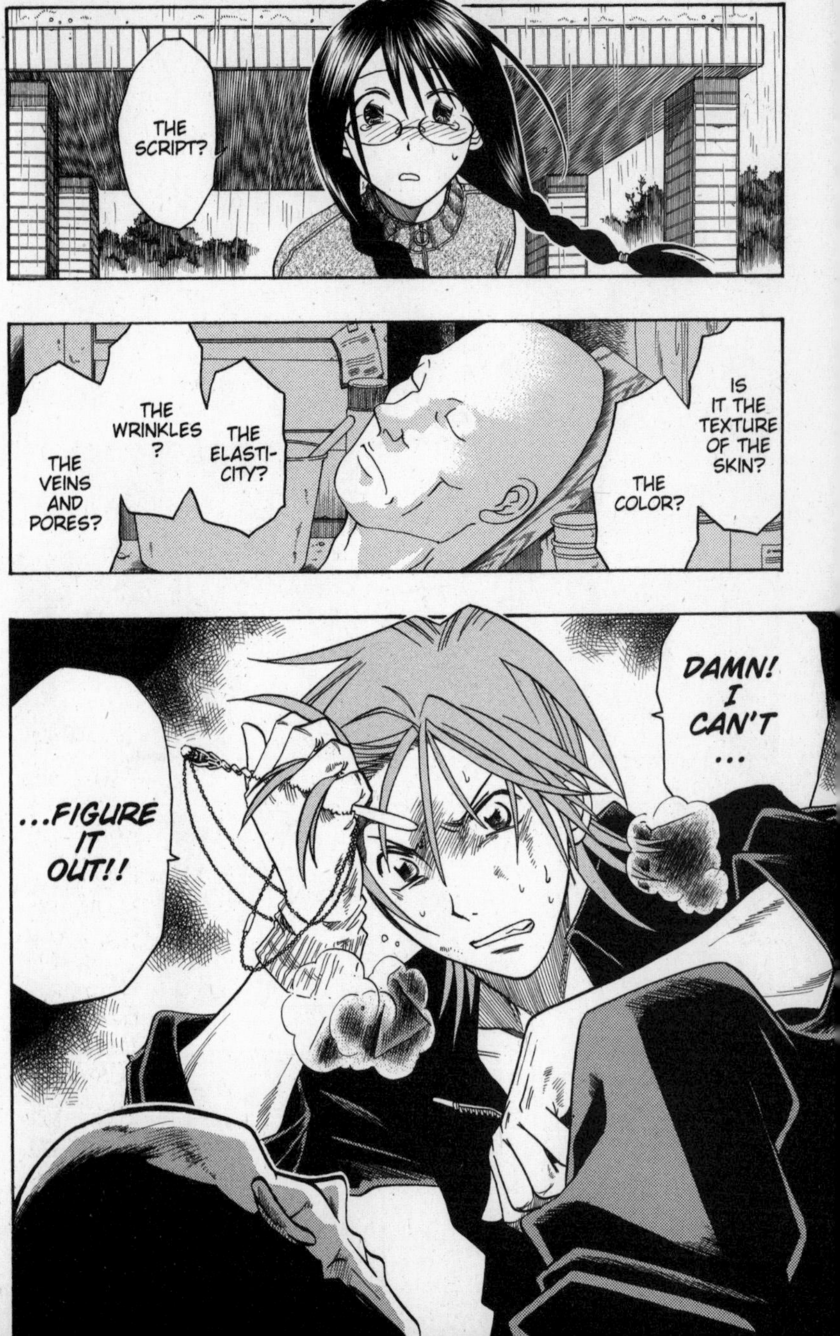
THE SCRIPT?
IS IT THE TEXTURE OF THE SKIN?
THE COLOR?
THE ELASTICITY?
THE WRINKLES?
THE VEINS AND PORES?
DAMN! I CAN'T ...
...FIGURE IT OUT!!

GIMMICK!

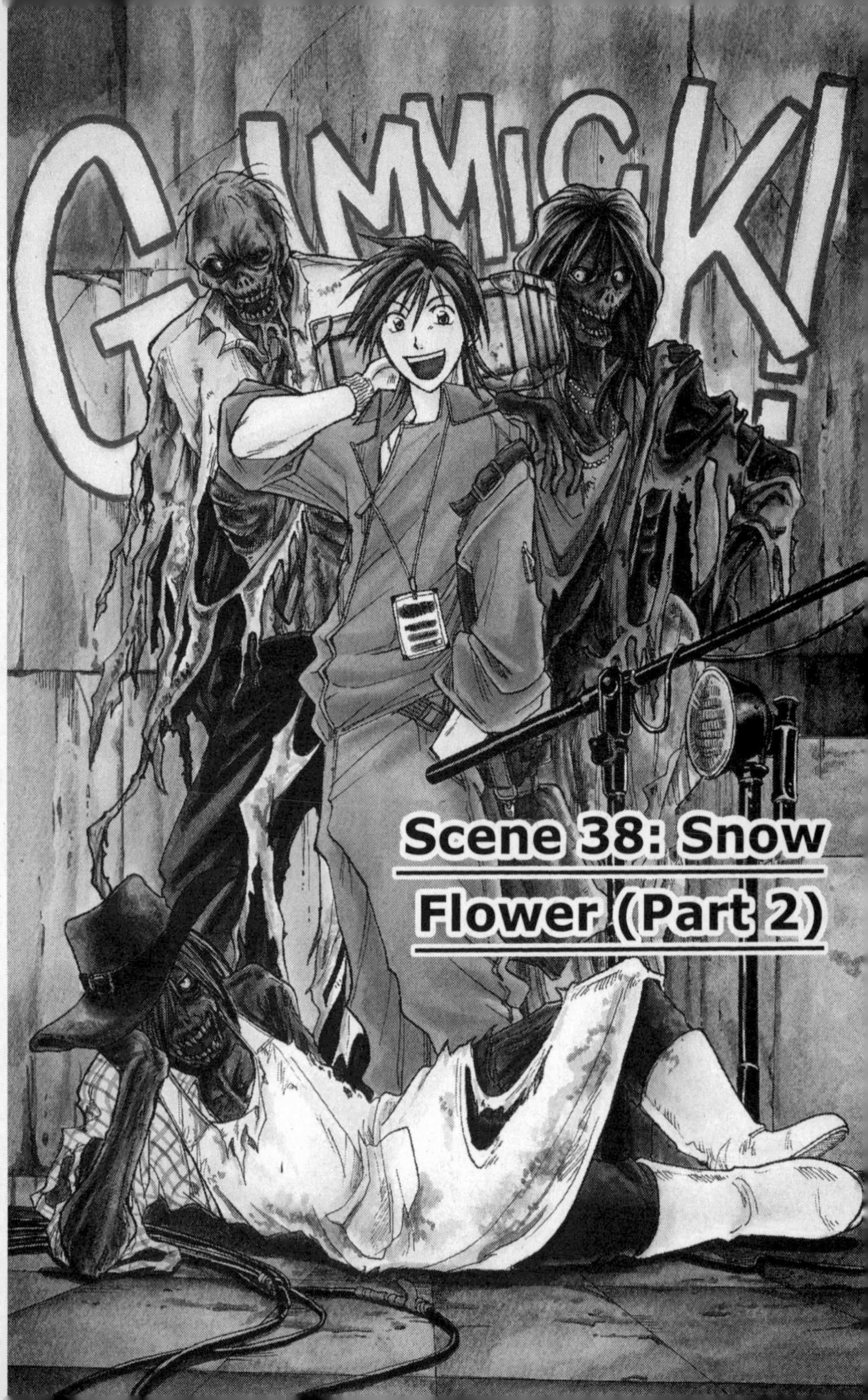
GIMMICK!
Scene 38: Snow Flower (Part 2)

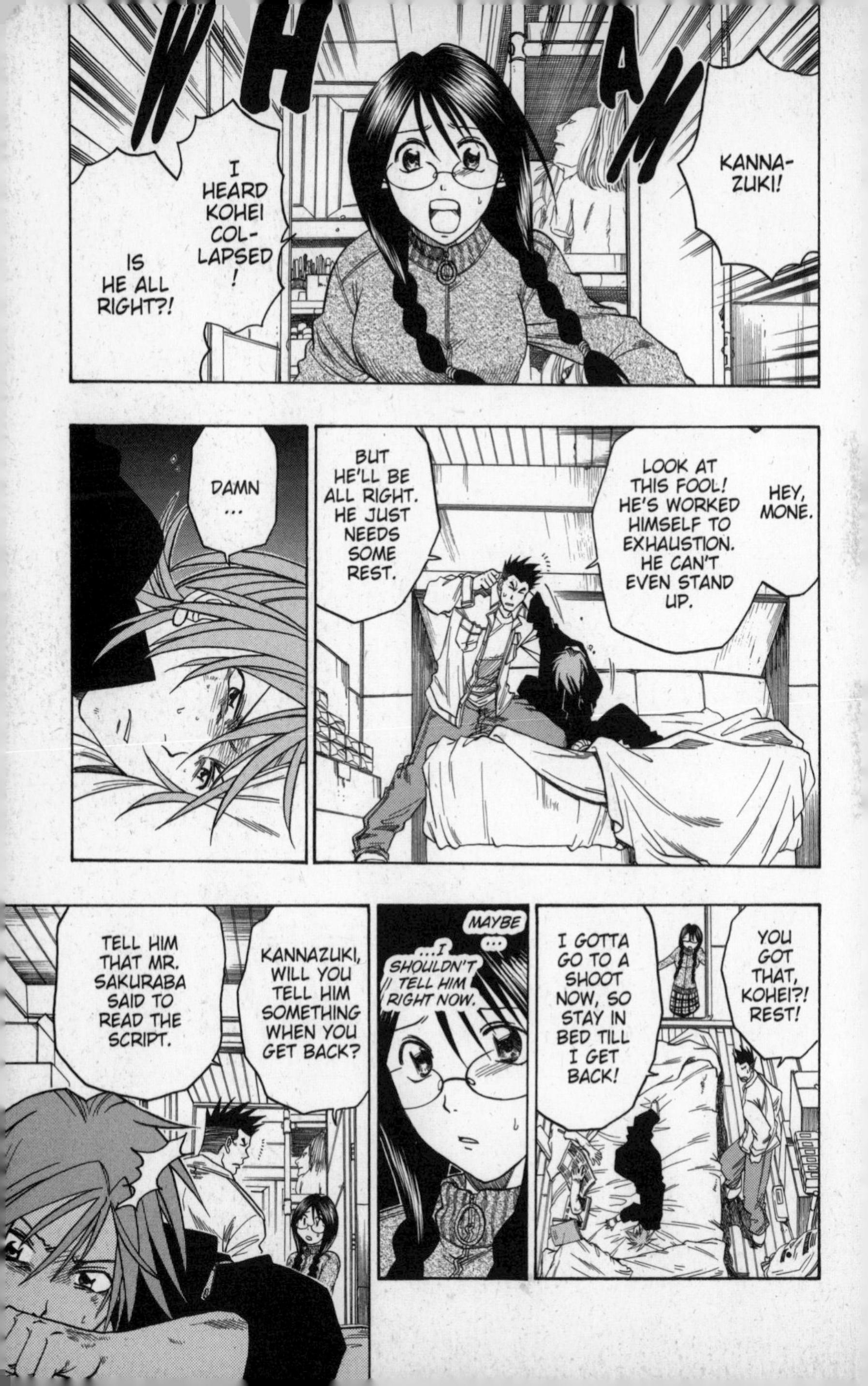

WHAM
KANNA-ZUKI!
I HEARD KOHEI COL-LAPSED!
IS HE ALL RIGHT?!
HEY, MONE.
LOOK AT THIS FOOL! HE'S WORKED HIMSELF TO EXHAUSTION. HE CAN'T EVEN STAND UP.
BUT HE'LL BE ALL RIGHT. HE JUST NEEDS SOME REST.
DAMN ...
YOU GOT THAT, KOHEI?! REST!
I GOTTA GO TO A SHOOT NOW, SO STAY IN BED TILL I GET BACK!
MAYBE ...
...I SHOULDN'T TELL HIM RIGHT NOW.
KANNAZUKI, WILL YOU TELL HIM SOMETHING WHEN YOU GET BACK?
TELL HIM THAT MR. SAKURABA SAID TO READ THE SCRIPT.

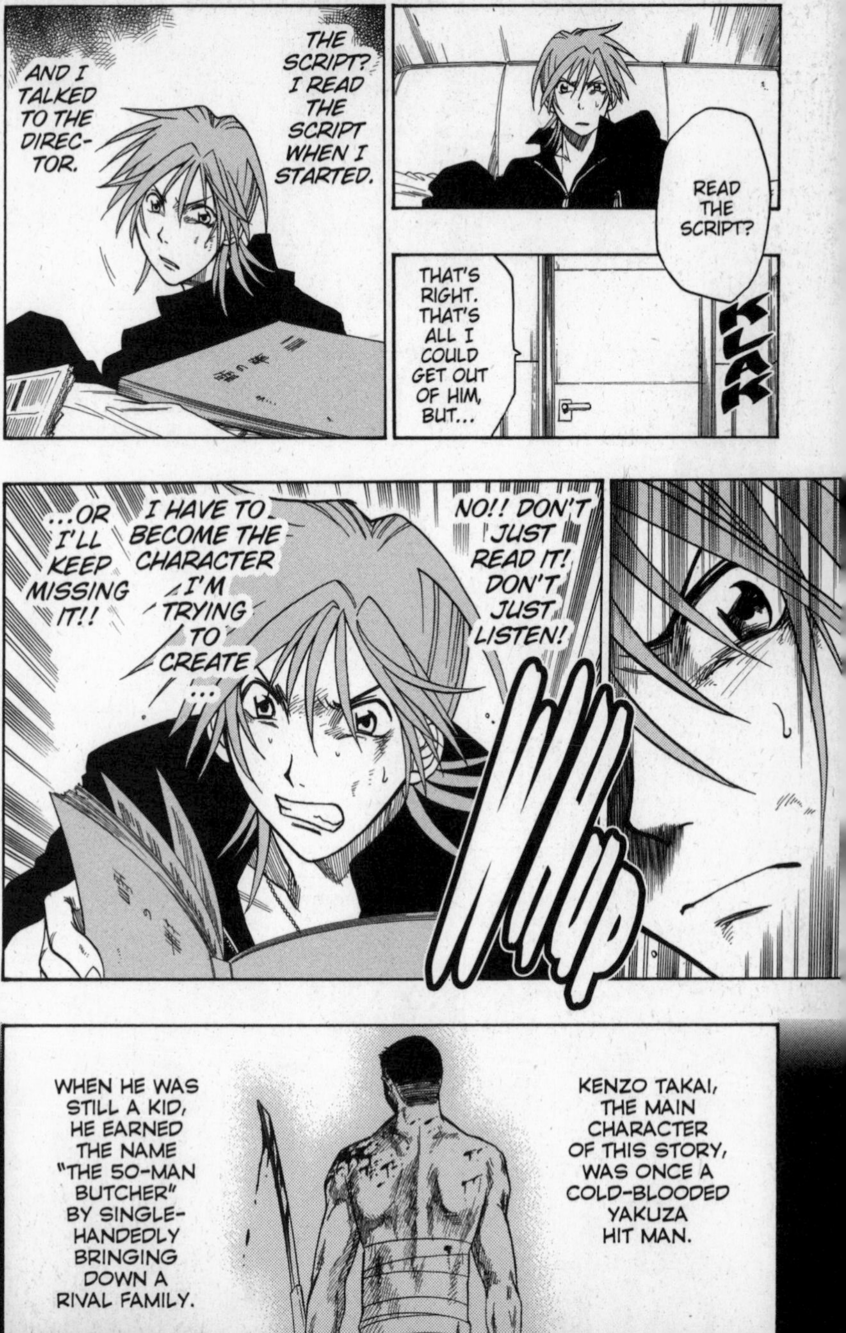
READ THE SCRIPT?
THE SCRIPT? I READ THE SCRIPT WHEN I STARTED.
AND I TALKED TO THE DIRECTOR.
KLAK
THAT'S RIGHT. THAT'S ALL I COULD GET OUT OF HIM, BUT...
WHUP
NO!! DON'T JUST READ IT! DON'T JUST LISTEN!
I HAVE TO BECOME THE CHARACTER I'M TRYING TO CREATE...
...OR I'LL KEEP MISSING IT!!
KENZO TAKAI, THE MAIN CHARACTER OF THIS STORY, WAS ONCE A COLD-BLOODED YAKUZA HIT MAN.
WHEN HE WAS STILL A KID, HE EARNED THE NAME "THE 50-MAN BUTCHER" BY SINGLE-HANDEDLY BRINGING DOWN A RIVAL FAMILY.

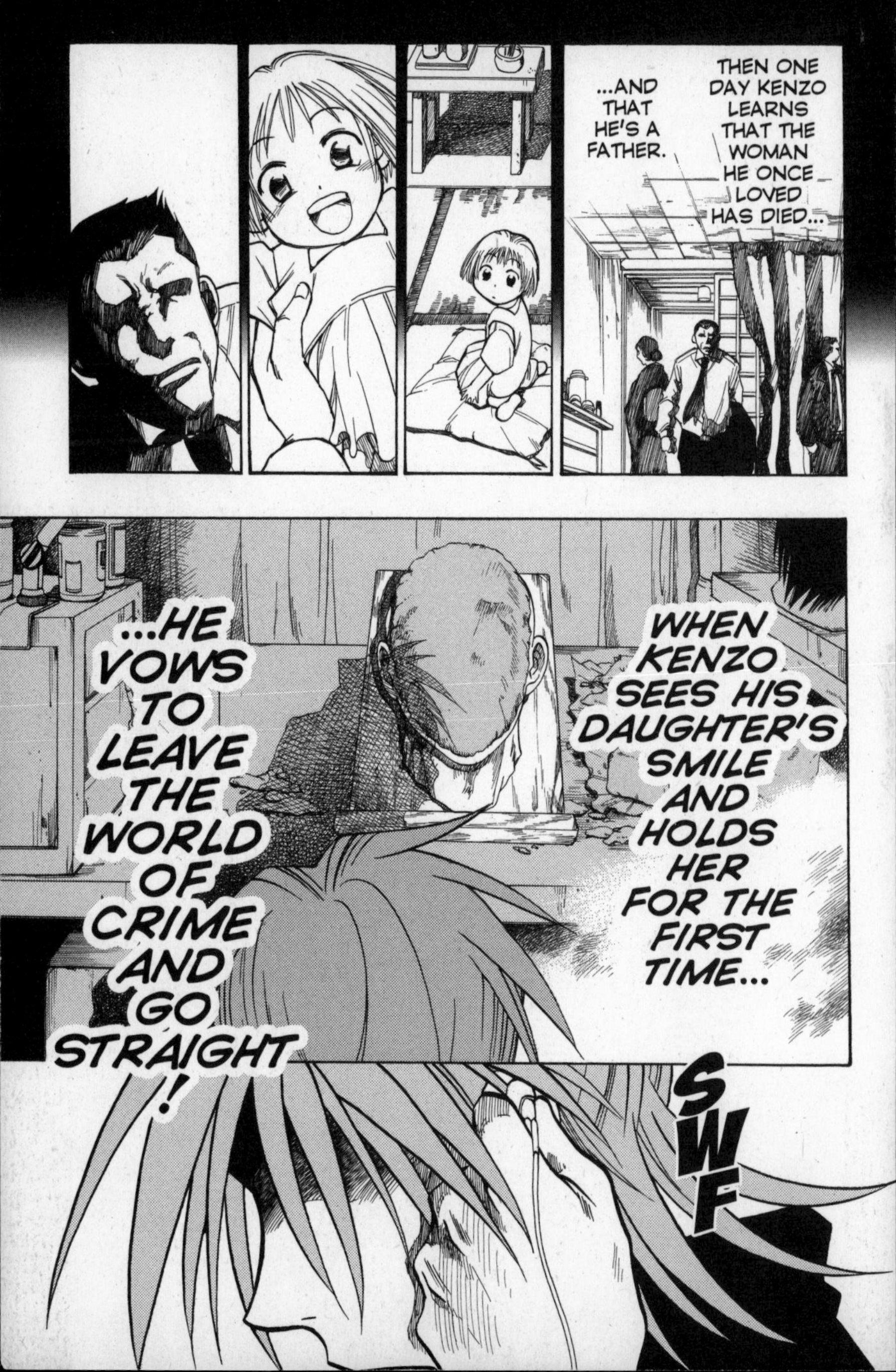
THEN ONE DAY KENZO LEARNS THAT THE WOMAN HE ONCE LOVED HAS DIED...
...AND THAT HE'S A FATHER.
WHEN KENZO SEES HIS DAUGHTER'S SMILE AND HOLDS HER FOR THE FIRST TIME...
...HE VOWS TO LEAVE THE WORLD OF CRIME AND GO STRAIGHT!
SWF

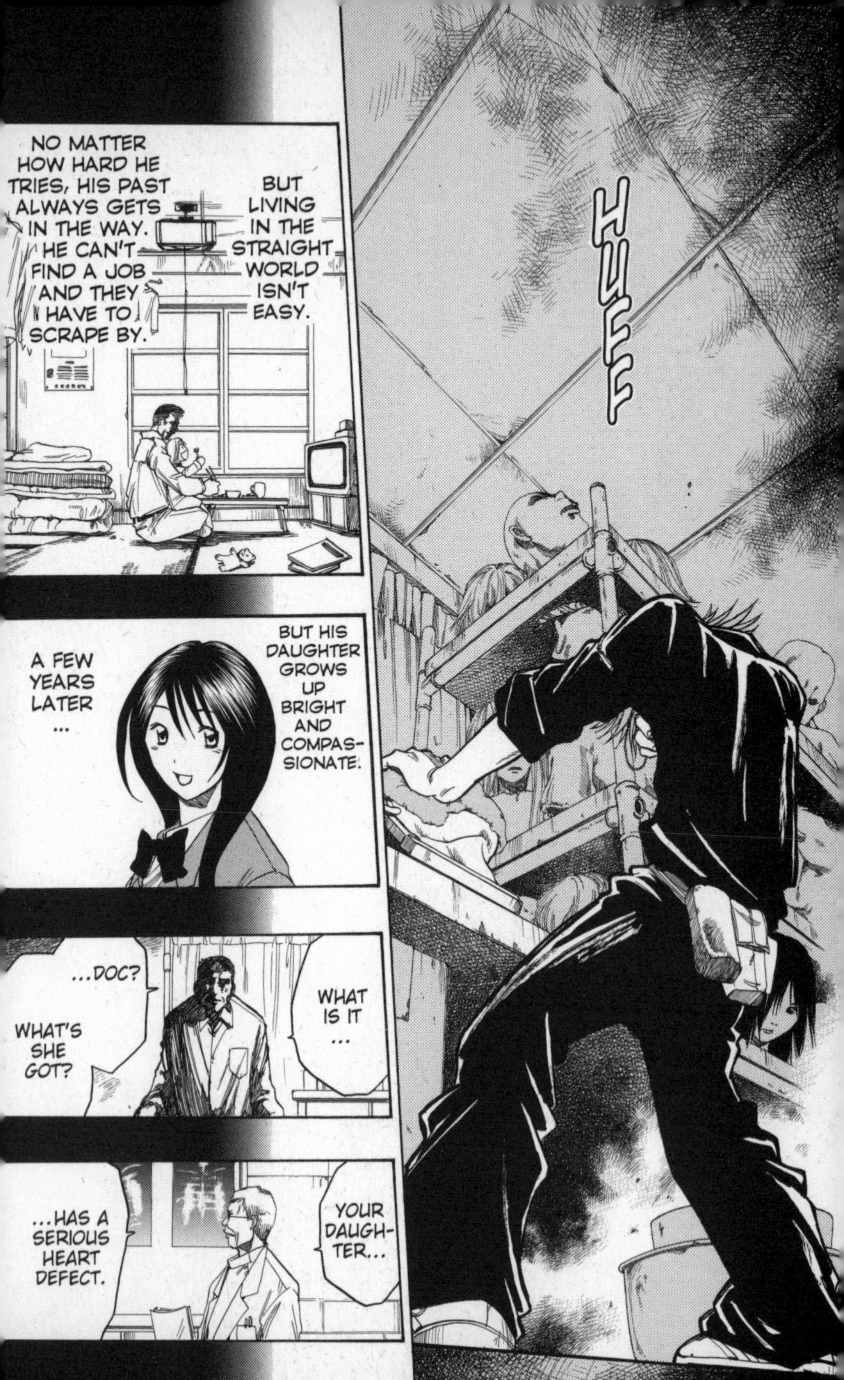
HUFF
BUT LIVING IN THE STRAIGHT WORLD ISN'T EASY.
NO MATTER HOW HARD HE TRIES, HIS PAST ALWAYS GETS IN THE WAY. HE CAN'T FIND A JOB AND THEY HAVE TO SCRAPE BY.
BUT HIS DAUGHTER GROWS UP BRIGHT AND COMPASSIONATE.
A FEW YEARS LATER ...
WHAT IS IT ...
...DOC?
WHAT'S SHE GOT?
YOUR DAUGHTER...
...HAS A SERIOUS HEART DEFECT.

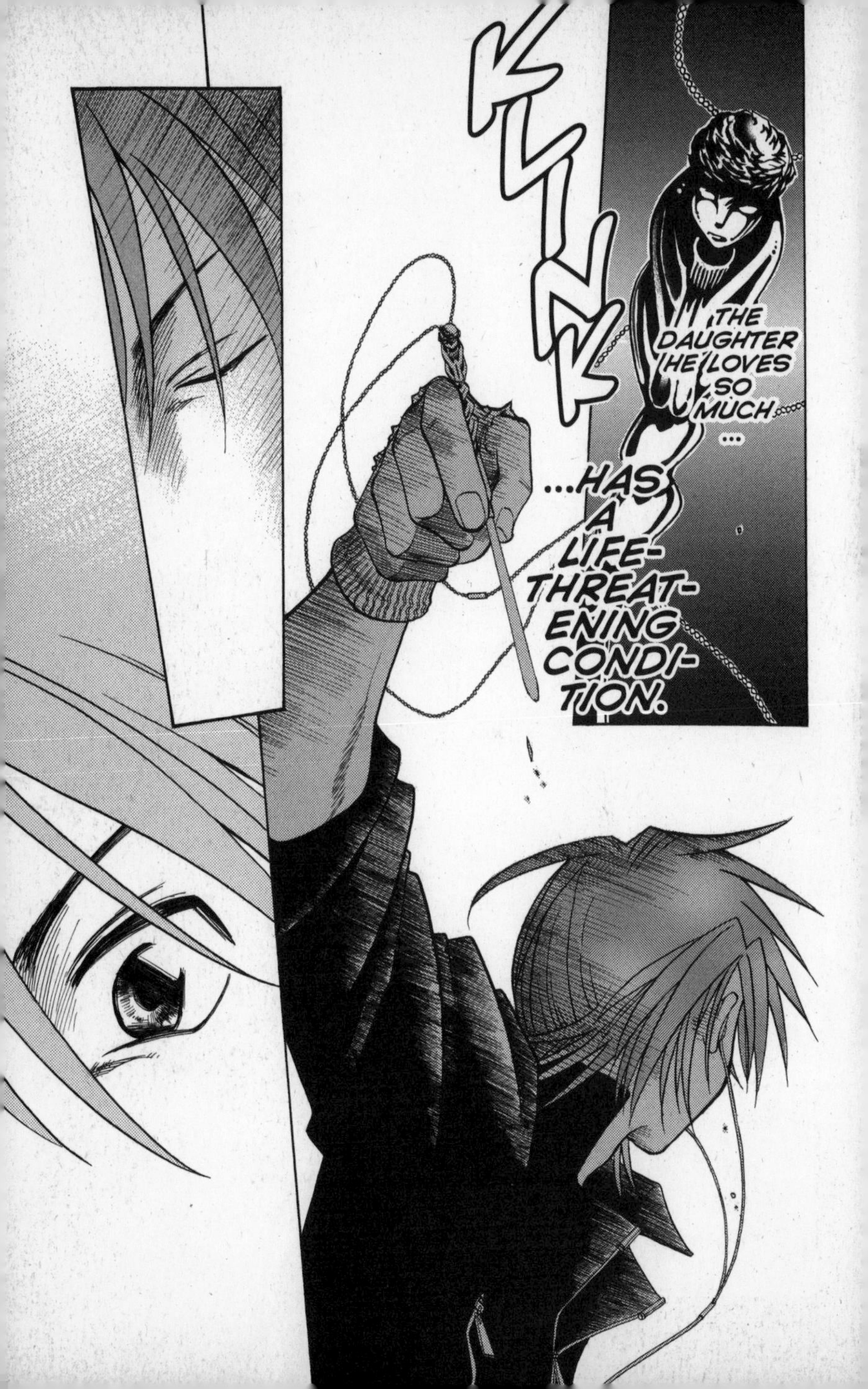
KLINK
THE DAUGHTER HE LOVES SO MUCH...
...HAS A LIFE-THREAT-ENING CONDI-TION.

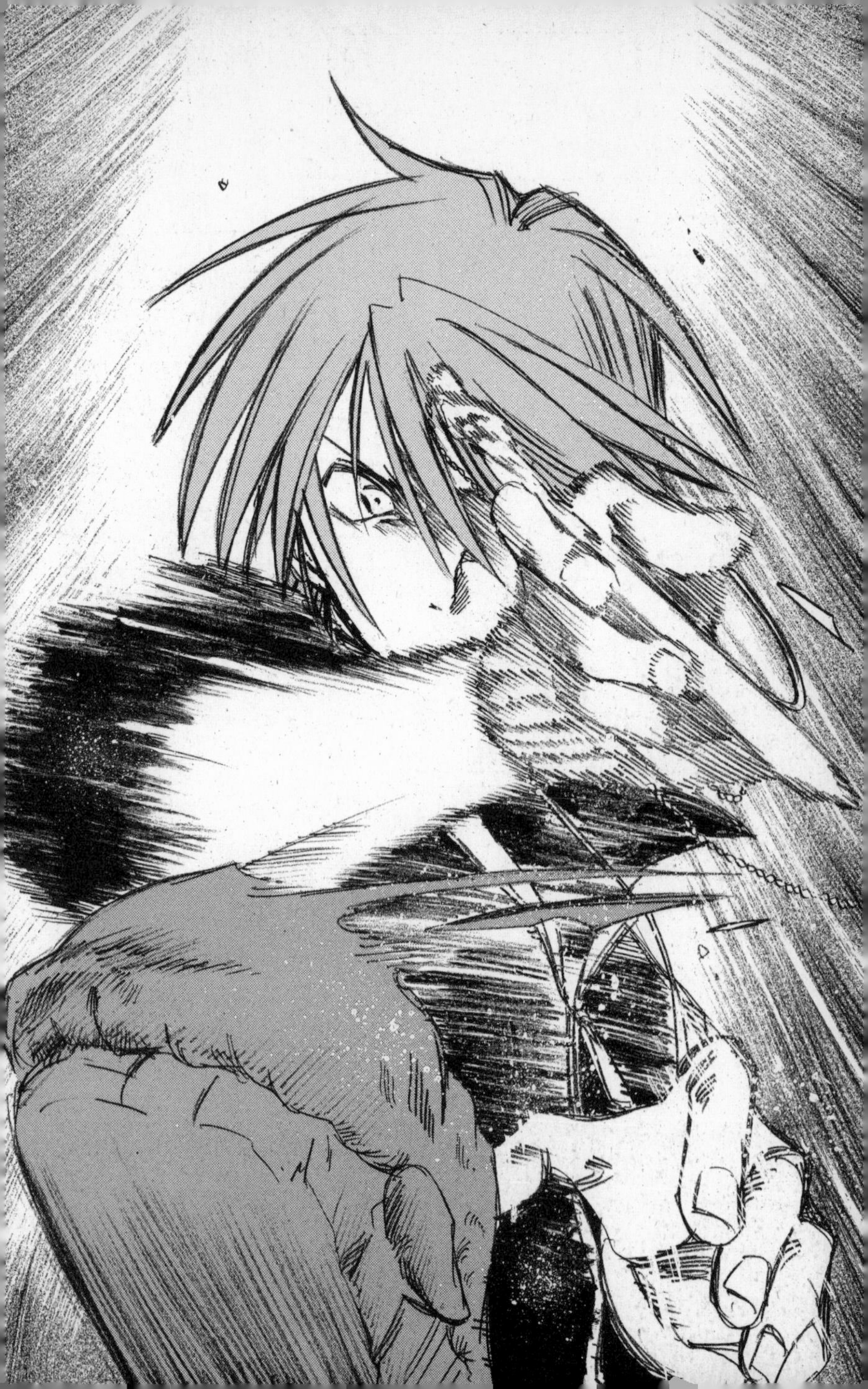

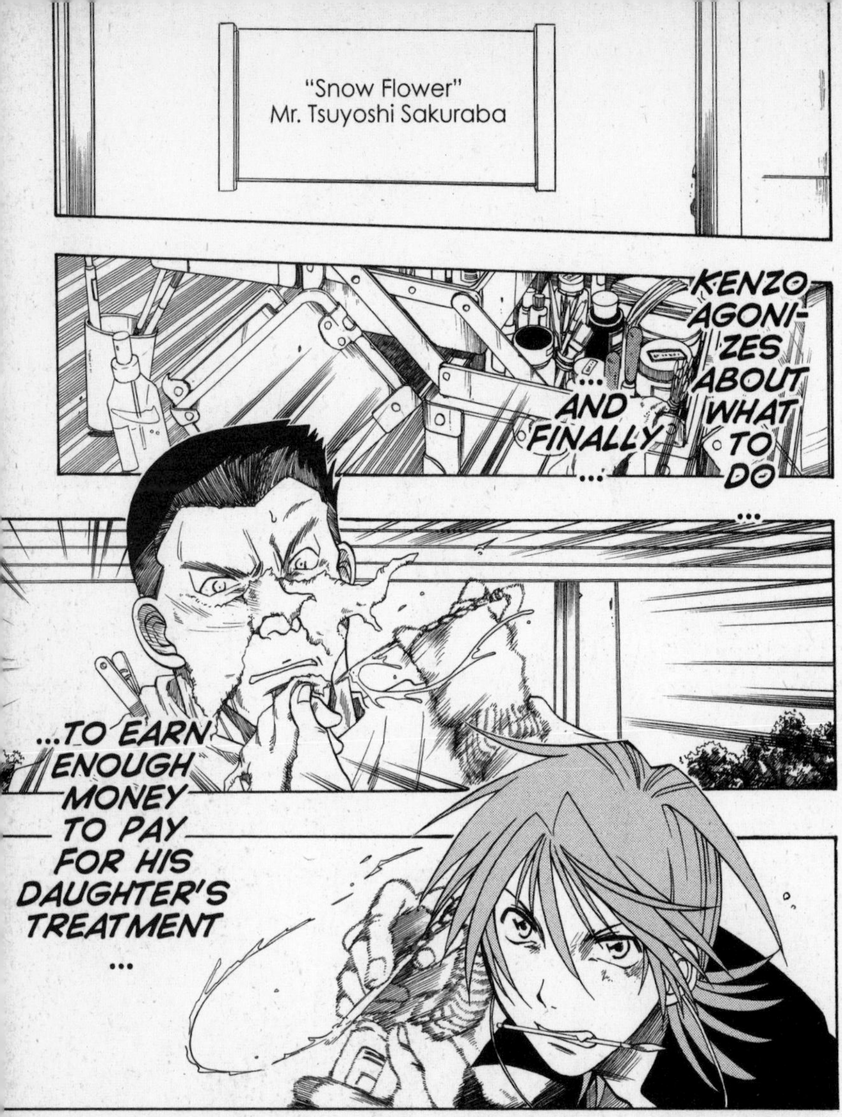
"Snow Flower"
Mr. Tsuyoshi Sakuraba
KENZO AGONIZES ABOUT WHAT TO DO...
...AND FINALLY...
...TO EARN ENOUGH MONEY TO PAY FOR HIS DAUGHTER'S TREATMENT...

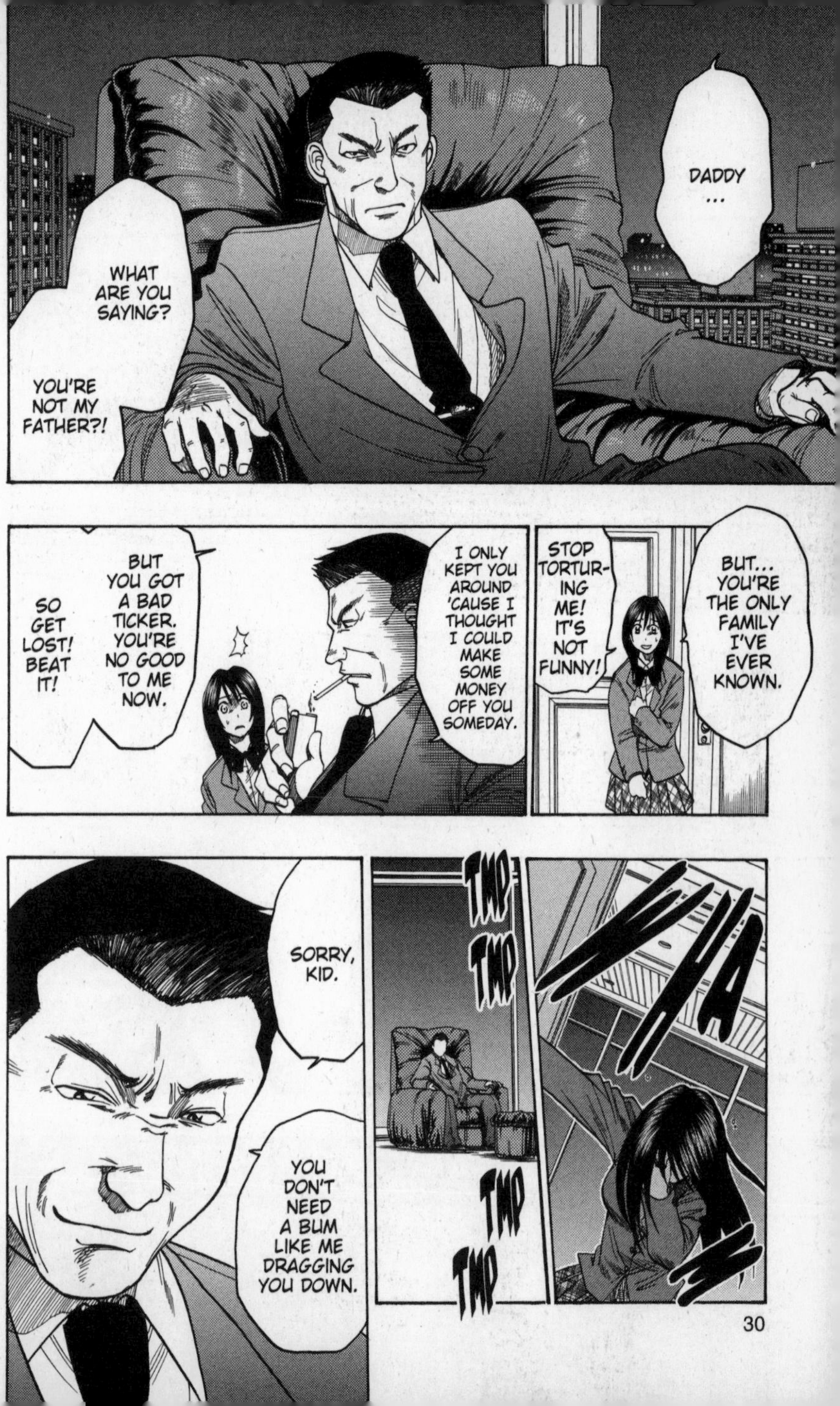
DADDY ...
WHAT ARE YOU SAYING?
YOU'RE NOT MY FATHER?!
BUT... YOU'RE THE ONLY FAMILY I'VE EVER KNOWN.
STOP TORTURING ME! IT'S NOT FUNNY!
I ONLY KEPT YOU AROUND 'CAUSE I THOUGHT I COULD MAKE SOME MONEY OFF YOU SOMEDAY.
BUT YOU GOT A BAD TICKER. YOU'RE NO GOOD TO ME NOW.
SO GET LOST! BEAT IT!
WHA
TMP TMP
TMP TMP
SORRY, KID.
YOU DON'T NEED A BUM LIKE ME DRAGGING YOU DOWN.

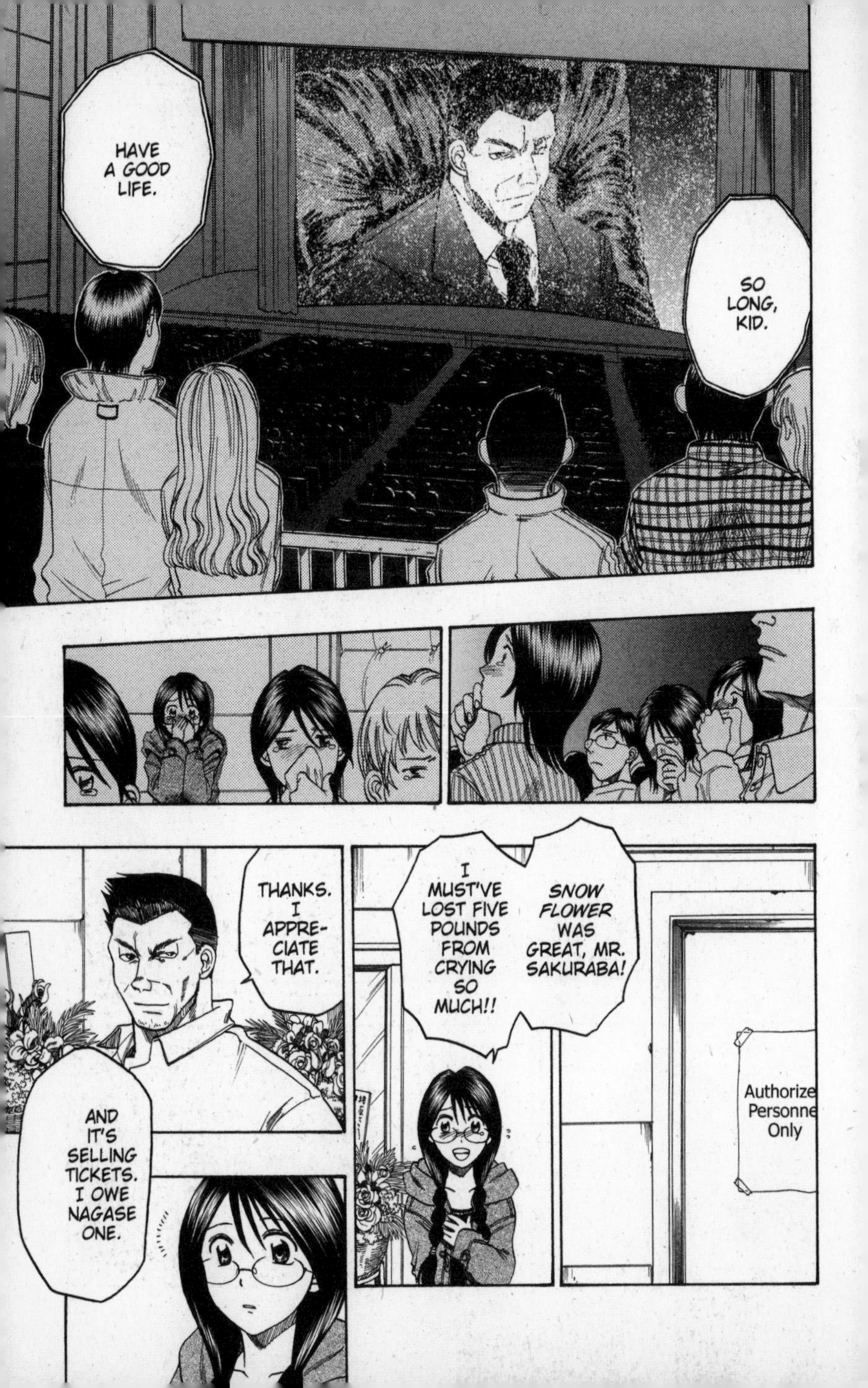
SO LONG, KID.
HAVE A GOOD LIFE.
Authorize Personne Only
SNOW FLOWER WAS GREAT, MR. SAKURABA!
I MUST'VE LOST FIVE POUNDS FROM CRYING SO MUCH!!
THANKS. I APPRE-CIATE THAT.
AND IT'S SELLING TICKETS. I OWE NAGASE ONE.

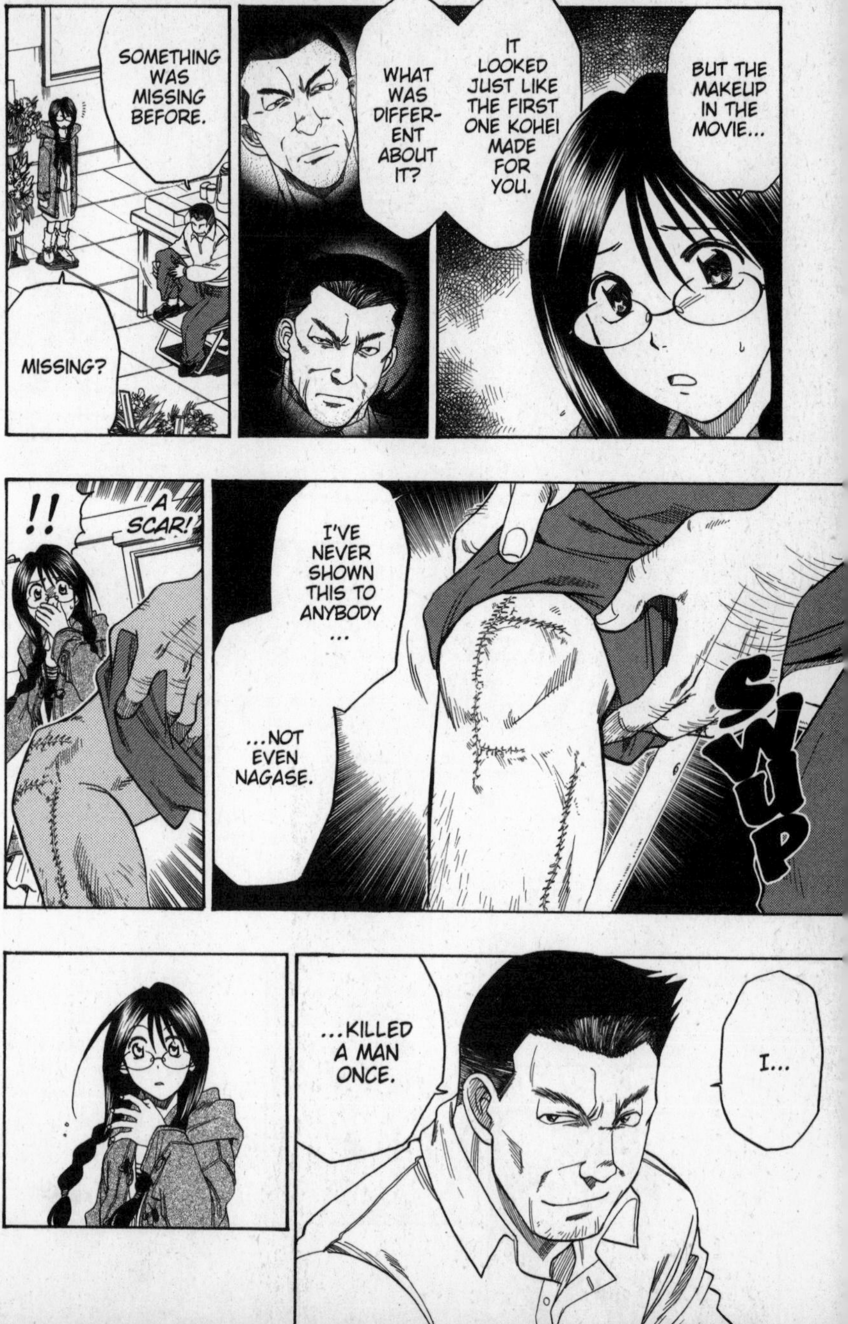
BUT THE MAKEUP IN THE MOVIE...
IT LOOKED JUST LIKE THE FIRST ONE KOHEI MADE FOR YOU.
WHAT WAS DIFFER-ENT ABOUT IT?
SOMETHING WAS MISSING BEFORE.
MISSING?
SWUP
I'VE NEVER SHOWN THIS TO ANYBODY ...
...NOT EVEN NAGASE.
!!
A SCAR!
I...
...KILLED A MAN ONCE.

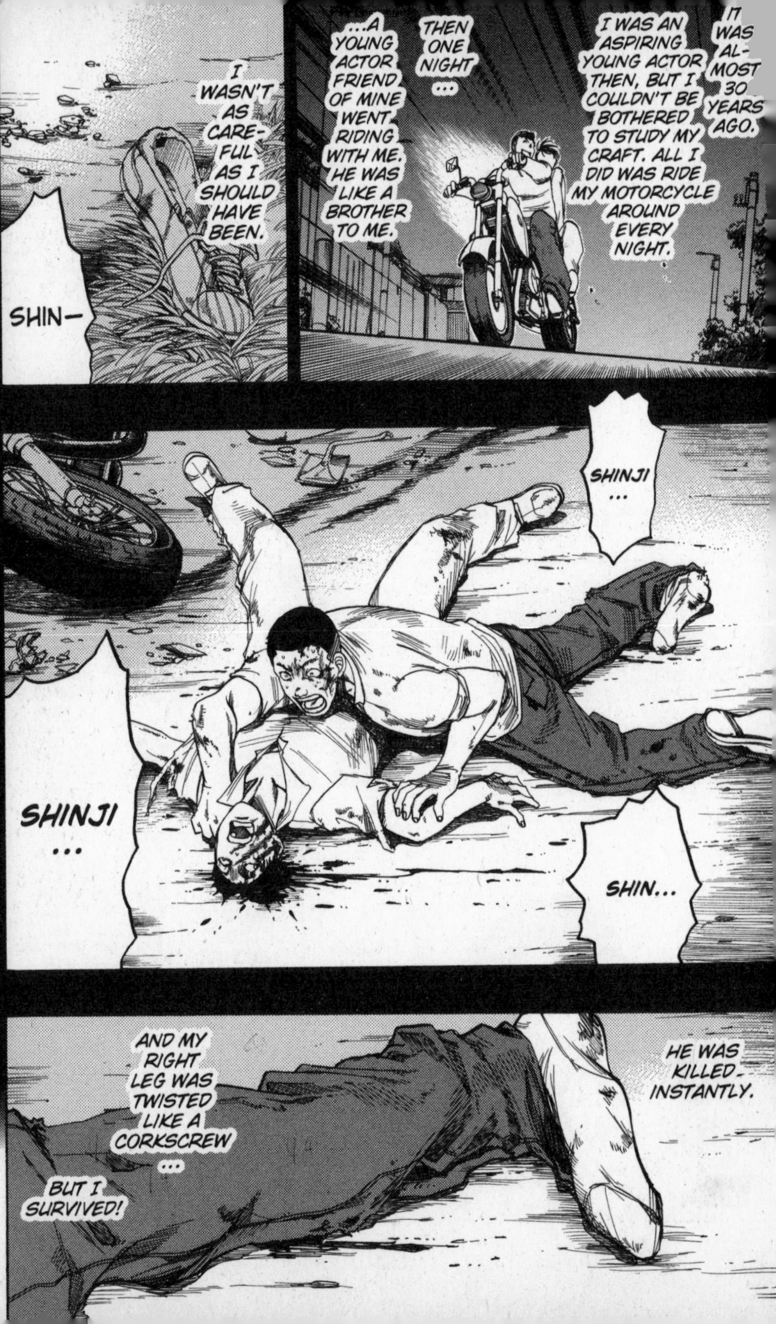
IT WAS ALMOST 30 YEARS AGO.
I WAS AN ASPIRING YOUNG ACTOR THEN, BUT I COULDN'T BE BOTHERED TO STUDY MY CRAFT. ALL I DID WAS RIDE MY MOTORCYCLE AROUND EVERY NIGHT.
THEN ONE NIGHT...
...A YOUNG ACTOR FRIEND OF MINE WENT RIDING WITH ME. HE WAS LIKE A BROTHER TO ME.
I WASN'T AS CAREFUL AS I SHOULD HAVE BEEN.
SHIN—
SHINJI...
SHIN...
SHINJI...
HE WAS KILLED INSTANTLY.
AND MY RIGHT LEG WAS TWISTED LIKE A CORKSCREW...
BUT I SURVIVED!

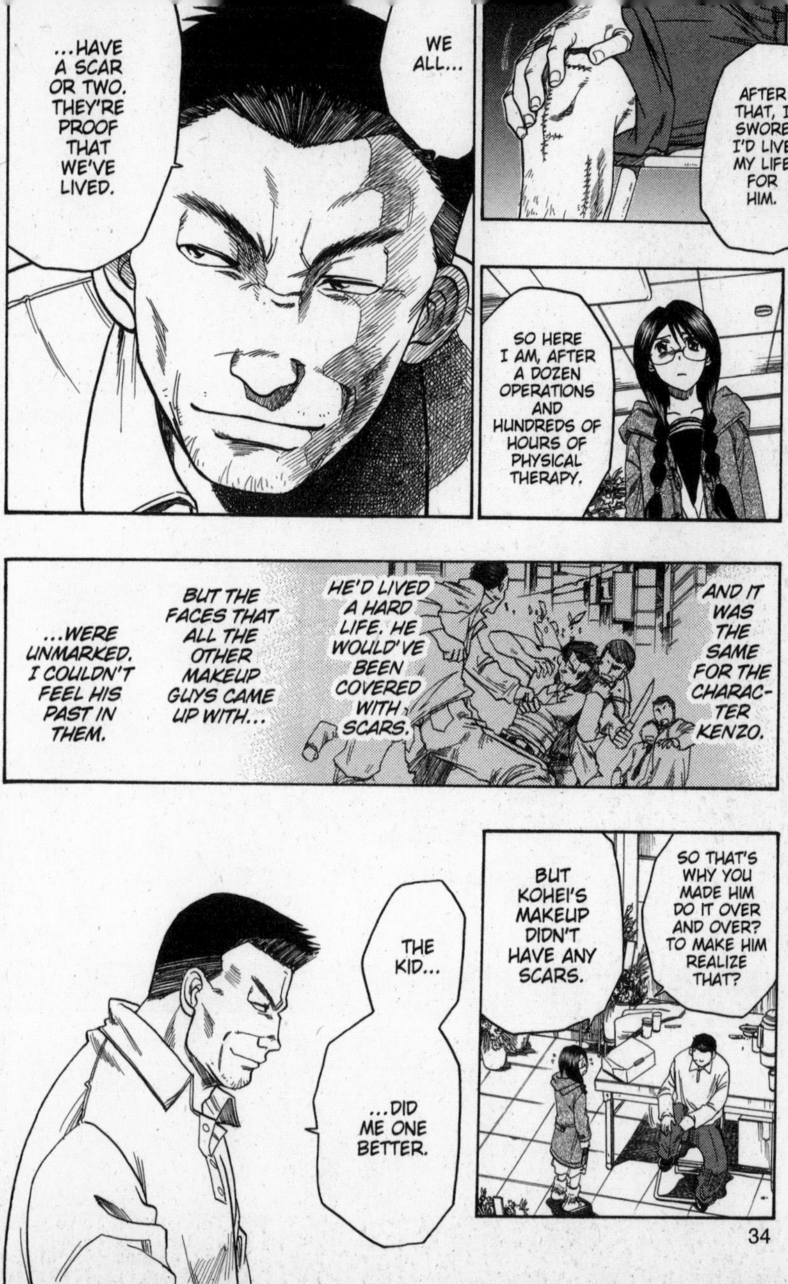
AFTER THAT, I SWORE I'D LIVE MY LIFE FOR HIM.
SO HERE I AM, AFTER A DOZEN OPERATIONS AND HUNDREDS OF HOURS OF PHYSICAL THERAPY.
WE ALL...
...HAVE A SCAR OR TWO. THEY'RE PROOF THAT WE'VE LIVED.
AND IT WAS THE SAME FOR THE CHARAC-TER KENZO.
HE'D LIVED A HARD LIFE. HE WOULD'VE BEEN COVERED WITH SCARS.
BUT THE FACES THAT ALL THE OTHER MAKEUP GUYS CAME UP WITH...
...WERE UNMARKED. I COULDN'T FEEL HIS PAST IN THEM.
SO THAT'S WHY YOU MADE HIM DO IT OVER AND OVER? TO MAKE HIM REALIZE THAT?
BUT KOHEI'S MAKEUP DIDN'T HAVE ANY SCARS.
THE KID...
...DID ME ONE BETTER.

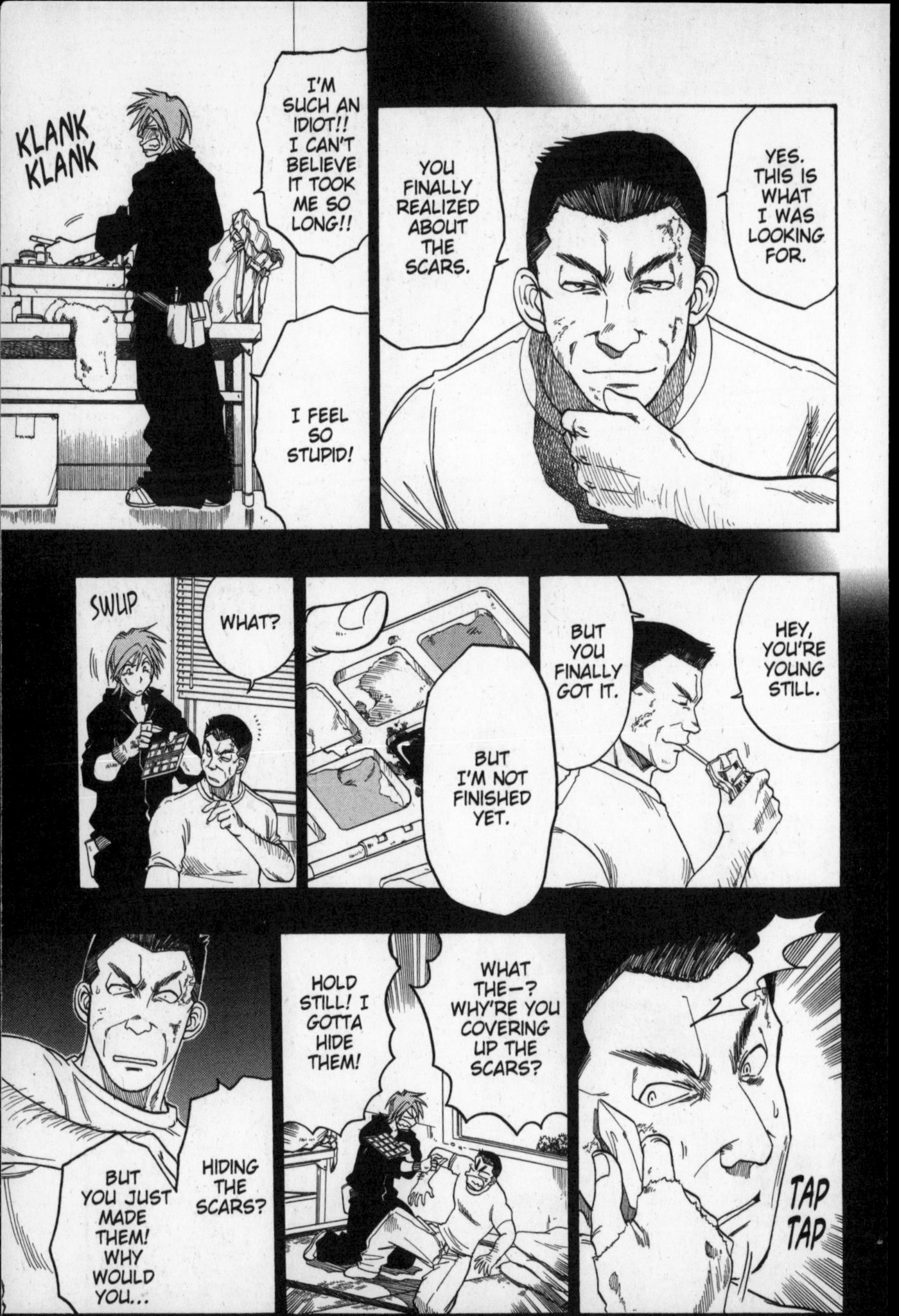
YES. THIS IS WHAT I WAS LOOKING FOR.
YOU FINALLY REALIZED ABOUT THE SCARS.
I'M SUCH AN IDIOT!! I CAN'T BELIEVE IT TOOK ME SO LONG!!
KLANK KLANK
I FEEL SO STUPID!
HEY, YOU'RE YOUNG STILL.
BUT YOU FINALLY GOT IT.
BUT I'M NOT FINISHED YET.
SWUP
WHAT?
TAP TAP
WHAT THE—? WHY'RE YOU COVERING UP THE SCARS?
HOLD STILL! I GOTTA HIDE THEM!
HIDING THE SCARS?
BUT YOU JUST MADE THEM! WHY WOULD YOU...

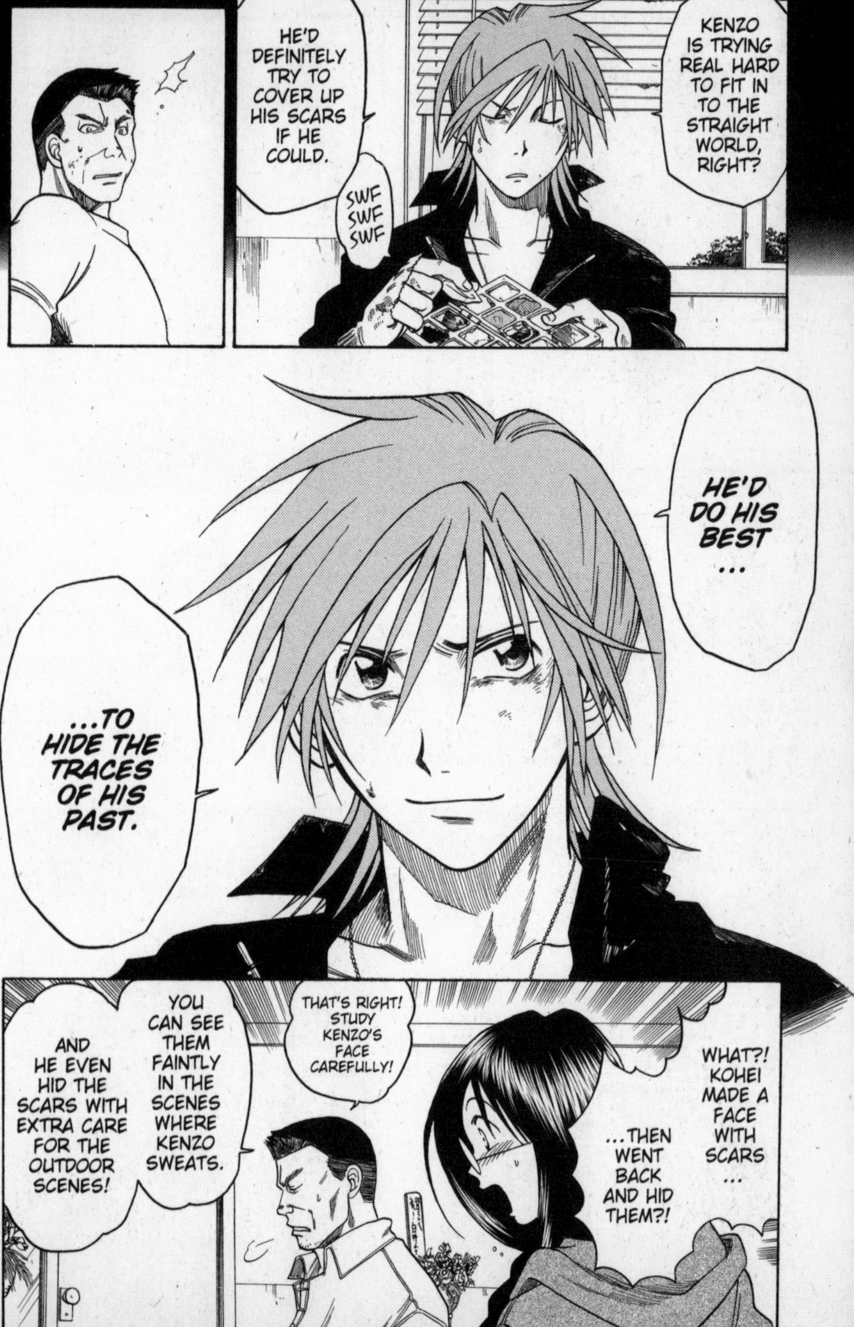
KENZO IS TRYING REAL HARD TO FIT IN TO THE STRAIGHT WORLD, RIGHT?
HE'D DEFINITELY TRY TO COVER UP HIS SCARS IF HE COULD.
SWF SWF SWF
HE'D DO HIS BEST...
...TO HIDE THE TRACES OF HIS PAST.
WHAT?! KOHEI MADE A FACE WITH SCARS...
...THEN WENT BACK AND HID THEM?!
THAT'S RIGHT! STUDY KENZO'S FACE CAREFULLY!
YOU CAN SEE THEM FAINTLY IN THE SCENES WHERE KENZO SWEATS.
AND HE EVEN HID THE SCARS WITH EXTRA CARE FOR THE OUTDOOR SCENES!

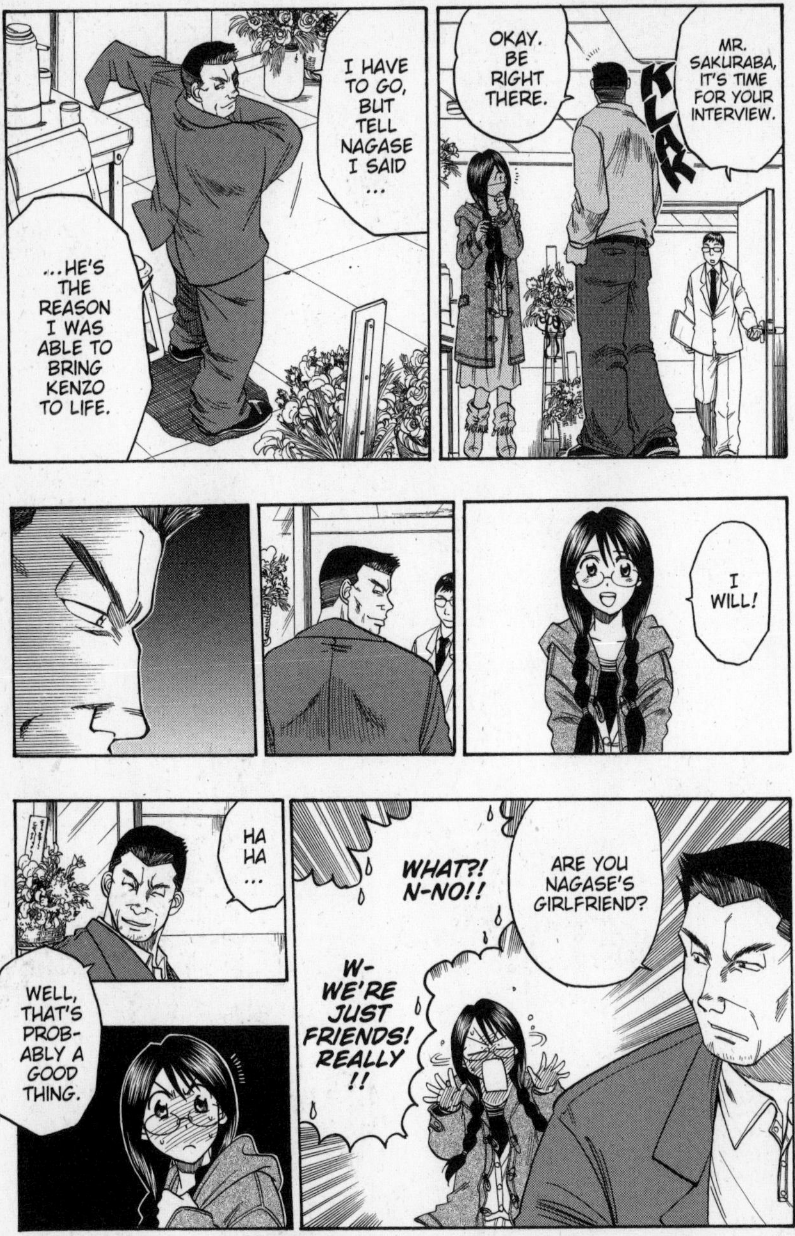
MR. SAKURABA, IT'S TIME FOR YOUR INTERVIEW.
KLAK
OKAY. BE RIGHT THERE.
I HAVE TO GO, BUT TELL NAGASE I SAID ...
...HE'S THE REASON I WAS ABLE TO BRING KENZO TO LIFE.
I WILL!
ARE YOU NAGASE'S GIRLFRIEND?
WHAT?! N-NO!!
W-WE'RE JUST FRIENDS! REALLY!!
HA HA ...
WELL, THAT'S PROB-ABLY A GOOD THING.

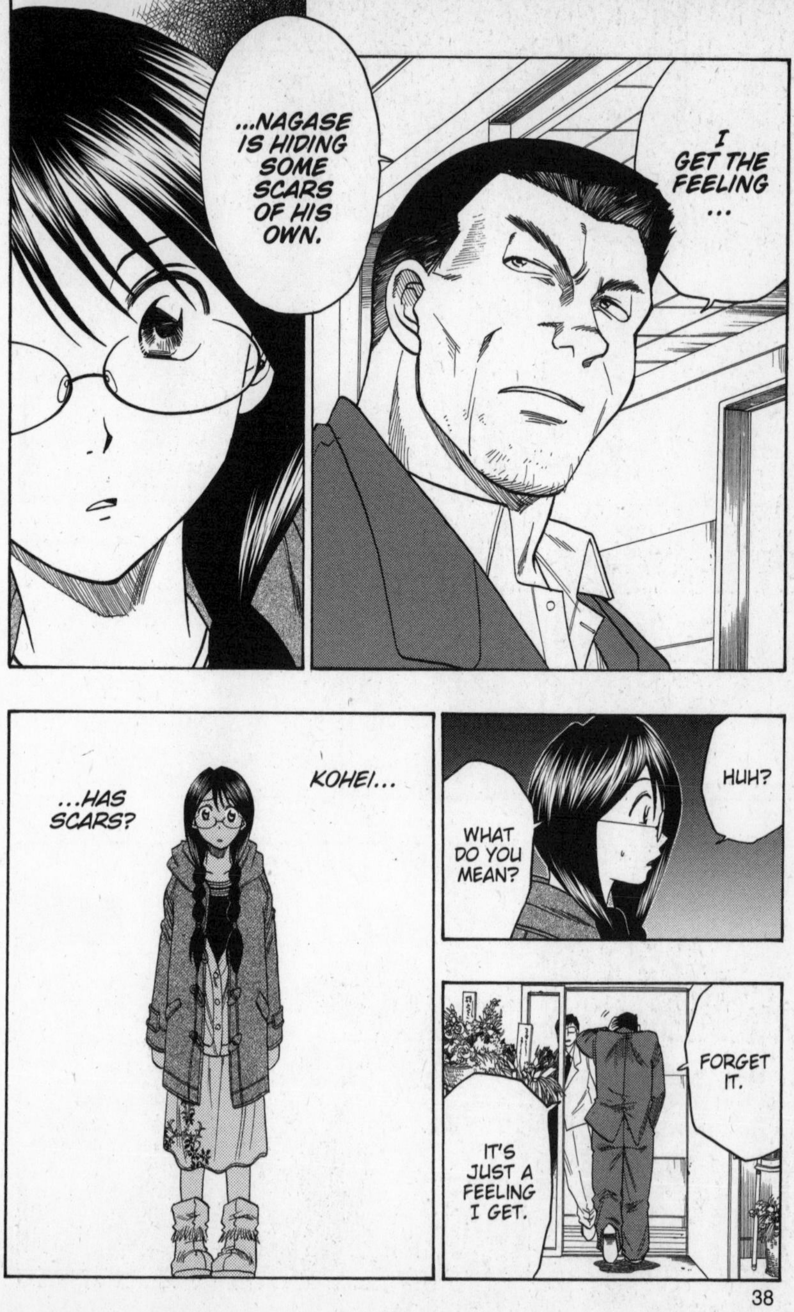
I GET THE FEELING ...
...NAGASE IS HIDING SOME SCARS OF HIS OWN.
HUH?
WHAT DO YOU MEAN?
FORGET IT.
IT'S JUST A FEELING I GET.
KOHEI...
...HAS SCARS?

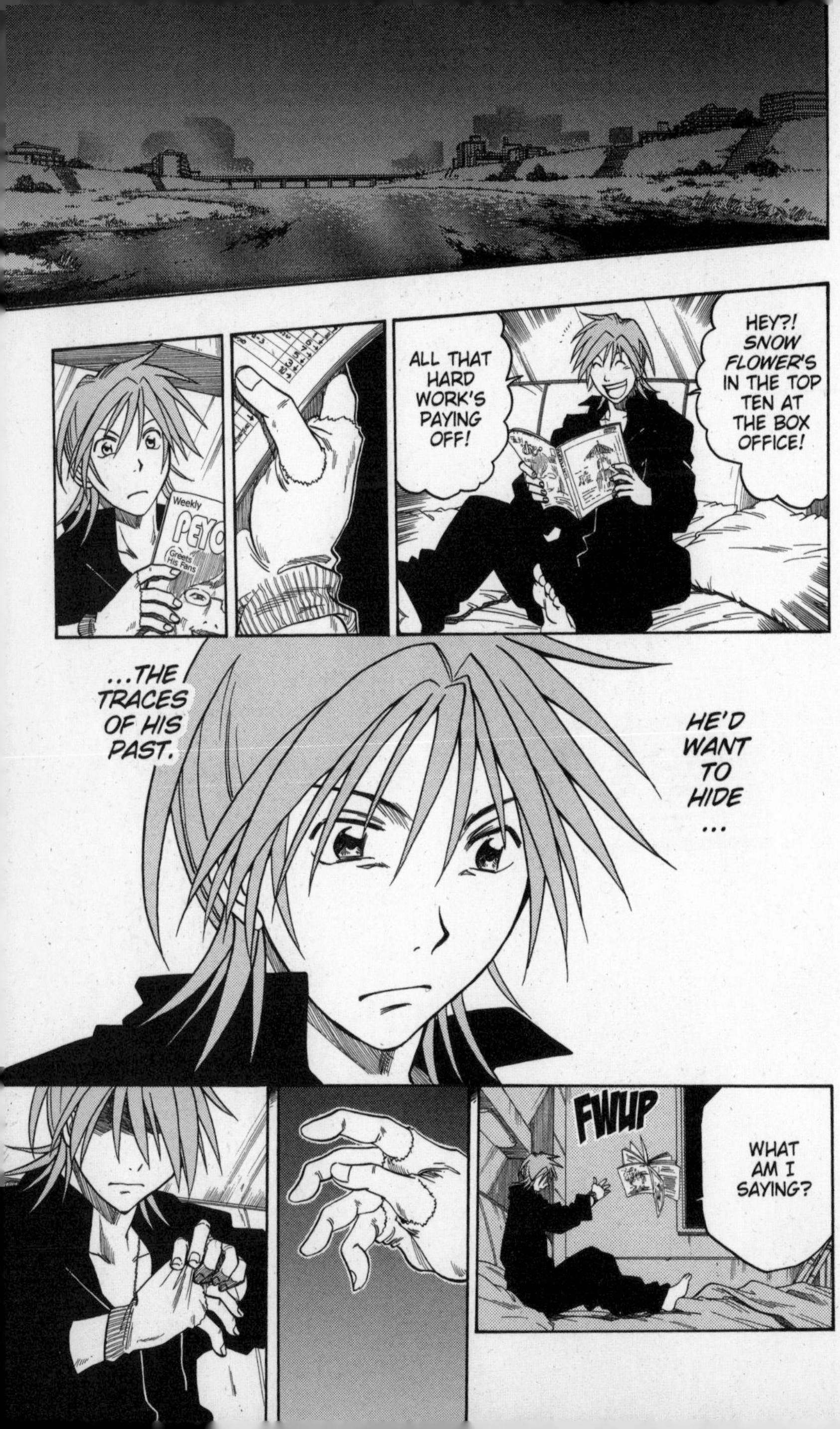
HEY?! SNOW FLOWER'S IN THE TOP TEN AT THE BOX OFFICE!
ALL THAT HARD WORK'S PAYING OFF!
Weekly PEYO Greets His Fans
HE'D WANT TO HIDE ...
...THE TRACES OF HIS PAST.
FWUP
WHAT AM I SAYING?

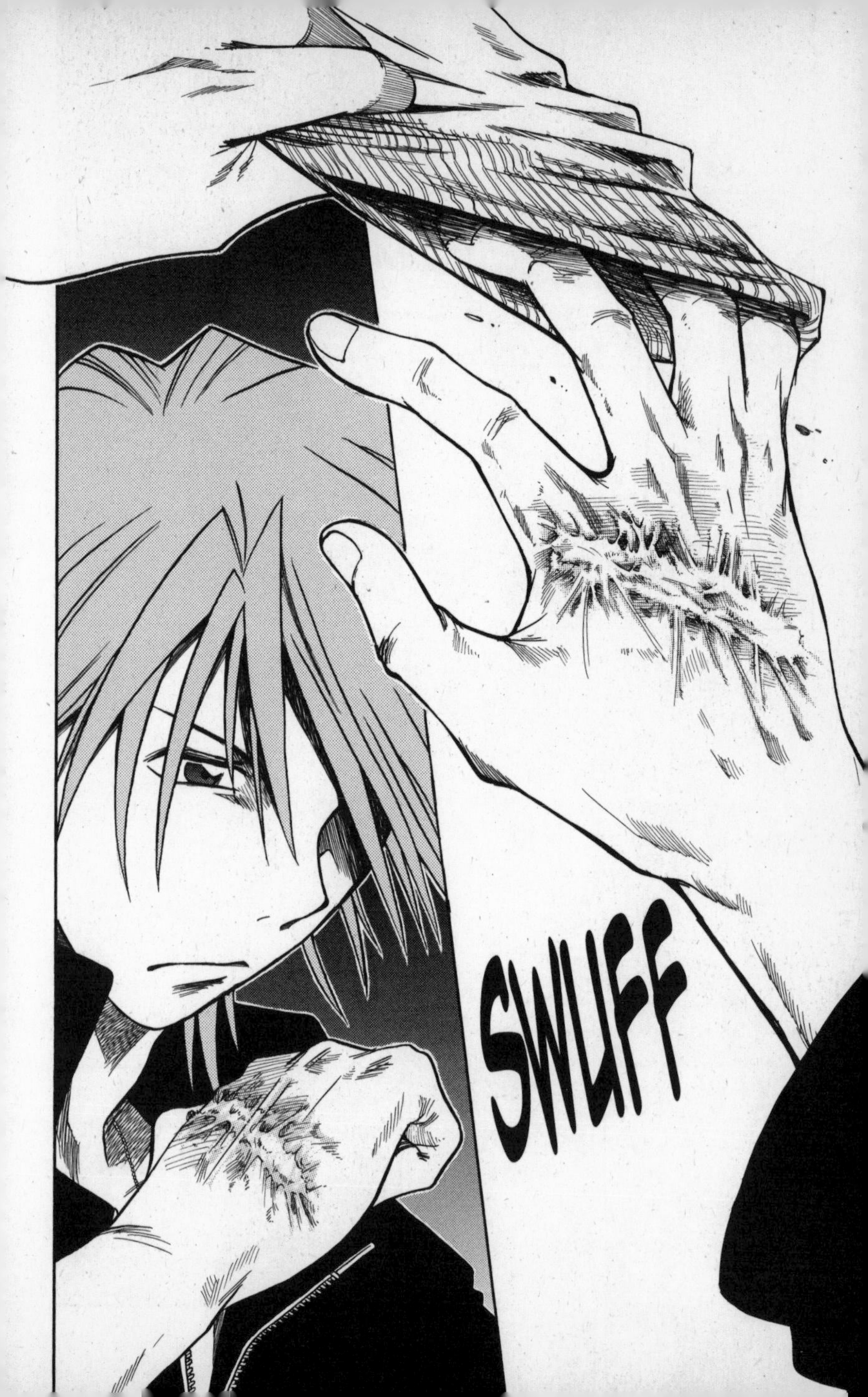
SWUFF

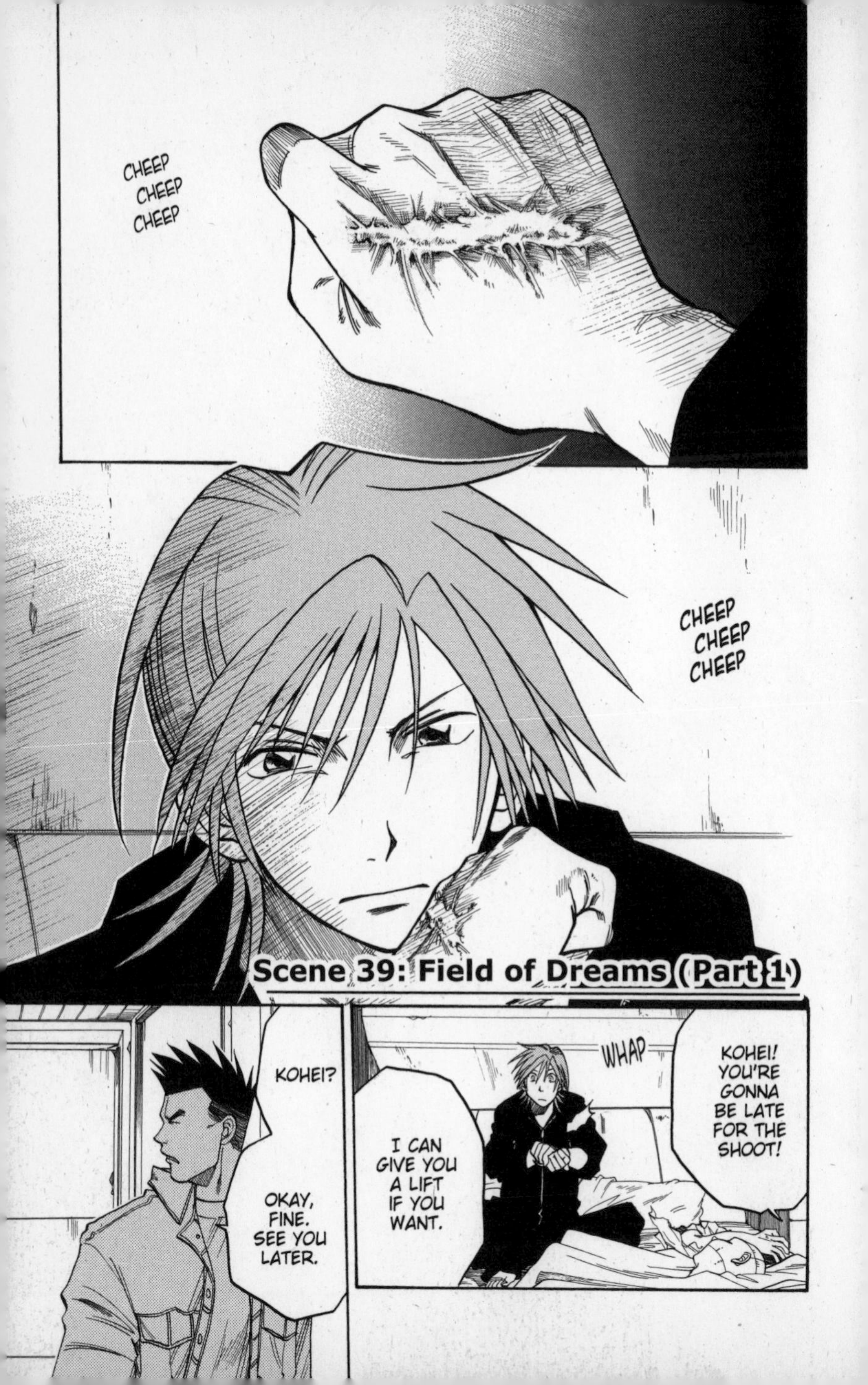
CHEEP CHEEP CHEEP
CHEEP CHEEP CHEEP
Scene 39: Field of Dreams (Part 1)
KOHEI! YOU'RE GONNA BE LATE FOR THE SHOOT!
WHAP
I CAN GIVE YOU A LIFT IF YOU WANT.
KOHEI?
OKAY, FINE. SEE YOU LATER.

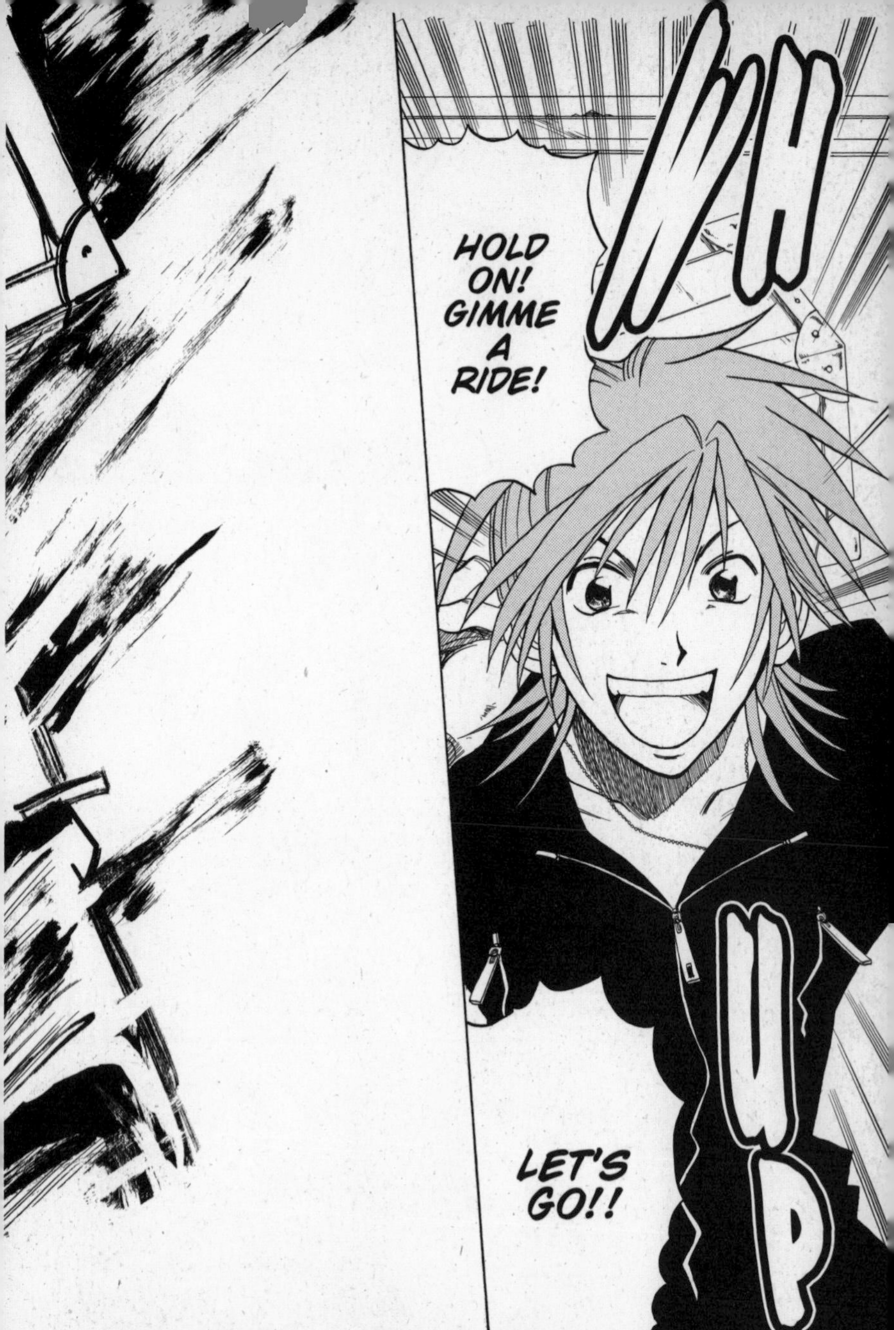
WH
HOLD ON! GIMME A RIDE!
UUP
LET'S GO!!

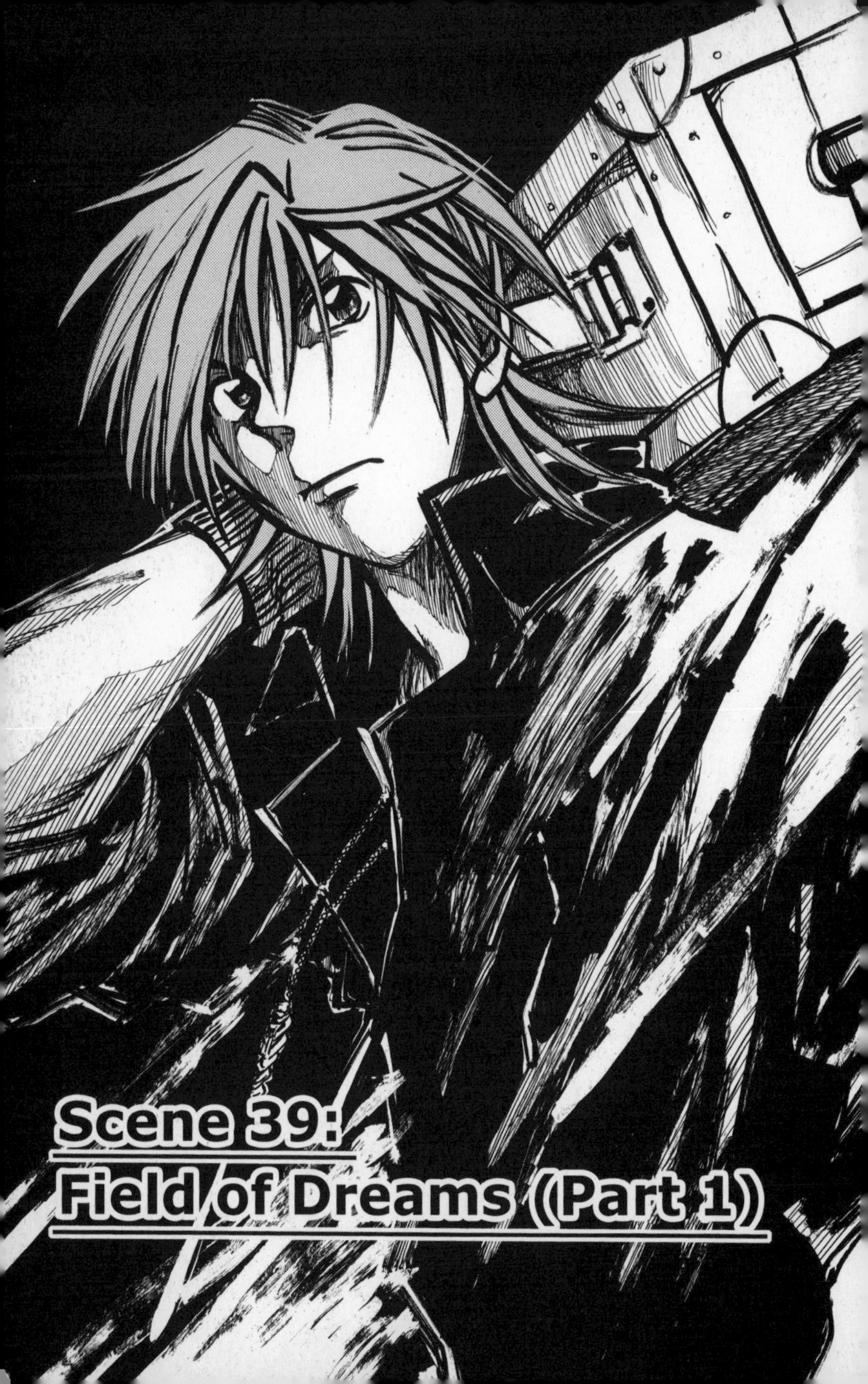
Scene 39:
Field of Dreams (Part 1)

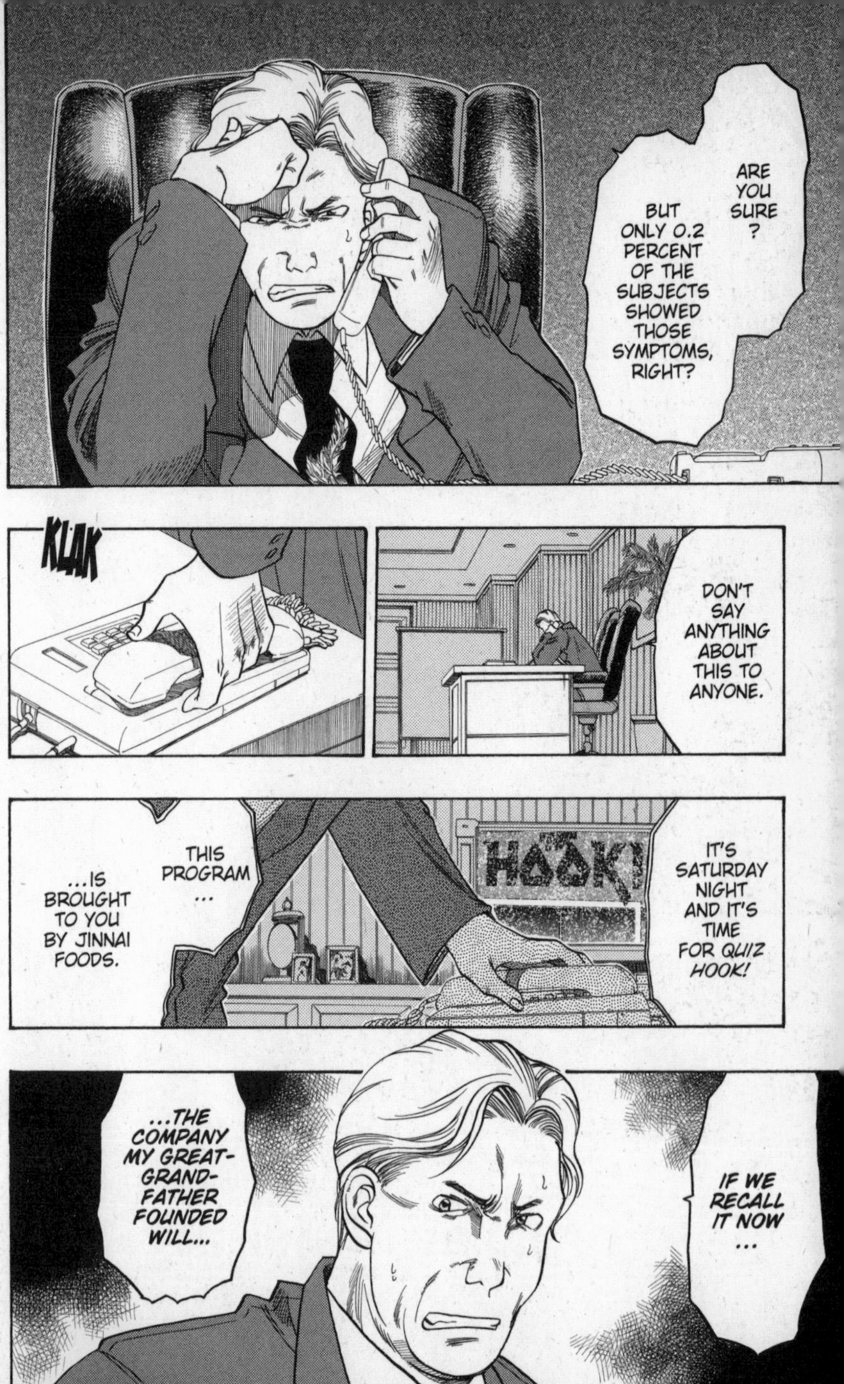
ARE YOU SURE?
BUT ONLY 0.2 PERCENT OF THE SUBJECTS SHOWED THOSE SYMPTOMS, RIGHT?
DON'T SAY ANYTHING ABOUT THIS TO ANYONE.
KLAK
IT'S SATURDAY NIGHT AND IT'S TIME FOR QUIZ *HOOK!*
HOOK!
THIS PROGRAM...
...IS BROUGHT TO YOU BY JINNAI FOODS.
IF WE RECALL IT NOW...
...THE COMPANY MY GREAT-GRANDFATHER FOUNDED WILL...

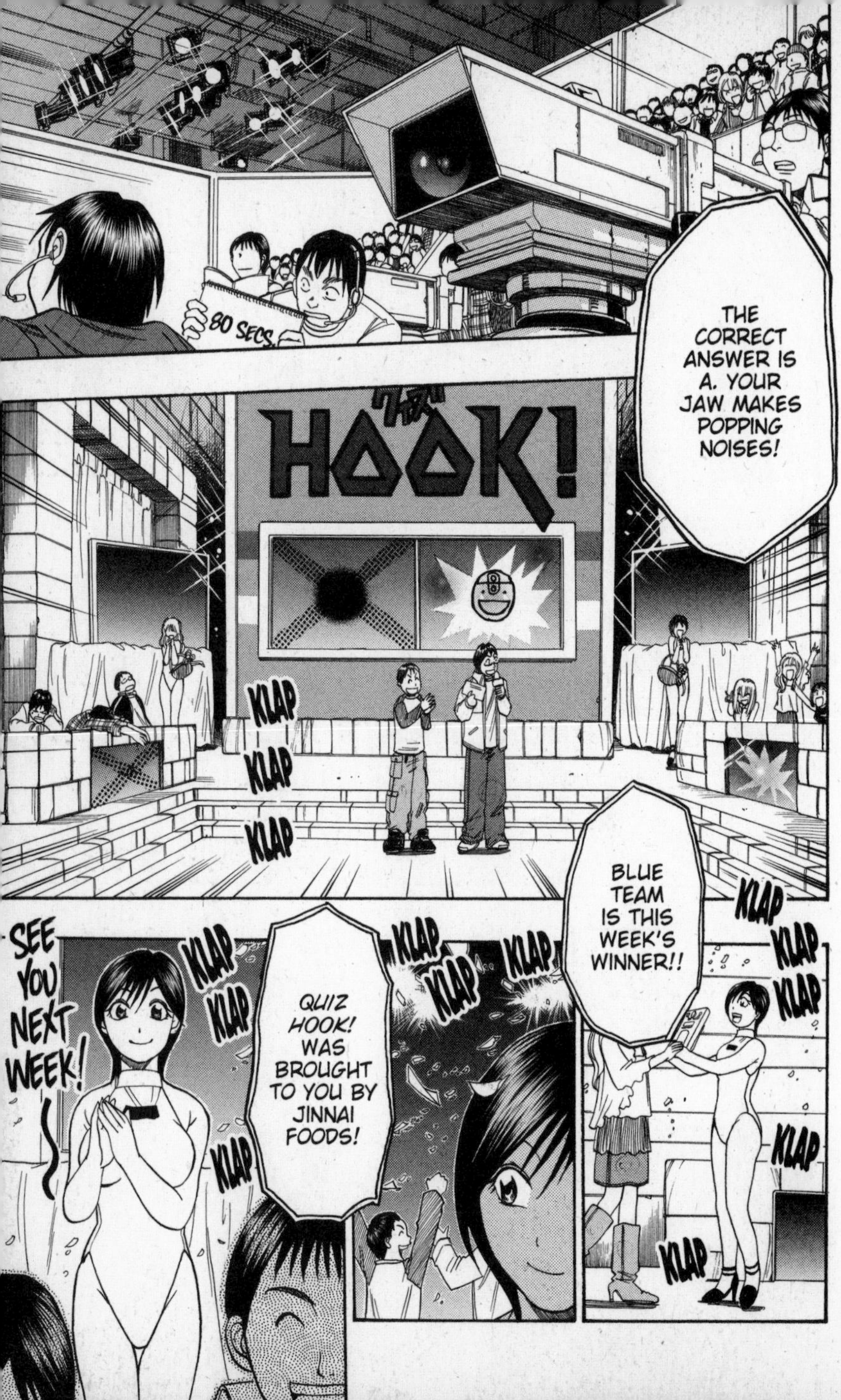

THE CORRECT ANSWER IS A. YOUR JAW MAKES POPPING NOISES!
80 SECS
HOOK!
KLAP
KLAP
KLAP
BLUE TEAM IS THIS WEEK'S WINNER!!
KLAP
KLAP
KLAP
KLAP
KLAP
KLAP
KLAP
KLAP
QUIZ HOOK! WAS BROUGHT TO YOU BY JINNAI FOODS!
SEE YOU NEXT WEEK!
KLAP
KLAP
KLAP

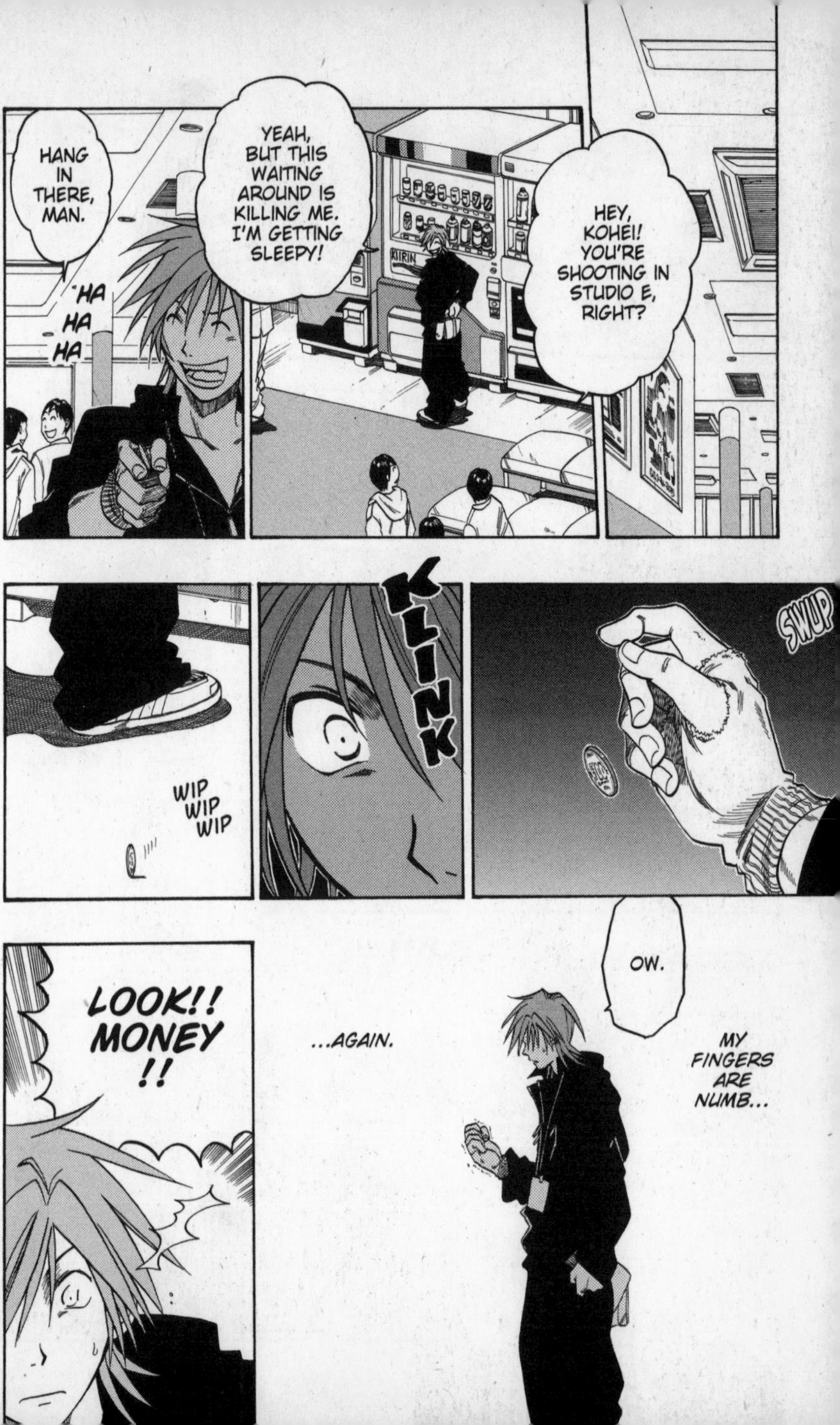
HEY, KOHEI! YOU'RE SHOOTING IN STUDIO E, RIGHT?
KIRIN
YEAH, BUT THIS WAITING AROUND IS KILLING ME. I'M GETTING SLEEPY!
HANG IN THERE, MAN.
HA HA HA
SWUP
KLINK
WIP WIP WIP
OW.
MY FINGERS ARE NUMB...
...AGAIN.
LOOK!! MONEY !!

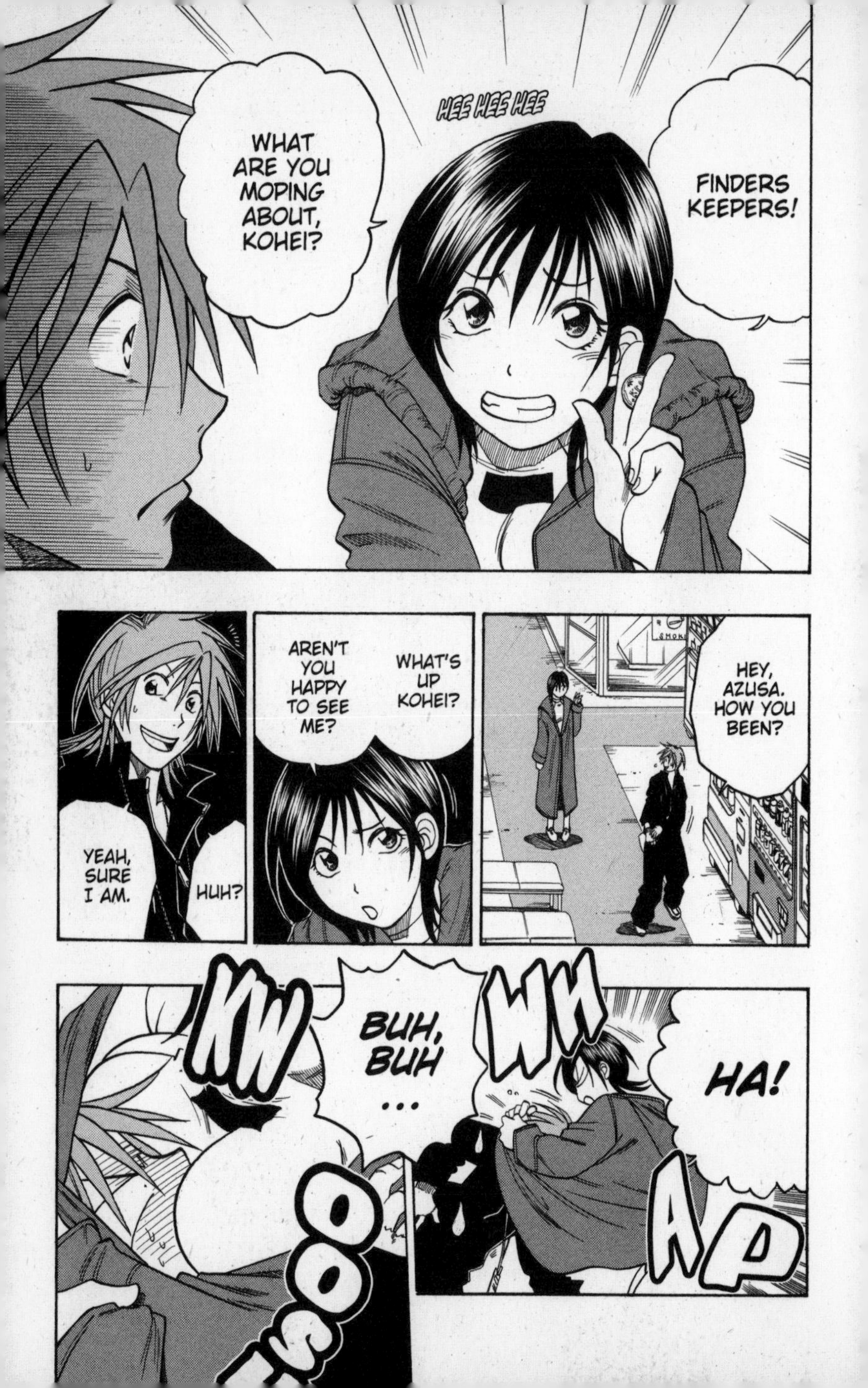
FINDERS KEEPERS!
HEE HEE HEE
WHAT ARE YOU MOPING ABOUT, KOHEI?
HEY, AZUSA. HOW YOU BEEN?
WHAT'S UP KOHEI?
AREN'T YOU HAPPY TO SEE ME?
HUH?
YEAH, SURE I AM.
HA!
WH
AP
BUH, BUH ...
KW
OOSH

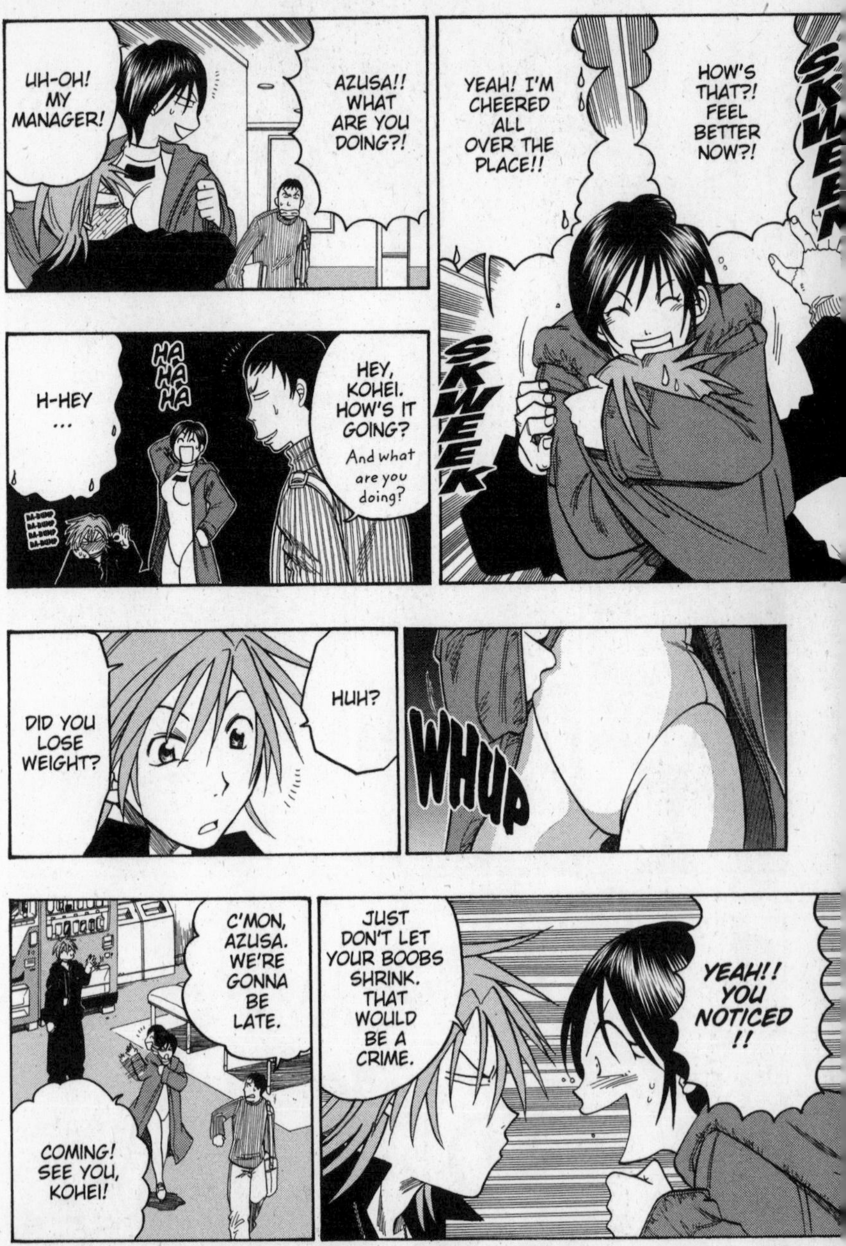
SKWEE
HOW'S THAT?! FEEL BETTER NOW?!
YEAH! I'M CHEERED ALL OVER THE PLACE!!
SKWEEK
AZUSA!! WHAT ARE YOU DOING?!
UH-OH! MY MANAGER!
HEY, KOHEI. HOW'S IT GOING? And what are you doing?
HA HA HA
H-HEY ...
WHUP
HUH?
DID YOU LOSE WEIGHT?
YEAH!! YOU NOTICED !!
JUST DON'T LET YOUR BOOBS SHRINK. THAT WOULD BE A CRIME.
C'MON, AZUSA. WE'RE GONNA BE LATE.
COMING! SEE YOU, KOHEI!

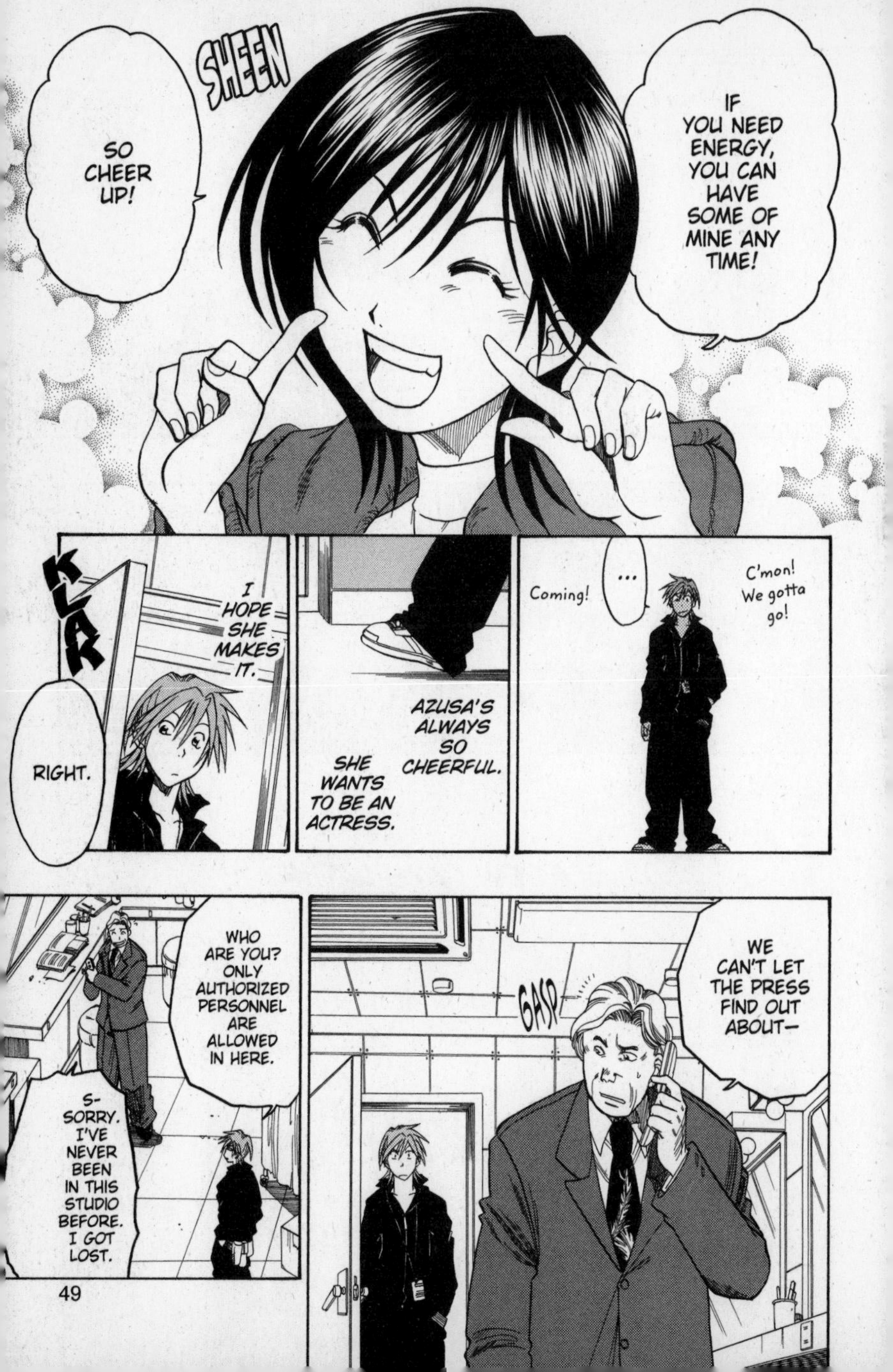
IF YOU NEED ENERGY, YOU CAN HAVE SOME OF MINE ANY TIME!
SHEEN
SO CHEER UP!
C'mon! We gotta go!
...
Coming!
AZUSA'S ALWAYS SO CHEERFUL.
SHE WANTS TO BE AN ACTRESS.
I HOPE SHE MAKES IT.
KLAK
RIGHT.
WE CAN'T LET THE PRESS FIND OUT ABOUT—
GASP
WHO ARE YOU? ONLY AUTHORIZED PERSONNEL ARE ALLOWED IN HERE.
S-SORRY. I'VE NEVER BEEN IN THIS STUDIO BEFORE. I GOT LOST.

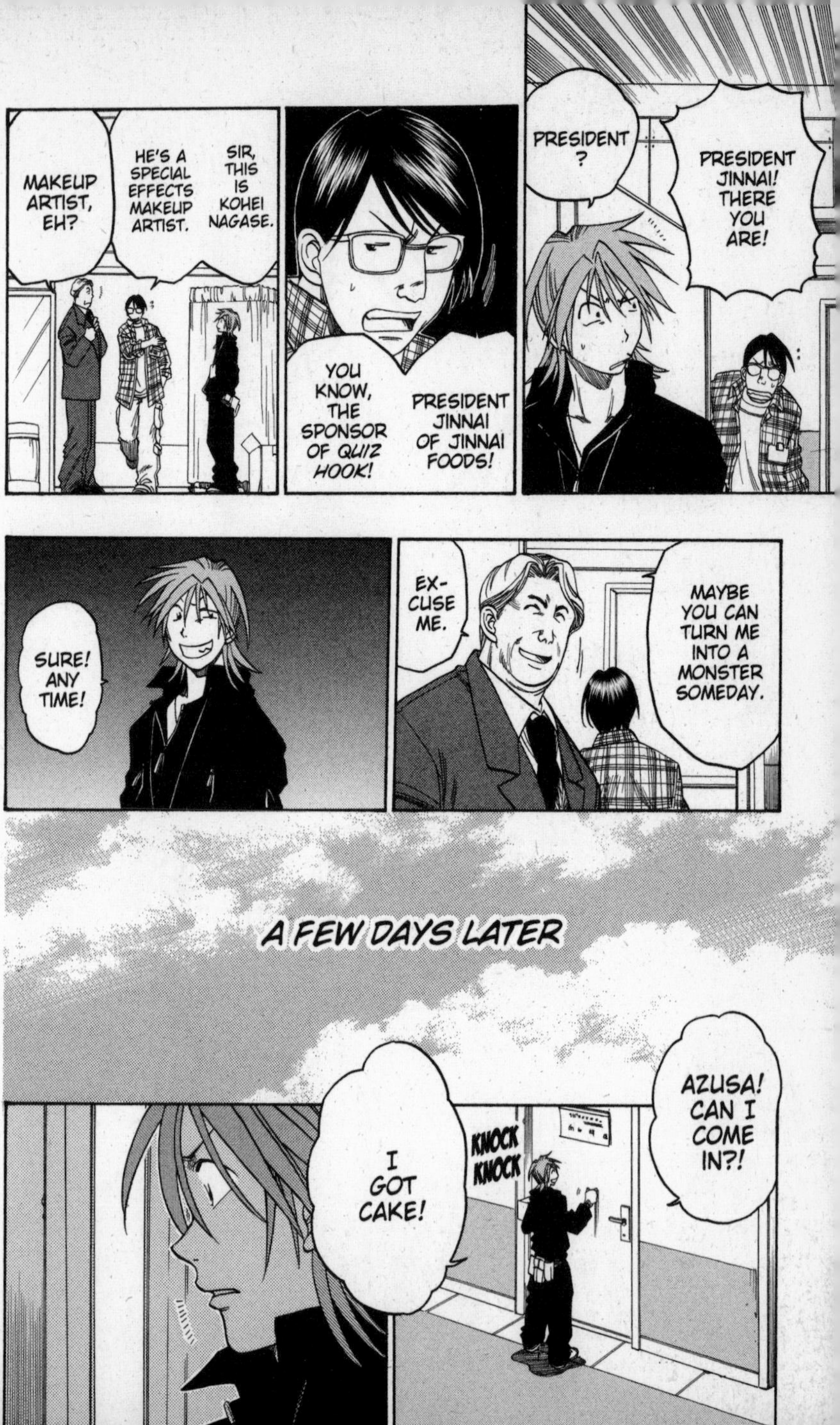
PRESIDENT JINNAI! THERE YOU ARE!
PRESIDENT ?
PRESIDENT JINNAI OF JINNAI FOODS!
YOU KNOW, THE SPONSOR OF QUIZ HOOK!
SIR, THIS IS KOHEI NAGASE.
HE'S A SPECIAL EFFECTS MAKEUP ARTIST.
MAKEUP ARTIST, EH?
MAYBE YOU CAN TURN ME INTO A MONSTER SOMEDAY.
EX-CUSE ME.
SURE! ANY TIME!
A FEW DAYS LATER
AZUSA! CAN I COME IN?!
KNOCK KNOCK
I GOT CAKE!

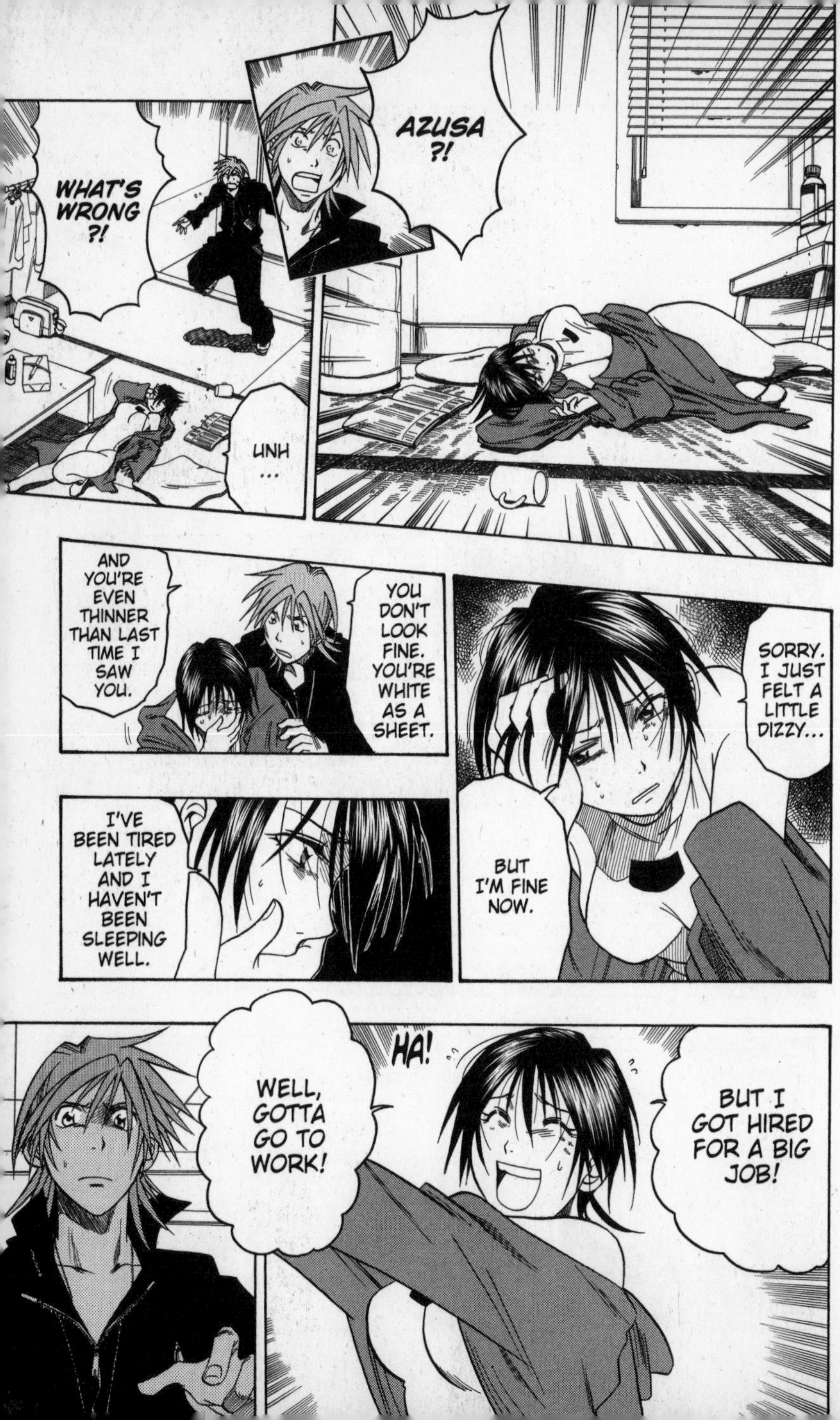
AZUSA ?!
WHAT'S WRONG ?!
UNH ...
SORRY. I JUST FELT A LITTLE DIZZY...
BUT I'M FINE NOW.
YOU DON'T LOOK FINE. YOU'RE WHITE AS A SHEET.
AND YOU'RE EVEN THINNER THAN LAST TIME I SAW YOU.
I'VE BEEN TIRED LATELY AND I HAVEN'T BEEN SLEEPING WELL.
BUT I GOT HIRED FOR A BIG JOB!
HA!
WELL, GOTTA GO TO WORK!

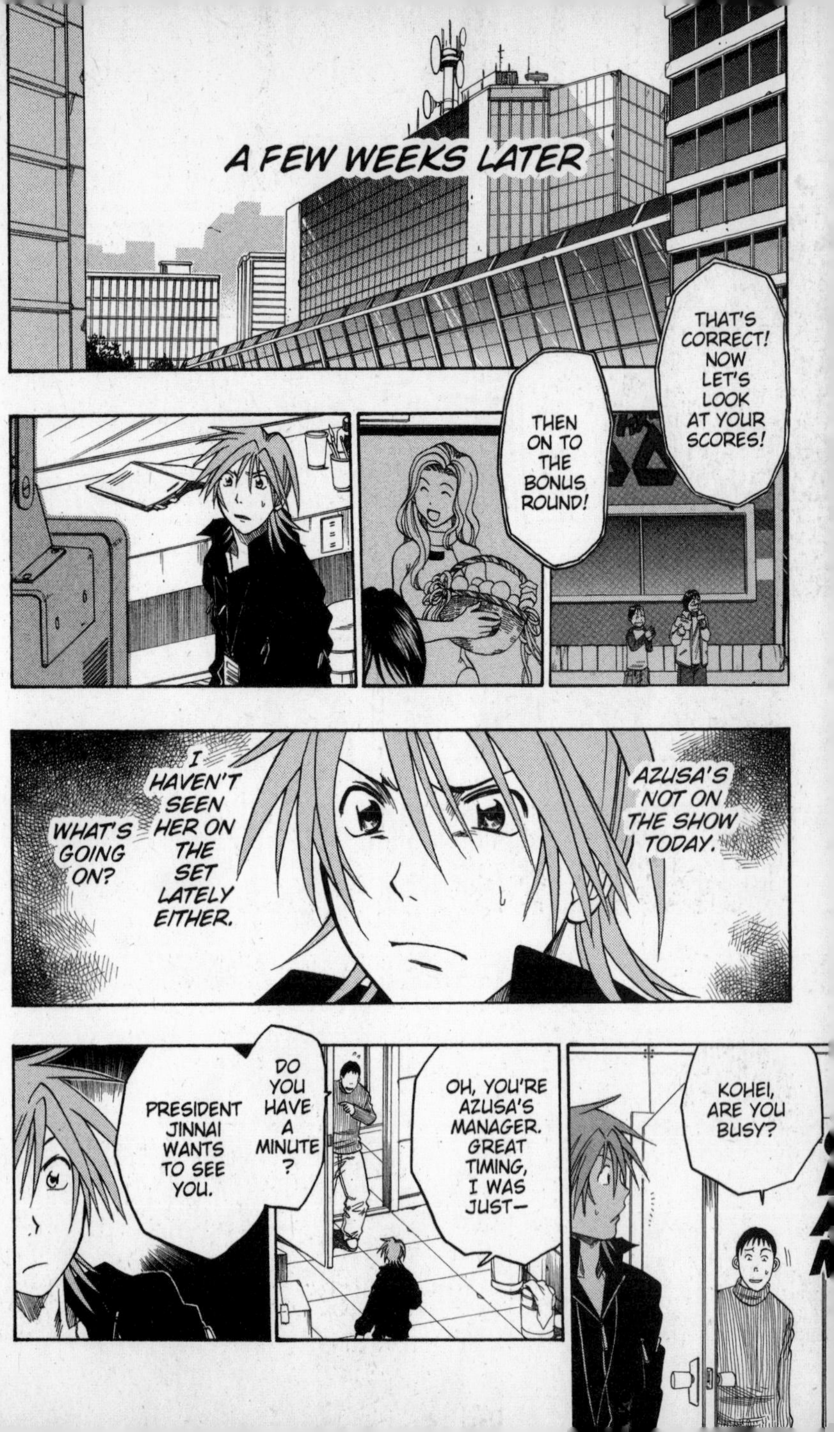
A FEW WEEKS LATER
THAT'S CORRECT! NOW LET'S LOOK AT YOUR SCORES!
THEN ON TO THE BONUS ROUND!
AZUSA'S NOT ON THE SHOW TODAY.
I HAVEN'T SEEN HER ON THE SET LATELY EITHER.
WHAT'S GOING ON?
KOHEI, ARE YOU BUSY?
OH, YOU'RE AZUSA'S MANAGER. GREAT TIMING, I WAS JUST—
DO YOU HAVE A MINUTE?
PRESIDENT JINNAI WANTS TO SEE YOU.

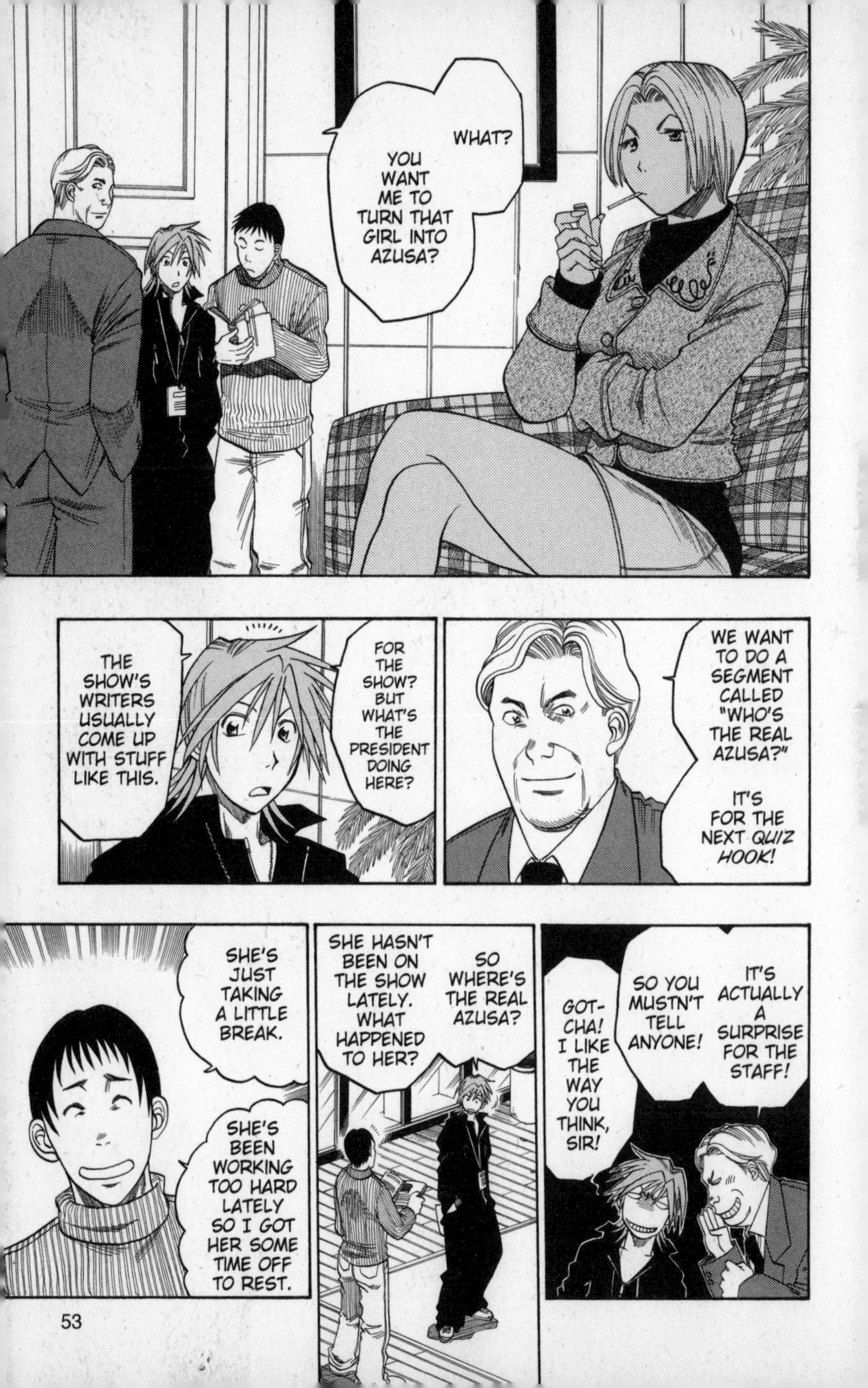
WHAT?
YOU WANT ME TO TURN THAT GIRL INTO AZUSA?
WE WANT TO DO A SEGMENT CALLED "WHO'S THE REAL AZUSA?"
IT'S FOR THE NEXT *QUIZ HOOK!*
FOR THE SHOW? BUT WHAT'S THE PRESIDENT DOING HERE?
THE SHOW'S WRITERS USUALLY COME UP WITH STUFF LIKE THIS.
IT'S ACTUALLY A SURPRISE FOR THE STAFF!
SO YOU MUSTN'T TELL ANYONE!
GOT-CHA! I LIKE THE WAY YOU THINK, SIR!
SO WHERE'S THE REAL AZUSA?
SHE HASN'T BEEN ON THE SHOW LATELY. WHAT HAPPENED TO HER?
SHE'S JUST TAKING A LITTLE BREAK.
SHE'S BEEN WORKING TOO HARD LATELY SO I GOT HER SOME TIME OFF TO REST.

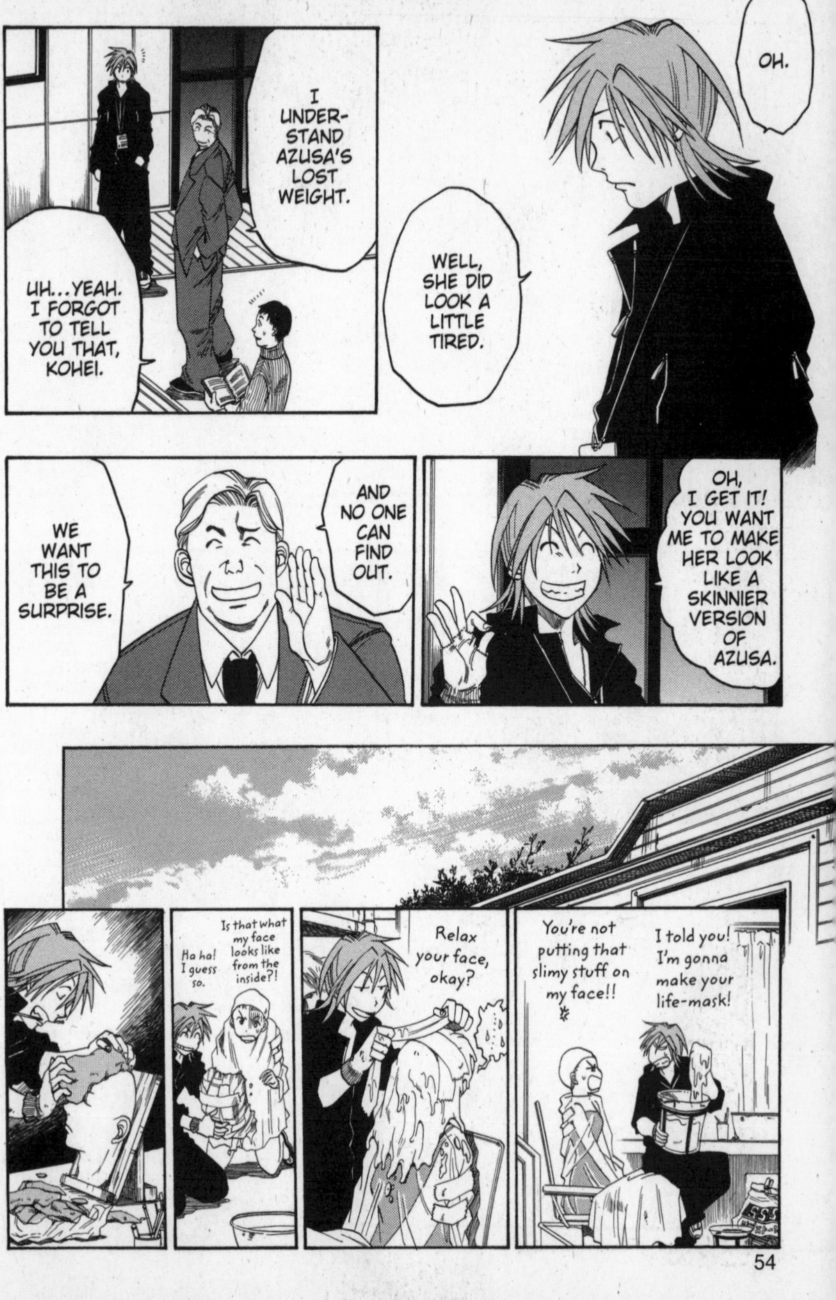
OH.
WELL, SHE DID LOOK A LITTLE TIRED.
I UNDER-STAND AZUSA'S LOST WEIGHT.
UH...YEAH. I FORGOT TO TELL YOU THAT, KOHEI.
OH, I GET IT! YOU WANT ME TO MAKE HER LOOK LIKE A SKINNIER VERSION OF AZUSA.
AND NO ONE CAN FIND OUT.
WE WANT THIS TO BE A SURPRISE.
I told you! I'm gonna make your life-mask!
You're not putting that slimy stuff on my face!!
Relax your face, okay?
Is that what my face looks like from the inside?!
Ha ha! I guess so.

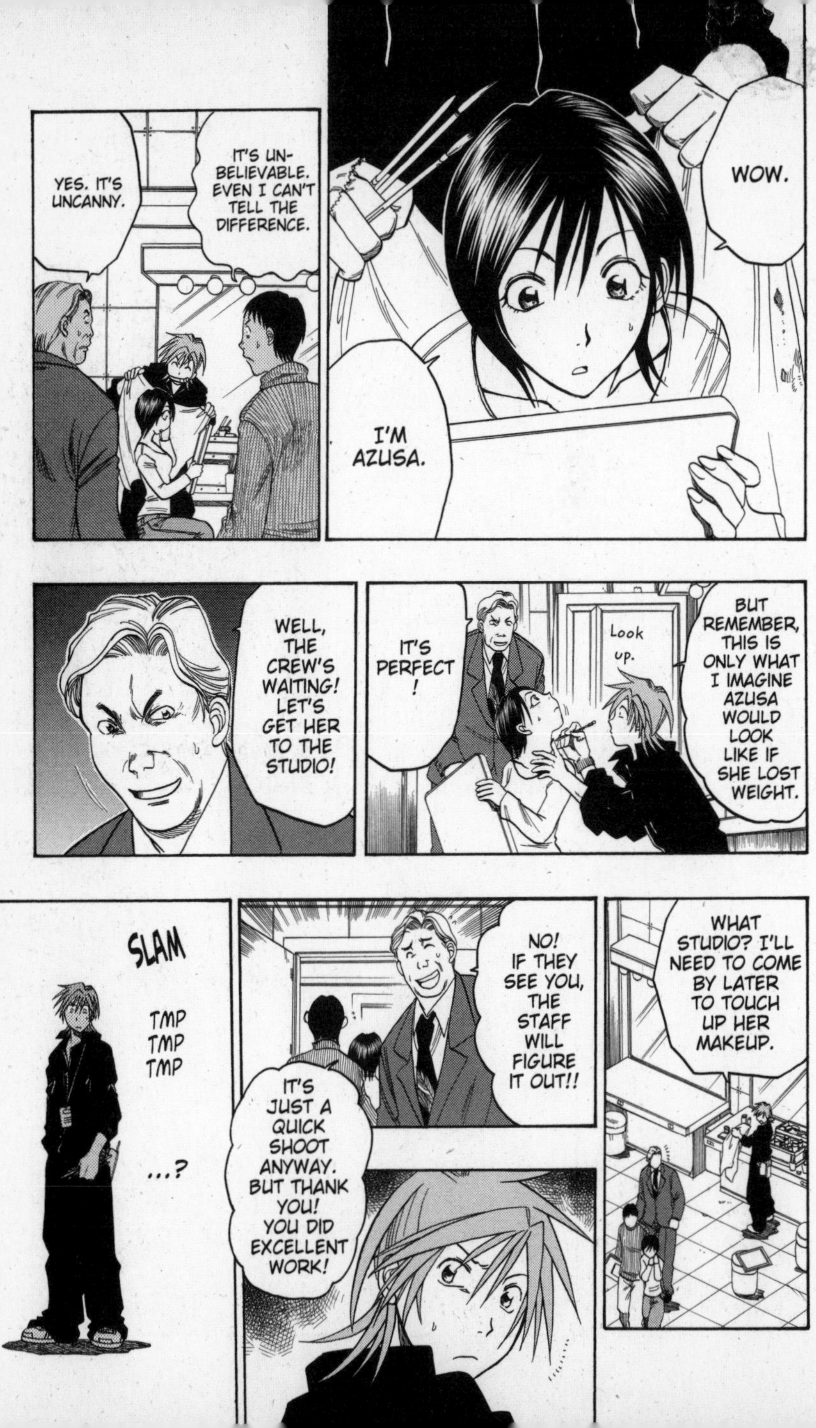
WOW.
I'M AZUSA.
IT'S UN-BELIEVABLE. EVEN I CAN'T TELL THE DIFFERENCE.
YES. IT'S UNCANNY.
BUT REMEMBER, THIS IS ONLY WHAT I IMAGINE AZUSA WOULD LOOK LIKE IF SHE LOST WEIGHT.
Look up.
IT'S PERFECT!
WELL, THE CREW'S WAITING! LET'S GET HER TO THE STUDIO!
WHAT STUDIO? I'LL NEED TO COME BY LATER TO TOUCH UP HER MAKEUP.
NO! IF THEY SEE YOU, THE STAFF WILL FIGURE IT OUT!!
IT'S JUST A QUICK SHOOT ANYWAY. BUT THANK YOU! YOU DID EXCELLENT WORK!
SLAM
TMP TMP TMP
...?

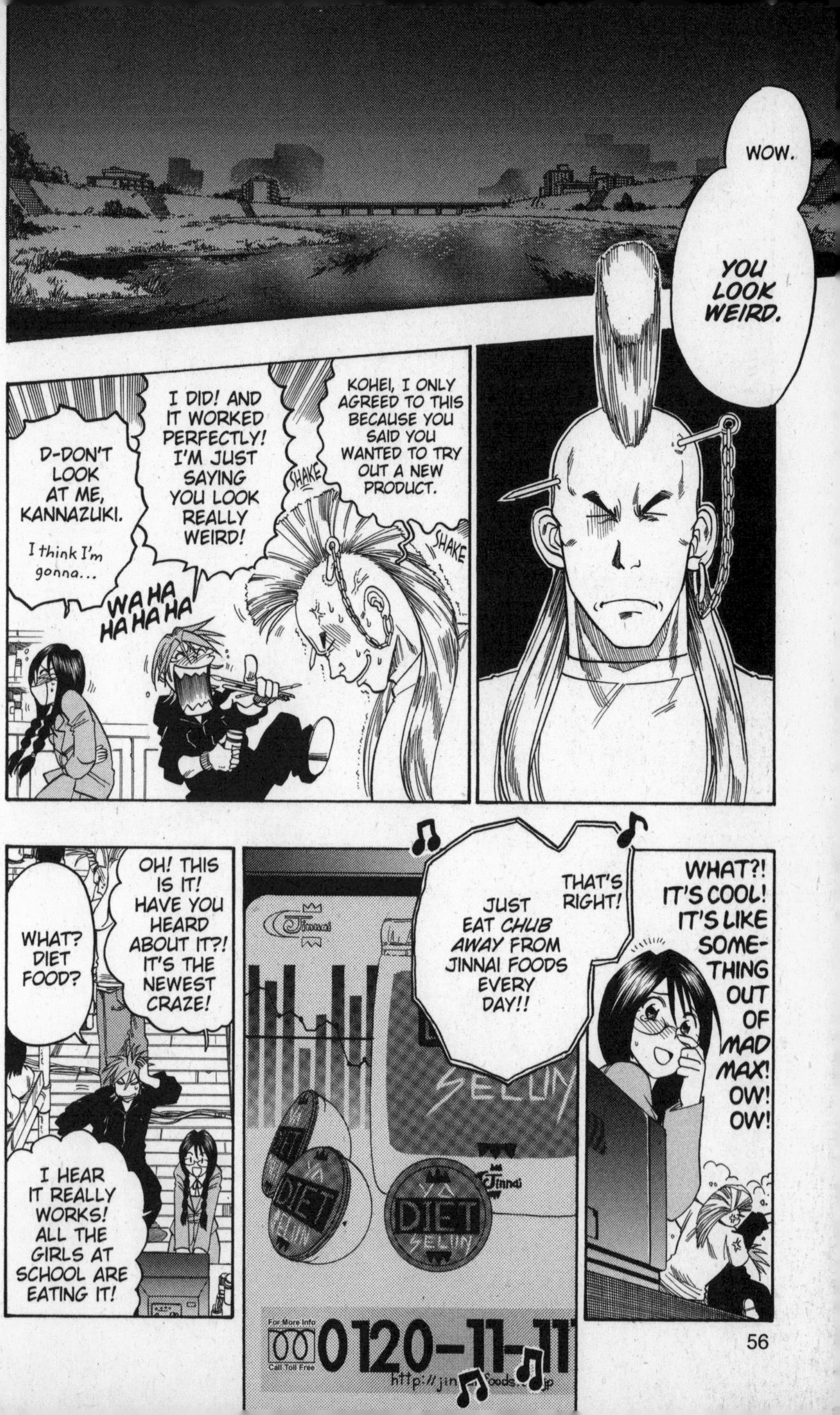
WOW.
YOU LOOK WEIRD.
KOHEI, I ONLY AGREED TO THIS BECAUSE YOU SAID YOU WANTED TO TRY OUT A NEW PRODUCT.
SHAKE
SHAKE
I DID! AND IT WORKED PERFECTLY! I'M JUST SAYING YOU LOOK REALLY WEIRD!
D-DON'T LOOK AT ME, KANNAZUKI.
I think I'm gonna...
WA HA HA HA HA HA
WHAT?! IT'S COOL! IT'S LIKE SOME-THING OUT OF MAD MAX! OW! OW!
THAT'S RIGHT!
JUST EAT CHUB AWAY FROM JINNAI FOODS EVERY DAY!!
DIET
SELUN
For More Info
0120-11-11
Call Toll Free
OH! THIS IS IT! HAVE YOU HEARD ABOUT IT?! IT'S THE NEWEST CRAZE!
WHAT? DIET FOOD?
I HEAR IT REALLY WORKS! ALL THE GIRLS AT SCHOOL ARE EATING IT!

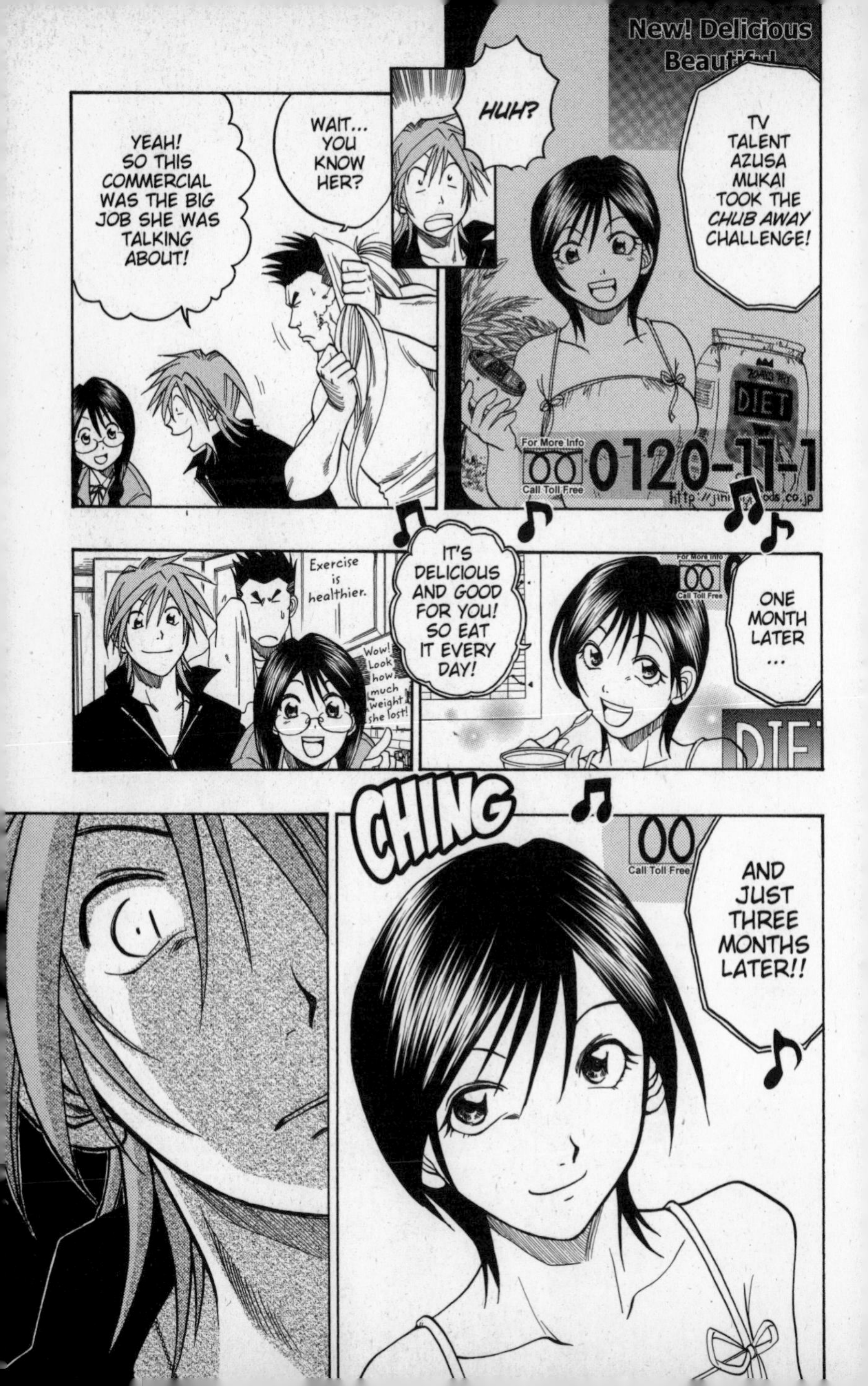

New! Delicious
TV TALENT AZUSA MUKAI TOOK THE CHUB AWAY CHALLENGE!
DIET
For More Info
0120-11-1
Call Toll Free
HUH?
WAIT... YOU KNOW HER?
YEAH! SO THIS COMMERCIAL WAS THE BIG JOB SHE WAS TALKING ABOUT!
For More Info
Call Toll Free
ONE MONTH LATER...
IT'S DELICIOUS AND GOOD FOR YOU! SO EAT IT EVERY DAY!
Exercise is healthier.
Wow! Look how much weight she lost!
CHING
Call Toll Free
AND JUST THREE MONTHS LATER!!

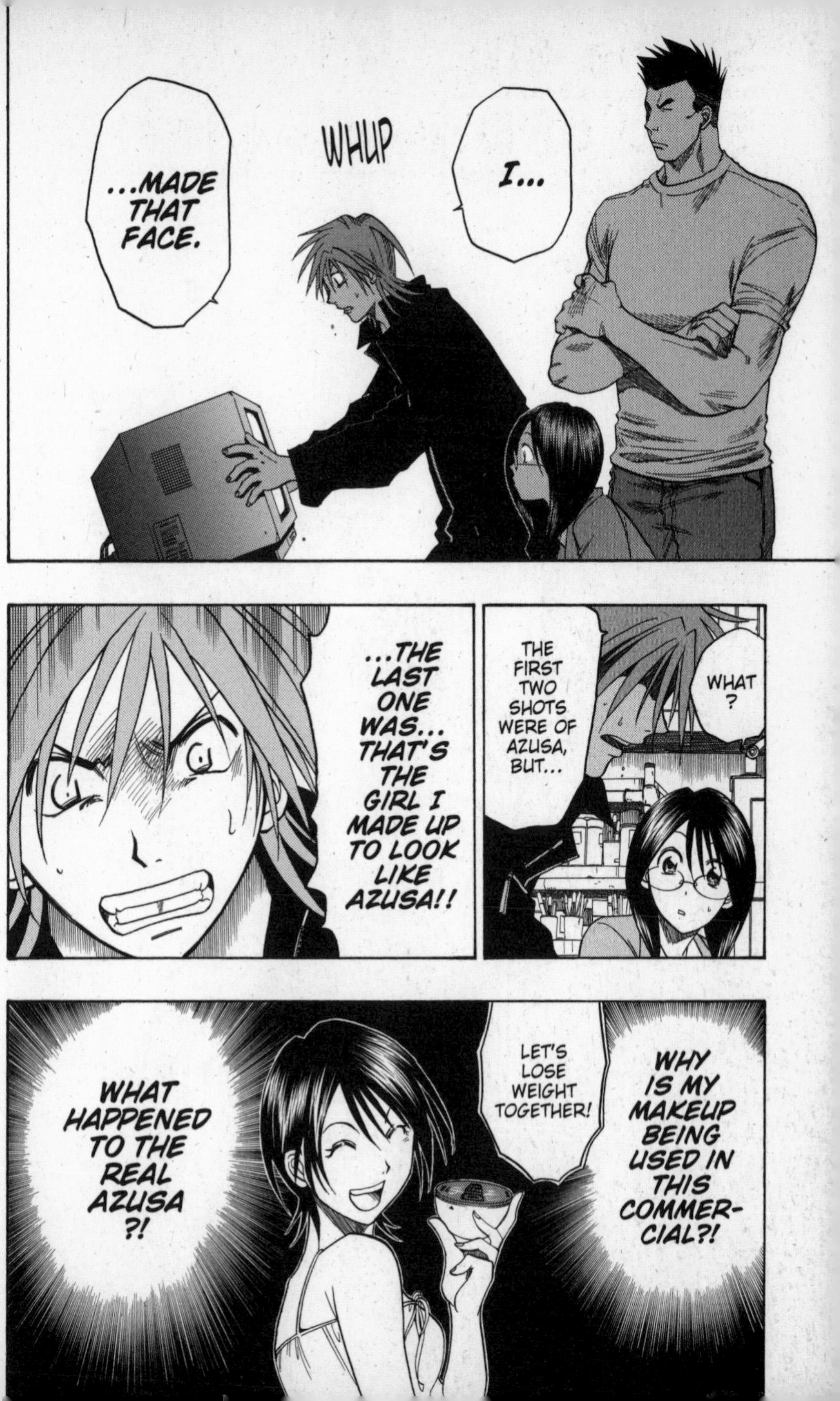
I...
WHUP
...MADE THAT FACE.
WHAT?
THE FIRST TWO SHOTS WERE OF AZUSA, BUT...
...THE LAST ONE WAS... THAT'S THE GIRL I MADE UP TO LOOK LIKE AZUSA!!
WHY IS MY MAKEUP BEING USED IN THIS COMMER-CIAL?!
LET'S LOSE WEIGHT TOGETHER!
WHAT HAPPENED TO THE REAL AZUSA?!

Scene 40:
Field of Dreams (Part 2)

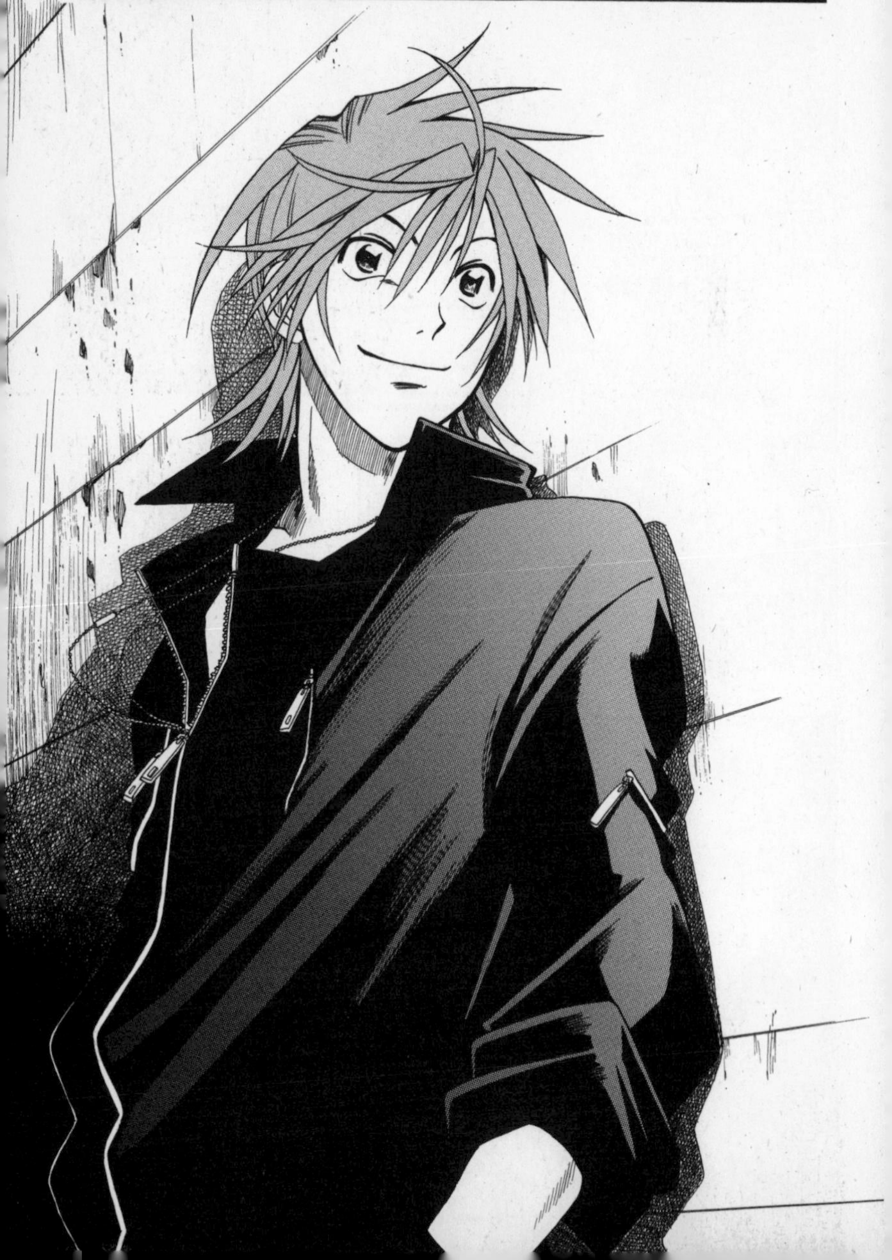

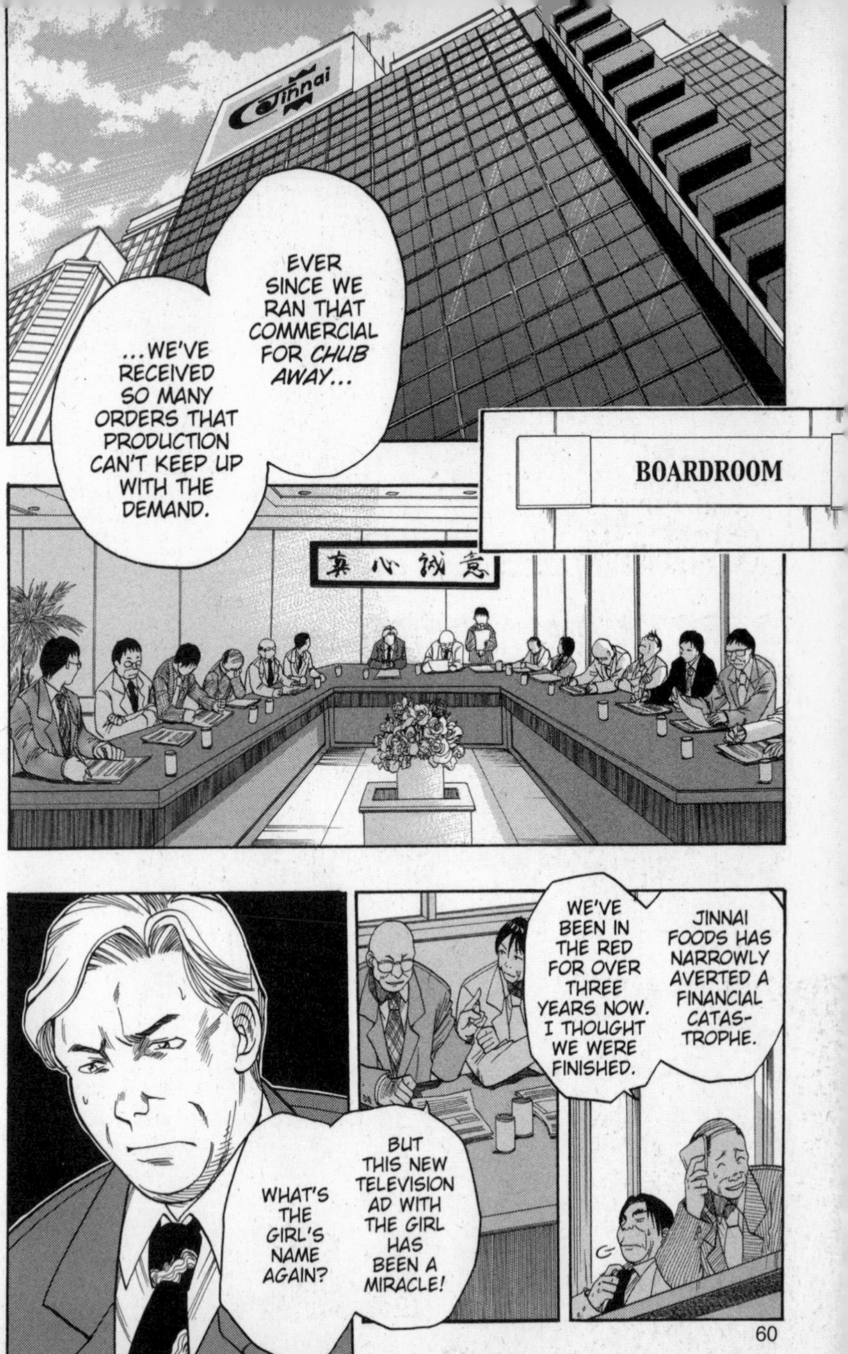
Jinnai
EVER SINCE WE RAN THAT COMMERCIAL FOR *CHUB AWAY*...
...WE'VE RECEIVED SO MANY ORDERS THAT PRODUCTION CAN'T KEEP UP WITH THE DEMAND.
BOARDROOM
真心誠意
JINNAI FOODS HAS NARROWLY AVERTED A FINANCIAL CATAS-TROPHE.
WE'VE BEEN IN THE RED FOR OVER THREE YEARS NOW. I THOUGHT WE WERE FINISHED.
BUT THIS NEW TELEVISION AD WITH THE GIRL HAS BEEN A MIRACLE!
WHAT'S THE GIRL'S NAME AGAIN?

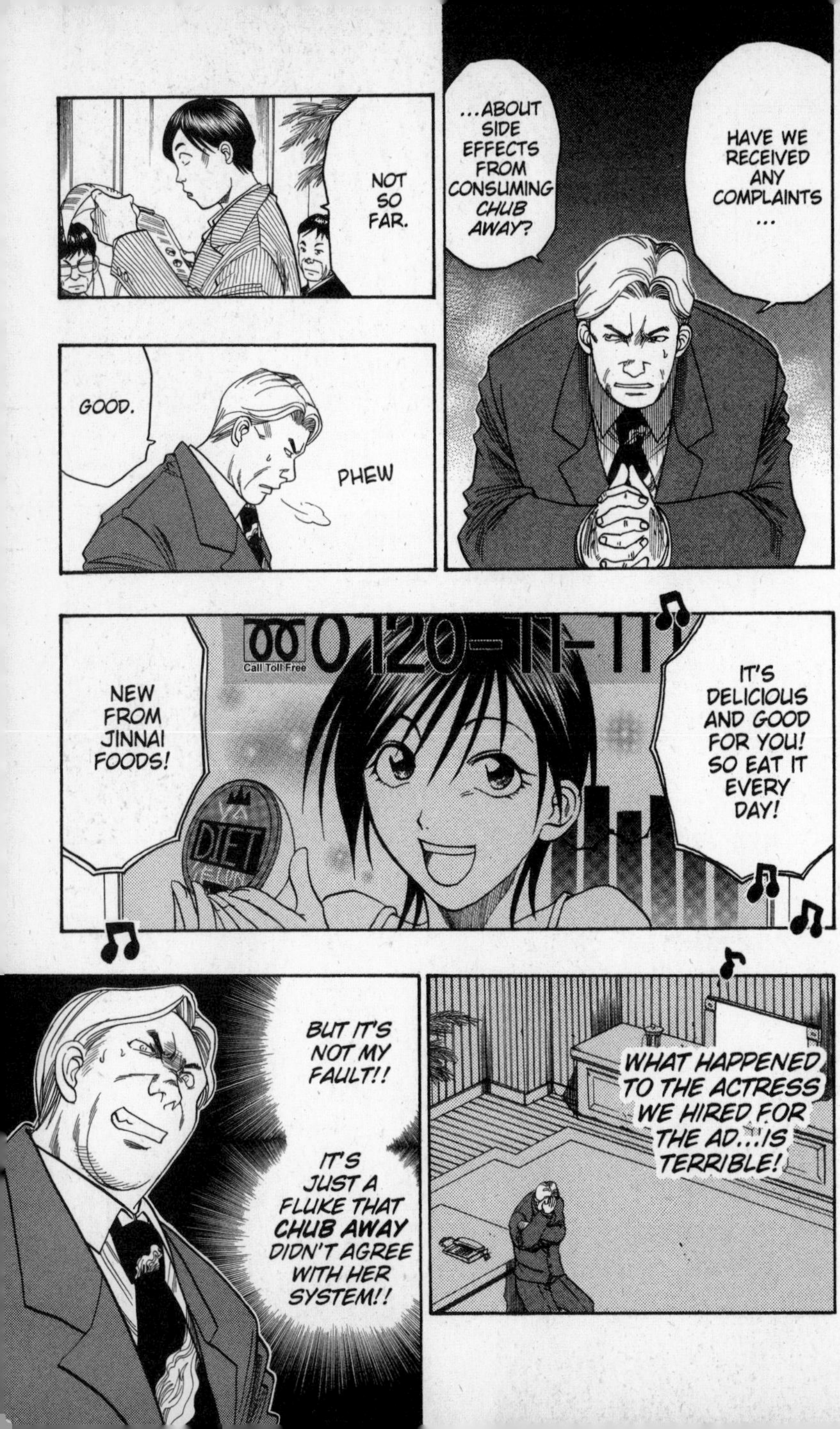
HAVE WE RECEIVED ANY COMPLAINTS...
...ABOUT SIDE EFFECTS FROM CONSUMING CHUB AWAY?
NOT SO FAR.
GOOD.
PHEW
Call Toll Free
IT'S DELICIOUS AND GOOD FOR YOU! SO EAT IT EVERY DAY!
NEW FROM JINNAI FOODS!
DIET
WHAT HAPPENED TO THE ACTRESS WE HIRED FOR THE AD...IS TERRIBLE!
BUT IT'S NOT MY FAULT!!
IT'S JUST A FLUKE THAT CHUB AWAY DIDN'T AGREE WITH HER SYSTEM!!

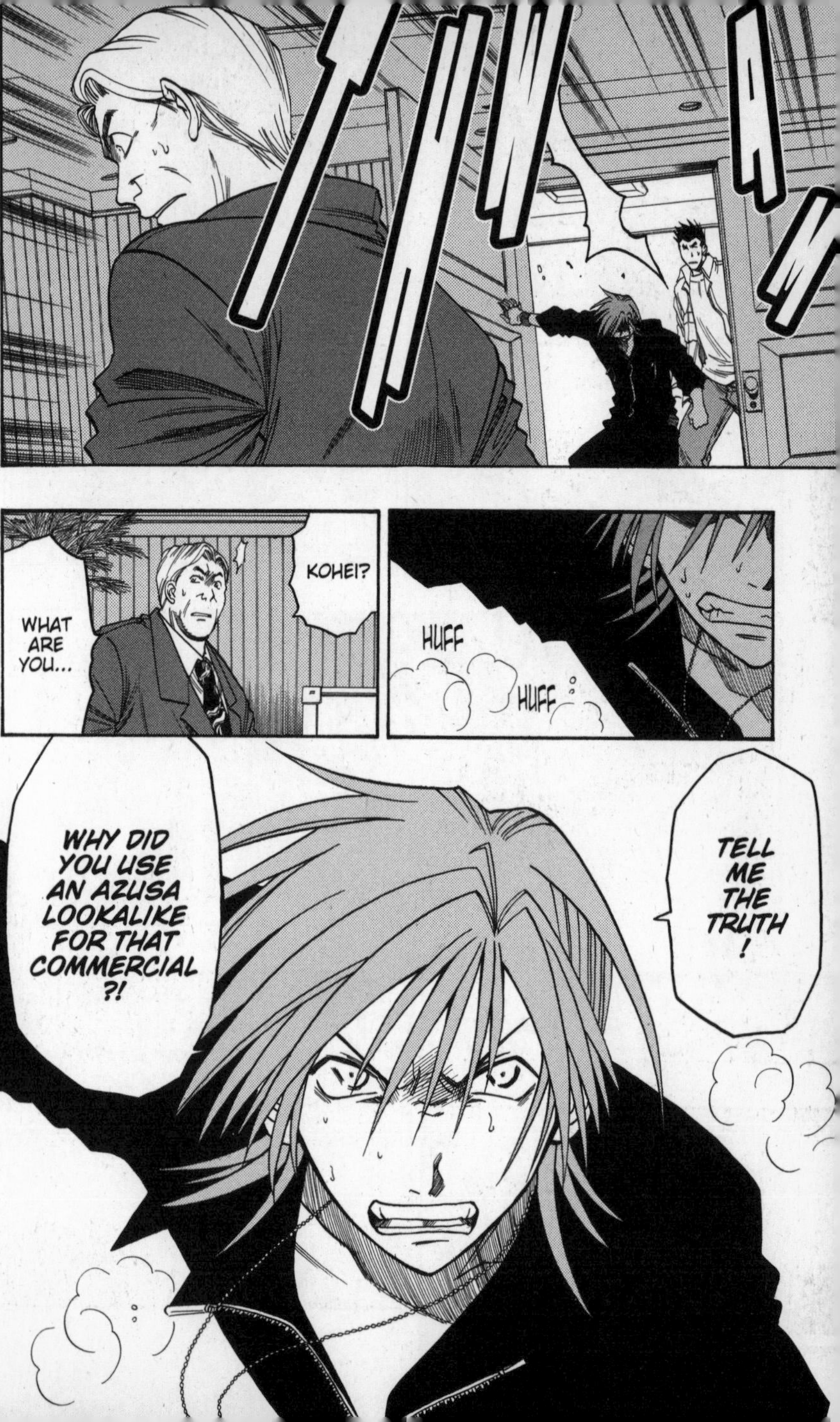
HUFF
HUFF
KOHEI?
WHAT ARE YOU...
TELL ME THE TRUTH!
WHY DID YOU USE AN AZUSA LOOKALIKE FOR THAT COMMERCIAL?!

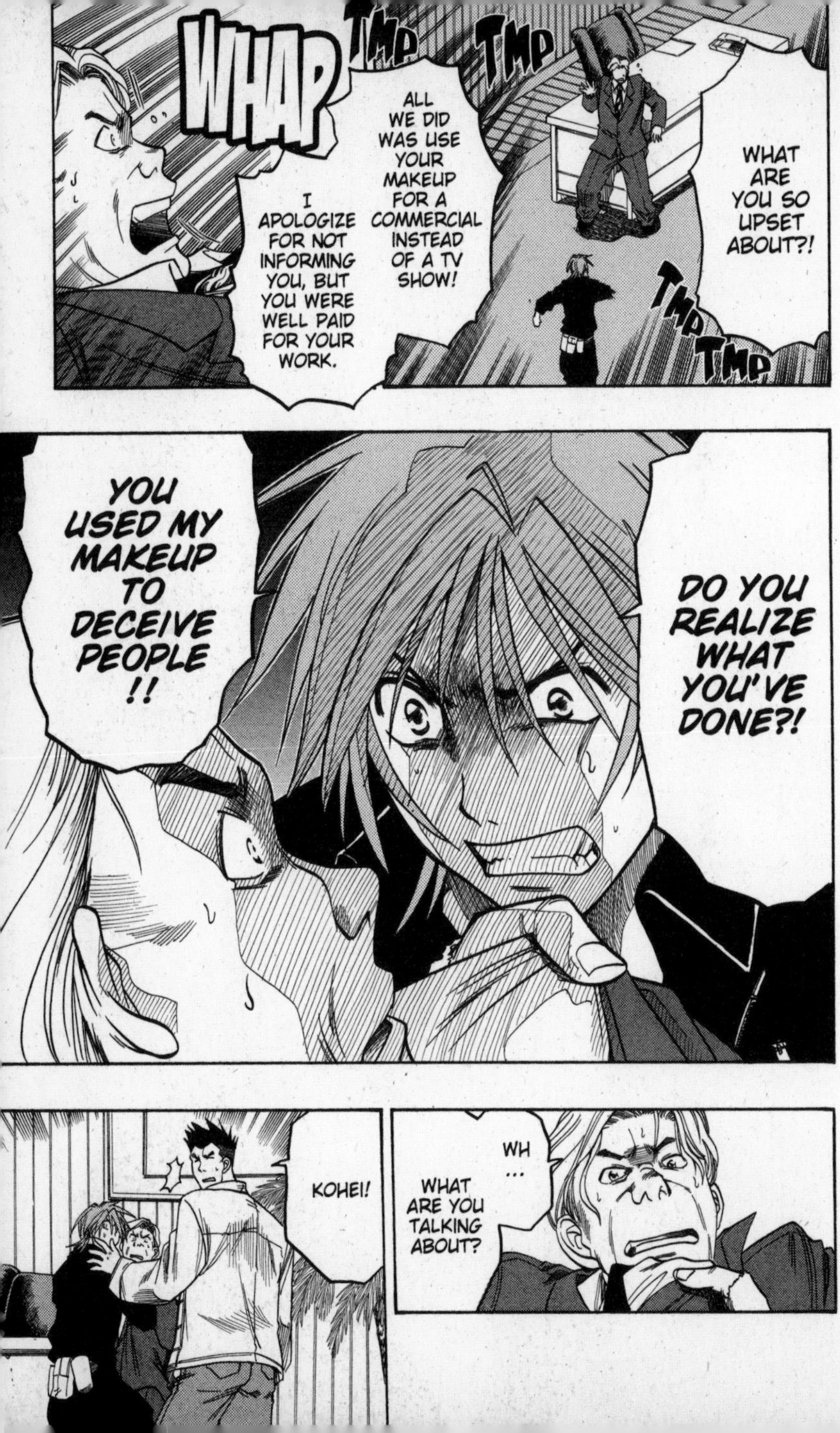
TMP TMP
WHAT ARE YOU SO UPSET ABOUT?!
WHAP
ALL WE DID WAS USE YOUR MAKEUP FOR A COMMERCIAL INSTEAD OF A TV SHOW!
I APOLOGIZE FOR NOT INFORMING YOU, BUT YOU WERE WELL PAID FOR YOUR WORK.
TMP TMP
DO YOU REALIZE WHAT YOU'VE DONE?!
YOU USED MY MAKEUP TO DECEIVE PEOPLE!!
WH...
WHAT ARE YOU TALKING ABOUT?
KOHEI!

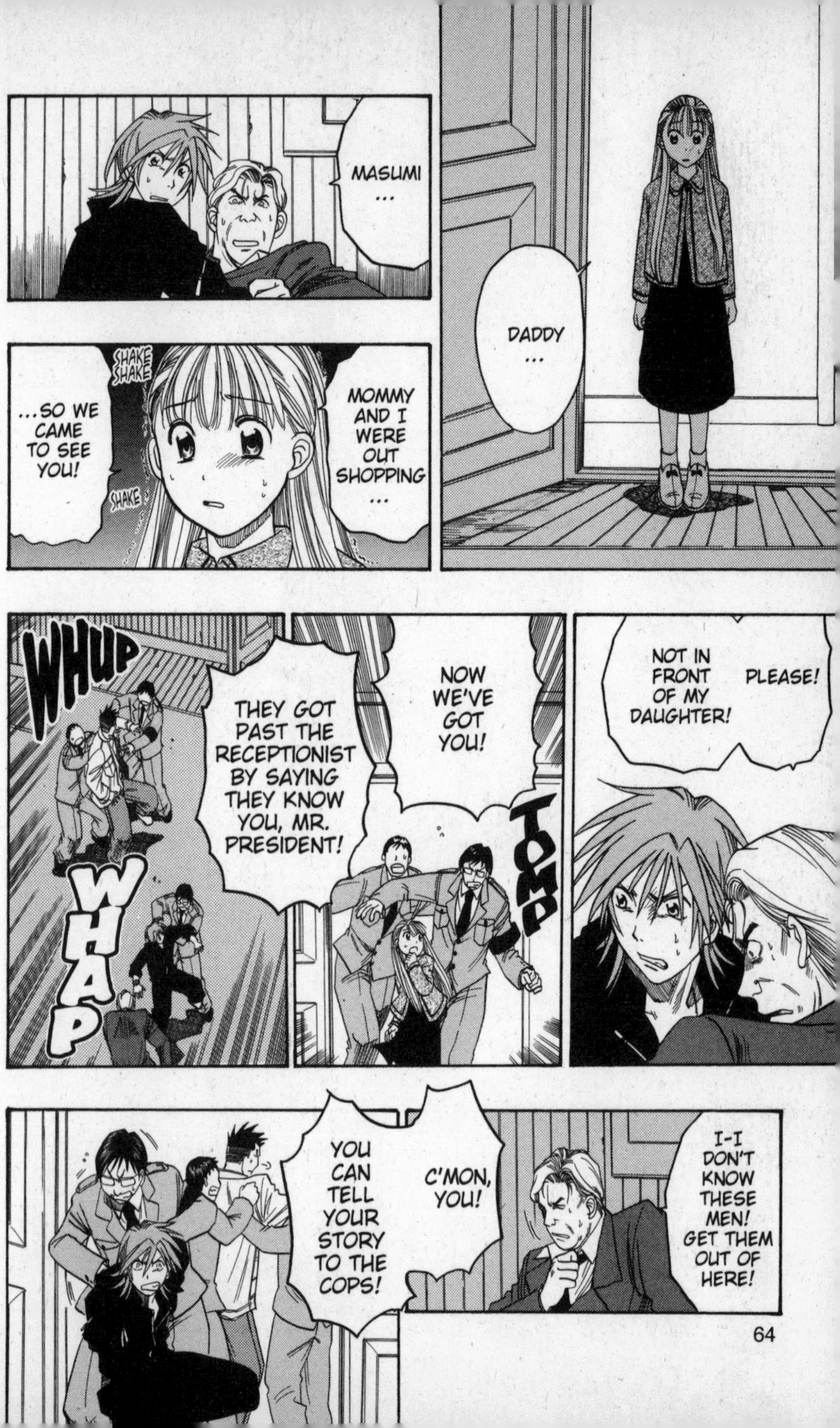
DADDY ...
MASUMI ...
MOMMY AND I WERE OUT SHOPPING ...
SHAKE SHAKE
...SO WE CAME TO SEE YOU!
SHAKE
PLEASE!
NOT IN FRONT OF MY DAUGHTER!
NOW WE'VE GOT YOU!
TOMP
THEY GOT PAST THE RECEPTIONIST BY SAYING THEY KNOW YOU, MR. PRESIDENT!
WHUP
WHAP
I-I DON'T KNOW THESE MEN! GET THEM OUT OF HERE!
C'MON, YOU!
YOU CAN TELL YOUR STORY TO THE COPS!

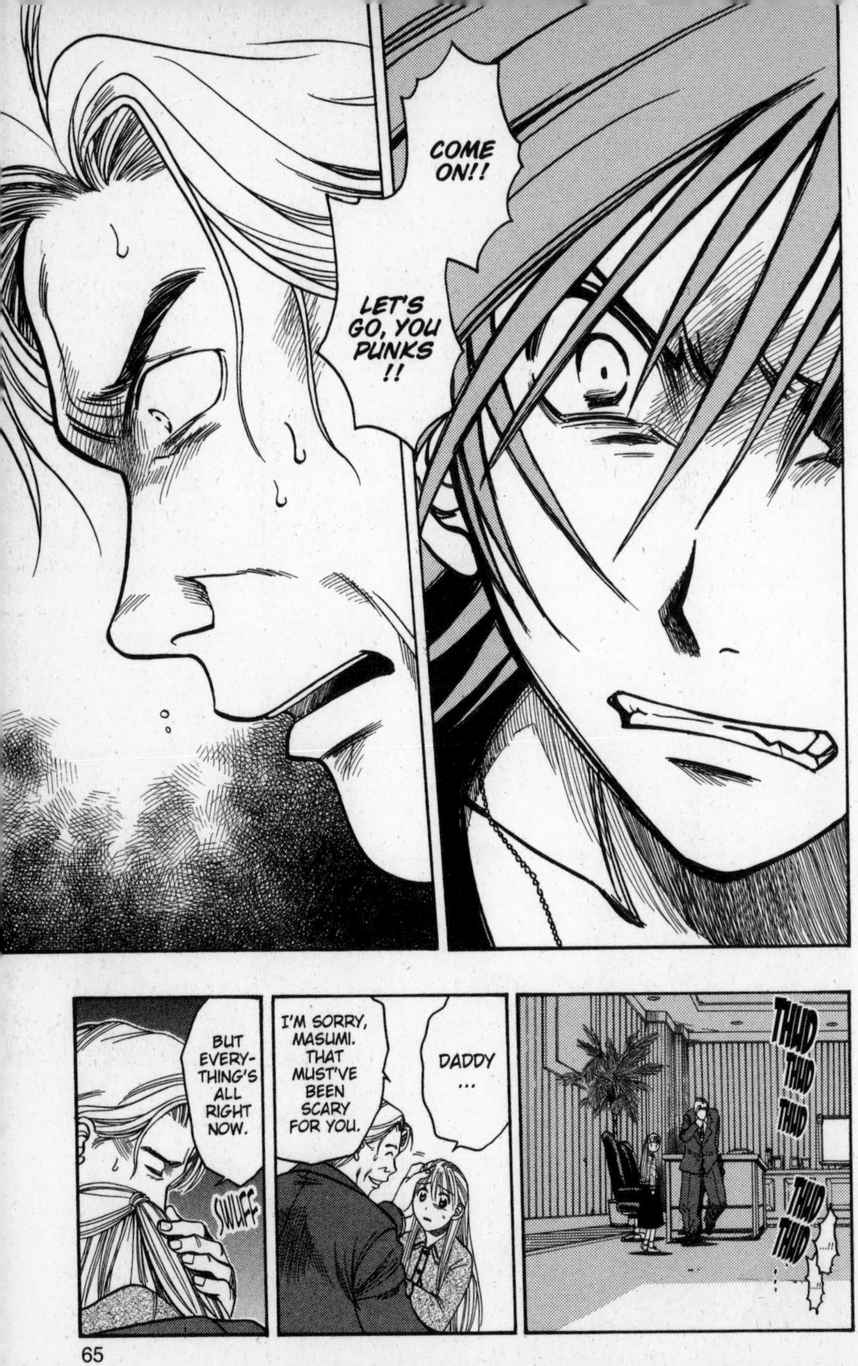
COME ON!!
LET'S GO, YOU PUNKS!!
THUD THUD THUD
THUD THUD
...!!
...!!
DADDY ...
I'M SORRY, MASUMI. THAT MUST'VE BEEN SCARY FOR YOU.
BUT EVERY-THING'S ALL RIGHT NOW.
SNUFF

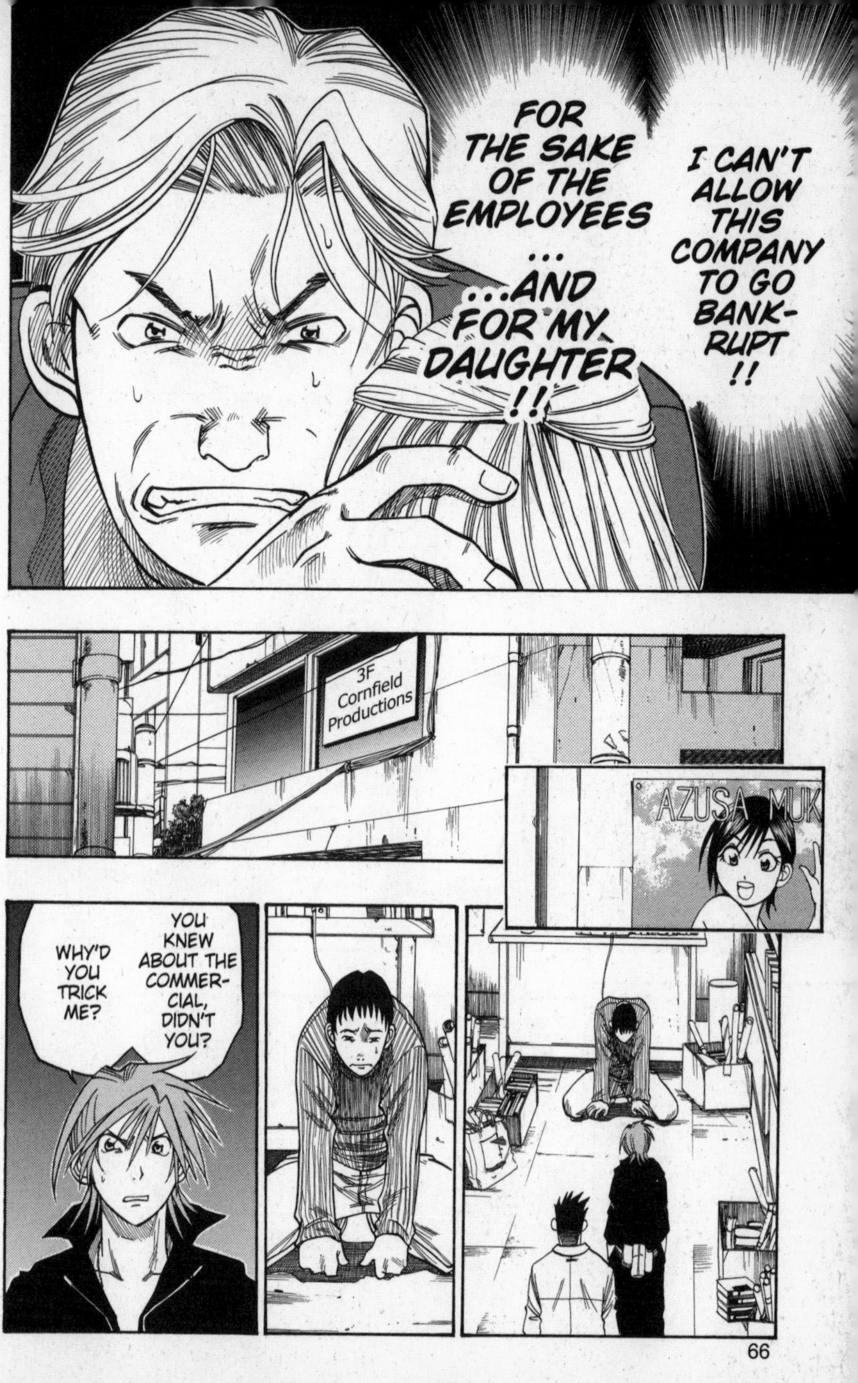
I CAN'T ALLOW THIS COMPANY TO GO BANK-RUPT!!
FOR THE SAKE OF THE EMPLOYEES...
...AND FOR MY DAUGHTER!!
3F Cornfield Productions
AZUSA MUK
YOU KNEW ABOUT THE COMMER-CIAL, DIDN'T YOU?
WHY'D YOU TRICK ME?

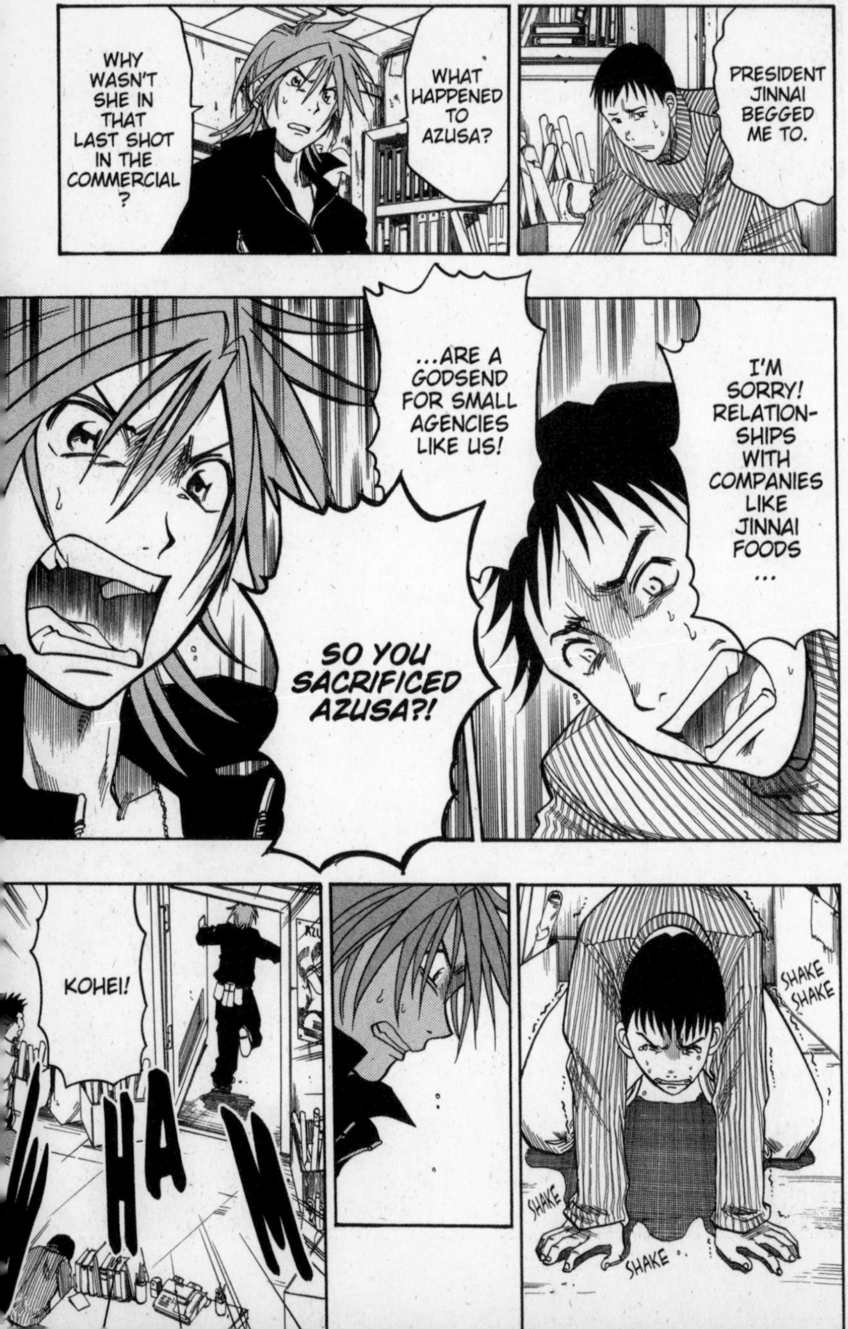
PRESIDENT JINNAI BEGGED ME TO.
WHAT HAPPENED TO AZUSA?
WHY WASN'T SHE IN THAT LAST SHOT IN THE COMMERCIAL?
I'M SORRY! RELATIONSHIPS WITH COMPANIES LIKE JINNAI FOODS...
...ARE A GODSEND FOR SMALL AGENCIES LIKE US!
SO YOU SACRIFICED AZUSA?!
SHAKE SHAKE
SHAKE
SHAKE
KOHEI!
WHAM

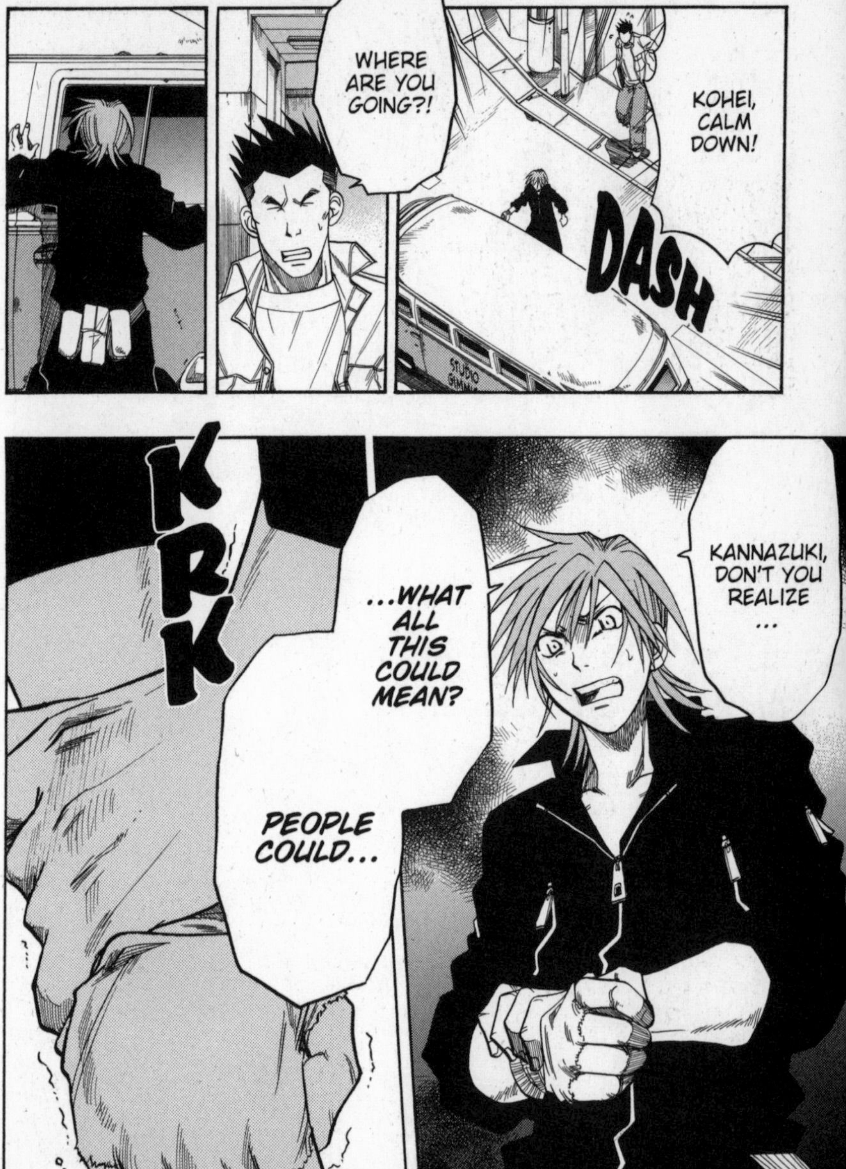
KOHEI, CALM DOWN!
DASH
WHERE ARE YOU GOING?!
KANNAZUKI, DON'T YOU REALIZE ...
...WHAT ALL THIS COULD MEAN?
PEOPLE COULD...
KRK

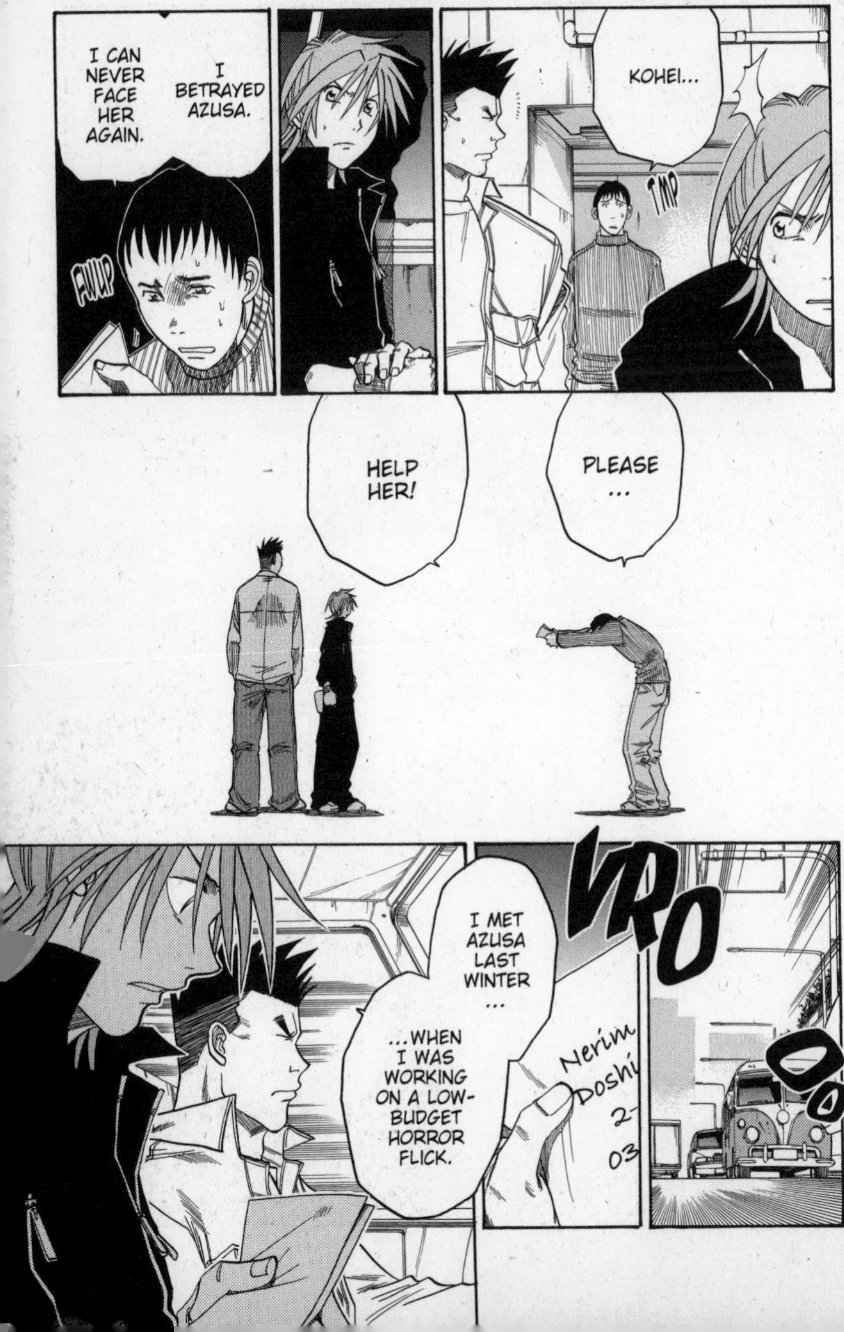
KOHEI...
TMP
I BETRAYED AZUSA.
I CAN NEVER FACE HER AGAIN.
FWUP
PLEASE ...
HELP HER!
VRO
OOO
Nerim Doshi 2- 03
I MET AZUSA LAST WINTER ...
...WHEN I WAS WORKING ON A LOW-BUDGET HORROR FLICK.

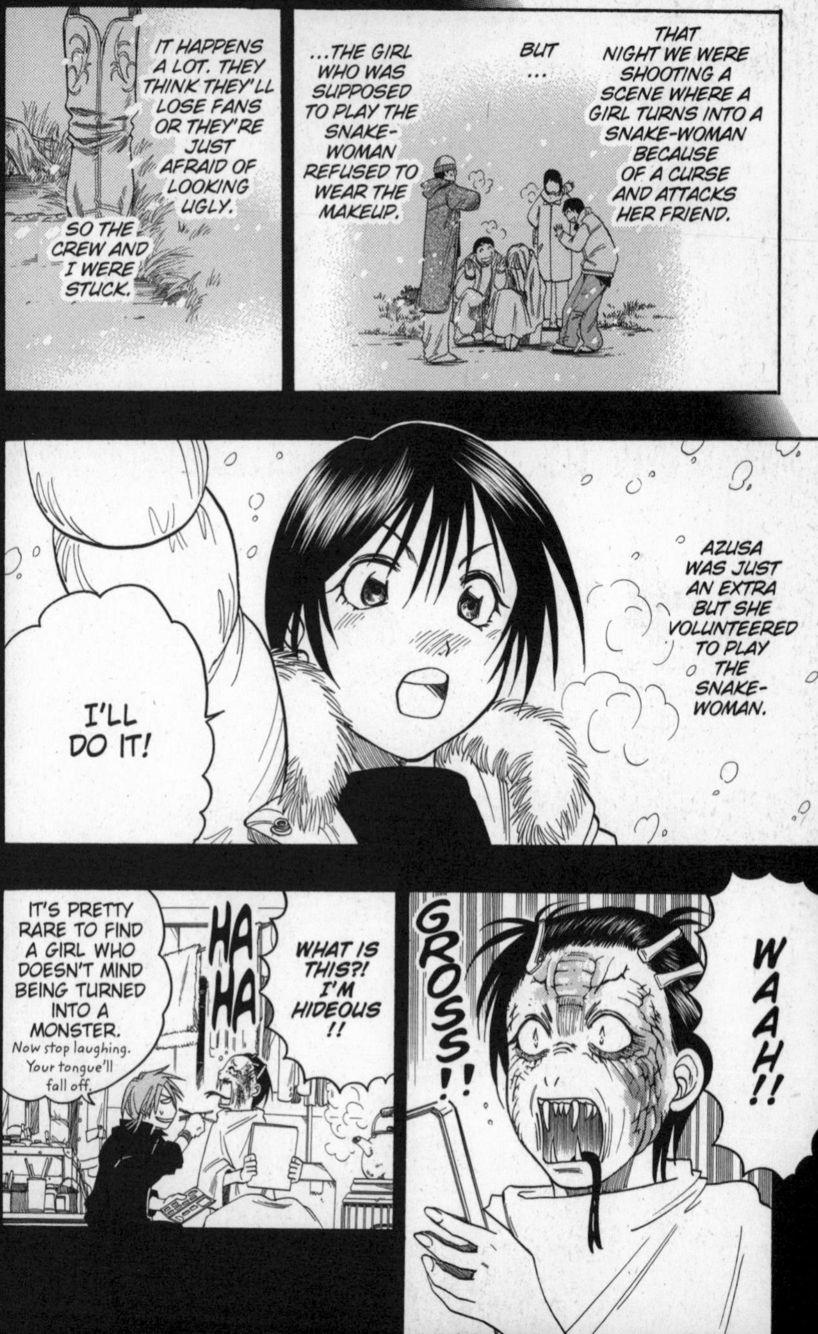
THAT NIGHT WE WERE SHOOTING A SCENE WHERE A GIRL TURNS INTO A SNAKE-WOMAN BECAUSE OF A CURSE AND ATTACKS HER FRIEND.
BUT ...
...THE GIRL WHO WAS SUPPOSED TO PLAY THE SNAKE-WOMAN REFUSED TO WEAR THE MAKEUP.
IT HAPPENS A LOT. THEY THINK THEY'LL LOSE FANS OR THEY'RE JUST AFRAID OF LOOKING UGLY.
SO THE CREW AND I WERE STUCK.
AZUSA WAS JUST AN EXTRA BUT SHE VOLUNTEERED TO PLAY THE SNAKE-WOMAN.
I'LL DO IT!
WAAAH!!
GROSS!!
WHAT IS THIS?! I'M HIDEOUS!!
HA HA
IT'S PRETTY RARE TO FIND A GIRL WHO DOESN'T MIND BEING TURNED INTO A MONSTER.
Now stop laughing. Your tongue'll fall off.

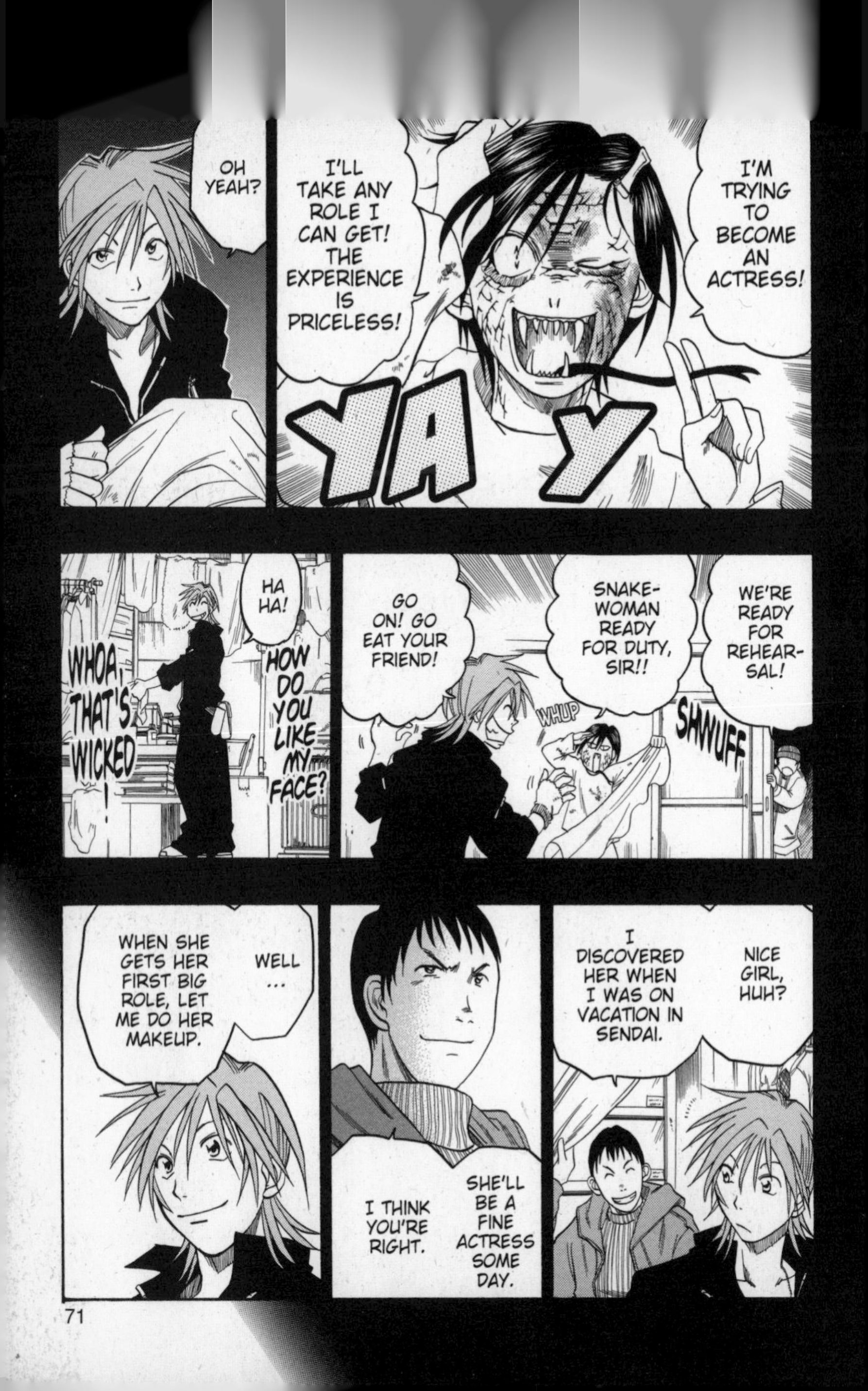
I'M TRYING TO BECOME AN ACTRESS!
I'LL TAKE ANY ROLE I CAN GET! THE EXPERIENCE IS PRICELESS!
YAY
OH YEAH?
WE'RE READY FOR REHEAR-SAL!
SHWUFF
SNAKE-WOMAN READY FOR DUTY, SIR!!
WHUP
GO ON! GO EAT YOUR FRIEND!
HA HA!
HOW DO YOU LIKE MY FACE?
WHOA, THAT'S WICKED!
NICE GIRL, HUH?
I DISCOVERED HER WHEN I WAS ON VACATION IN SENDAI.
SHE'LL BE A FINE ACTRESS SOME DAY.
I THINK YOU'RE RIGHT.
WELL ...
WHEN SHE GETS HER FIRST BIG ROLE, LET ME DO HER MAKEUP.

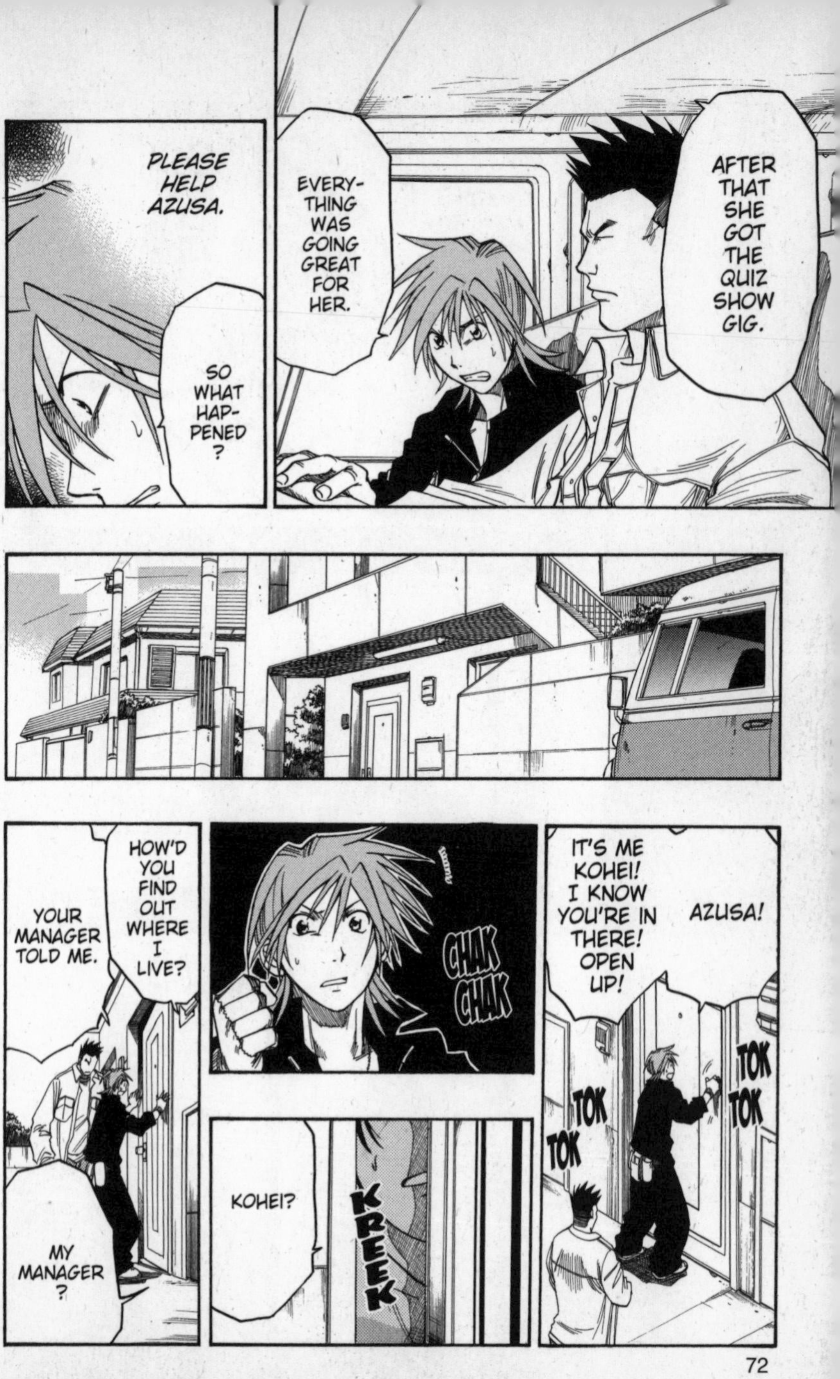
AFTER THAT SHE GOT THE QUIZ SHOW GIG.
EVERYTHING WAS GOING GREAT FOR HER.
PLEASE HELP AZUSA.
SO WHAT HAPPENED?
AZUSA!
IT'S ME KOHEI! I KNOW YOU'RE IN THERE! OPEN UP!
TOK TOK
TOK TOK
CHAK CHAK
KREEK
KOHEI?
HOW'D YOU FIND OUT WHERE I LIVE?
YOUR MANAGER TOLD ME.
MY MANAGER?

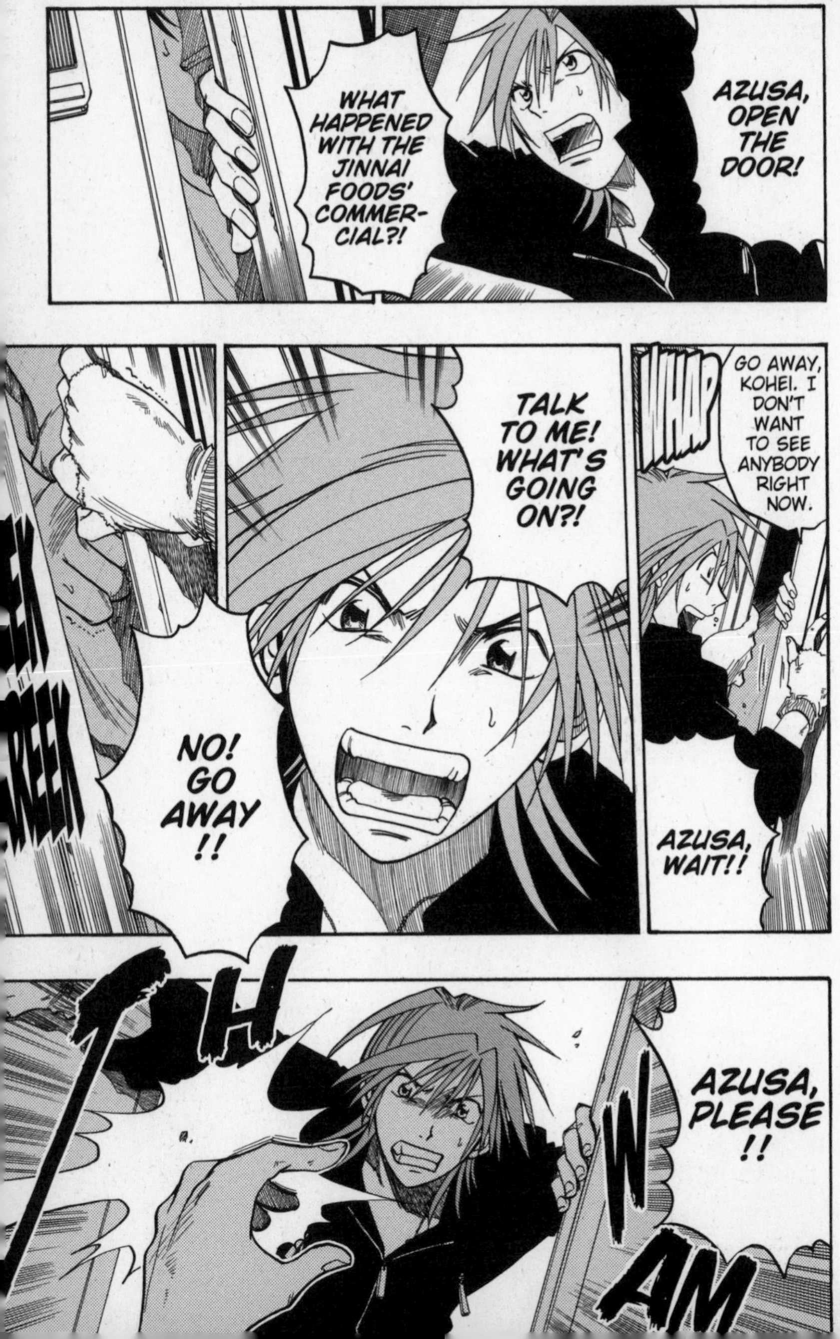
AZUSA, OPEN THE DOOR!
WHAT HAPPENED WITH THE JINNAI FOODS' COMMERCIAL?!
WHAP
GO AWAY, KOHEI. I DON'T WANT TO SEE ANYBODY RIGHT NOW.
AZUSA, WAIT!!
TALK TO ME! WHAT'S GOING ON?!
NO! GO AWAY!!
AZUSA, PLEASE!!

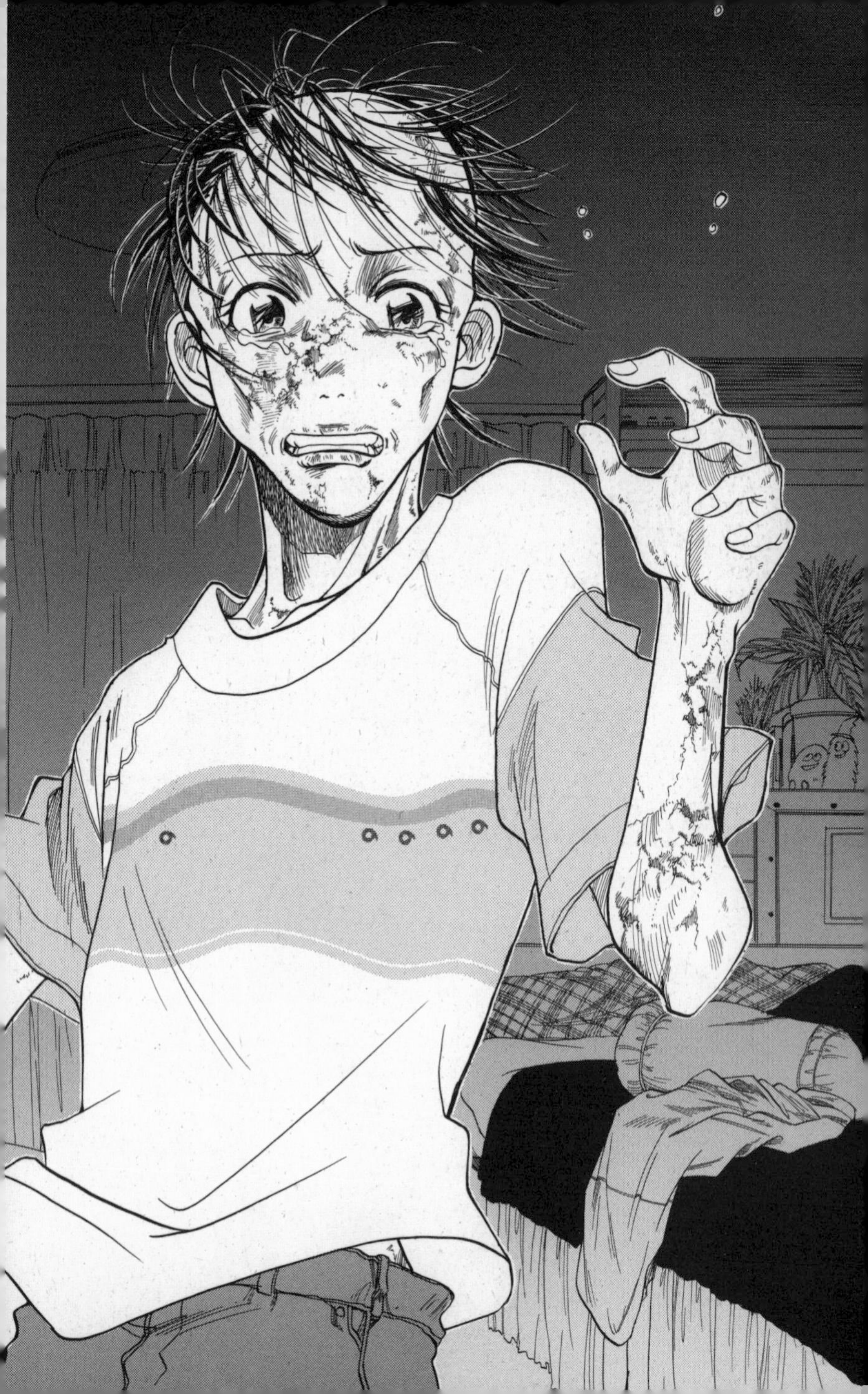

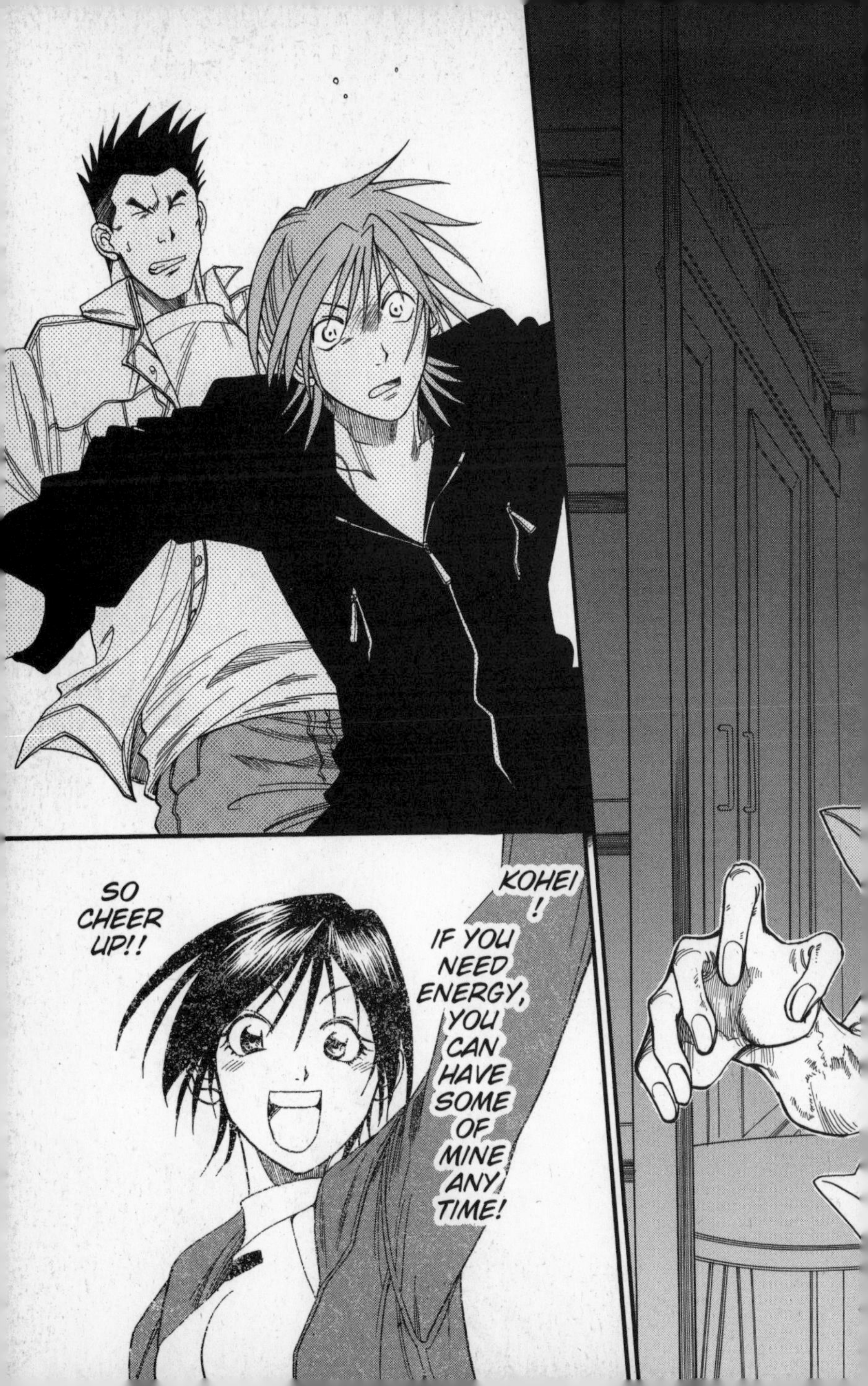
KOHEI!
IF YOU NEED ENERGY, YOU CAN HAVE SOME OF MINE ANY TIME!
SO CHEER UP!!

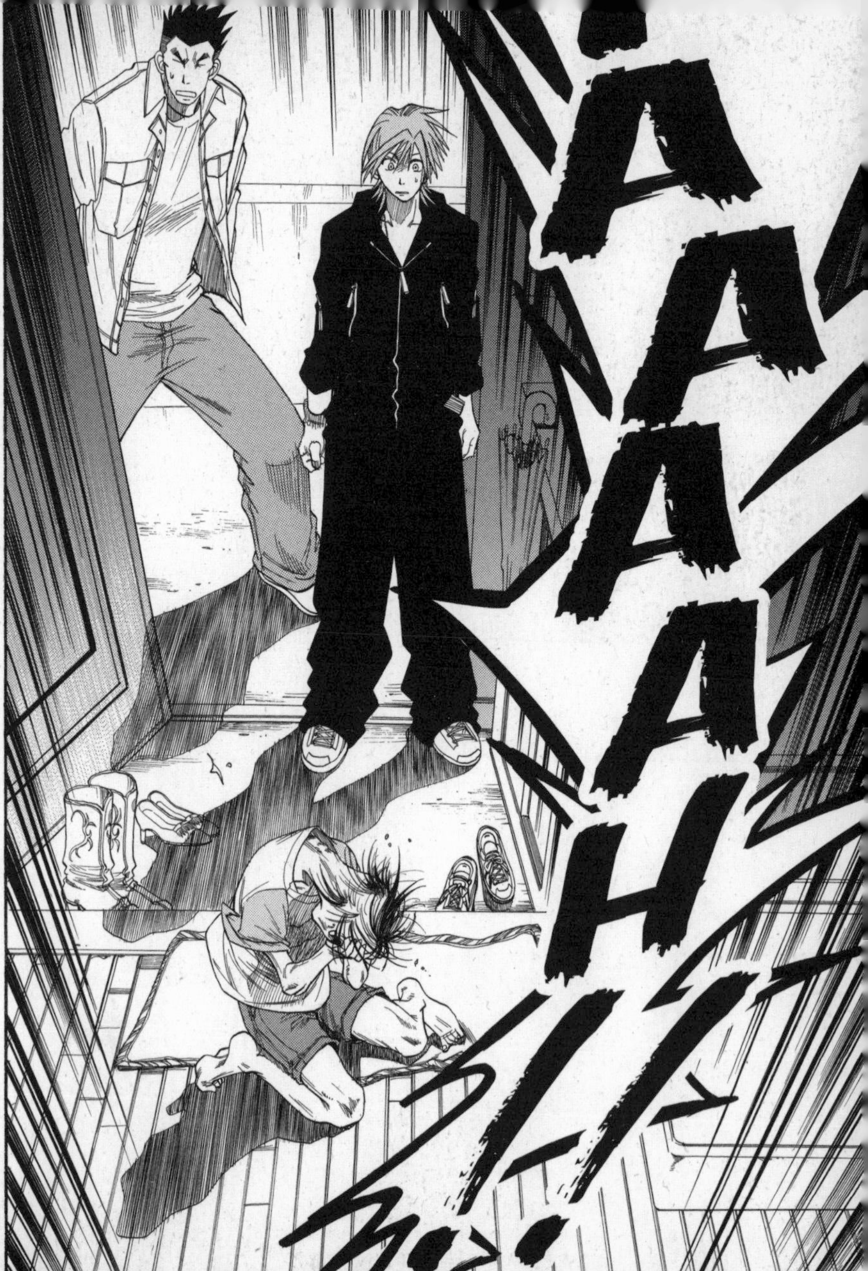
AAAAH!!

Scene 41: Field of Dreams (Part 3)

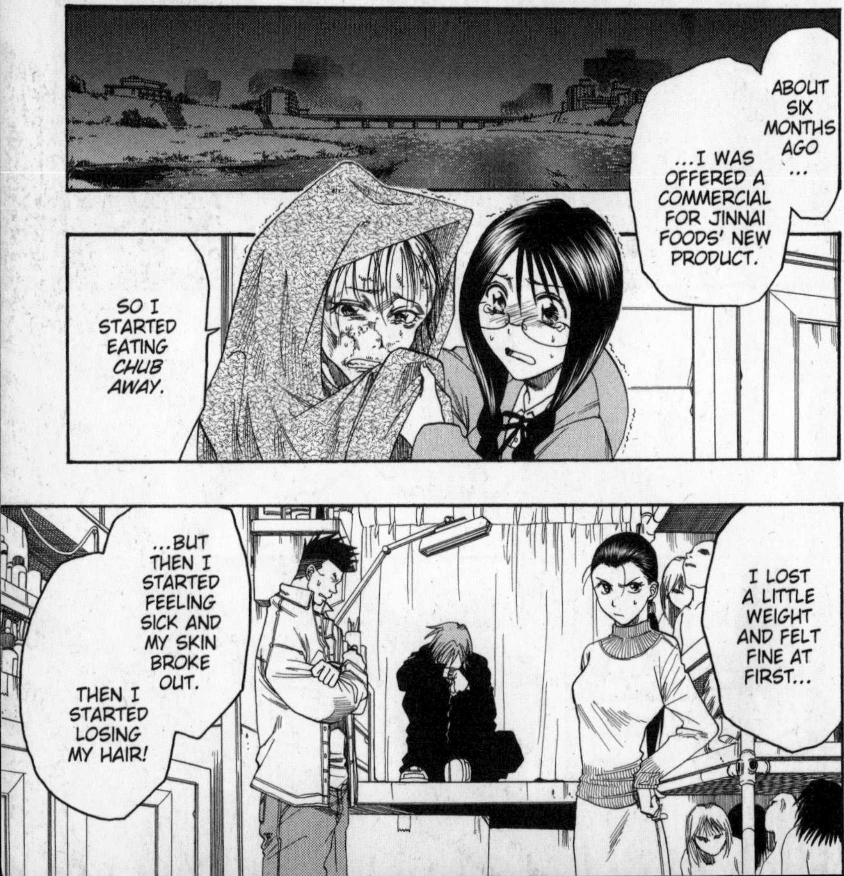
ABOUT SIX MONTHS AGO...
...I WAS OFFERED A COMMERCIAL FOR JINNAI FOODS' NEW PRODUCT.
SO I STARTED EATING CHUB AWAY.
I LOST A LITTLE WEIGHT AND FELT FINE AT FIRST...
...BUT THEN I STARTED FEELING SICK AND MY SKIN BROKE OUT.
THEN I STARTED LOSING MY HAIR!

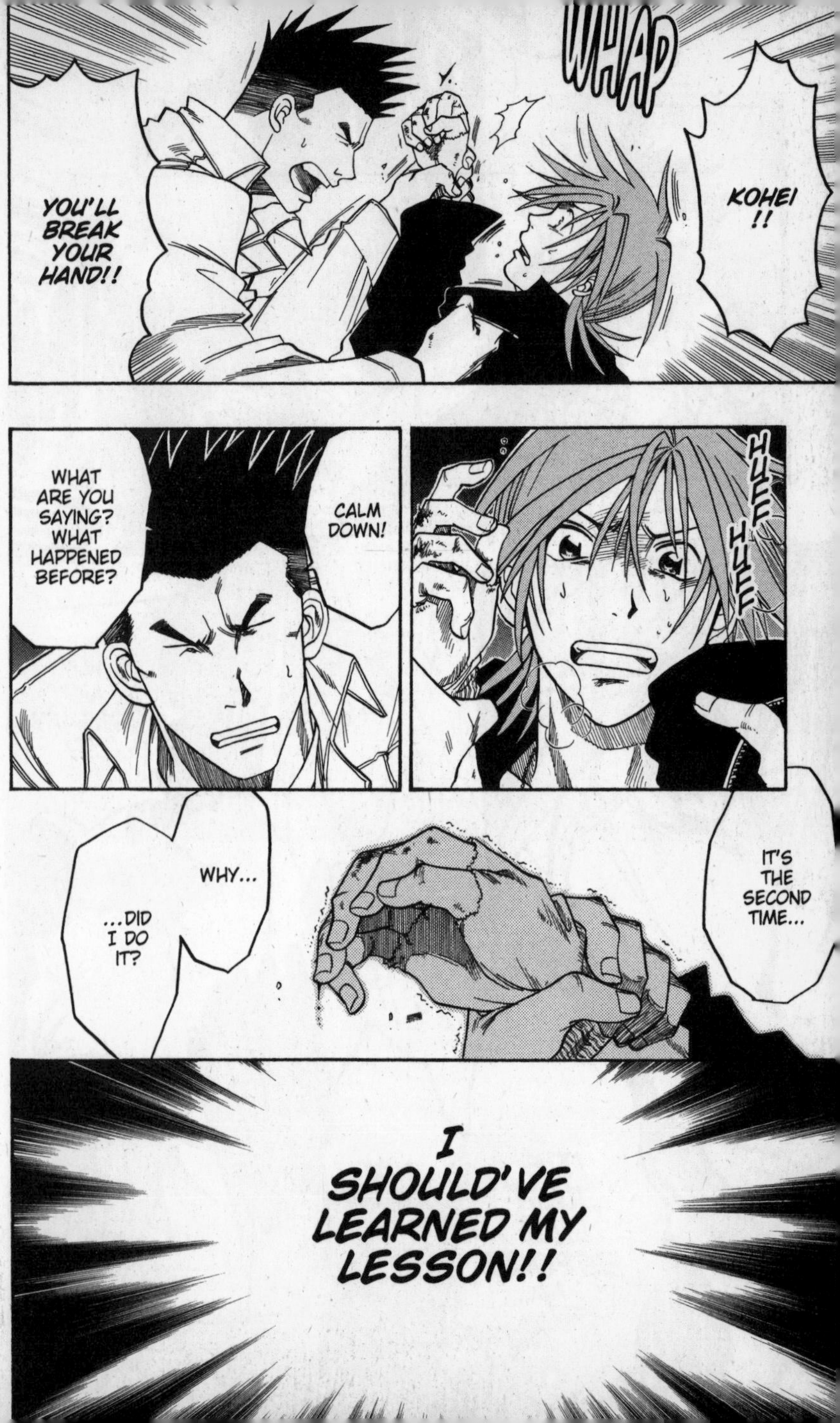
WHAP
KOHEI!!
YOU'LL BREAK YOUR HAND!!
HUFF HUFF
CALM DOWN!
WHAT ARE YOU SAYING? WHAT HAPPENED BEFORE?
IT'S THE SECOND TIME...
WHY...
...DID I DO IT?
I SHOULD'VE LEARNED MY LESSON!!

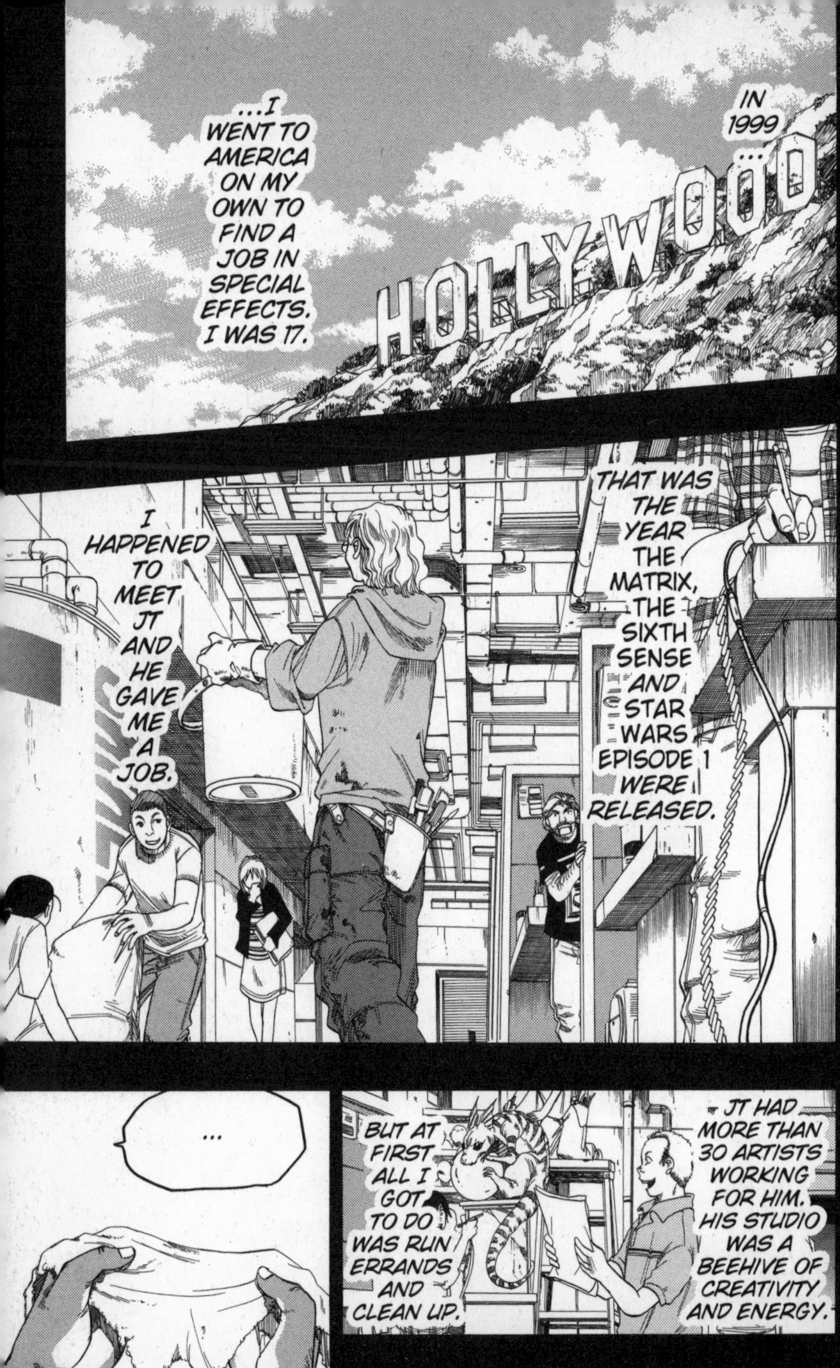
IN 1999 ...
HOLLYWOOD
...I WENT TO AMERICA ON MY OWN TO FIND A JOB IN SPECIAL EFFECTS. I WAS 17.
THAT WAS THE YEAR THE MATRIX, THE SIXTH SENSE AND STAR WARS EPISODE 1 WERE RELEASED.
I HAPPENED TO MEET JT AND HE GAVE ME A JOB.
JT HAD MORE THAN 30 ARTISTS WORKING FOR HIM. HIS STUDIO WAS A BEEHIVE OF CREATIVITY AND ENERGY.
BUT AT FIRST ALL I GOT TO DO WAS RUN ERRANDS AND CLEAN UP.
...

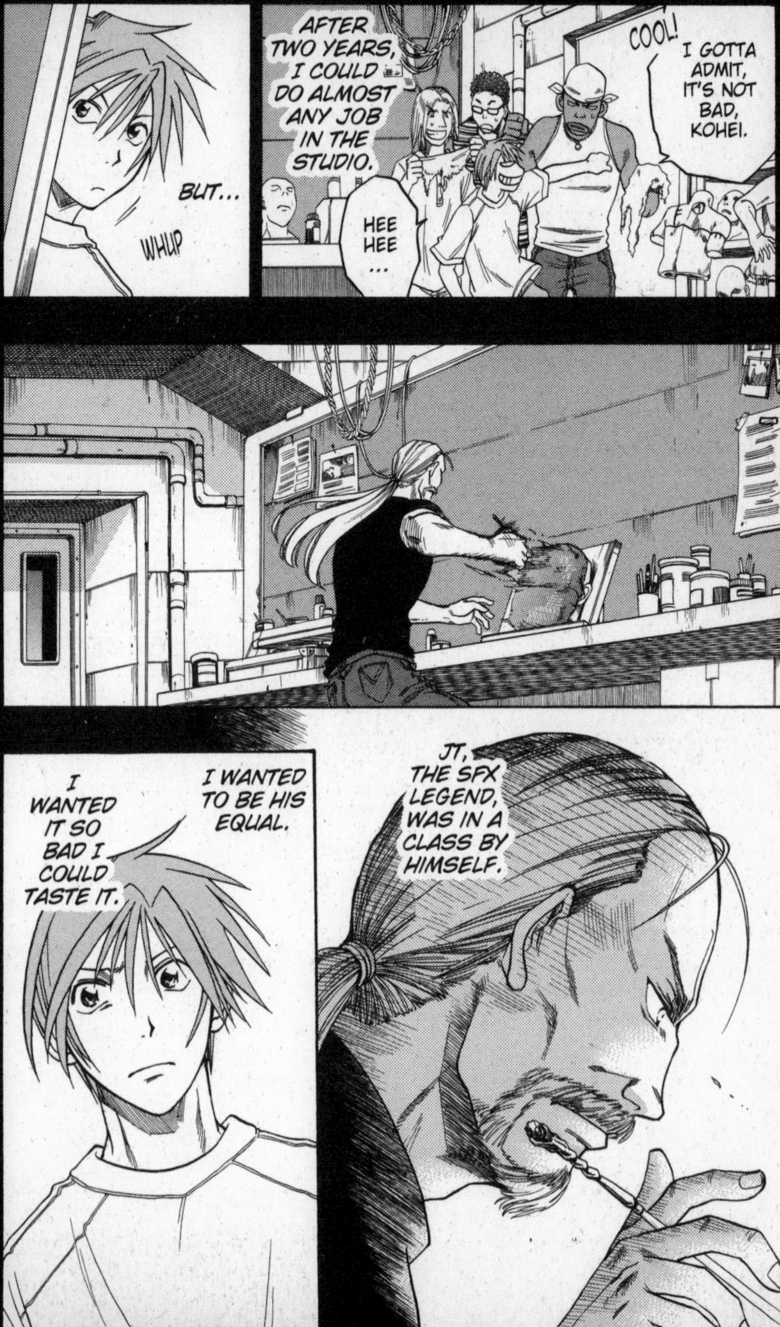
COOL!
I GOTTA ADMIT, IT'S NOT BAD, KOHEI.
AFTER TWO YEARS, I COULD DO ALMOST ANY JOB IN THE STUDIO.
HEE HEE ...
BUT...
WHUP
JT, THE SFX LEGEND, WAS IN A CLASS BY HIMSELF.
I WANTED TO BE HIS EQUAL.
I WANTED IT SO BAD I COULD TASTE IT.

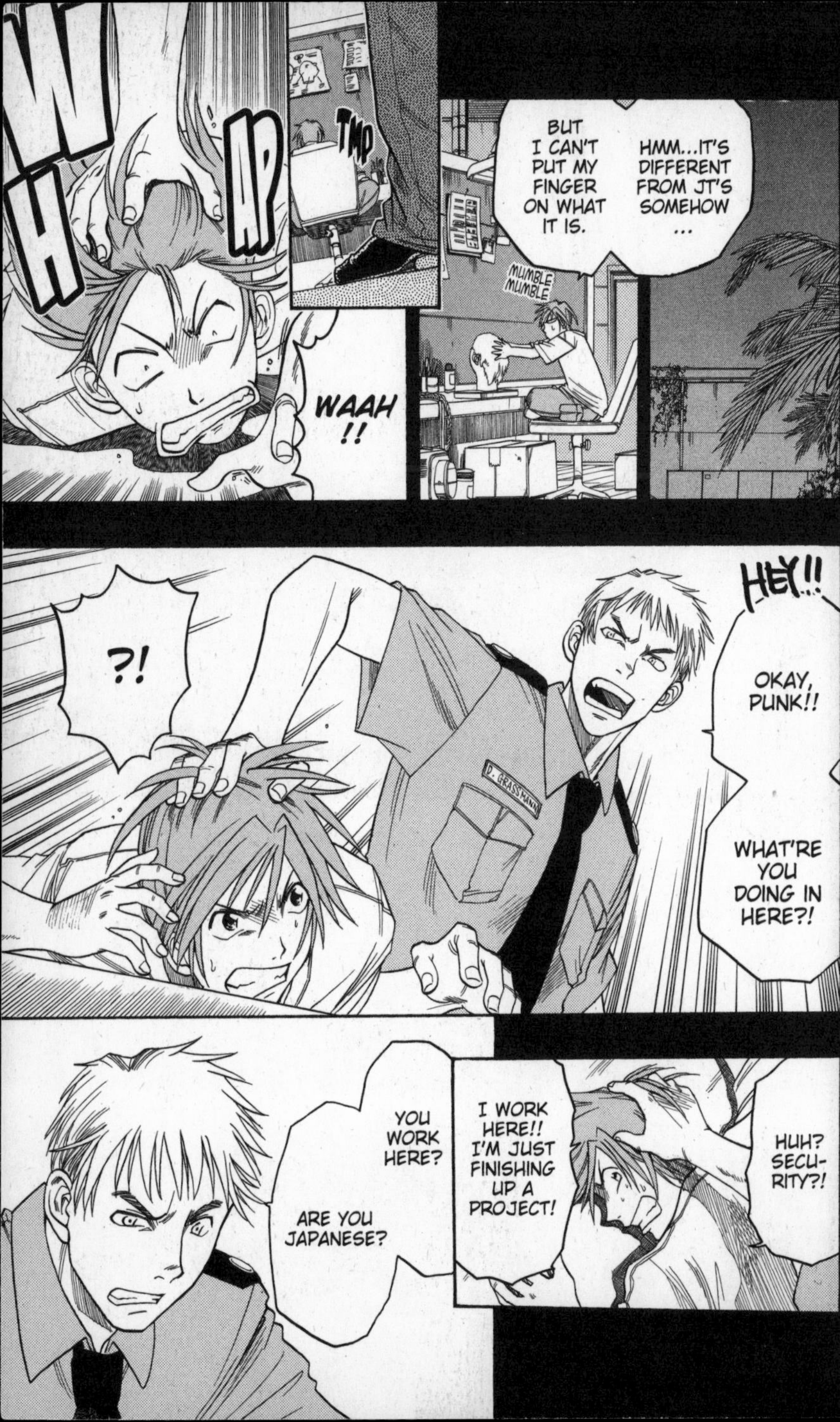
TMP
HMM...IT'S DIFFERENT FROM JT'S SOMEHOW ...
BUT I CAN'T PUT MY FINGER ON WHAT IT IS.
MUMBLE MUMBLE
WHAP
WAAH !!
HEY!!
OKAY, PUNK!!
WHAT'RE YOU DOING IN HERE?!
?!
HUH? SECURITY?!
I WORK HERE!! I'M JUST FINISHING UP A PROJECT!
YOU WORK HERE?
ARE YOU JAPANESE?

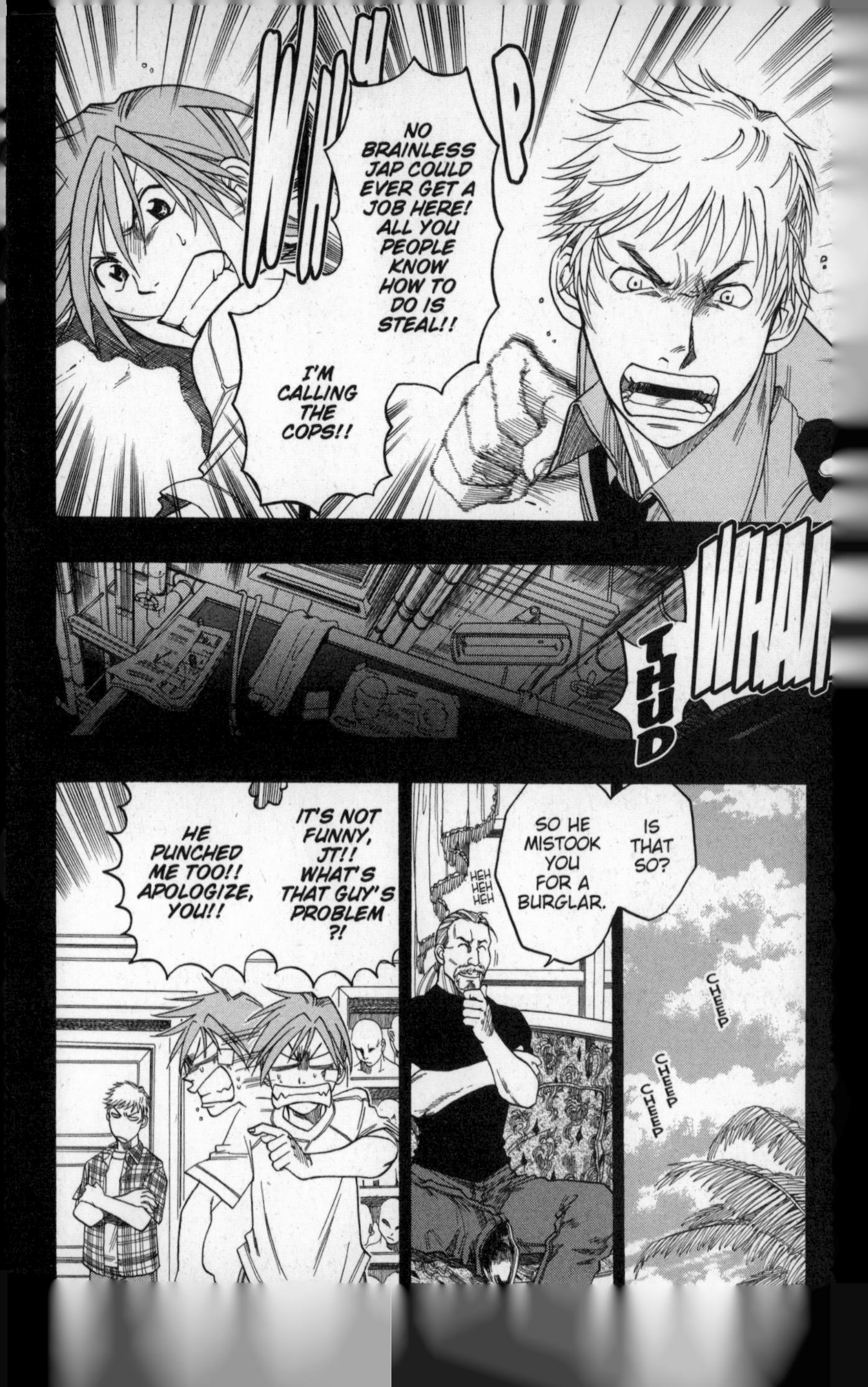
NO BRAINLESS JAP COULD EVER GET A JOB HERE! ALL YOU PEOPLE KNOW HOW TO DO IS STEAL!!
I'M CALLING THE COPS!!
THUD
IS THAT SO?
CHEEP
CHEEP
CHEEP
SO HE MISTOOK YOU FOR A BURGLAR.
HEH HEH HEH
IT'S NOT FUNNY, JT!! WHAT'S THAT GUY'S PROBLEM ?!
HE PUNCHED ME TOO!! APOLOGIZE, YOU!!

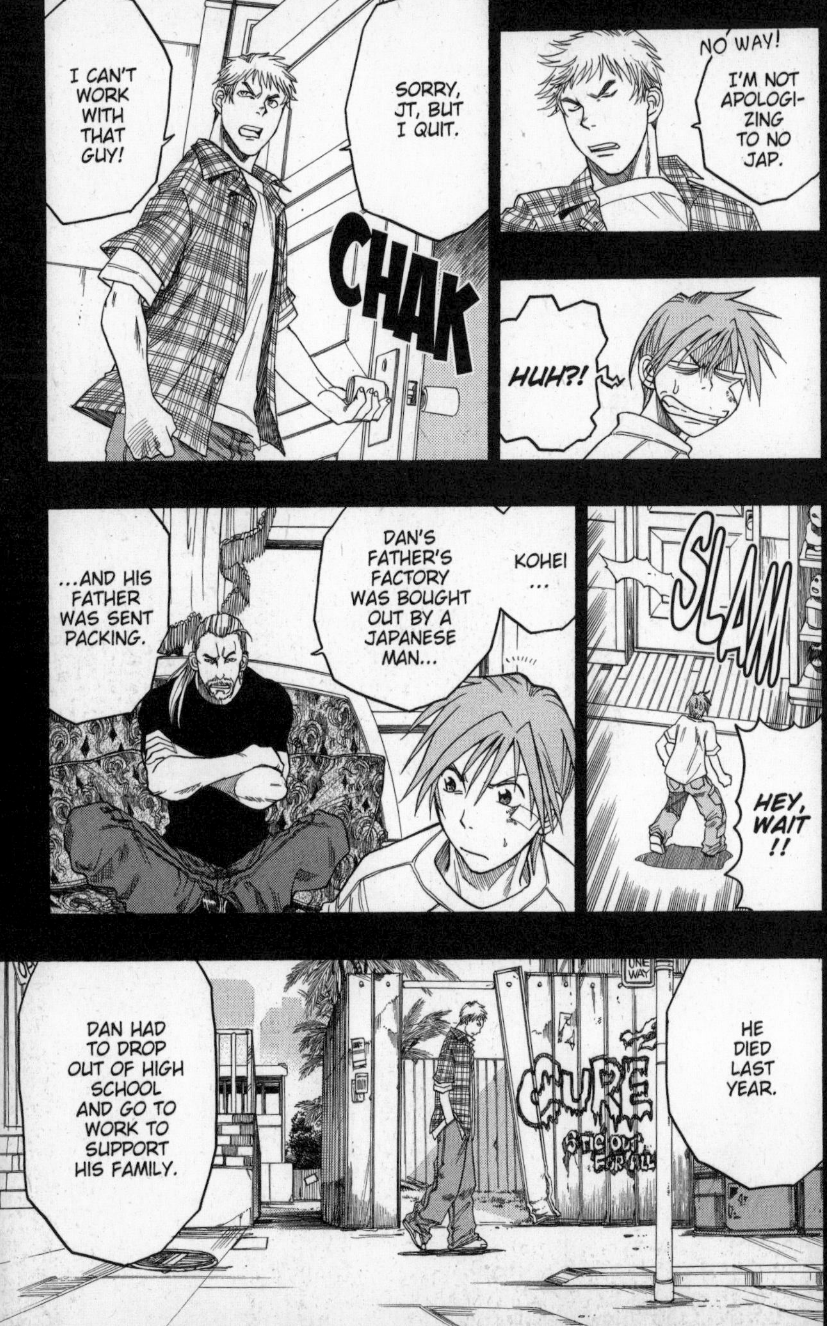
NO WAY!
I'M NOT APOLOGI-ZING TO NO JAP.
HUH?!
SORRY, JT, BUT I QUIT.
I CAN'T WORK WITH THAT GUY!
CHAK
SLAM
HEY, WAIT!!
KOHEI...
DAN'S FATHER'S FACTORY WAS BOUGHT OUT BY A JAPANESE MAN...
...AND HIS FATHER WAS SENT PACKING.
HE DIED LAST YEAR.
ONE WAY
CURE
DAN HAD TO DROP OUT OF HIGH SCHOOL AND GO TO WORK TO SUPPORT HIS FAMILY.

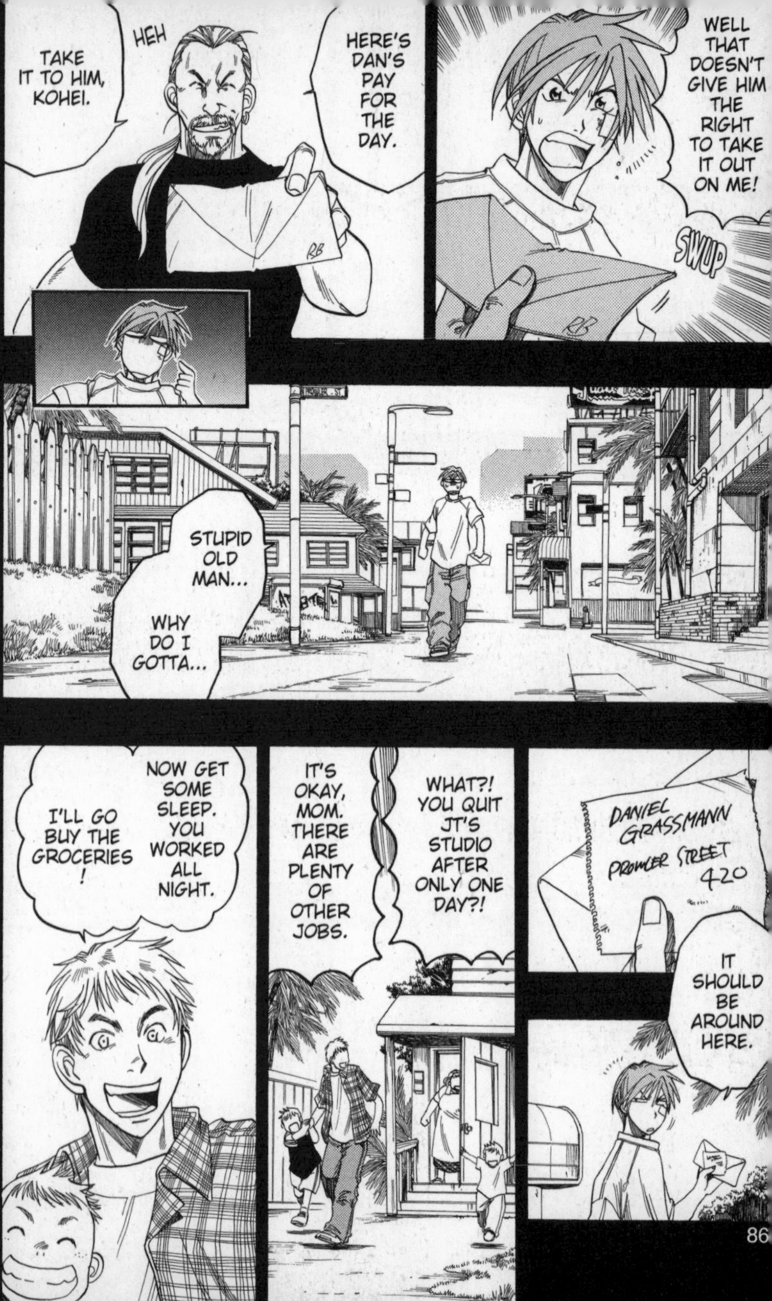
WELL THAT DOESN'T GIVE HIM THE RIGHT TO TAKE IT OUT ON ME!
SWUP
HERE'S DAN'S PAY FOR THE DAY.
HEH
TAKE IT TO HIM, KOHEI.
STUPID OLD MAN...
WHY DO I GOTTA...
DANIEL GRASSMANN
PROWLER STREET 420
IT SHOULD BE AROUND HERE.
WHAT?! YOU QUIT JT'S STUDIO AFTER ONLY ONE DAY?!
IT'S OKAY, MOM. THERE ARE PLENTY OF OTHER JOBS.
NOW GET SOME SLEEP. YOU WORKED ALL NIGHT.
I'LL GO BUY THE GROCERIES!

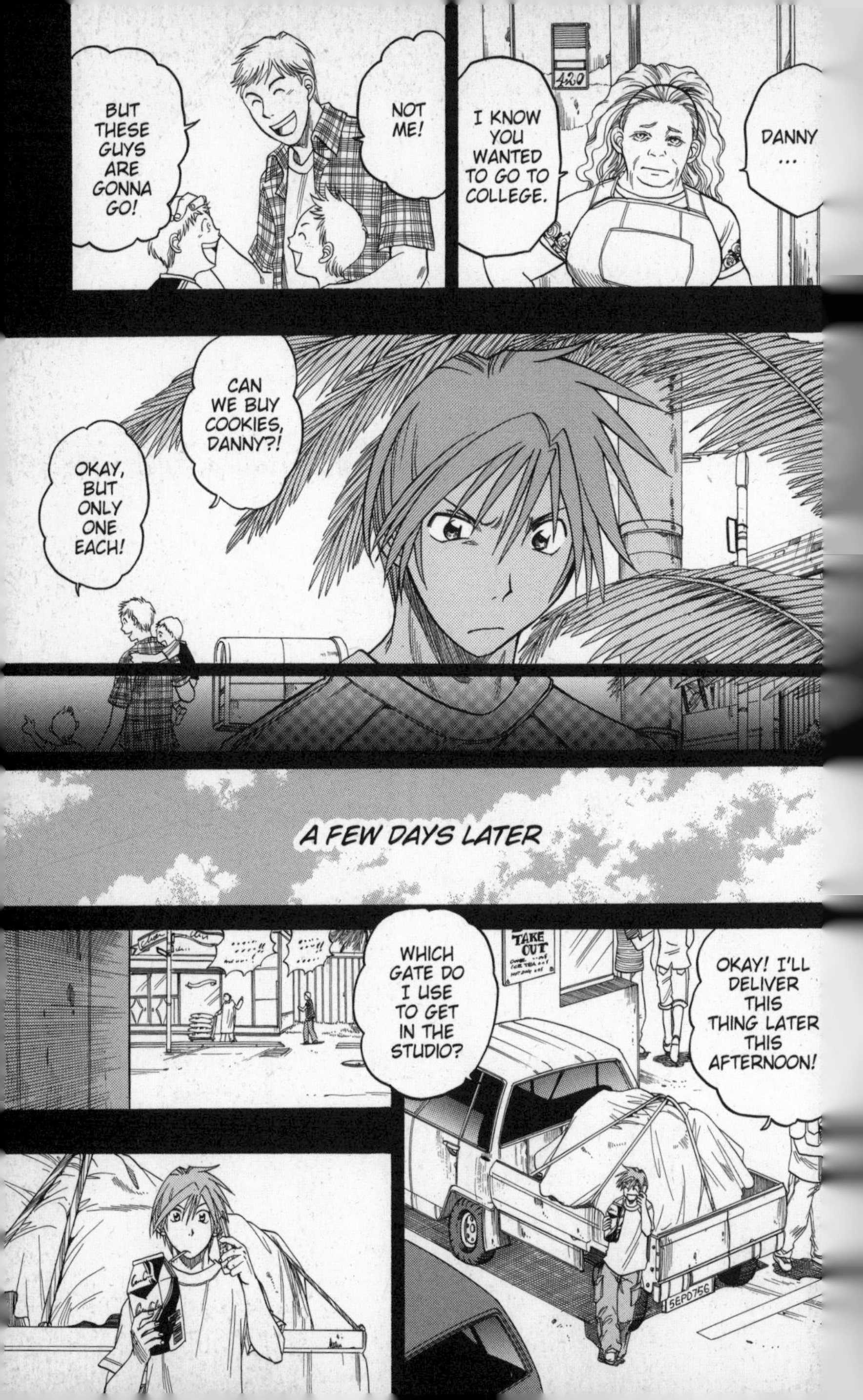
420
DANNY ...
I KNOW YOU WANTED TO GO TO COLLEGE.
NOT ME!
BUT THESE GUYS ARE GONNA GO!
CAN WE BUY COOKIES, DANNY?!
OKAY, BUT ONLY ONE EACH!
A FEW DAYS LATER
TAKE OUT
OKAY! I'LL DELIVER THIS THING LATER THIS AFTERNOON!
WHICH GATE DO I USE TO GET IN THE STUDIO?
5EPD756

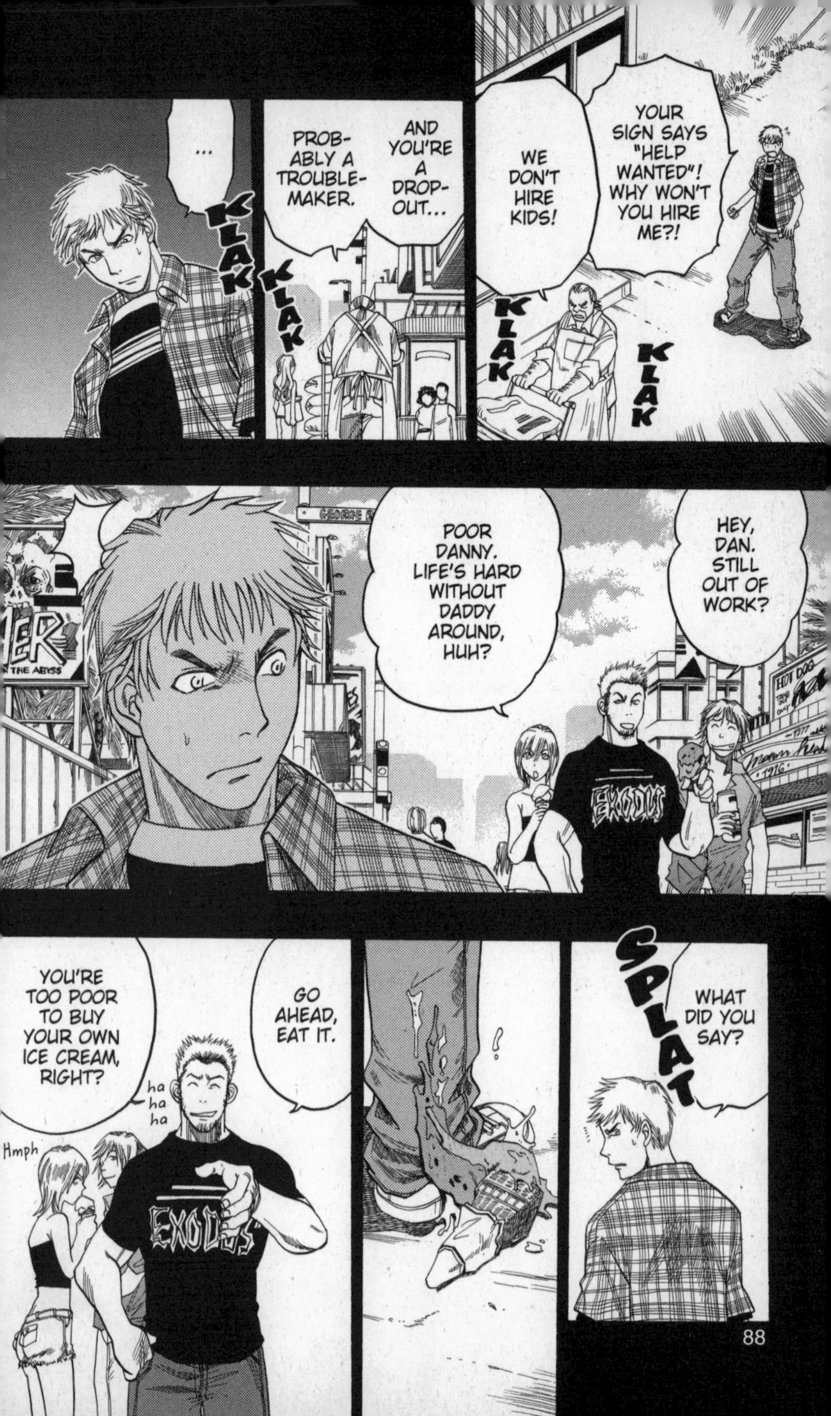
YOUR SIGN SAYS "HELP WANTED"! WHY WON'T YOU HIRE ME?!
KLAK
WE DON'T HIRE KIDS!
KLAK
AND YOU'RE A DROP-OUT...
PROB-ABLY A TROUBLE-MAKER.
KLAK
KLAK
...
HEY, DAN. STILL OUT OF WORK?
POOR DANNY. LIFE'S HARD WITHOUT DADDY AROUND, HUH?
SPLAT
WHAT DID YOU SAY?
GO AHEAD, EAT IT.
YOU'RE TOO POOR TO BUY YOUR OWN ICE CREAM, RIGHT?
ha ha ha
Hmph

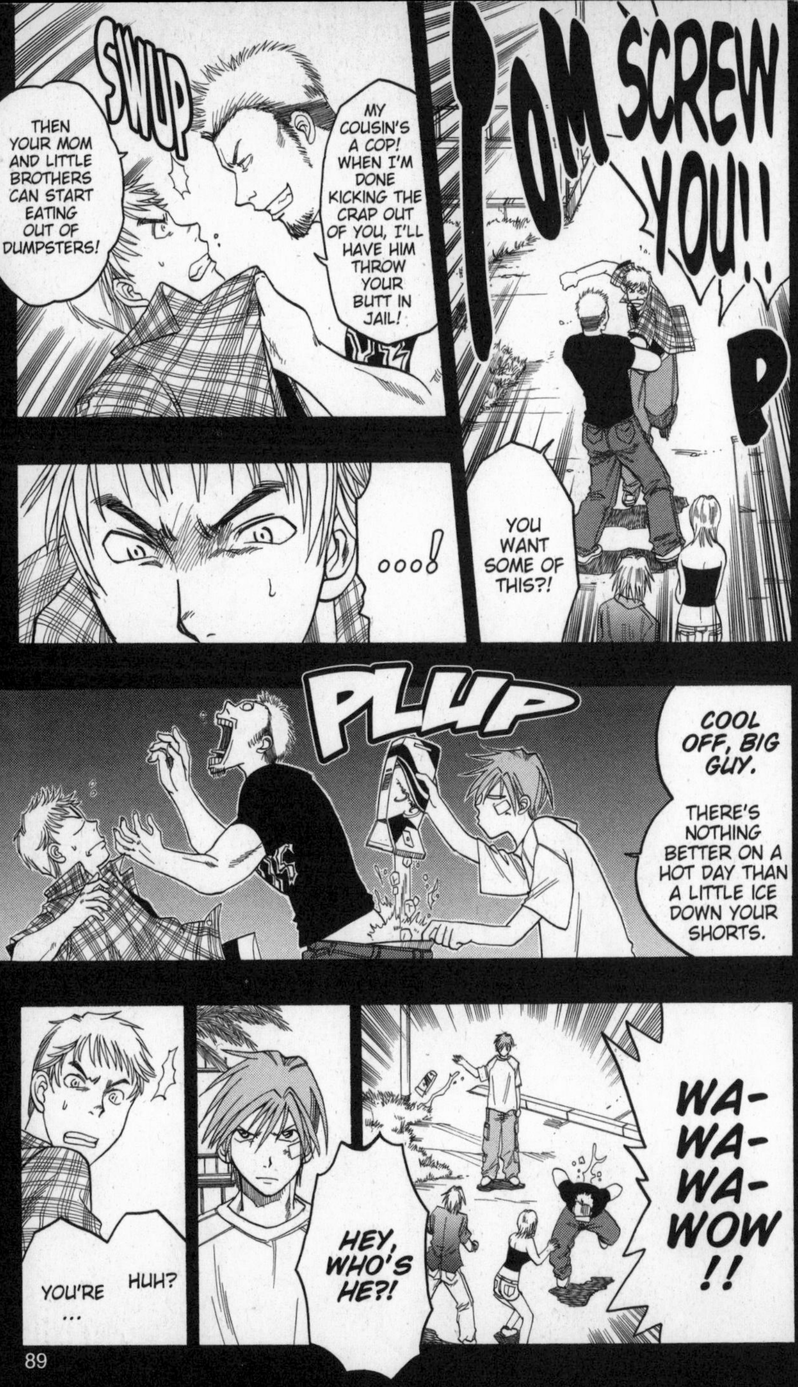
POM SCREW YOU!!
P
YOU WANT SOME OF THIS?!
MY COUSIN'S A COP! WHEN I'M DONE KICKING THE CRAP OUT OF YOU, I'LL HAVE HIM THROW YOUR BUTT IN JAIL!
SWUP
THEN YOUR MOM AND LITTLE BROTHERS CAN START EATING OUT OF DUMPSTERS!
OOO!
COOL OFF, BIG GUY.
THERE'S NOTHING BETTER ON A HOT DAY THAN A LITTLE ICE DOWN YOUR SHORTS.
PLUP
WA-WA-WA-WOW!!
HEY, WHO'S HE?!
HUH?
YOU'RE ...

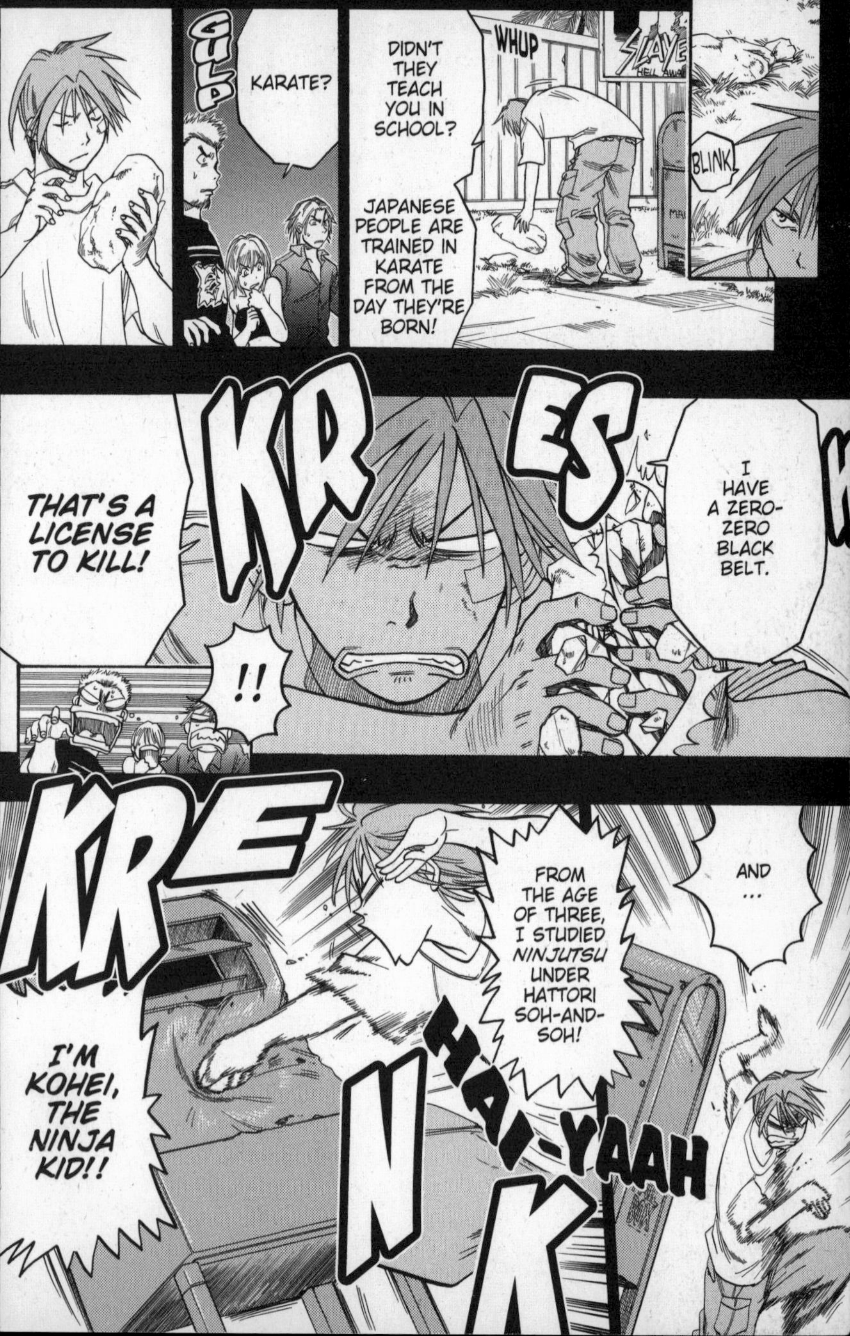
BLINK
WHUP
DIDN'T THEY TEACH YOU IN SCHOOL?
JAPANESE PEOPLE ARE TRAINED IN KARATE FROM THE DAY THEY'RE BORN!
GULP
KARATE?
I HAVE A ZERO-ZERO BLACK BELT.
ES
KR
THAT'S A LICENSE TO KILL!
!!
AND ...
FROM THE AGE OF THREE, I STUDIED *NINJUTSU* UNDER HATTORI SOH-AND-SOH!
HAI-YAAH
KRE
N
K
I'M KOHEI, THE NINJA KID!!

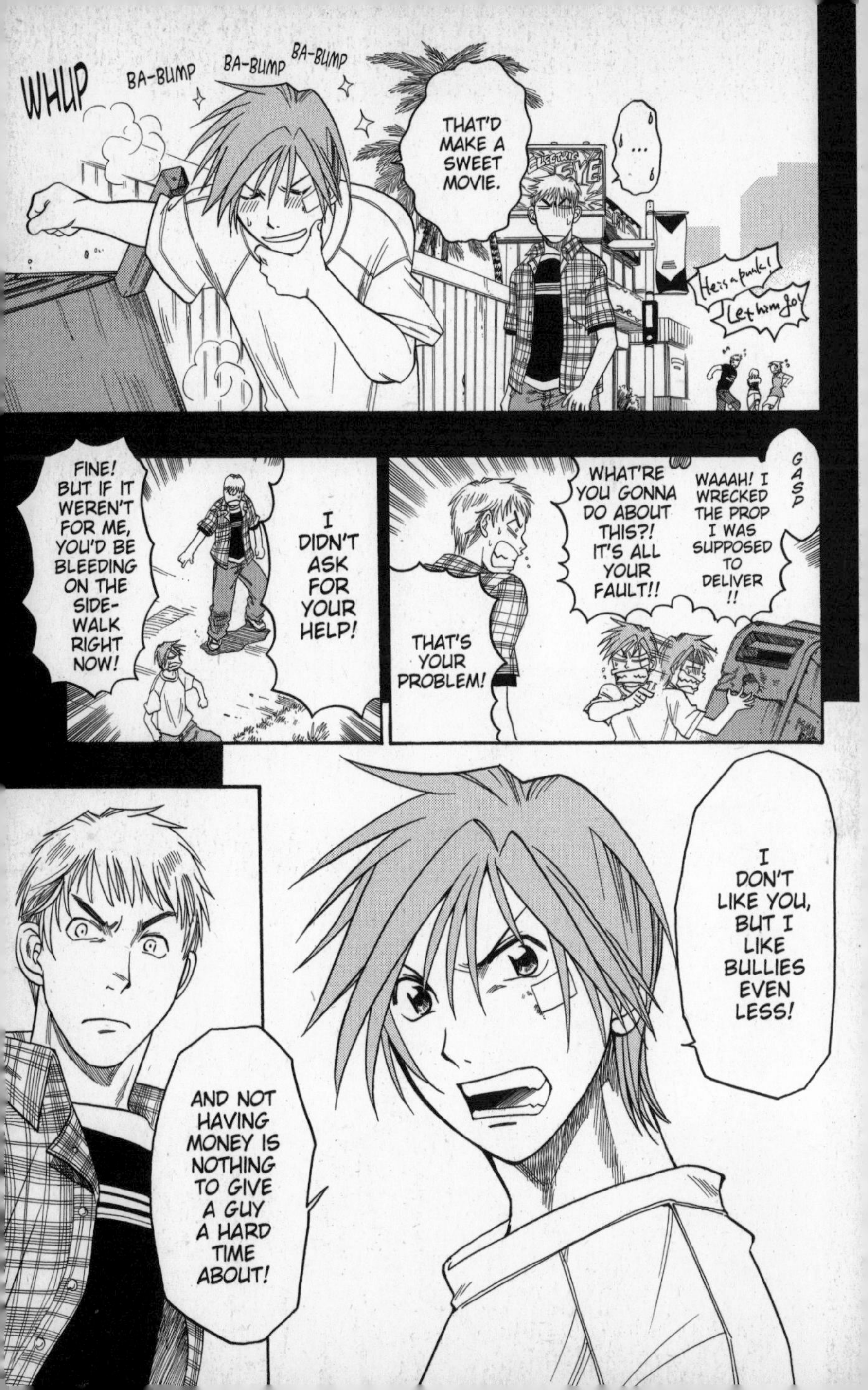
He is a punk!
Let him go!
...
THAT'D MAKE A SWEET MOVIE.
BA-BUMP
BA-BUMP
BA-BUMP
WHUP
GASP
WAAAH! I WRECKED THE PROP I WAS SUPPOSED TO DELIVER!!
WHAT'RE YOU GONNA DO ABOUT THIS?! IT'S ALL YOUR FAULT!!
THAT'S YOUR PROBLEM!
I DIDN'T ASK FOR YOUR HELP!
FINE! BUT IF IT WEREN'T FOR ME, YOU'D BE BLEEDING ON THE SIDE-WALK RIGHT NOW!
I DON'T LIKE YOU, BUT I LIKE BULLIES EVEN LESS!
AND NOT HAVING MONEY IS NOTHING TO GIVE A GUY A HARD TIME ABOUT!

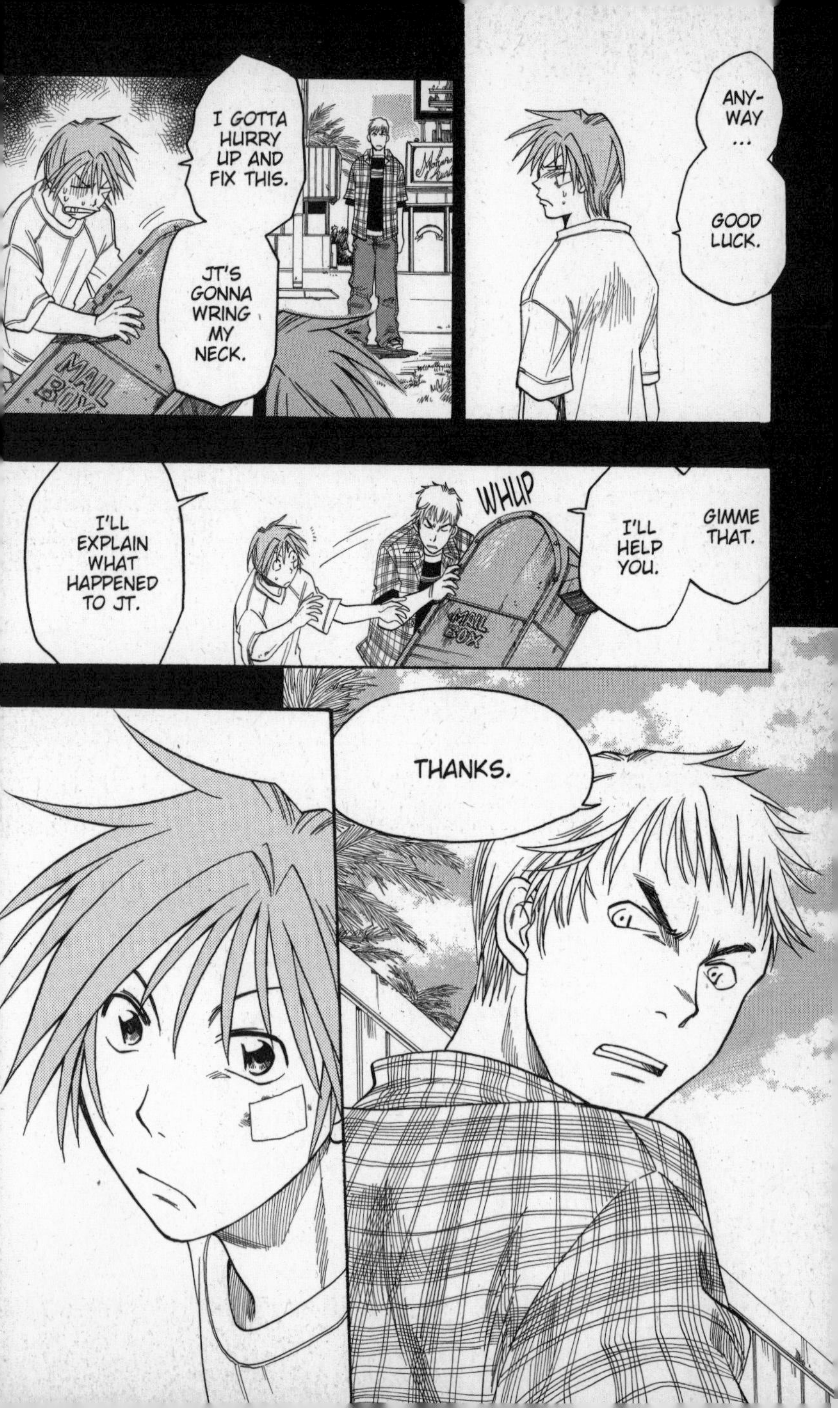
ANY-WAY...
GOOD LUCK.
I GOTTA HURRY UP AND FIX THIS.
JT'S GONNA WRING MY NECK.
MAIL BOX
GIMME THAT.
I'LL HELP YOU.
WHUP
I'LL EXPLAIN WHAT HAPPENED TO JT.
MAIL BOX
THANKS.

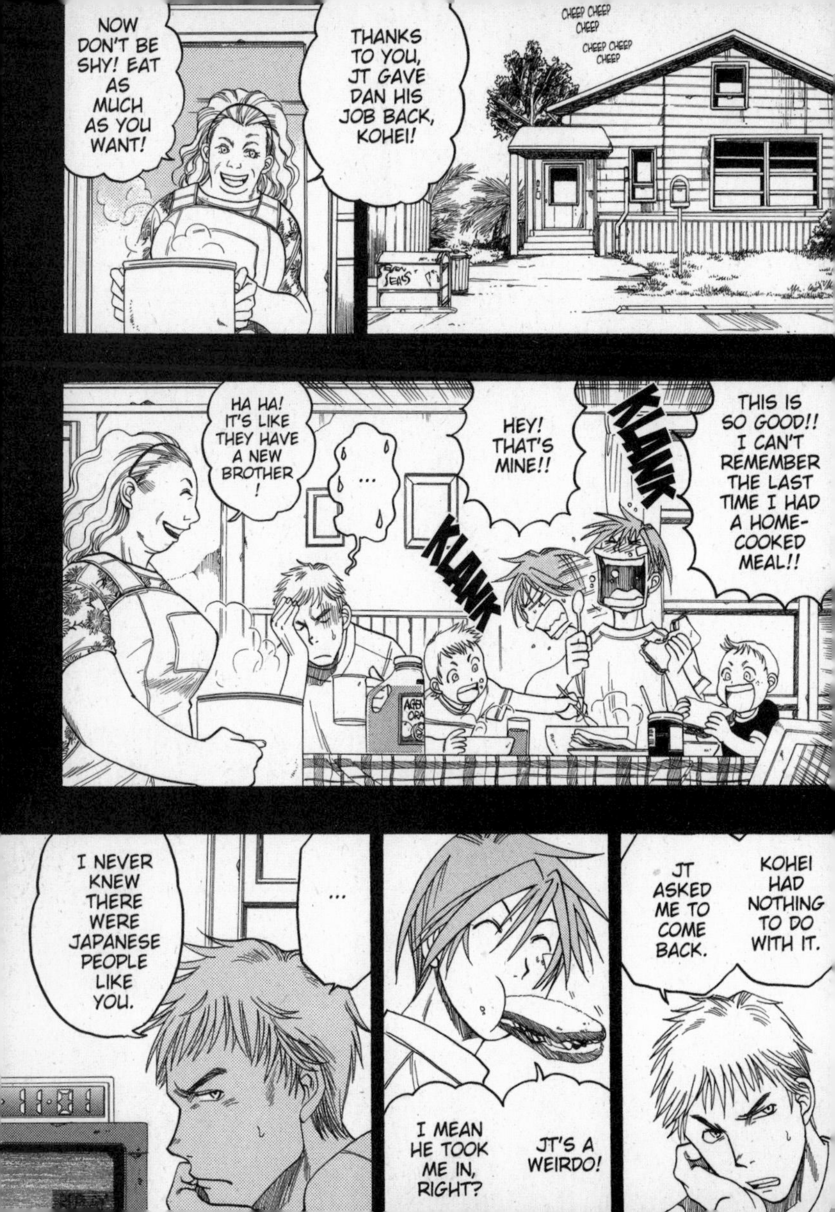
CHEEP CHEEP CHEEP
CHEEP CHEEP CHEEP
THANKS TO YOU, JT GAVE DAN HIS JOB BACK, KOHEI!
NOW DON'T BE SHY! EAT AS MUCH AS YOU WANT!
THIS IS SO GOOD!! I CAN'T REMEMBER THE LAST TIME I HAD A HOME-COOKED MEAL!!
KLANK
HEY! THAT'S MINE!!
KLANK
...
HA HA! IT'S LIKE THEY HAVE A NEW BROTHER!
KOHEI HAD NOTHING TO DO WITH IT.
JT ASKED ME TO COME BACK.
JT'S A WEIRDO!
I MEAN HE TOOK ME IN, RIGHT?
...
I NEVER KNEW THERE WERE JAPANESE PEOPLE LIKE YOU.

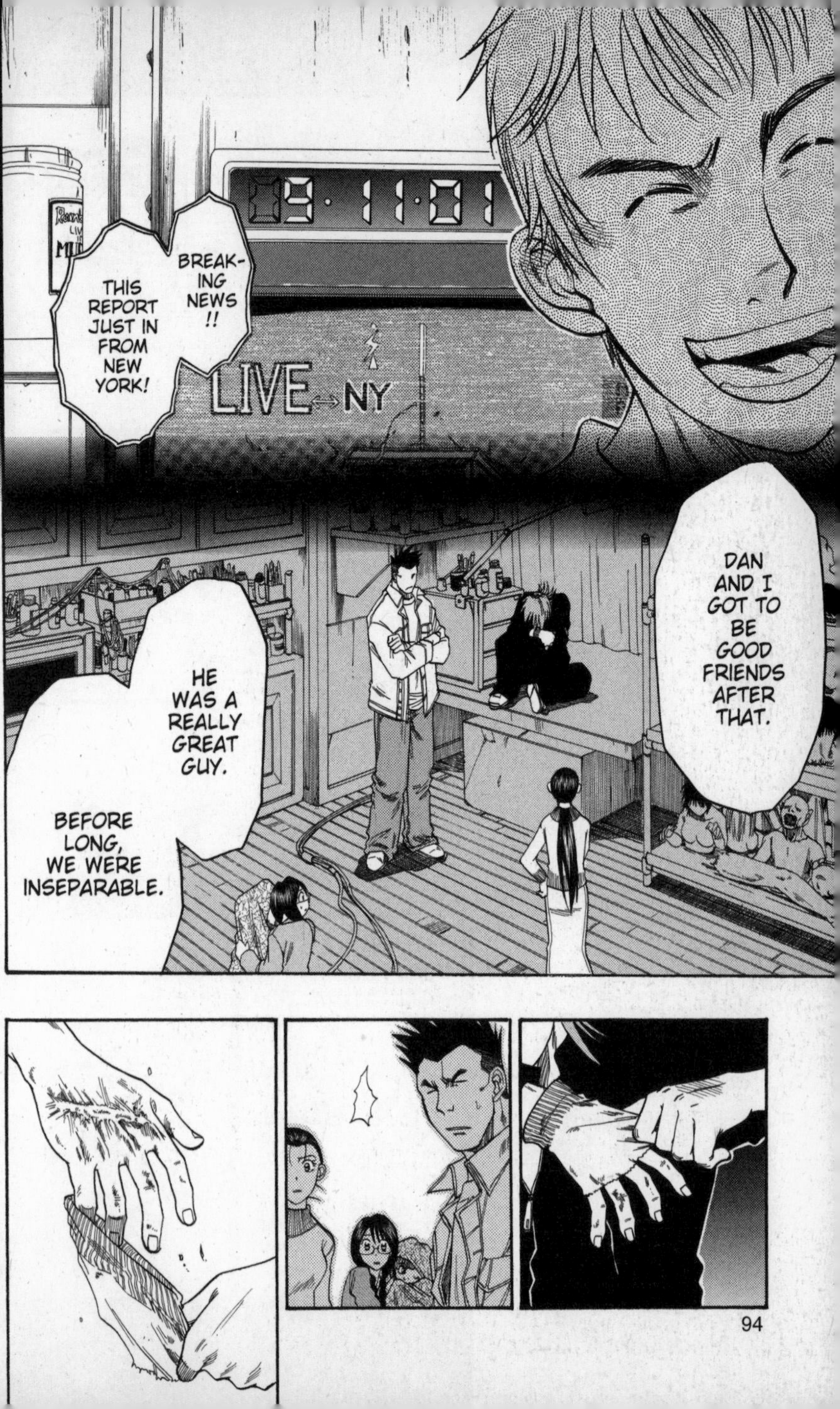
09·11·01
BREAKING-ING NEWS!!
THIS REPORT JUST IN FROM NEW YORK!
LIVE↔NY
DAN AND I GOT TO BE GOOD FRIENDS AFTER THAT.
HE WAS A REALLY GREAT GUY.
BEFORE LONG, WE WERE INSEPARABLE.

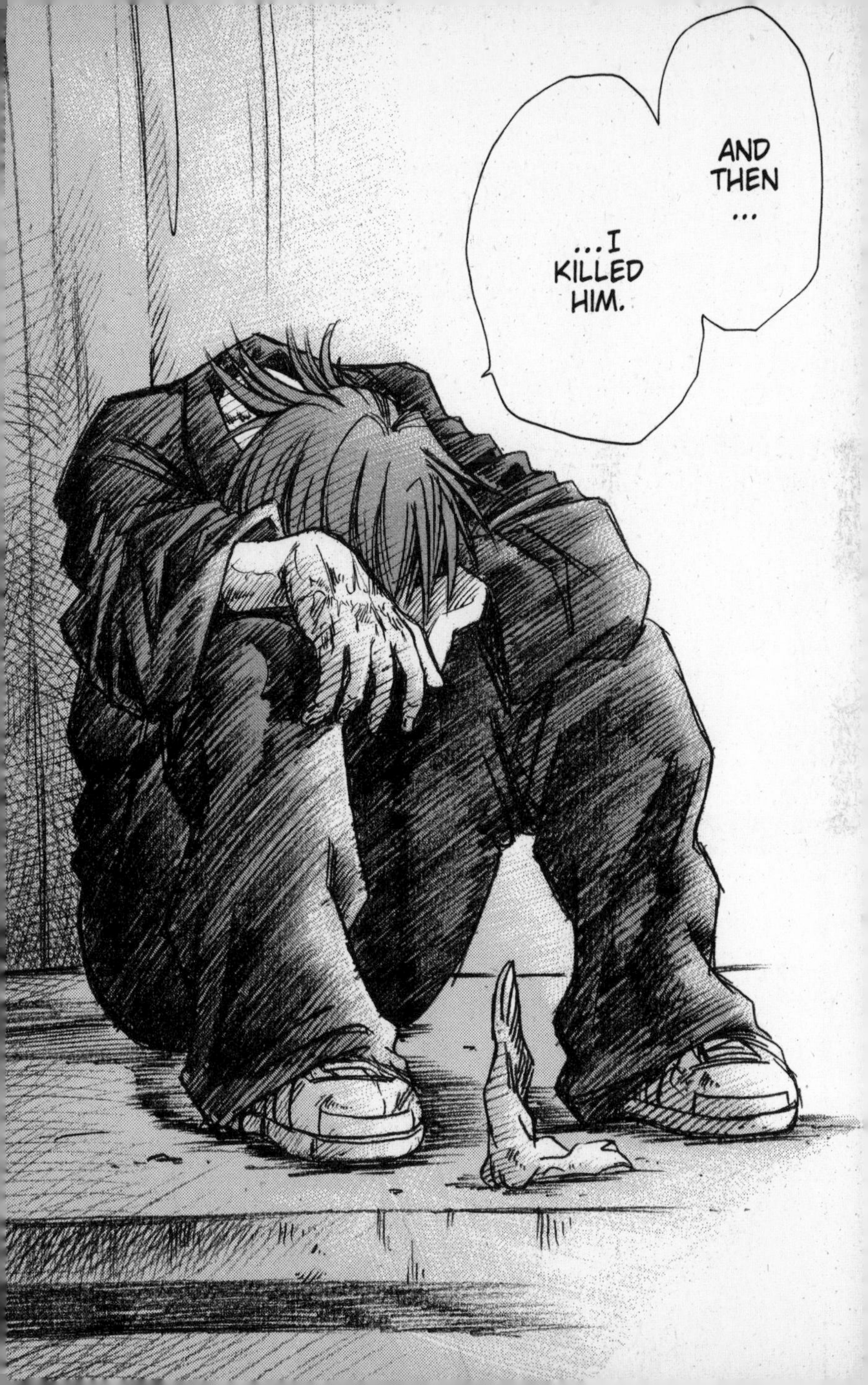
AND THEN ...
...I KILLED HIM.

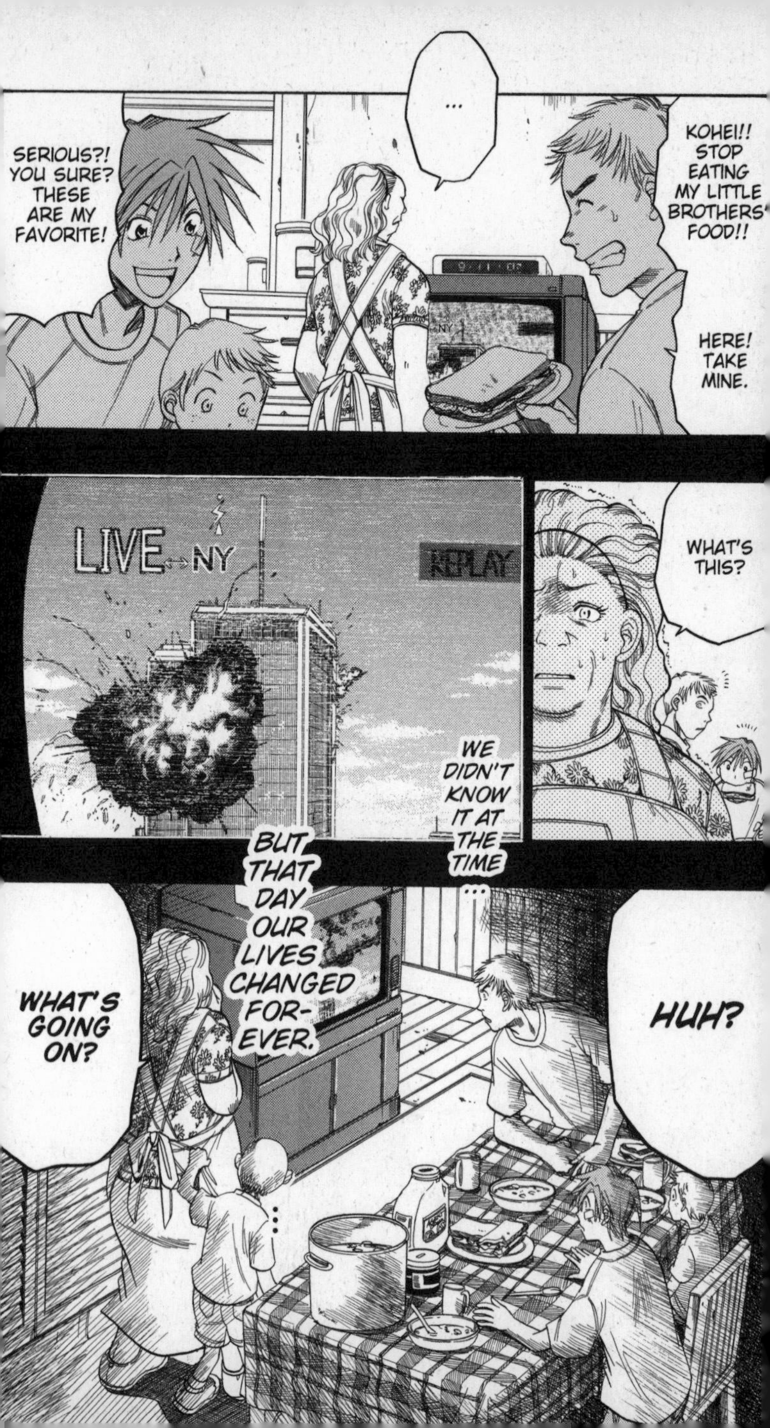
KOHEI!! STOP EATING MY LITTLE BROTHERS' FOOD!!
HERE! TAKE MINE.
...
SERIOUS?! YOU SURE? THESE ARE MY FAVORITE!
WHAT'S THIS?
LIVE↔NY
REPLAY
WE DIDN'T KNOW IT AT THE TIME...
BUT THAT DAY OUR LIVES CHANGED FOR-EVER.
HUH?
...
WHAT'S GOING ON?

Scene 42: Field of Dreams (Part 4)

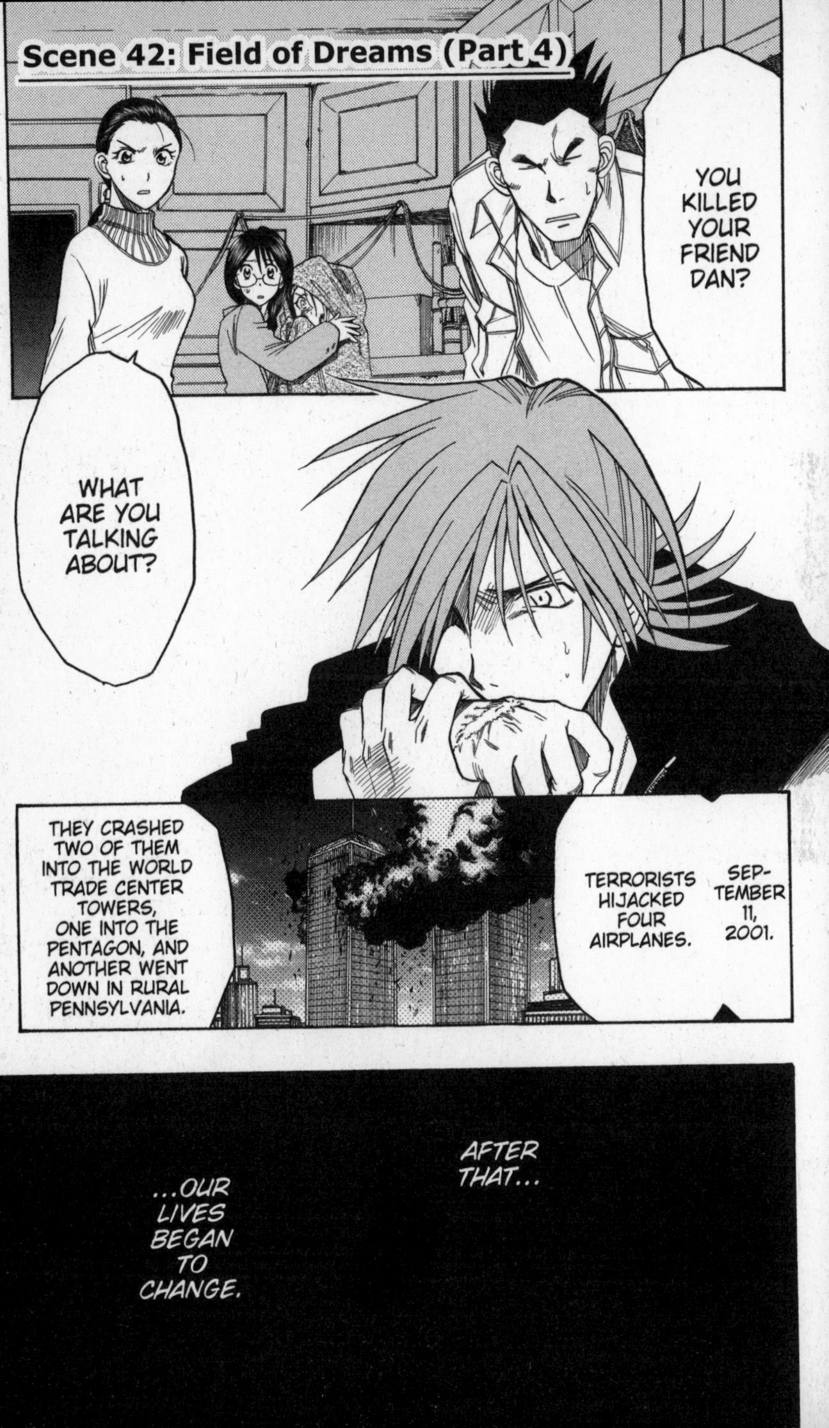
YOU KILLED YOUR FRIEND DAN?
WHAT ARE YOU TALKING ABOUT?
SEPTEMBER 11, 2001.
TERRORISTS HIJACKED FOUR AIRPLANES.
THEY CRASHED TWO OF THEM INTO THE WORLD TRADE CENTER TOWERS, ONE INTO THE PENTAGON, AND ANOTHER WENT DOWN IN RURAL PENNSYLVANIA.
AFTER THAT...
...OUR LIVES BEGAN TO CHANGE.

Scene 42:
Field of Dreams (Part 4)

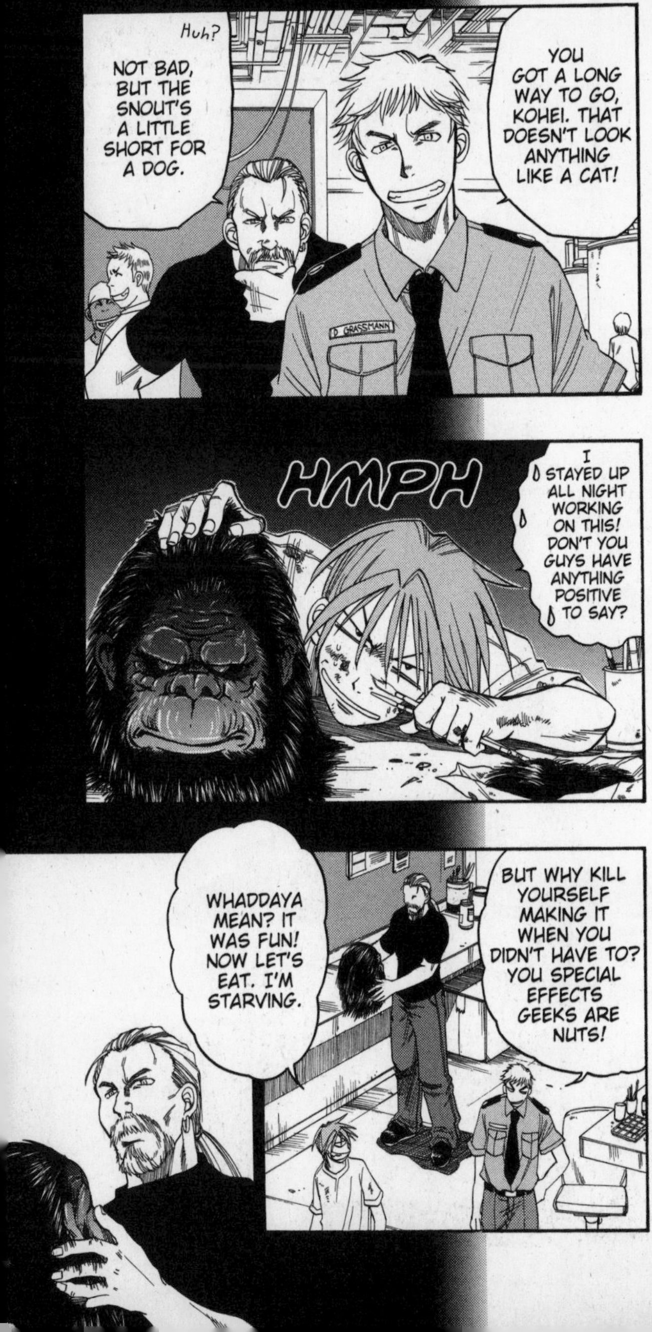
YOU GOT A LONG WAY TO GO, KOHEI. THAT DOESN'T LOOK ANYTHING LIKE A CAT!
Huh?
NOT BAD, BUT THE SNOUT'S A LITTLE SHORT FOR A DOG.
D GRASSMANN
I STAYED UP ALL NIGHT WORKING ON THIS! DON'T YOU GUYS HAVE ANYTHING POSITIVE TO SAY?
HMPH
BUT WHY KILL YOURSELF MAKING IT WHEN YOU DIDN'T HAVE TO? YOU SPECIAL EFFECTS GEEKS ARE NUTS!
WHADDAYA MEAN? IT WAS FUN! NOW LET'S EAT. I'M STARVING.

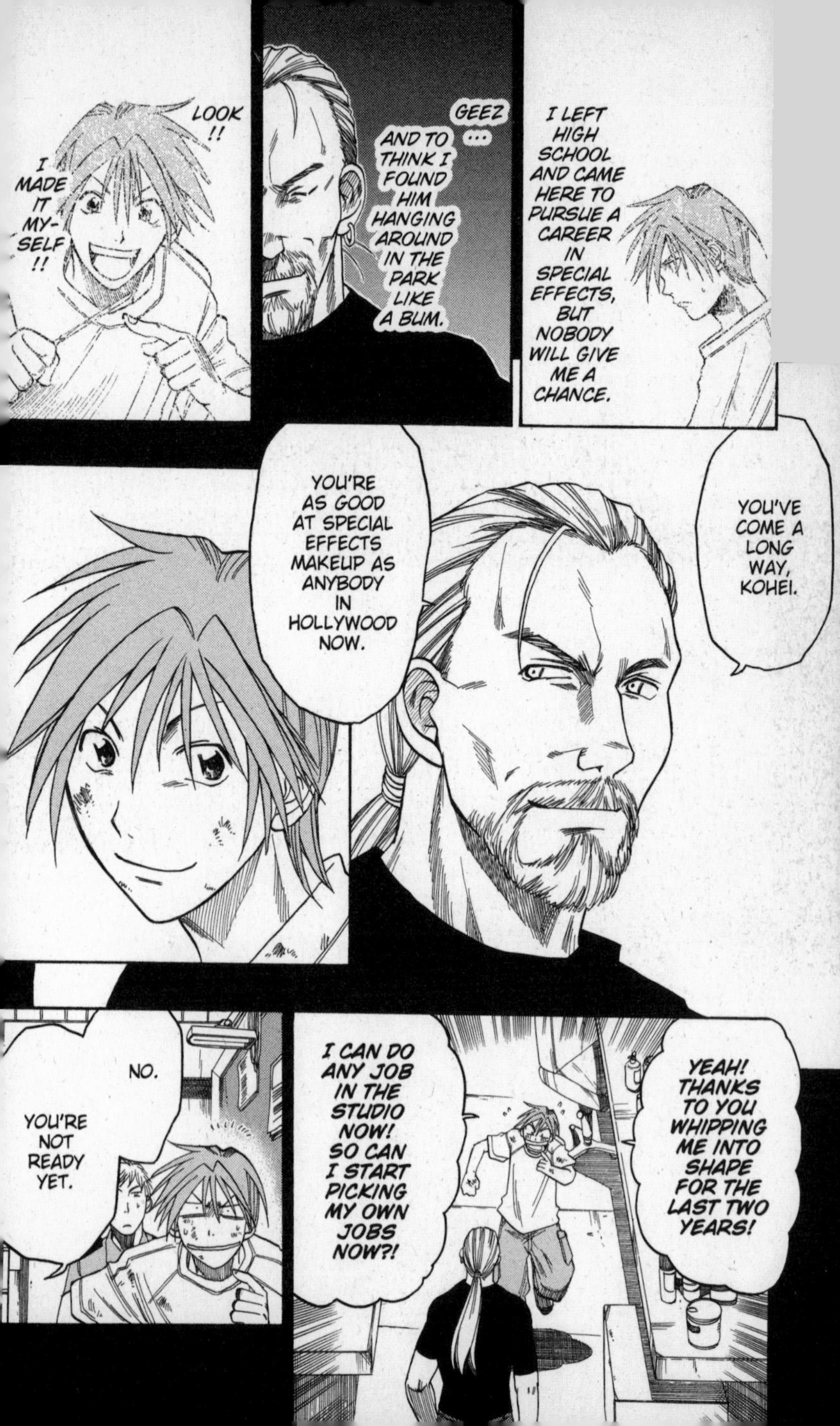
I LEFT HIGH SCHOOL AND CAME HERE TO PURSUE A CAREER IN SPECIAL EFFECTS, BUT NOBODY WILL GIVE ME A CHANCE.
GEEZ...
AND TO THINK I FOUND HIM HANGING AROUND IN THE PARK LIKE A BUM.
LOOK!!
I MADE IT MY-SELF!!
YOU'VE COME A LONG WAY, KOHEI.
YOU'RE AS GOOD AT SPECIAL EFFECTS MAKEUP AS ANYBODY IN HOLLYWOOD NOW.
YEAH! THANKS TO YOU WHIPPING ME INTO SHAPE FOR THE LAST TWO YEARS!
I CAN DO ANY JOB IN THE STUDIO NOW! SO CAN I START PICKING MY OWN JOBS NOW?!
NO.
YOU'RE NOT READY YET.

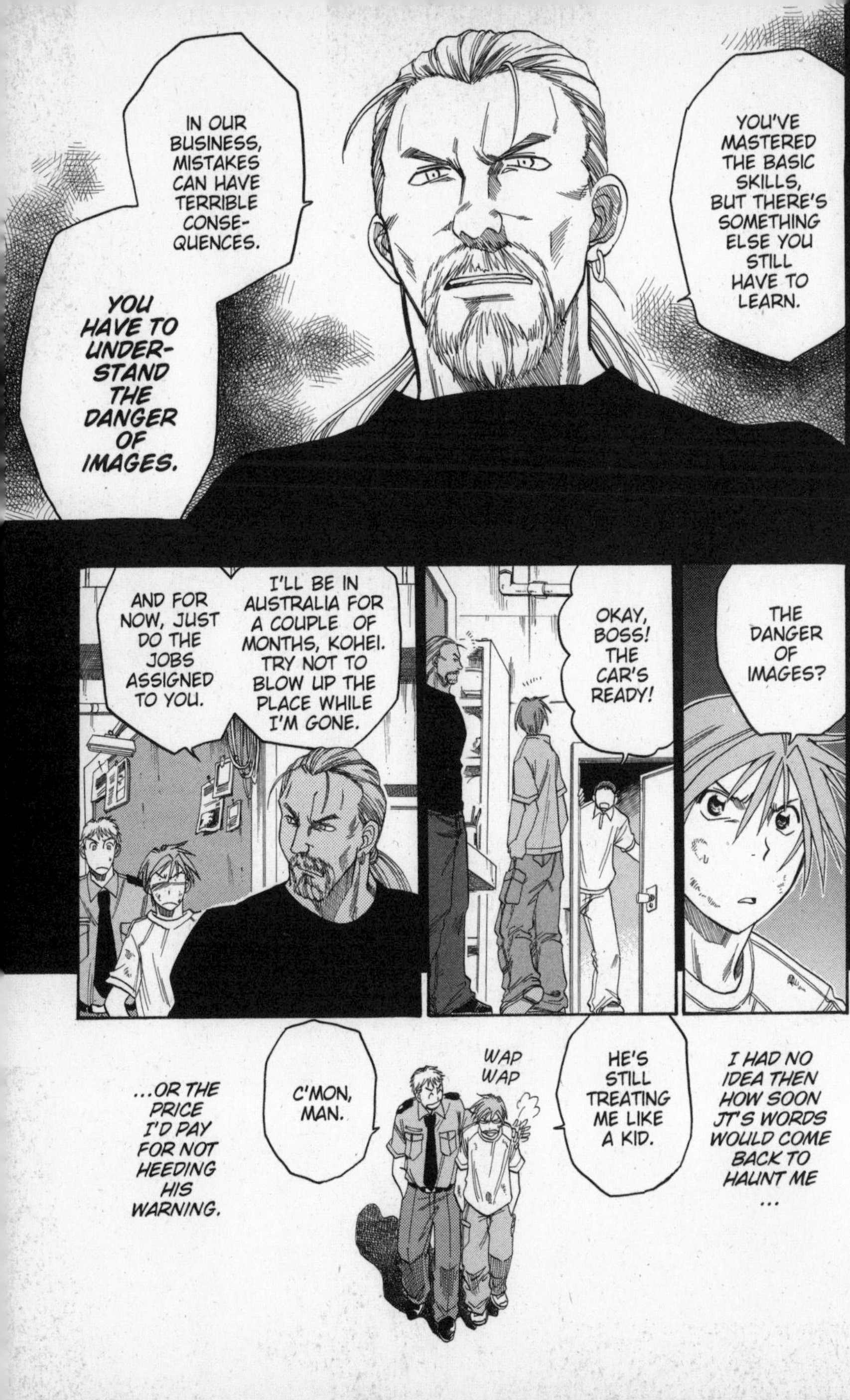
YOU'VE MASTERED THE BASIC SKILLS, BUT THERE'S SOMETHING ELSE YOU STILL HAVE TO LEARN.
IN OUR BUSINESS, MISTAKES CAN HAVE TERRIBLE CONSE-QUENCES.
YOU HAVE TO UNDER-STAND THE DANGER OF IMAGES.
THE DANGER OF IMAGES?
OKAY, BOSS! THE CAR'S READY!
I'LL BE IN AUSTRALIA FOR A COUPLE OF MONTHS, KOHEI. TRY NOT TO BLOW UP THE PLACE WHILE I'M GONE.
AND FOR NOW, JUST DO THE JOBS ASSIGNED TO YOU.
I HAD NO IDEA THEN HOW SOON JT'S WORDS WOULD COME BACK TO HAUNT ME ...
HE'S STILL TREATING ME LIKE A KID.
WAP WAP
C'MON, MAN.
...OR THE PRICE I'D PAY FOR NOT HEEDING HIS WARNING.

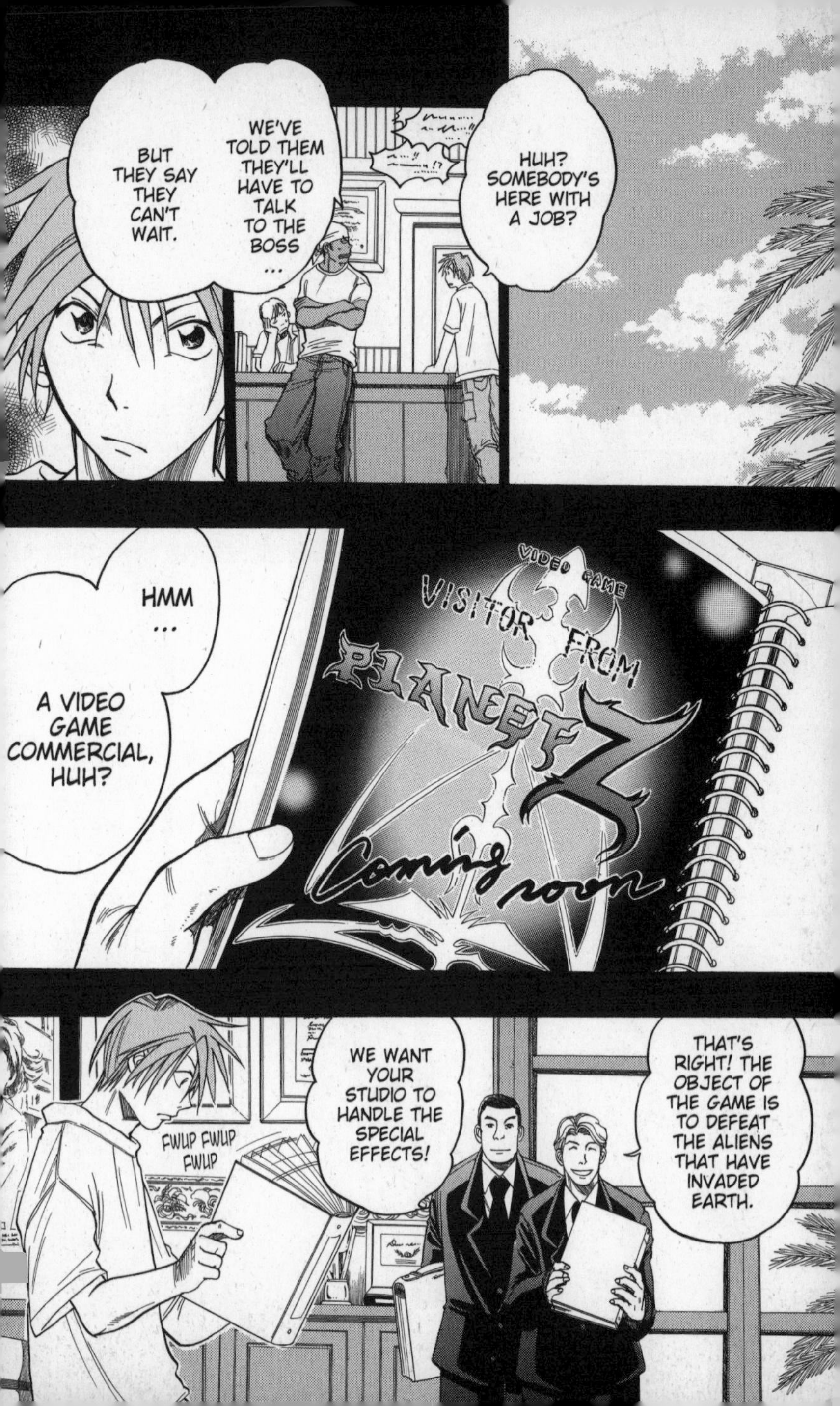
HUH? SOMEBODY'S HERE WITH A JOB?
WE'VE TOLD THEM THEY'LL HAVE TO TALK TO THE BOSS ...
BUT THEY SAY THEY CAN'T WAIT.
VIDEO GAME
VISITOR FROM PLANET Z
Coming soon
HMM ...
A VIDEO GAME COMMERCIAL, HUH?
THAT'S RIGHT! THE OBJECT OF THE GAME IS TO DEFEAT THE ALIENS THAT HAVE INVADED EARTH.
WE WANT YOUR STUDIO TO HANDLE THE SPECIAL EFFECTS!
FWUP FWUP FWUP

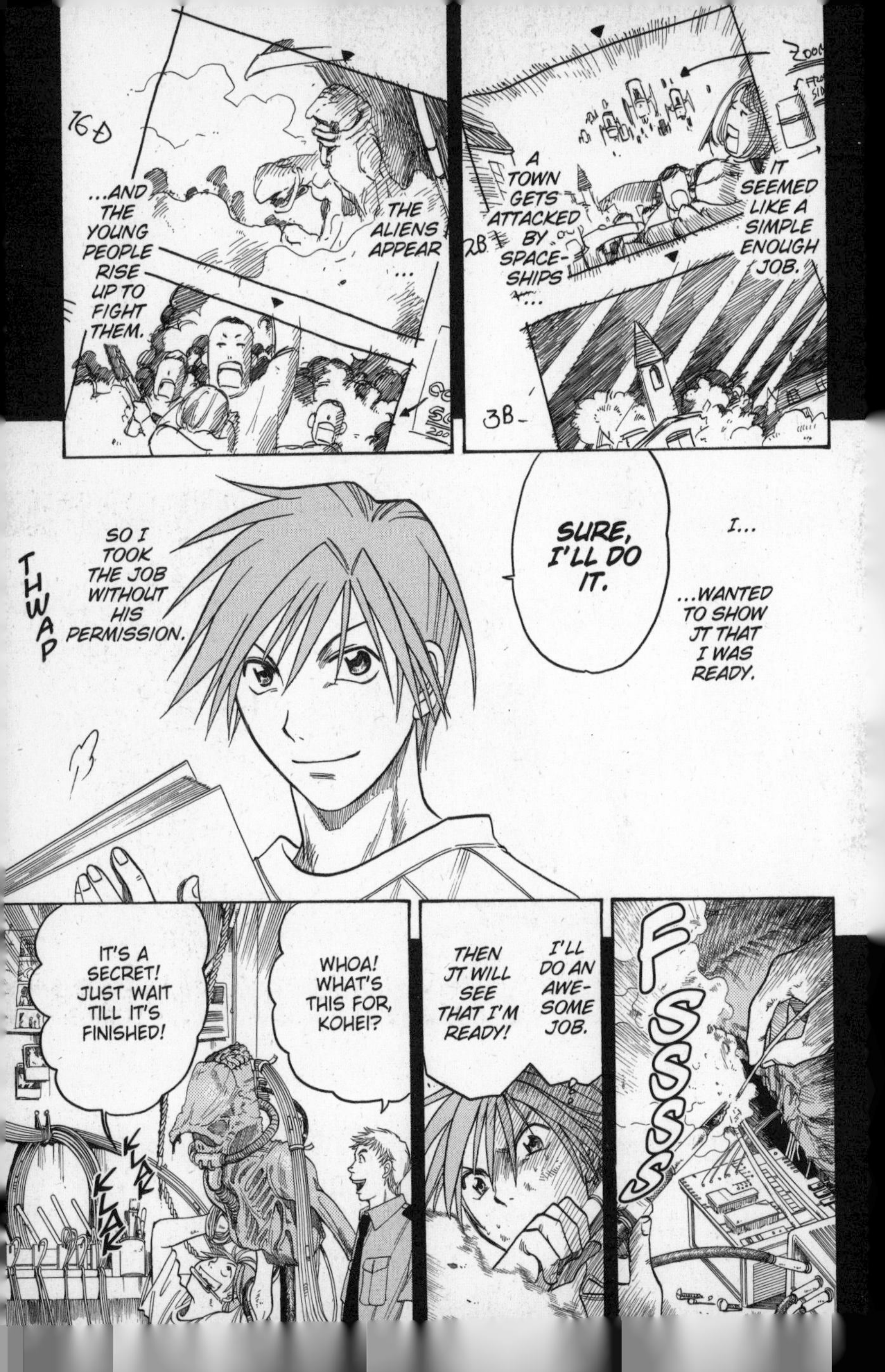
IT SEEMED LIKE A SIMPLE ENOUGH JOB.
A TOWN GETS ATTACKED BY SPACE-SHIPS...
THE ALIENS APPEAR...
...AND THE YOUNG PEOPLE RISE UP TO FIGHT THEM.
I...
...WANTED TO SHOW JT THAT I WAS READY.
SURE, I'LL DO IT.
SO I TOOK THE JOB WITHOUT HIS PERMISSION.
THWAP
FSSSSS
I'LL DO AN AWE-SOME JOB.
THEN JT WILL SEE THAT I'M READY!
WHOA! WHAT'S THIS FOR, KOHEI?
IT'S A SECRET! JUST WAIT TILL IT'S FINISHED!
KLAK
KLAK

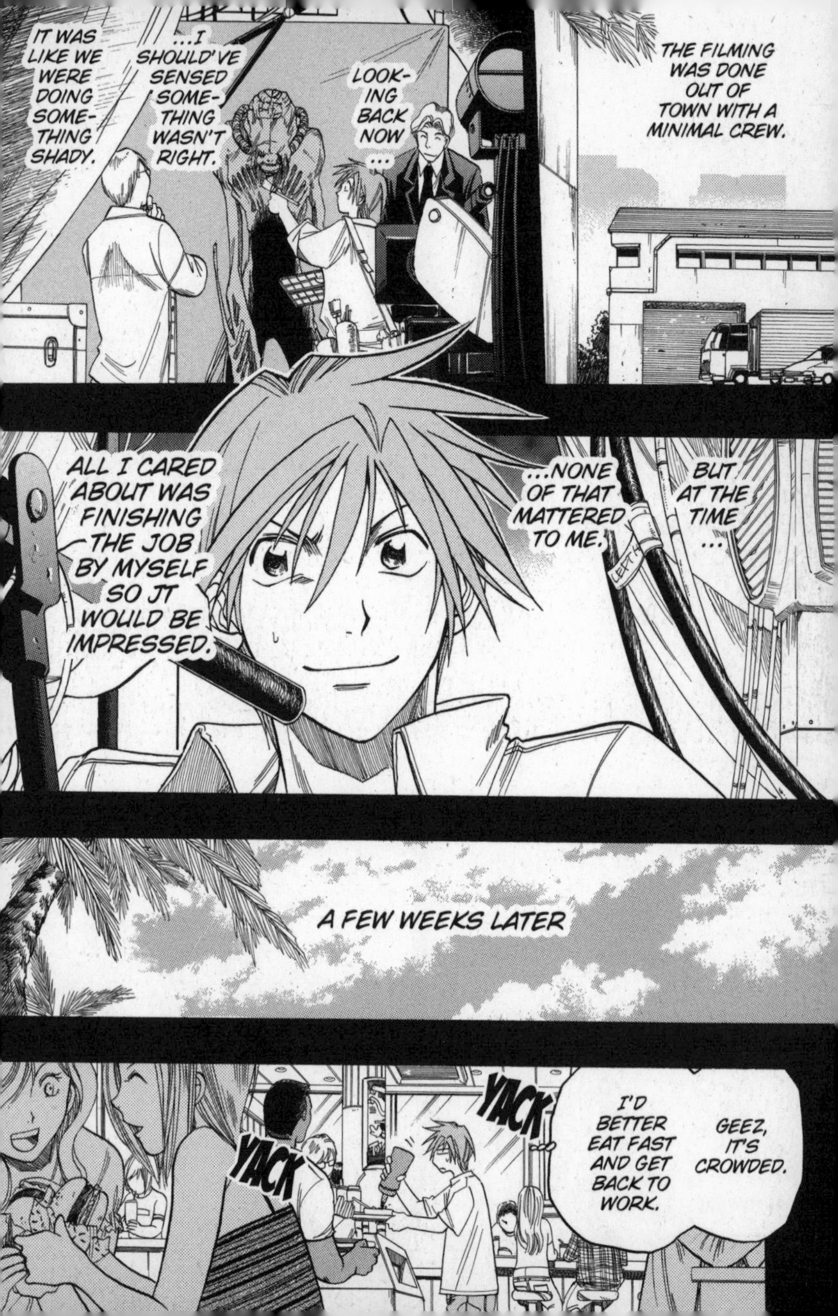
THE FILMING WAS DONE OUT OF TOWN WITH A MINIMAL CREW.
LOOKING BACK NOW ...
...I SHOULD'VE SENSED SOMETHING WASN'T RIGHT.
IT WAS LIKE WE WERE DOING SOMETHING SHADY.
BUT AT THE TIME ...
...NONE OF THAT MATTERED TO ME.
ALL I CARED ABOUT WAS FINISHING THE JOB BY MYSELF SO JT WOULD BE IMPRESSED.
A FEW WEEKS LATER
GEEZ, IT'S CROWDED.
I'D BETTER EAT FAST AND GET BACK TO WORK.
YACK
YACK

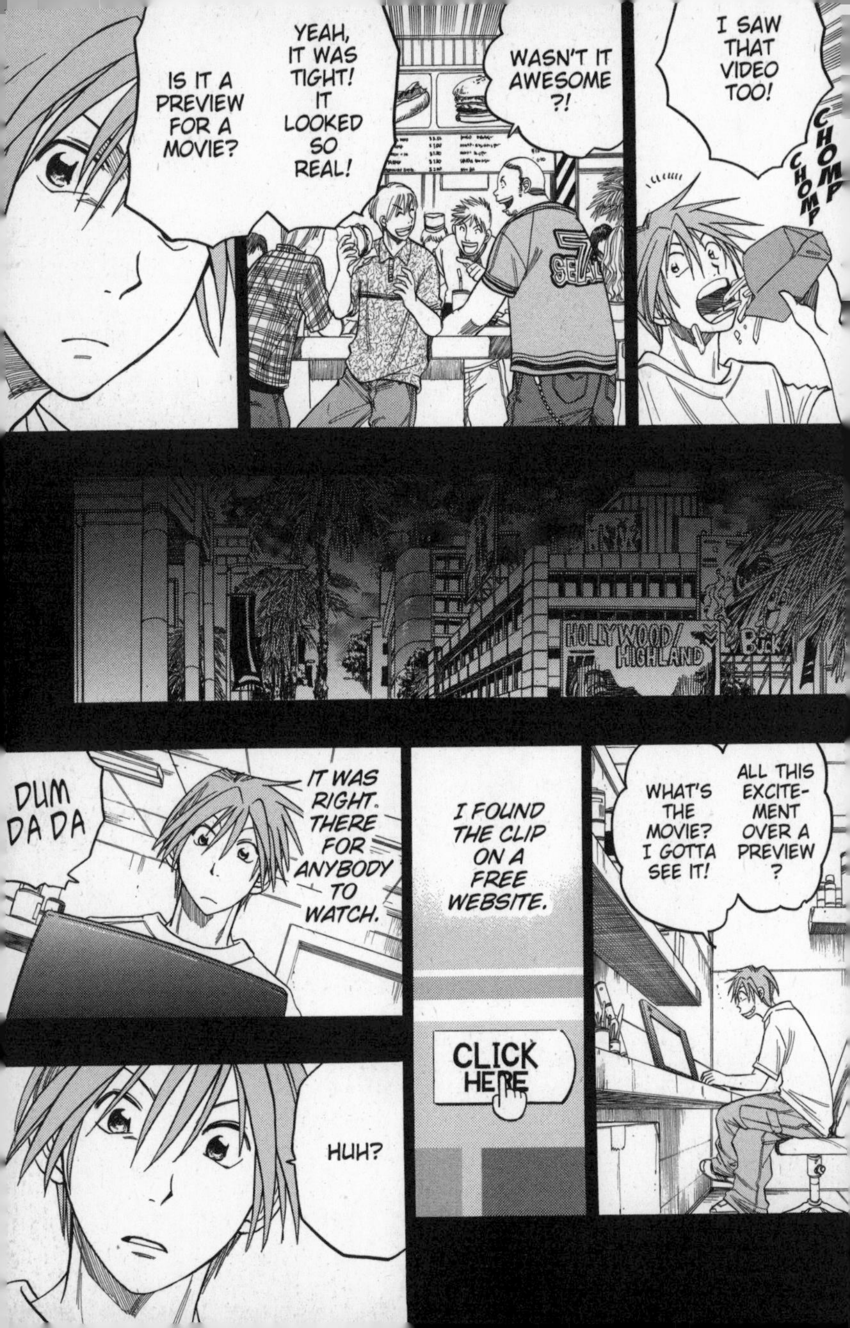
I SAW THAT VIDEO TOO!
CHOMP CHOMP
WASN'T IT AWESOME?!
YEAH, IT WAS TIGHT! IT LOOKED SO REAL!
IS IT A PREVIEW FOR A MOVIE?
HOLLYWOOD/HIGHLAND
ALL THIS EXCITE-MENT OVER A PREVIEW?
WHAT'S THE MOVIE? I GOTTA SEE IT!
I FOUND THE CLIP ON A FREE WEBSITE.
CLICK HERE
IT WAS RIGHT. THERE FOR ANYBODY TO WATCH.
DUM DA DA
HUH?

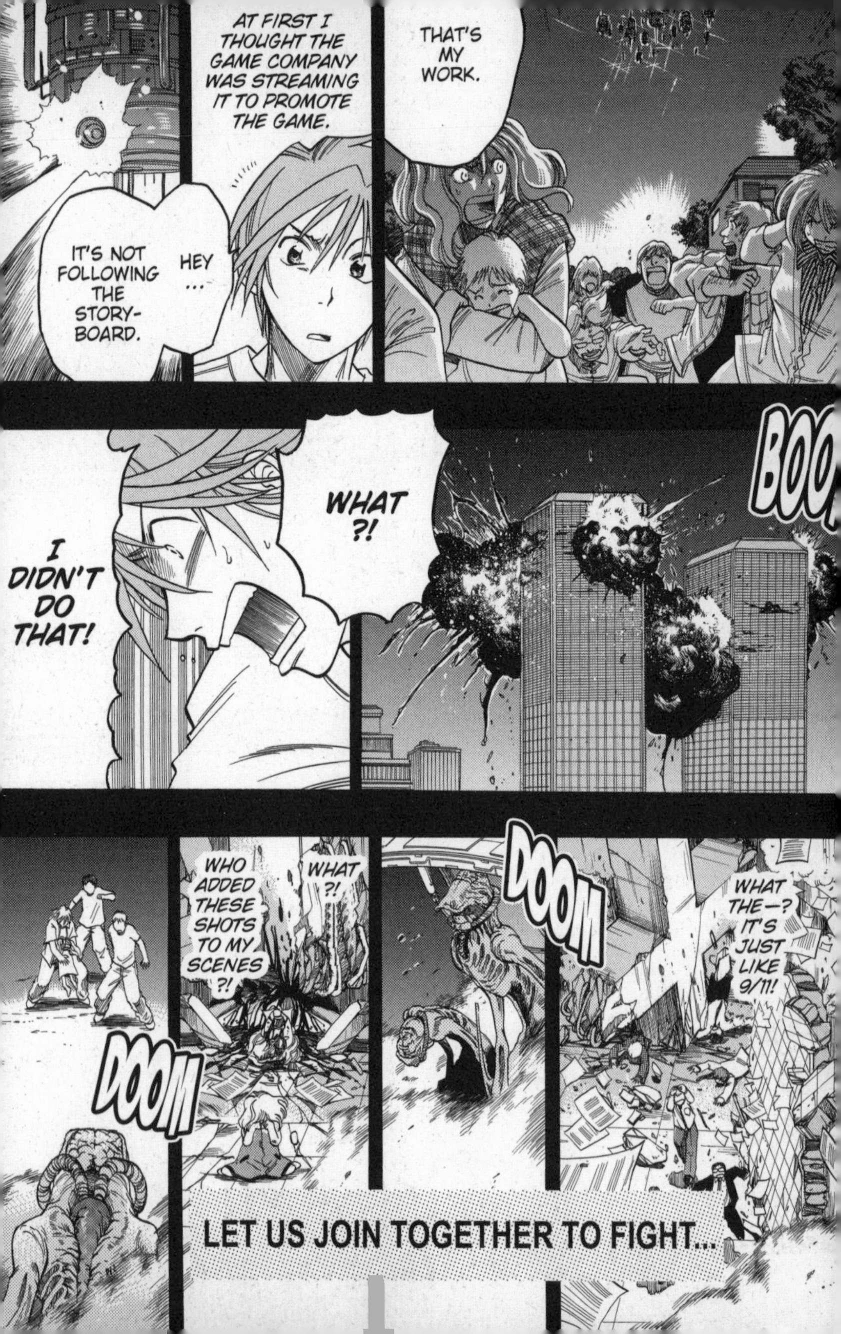
THAT'S MY WORK.
AT FIRST I THOUGHT THE GAME COMPANY WAS STREAMING IT TO PROMOTE THE GAME.
HEY...
IT'S NOT FOLLOWING THE STORY-BOARD.
BOO
WHAT?!
I DIDN'T DO THAT!
WHAT THE—? IT'S JUST LIKE 9/11!
DOOM
WHAT?!
WHO ADDED THESE SHOTS TO MY SCENES?!
DOOM
LET US JOIN TOGETHER TO FIGHT...

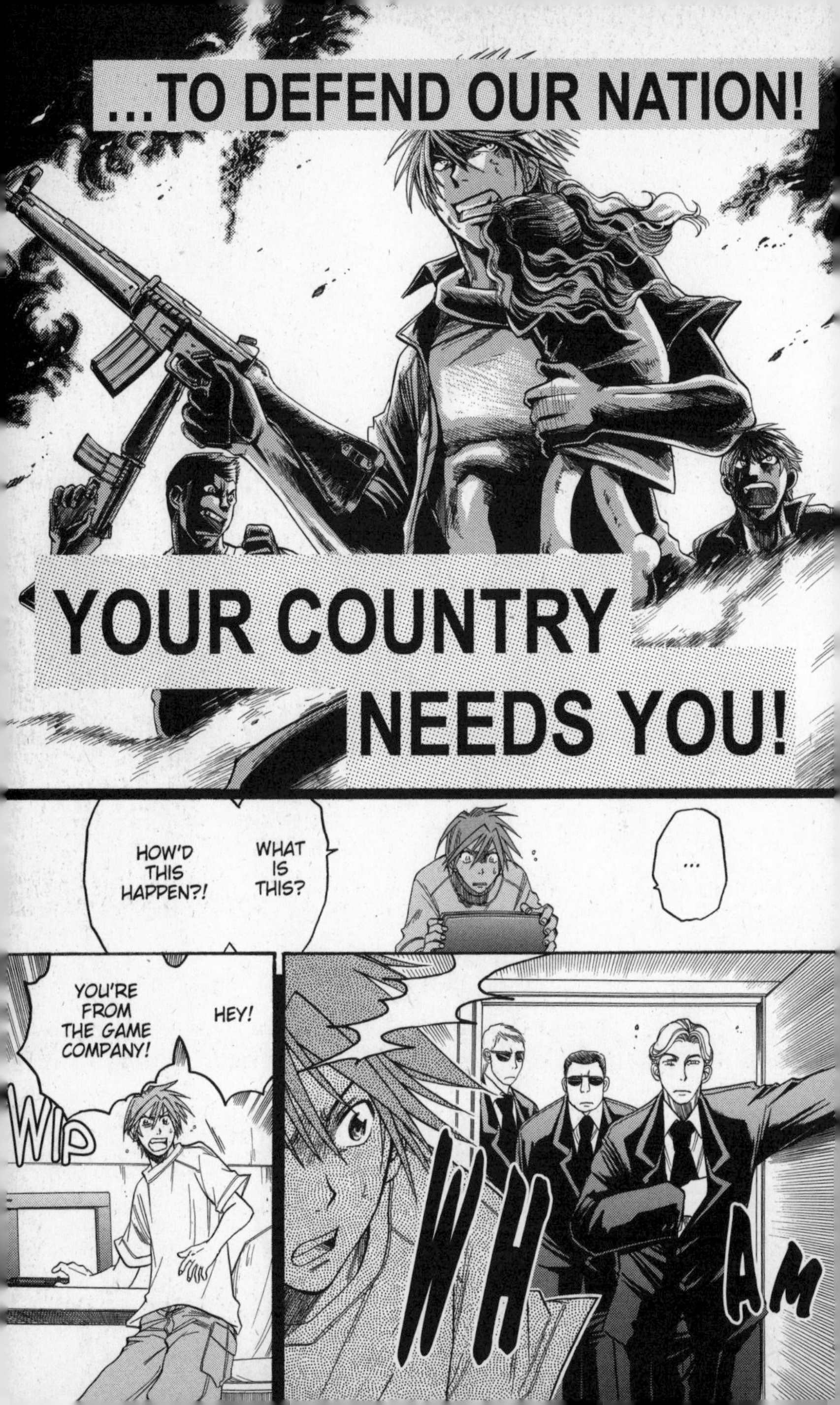
...TO DEFEND OUR NATION!
YOUR COUNTRY NEEDS YOU!
...
WHAT IS THIS?
HOW'D THIS HAPPEN?!
WHAM
HEY!
YOU'RE FROM THE GAME COMPANY!
WIP

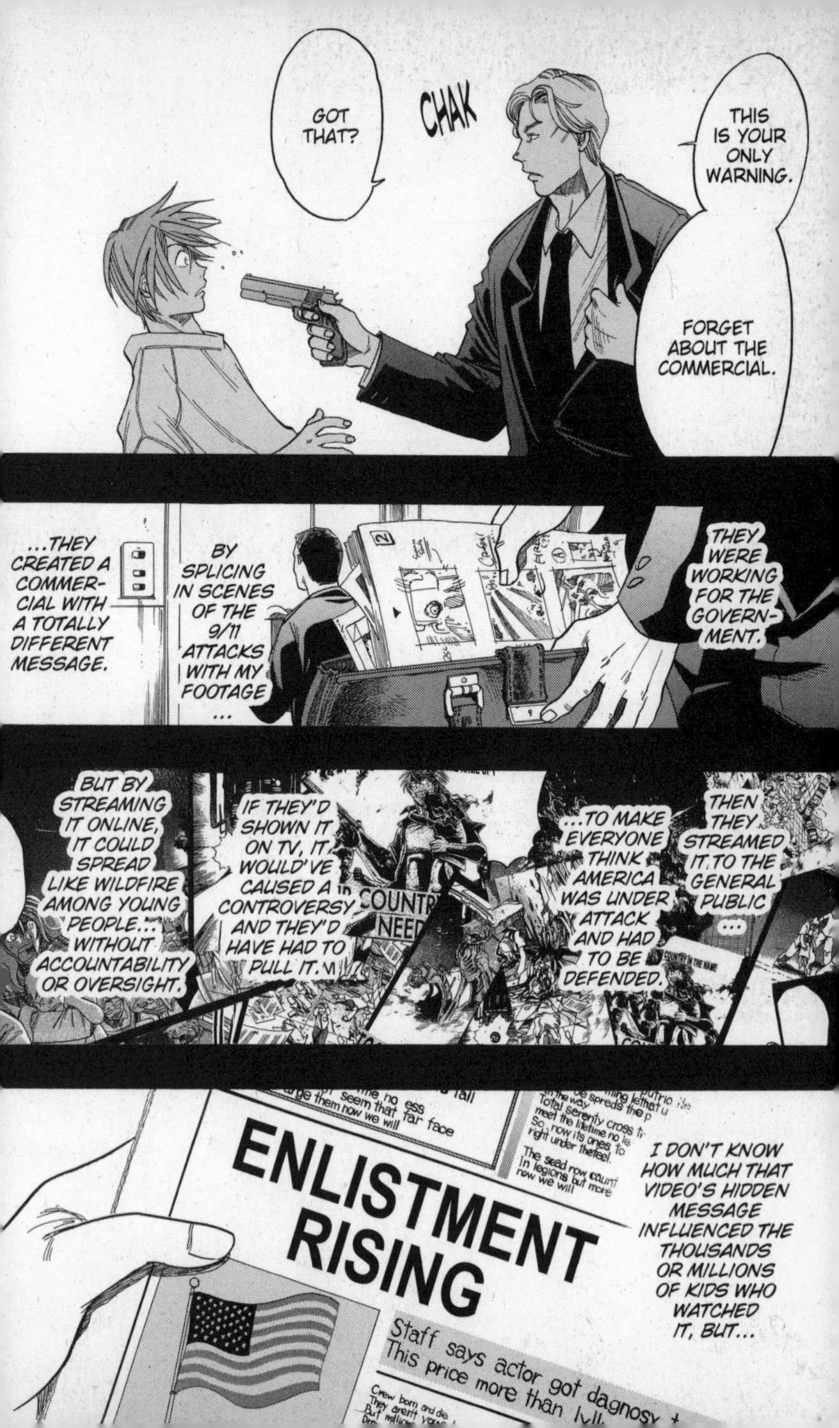
THIS IS YOUR ONLY WARNING.
FORGET ABOUT THE COMMERCIAL.
CHAK
GOT THAT?
THEY WERE WORKING FOR THE GOVERNMENT.
BY SPLICING IN SCENES OF THE 9/11 ATTACKS WITH MY FOOTAGE...
...THEY CREATED A COMMERCIAL WITH A TOTALLY DIFFERENT MESSAGE.
THEN THEY STREAMED IT TO THE GENERAL PUBLIC...
...TO MAKE EVERYONE THINK AMERICA WAS UNDER ATTACK AND HAD TO BE DEFENDED.
IF THEY'D SHOWN IT ON TV, IT WOULD'VE CAUSED A CONTROVERSY AND THEY'D HAVE HAD TO PULL IT.
BUT BY STREAMING IT ONLINE, IT COULD SPREAD LIKE WILDFIRE AMONG YOUNG PEOPLE... WITHOUT ACCOUNTABILITY OR OVERSIGHT.
I DON'T KNOW HOW MUCH THAT VIDEO'S HIDDEN MESSAGE INFLUENCED THE THOUSANDS OR MILLIONS OF KIDS WHO WATCHED IT, BUT...
ENLISTMENT RISING
Staff says actor got dagnosy
This price more than lyll

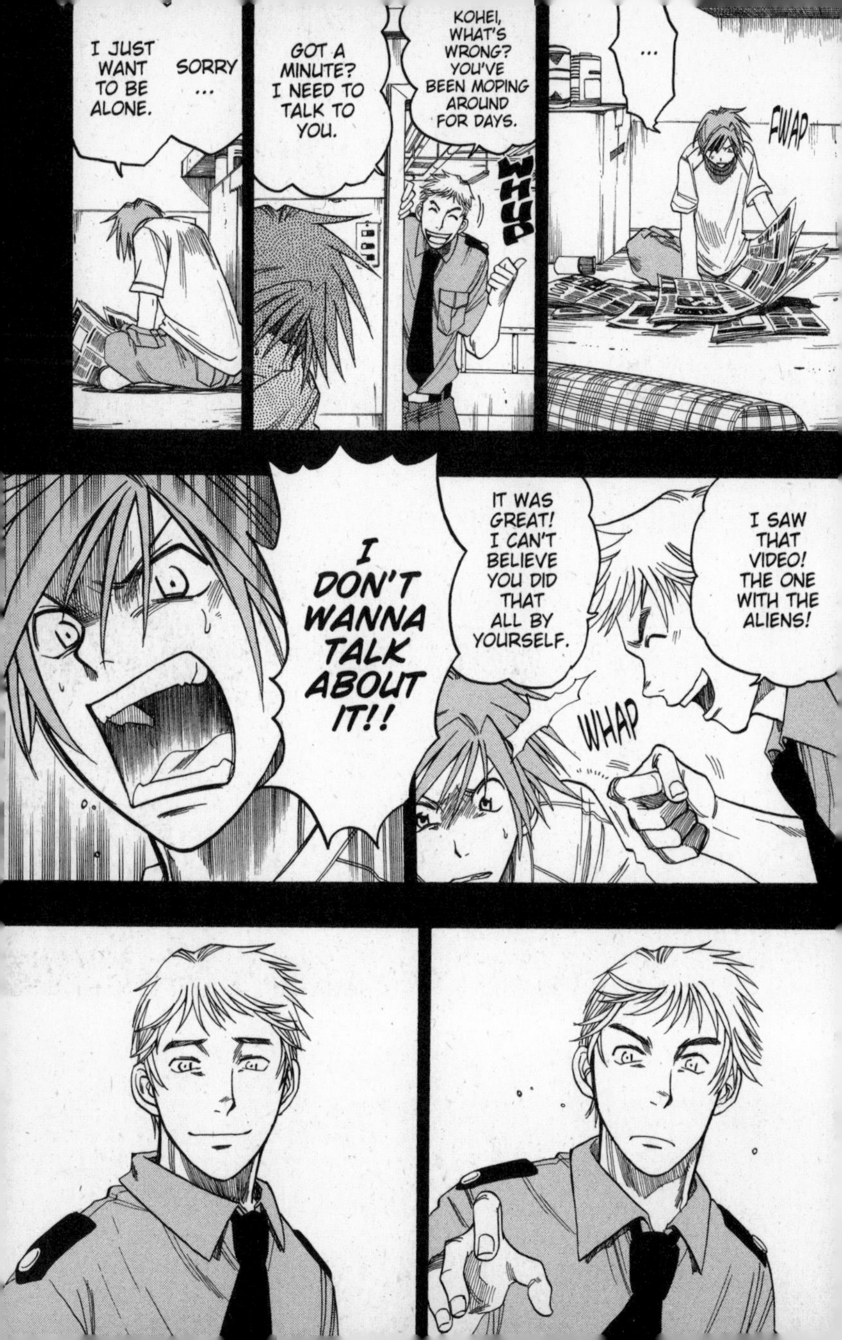
...
FWAP
KOHEI, WHAT'S WRONG? YOU'VE BEEN MOPING AROUND FOR DAYS.
GOT A MINUTE? I NEED TO TALK TO YOU.
WHUP
SORRY ...
I JUST WANT TO BE ALONE.
I SAW THAT VIDEO! THE ONE WITH THE ALIENS!
IT WAS GREAT! I CAN'T BELIEVE YOU DID THAT ALL BY YOURSELF.
WHAP
I DON'T WANNA TALK ABOUT IT!!

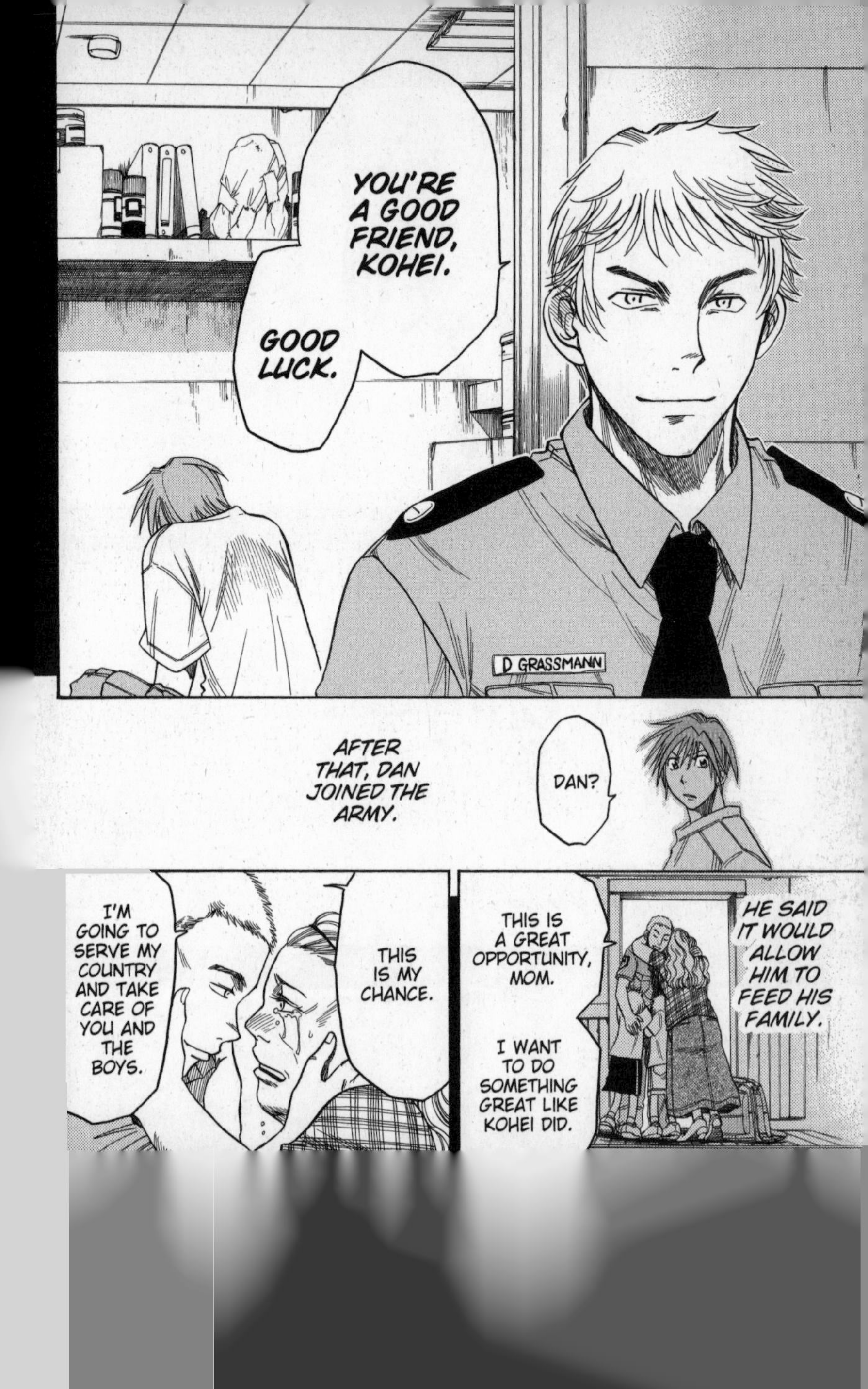
YOU'RE A GOOD FRIEND, KOHEI.
GOOD LUCK.
D GRASSMANN
DAN?
AFTER THAT, DAN JOINED THE ARMY.
HE SAID IT WOULD ALLOW HIM TO FEED HIS FAMILY.
THIS IS A GREAT OPPORTUNITY, MOM.
I WANT TO DO SOMETHING GREAT LIKE KOHEI DID.
THIS IS MY CHANCE.
I'M GOING TO SERVE MY COUNTRY AND TAKE CARE OF YOU AND THE BOYS.

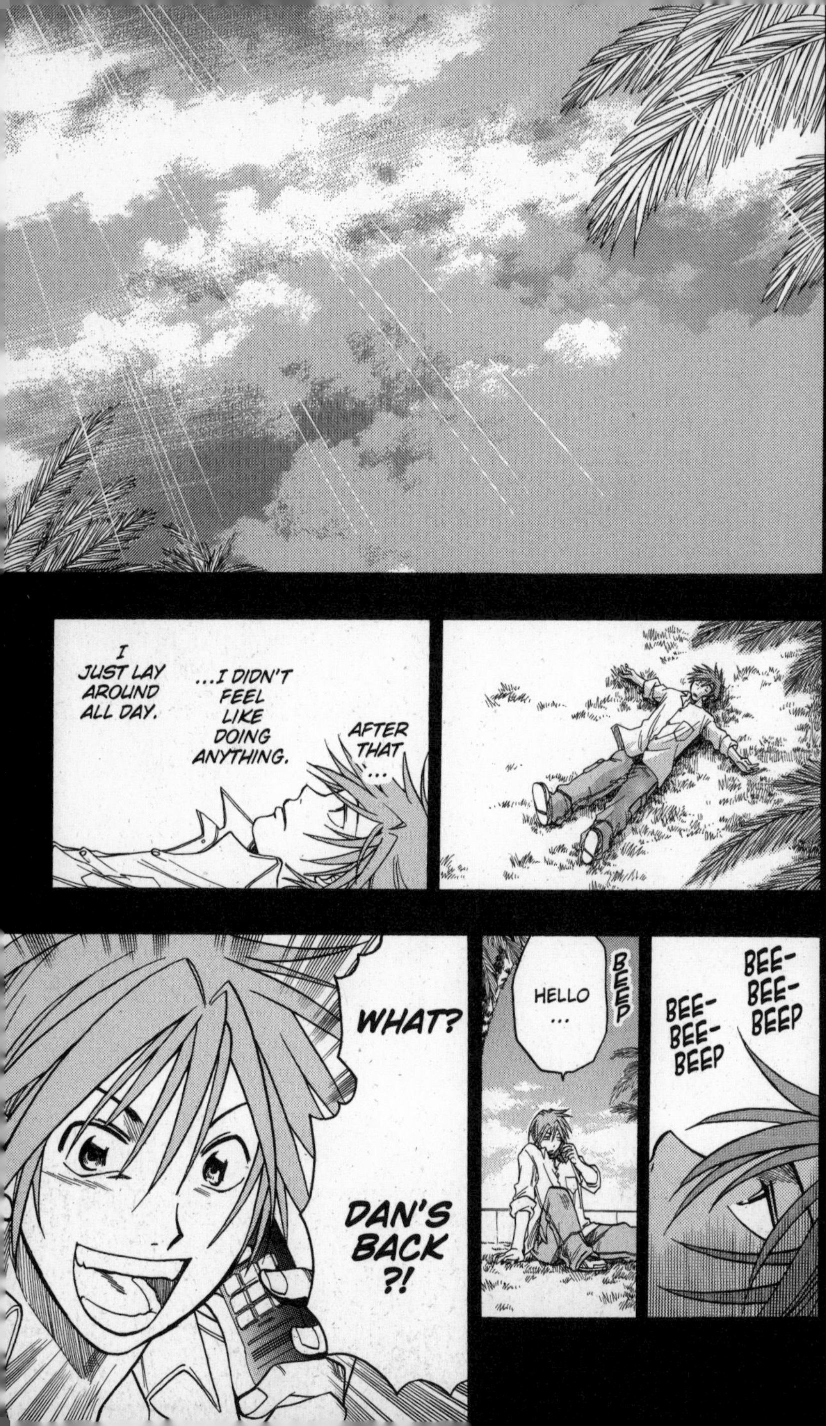
AFTER THAT...
...I DIDN'T FEEL LIKE DOING ANYTHING.
I JUST LAY AROUND ALL DAY.
BEE-BEE-BEEP
BEE-BEE-BEEP
BEEP
HELLO...
WHAT?
DAN'S BACK?!

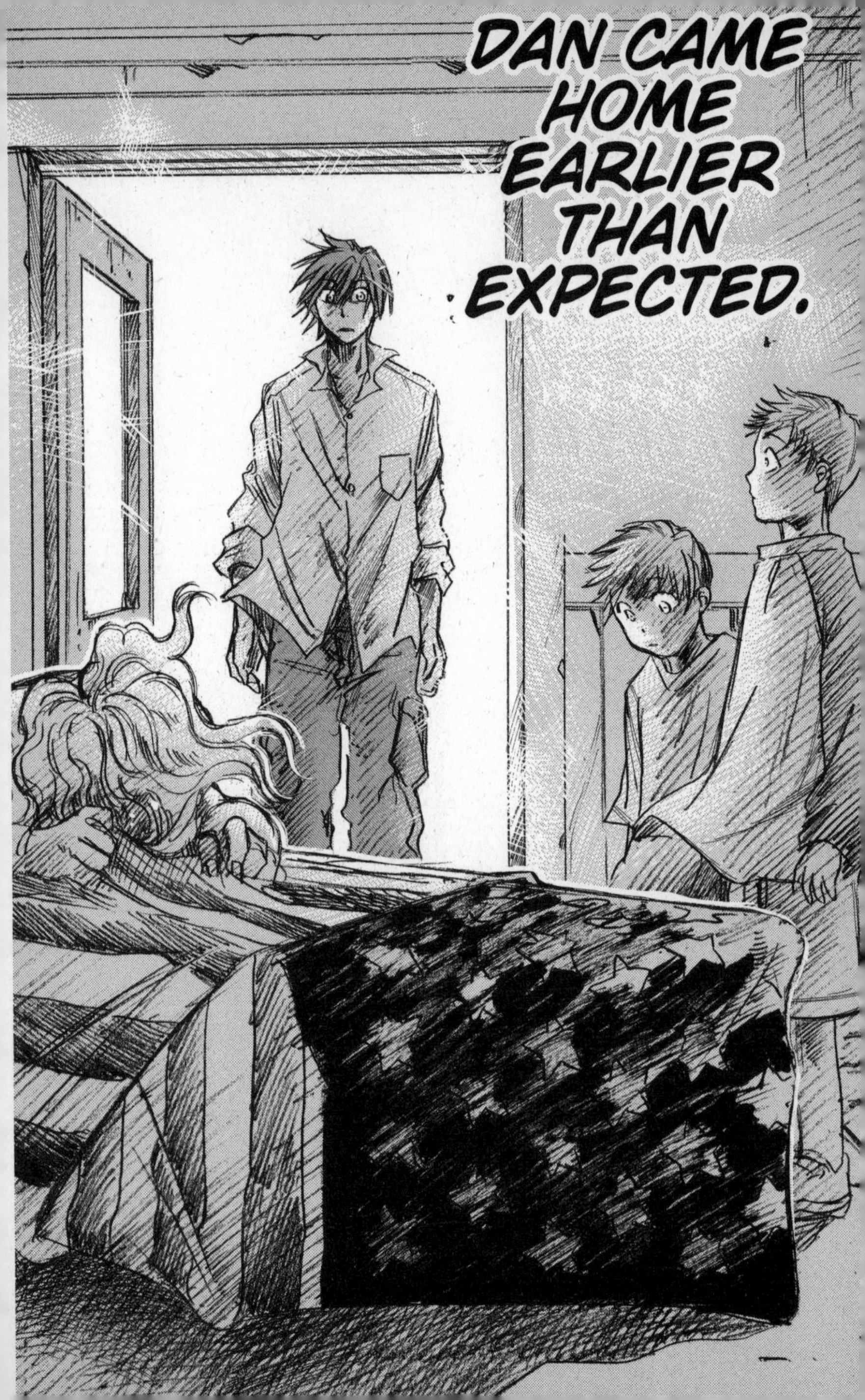
DAN CAME HOME EARLIER THAN EXPECTED.

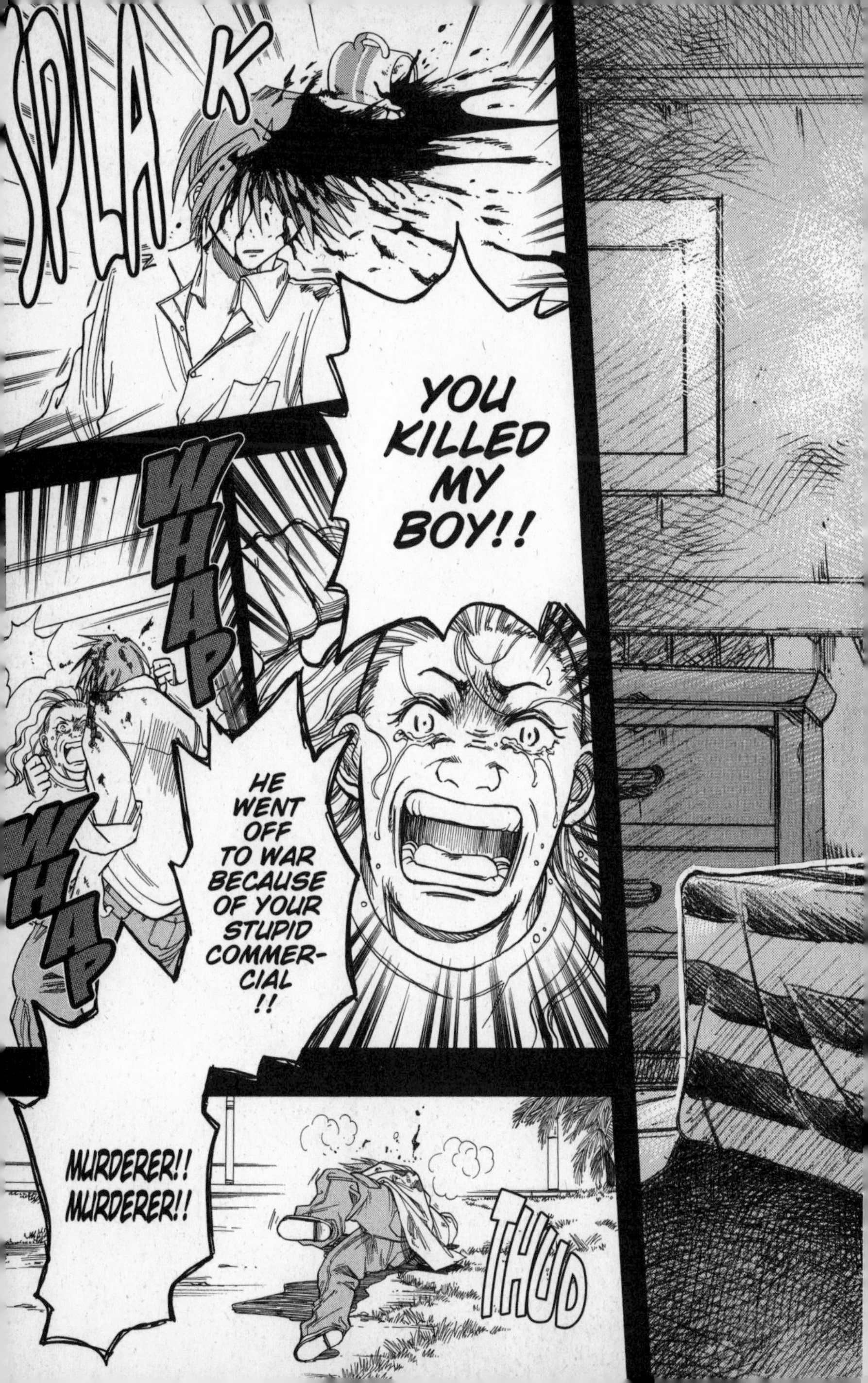
SPLAK
YOU KILLED MY BOY!!
WHAP
HE WENT OFF TO WAR BECAUSE OF YOUR STUPID COMMER-CIAL!!
WHAP
THUD
MURDERER!! MURDERER!!

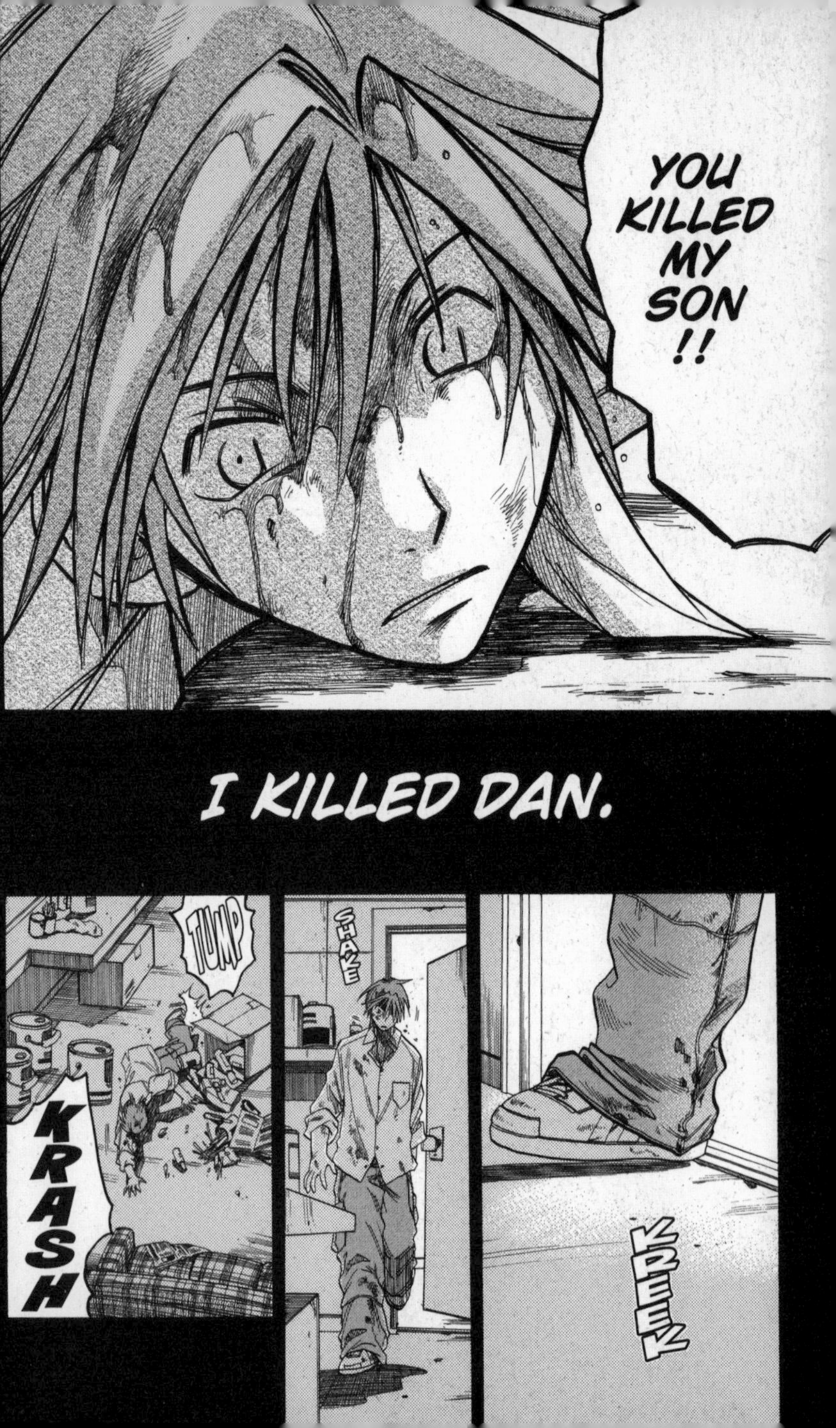
YOU KILLED MY SON !!
I KILLED DAN.
KREEK
SHAKE
TUMP
KRASH

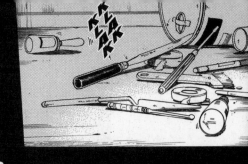

KLAK KLAK

I MUR- DERED MY BEST FRIEND !!

CHONK

I...

KLAK

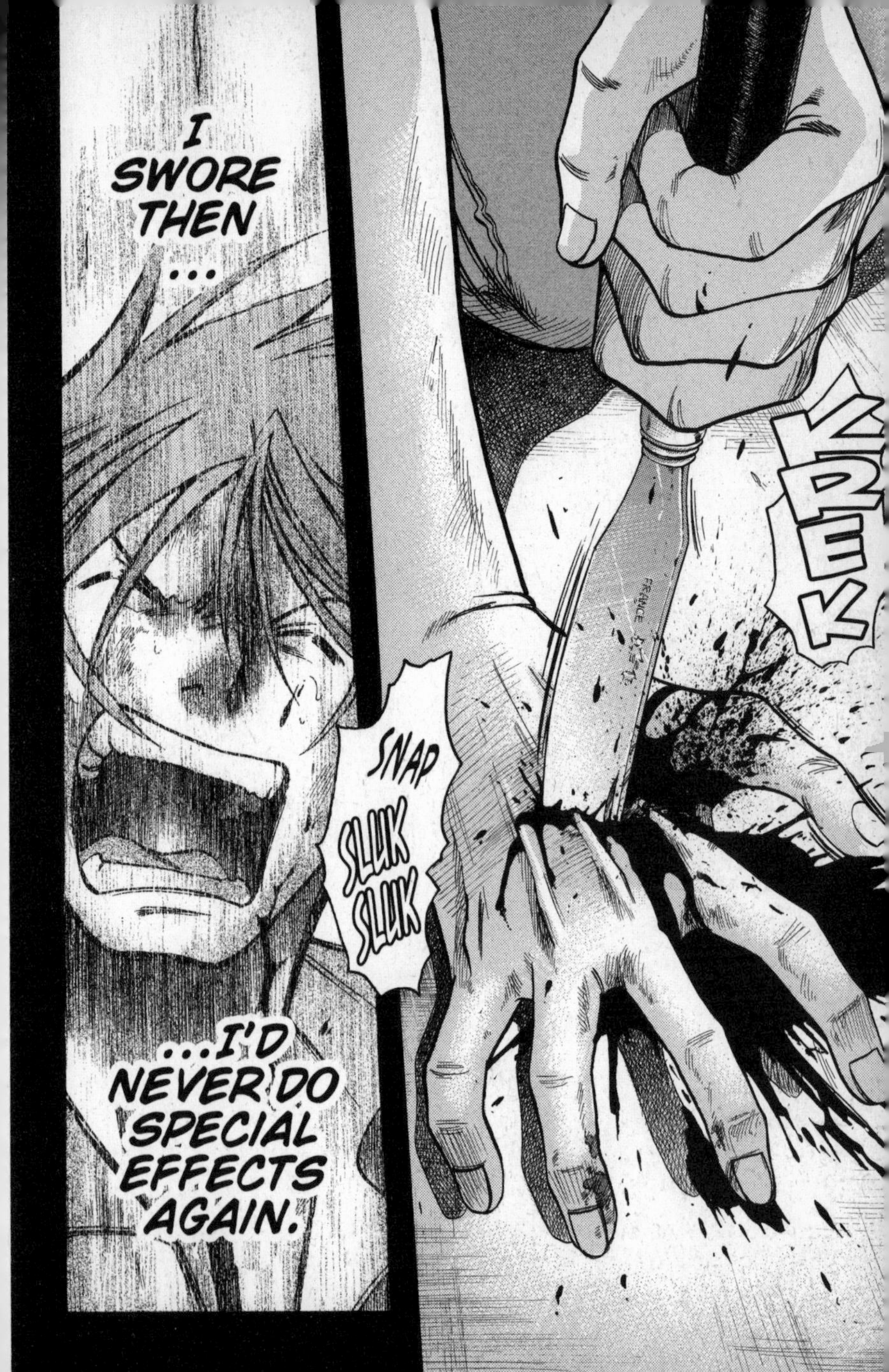
KREK
SNAP
SLUK SLUK
I SWORE THEN...
...I'D NEVER DO SPECIAL EFFECTS AGAIN.

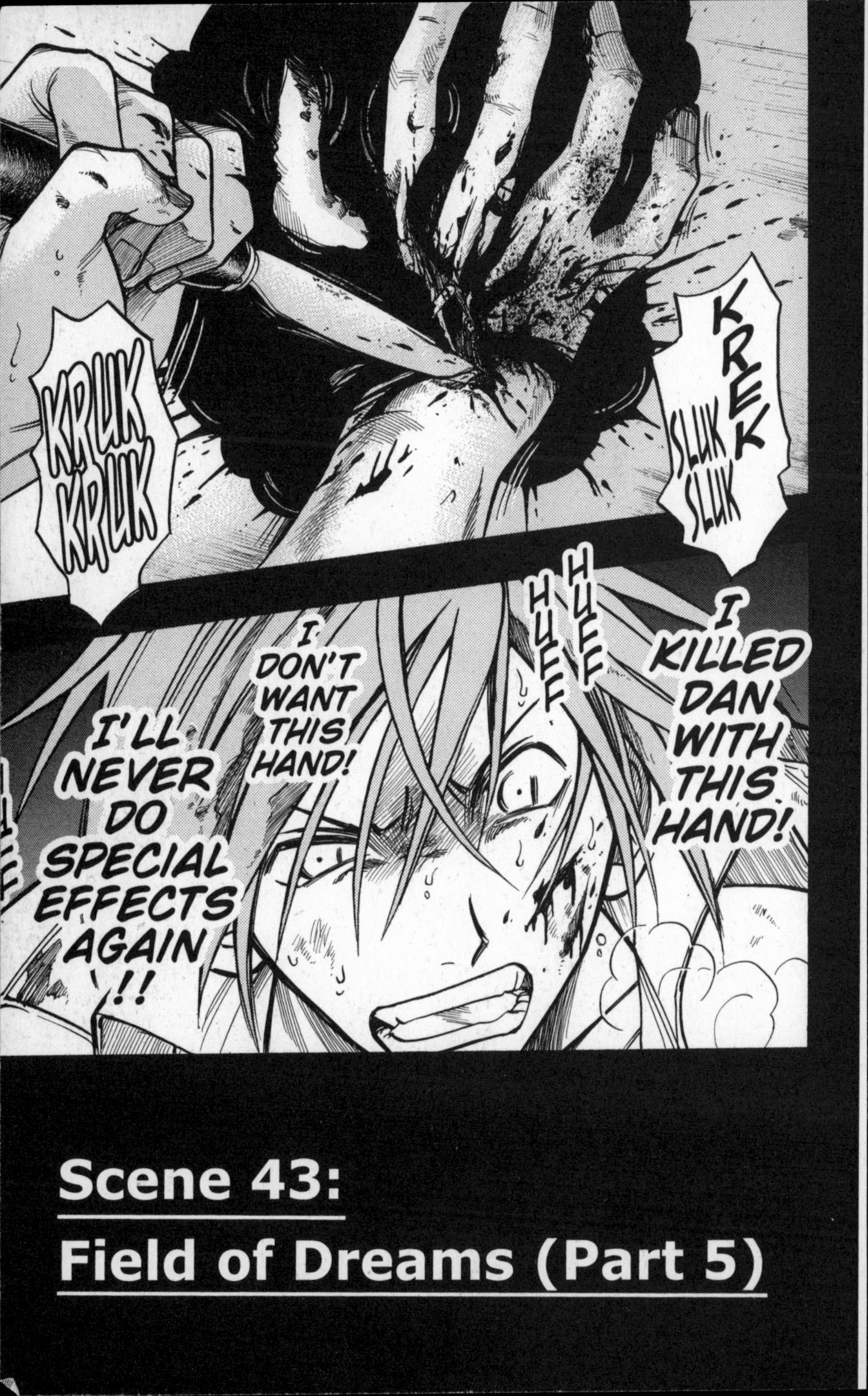
KREK
SLUK SLUK
KRUK KRUK
I KILLED DAN WITH THIS HAND!
HUFF HUFF
I DON'T WANT THIS HAND!
I'LL NEVER DO SPECIAL EFFECTS AGAIN!!

Scene 43: Field of Dreams (Part 5)

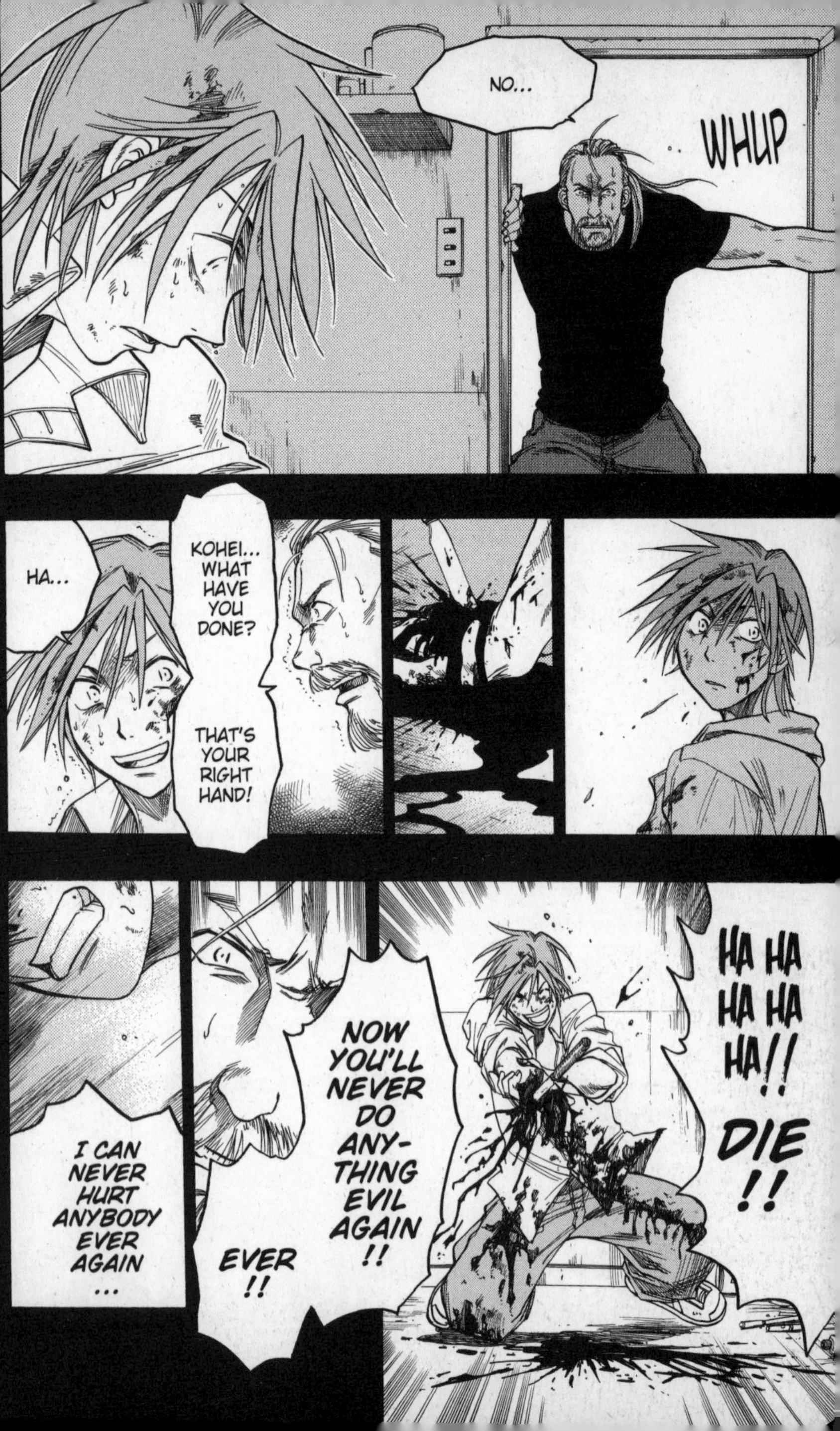
NO...
WHUP
KOHEI... WHAT HAVE YOU DONE?
THAT'S YOUR RIGHT HAND!
HA...
HA HA HA HA HA!!
DIE!!
NOW YOU'LL NEVER DO ANY-THING EVIL AGAIN!!
EVER!!
I CAN NEVER HURT ANYBODY EVER AGAIN...

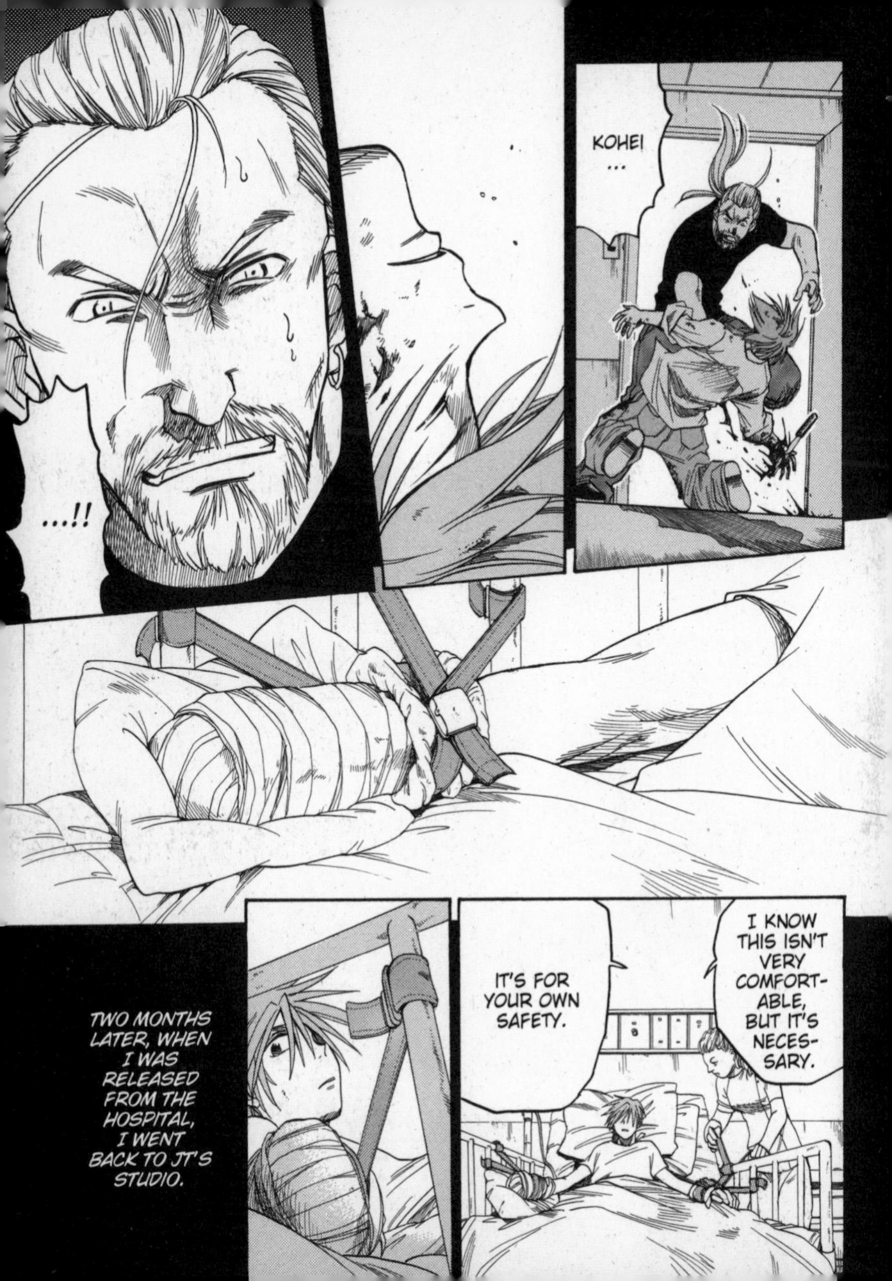
KOHEI ...
...!!
I KNOW THIS ISN'T VERY COMFORTABLE, BUT IT'S NECESSARY.
IT'S FOR YOUR OWN SAFETY.
TWO MONTHS LATER, WHEN I WAS RELEASED FROM THE HOSPITAL, I WENT BACK TO JT'S STUDIO.

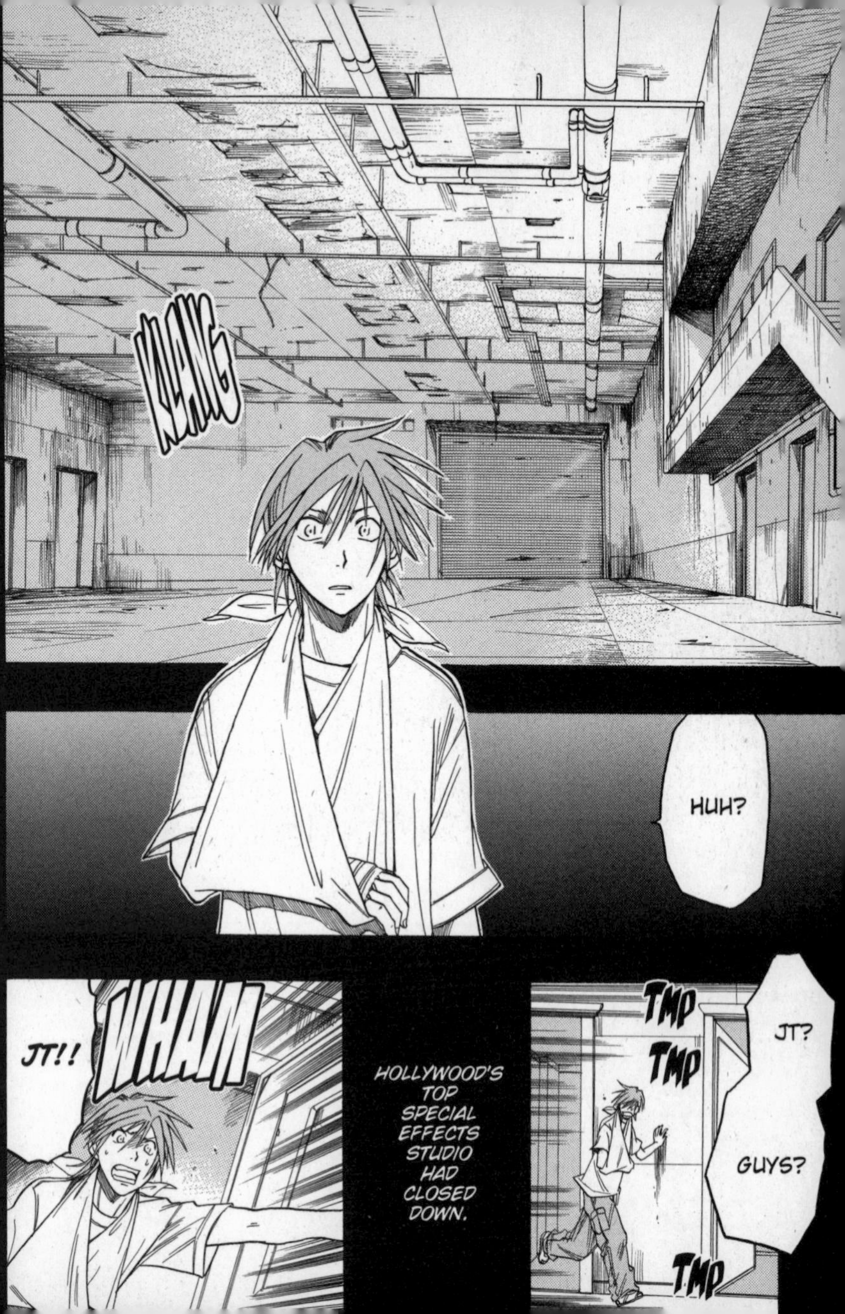
KLANG
HUH?
JT?
GUYS?
TMP
TMP
TMP
HOLLYWOOD'S TOP SPECIAL EFFECTS STUDIO HAD CLOSED DOWN.
WHAM
JT!!

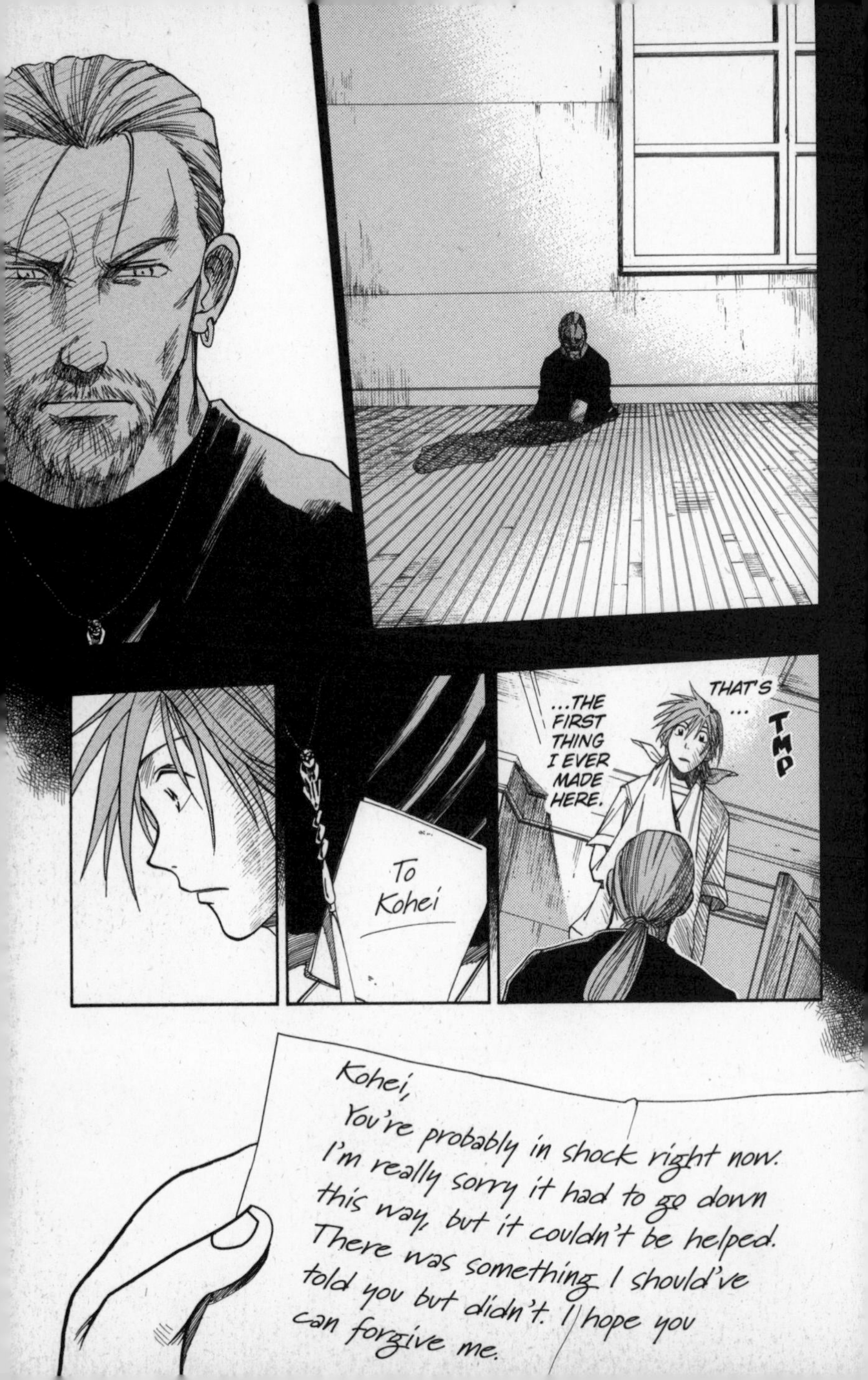
THAT'S ...
...THE FIRST THING I EVER MADE HERE.
TMP
To Kohei
Kohei,
You're probably in shock right now. I'm really sorry it had to go down this way, but it couldn't be helped. There was something I should've told you but didn't. I hope you can forgive me.

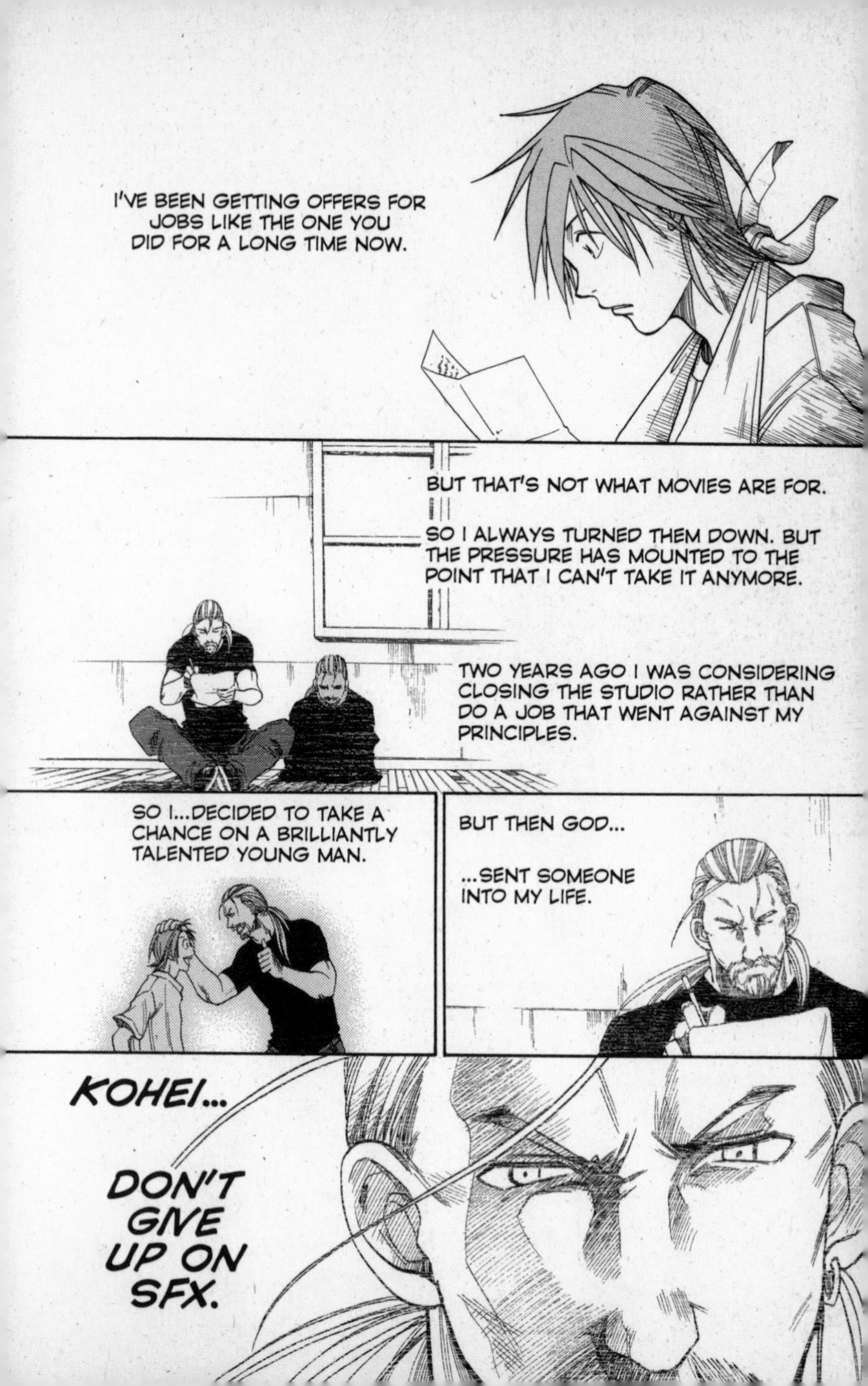
I'VE BEEN GETTING OFFERS FOR JOBS LIKE THE ONE YOU DID FOR A LONG TIME NOW.
BUT THAT'S NOT WHAT MOVIES ARE FOR.
SO I ALWAYS TURNED THEM DOWN. BUT THE PRESSURE HAS MOUNTED TO THE POINT THAT I CAN'T TAKE IT ANYMORE.
TWO YEARS AGO I WAS CONSIDERING CLOSING THE STUDIO RATHER THAN DO A JOB THAT WENT AGAINST MY PRINCIPLES.
BUT THEN GOD...
...SENT SOMEONE INTO MY LIFE.
SO I...DECIDED TO TAKE A CHANCE ON A BRILLIANTLY TALENTED YOUNG MAN.
KOHEI...
DON'T GIVE UP ON SFX.

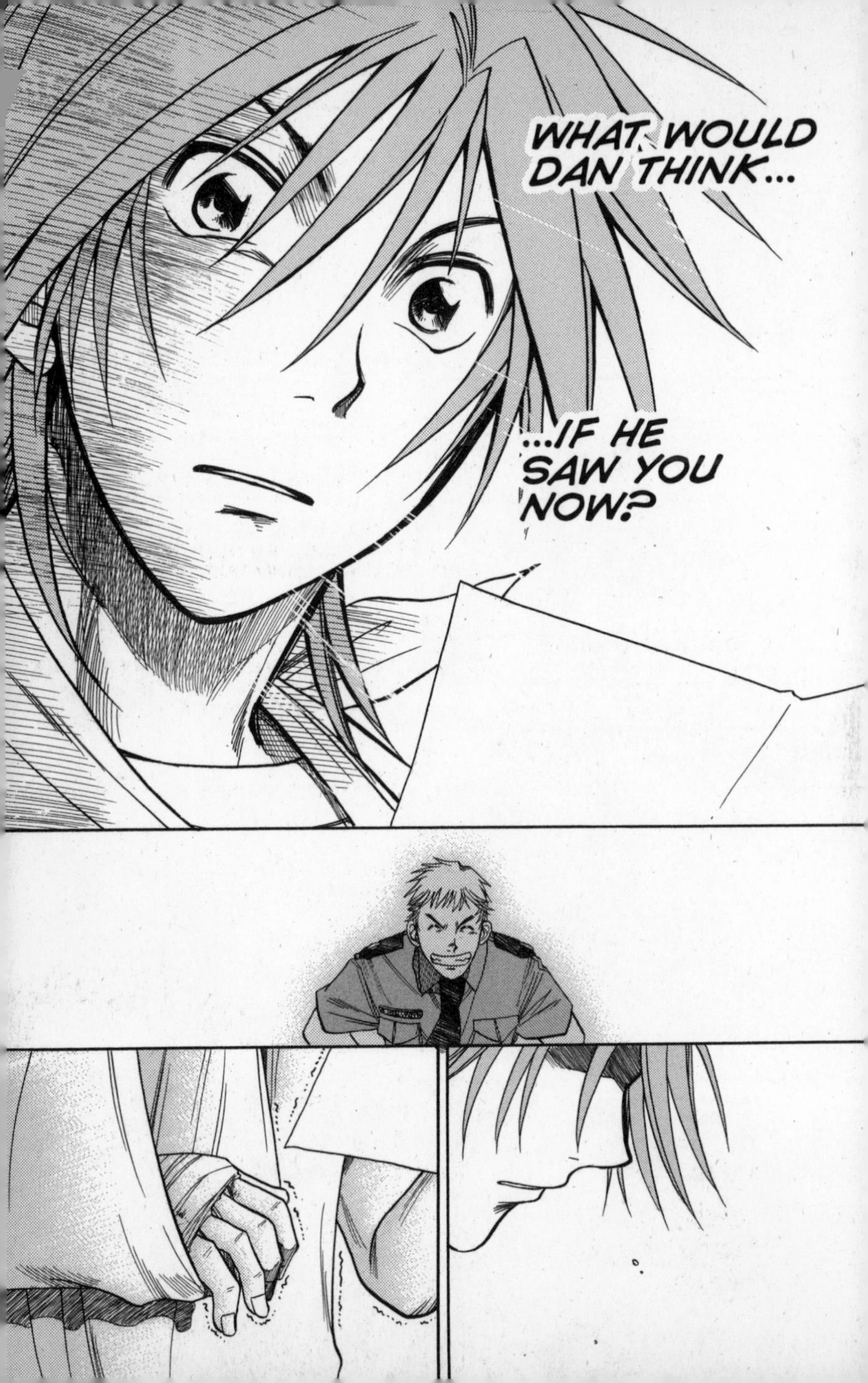
WHAT WOULD DAN THINK...
...IF HE SAW YOU NOW?

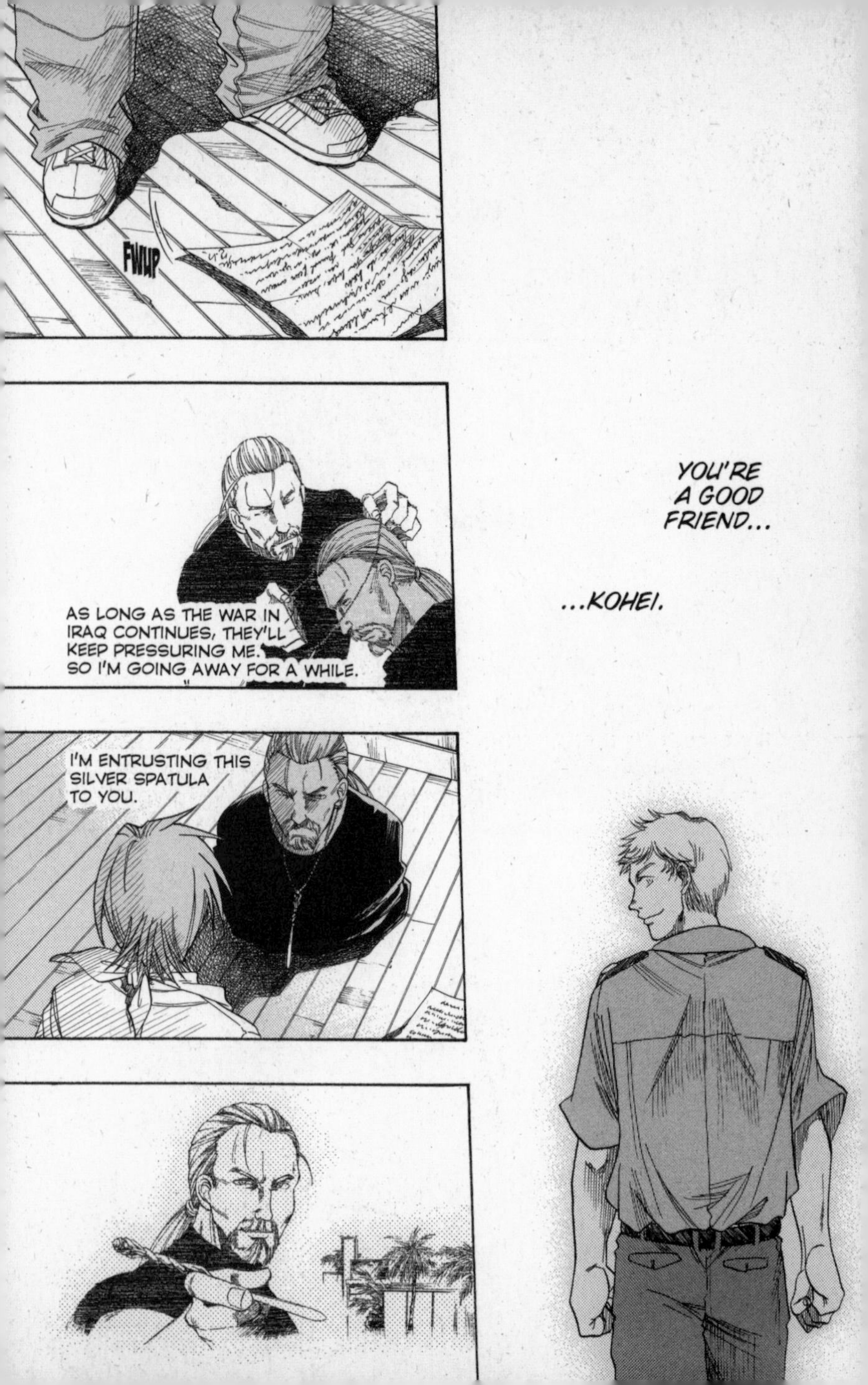
YOU'RE A GOOD FRIEND...
...KOHEI.
FWUP
AS LONG AS THE WAR IN IRAQ CONTINUES, THEY'LL KEEP PRESSURING ME. SO I'M GOING AWAY FOR A WHILE.
I'M ENTRUSTING THIS SILVER SPATULA TO YOU.

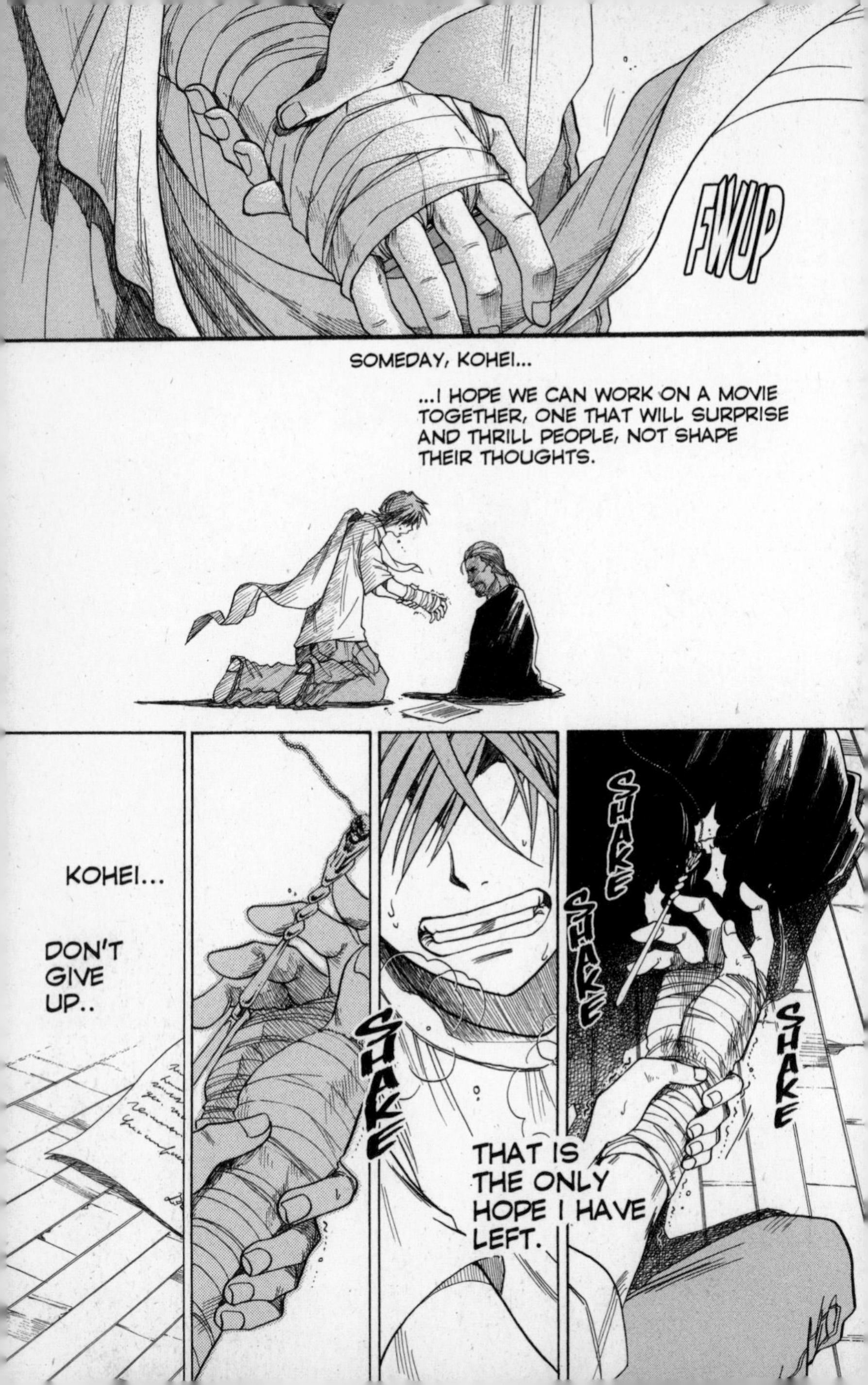
FWUP
SOMEDAY, KOHEI...
...I HOPE WE CAN WORK ON A MOVIE TOGETHER, ONE THAT WILL SURPRISE AND THRILL PEOPLE, NOT SHAPE THEIR THOUGHTS.
SHAKE
SHAKE
SHAKE
THAT IS THE ONLY HOPE I HAVE LEFT.
SHAKE
KOHEI...
DON'T GIVE UP..

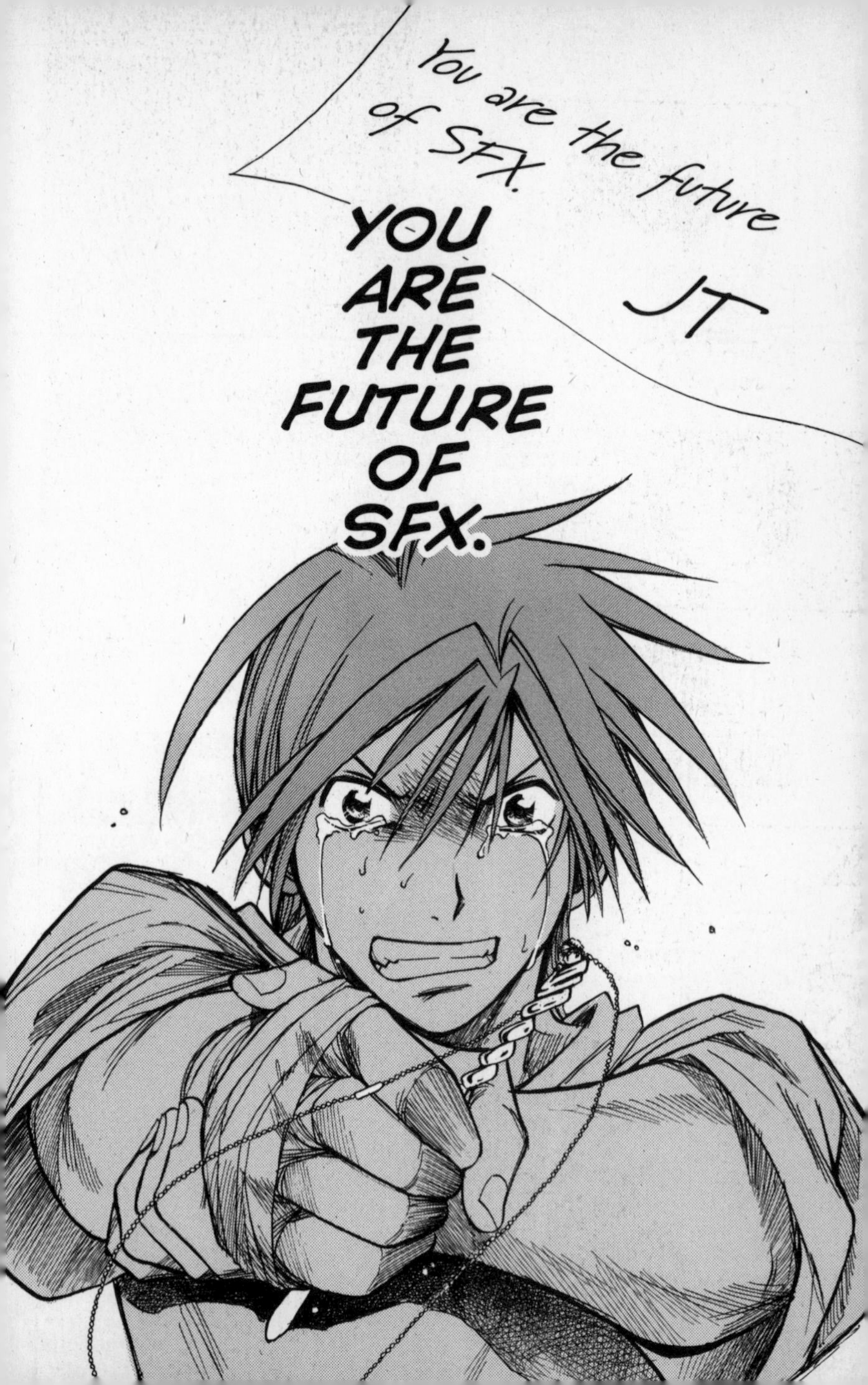
You are the future of SFX.
JT
YOU ARE THE FUTURE OF SFX.

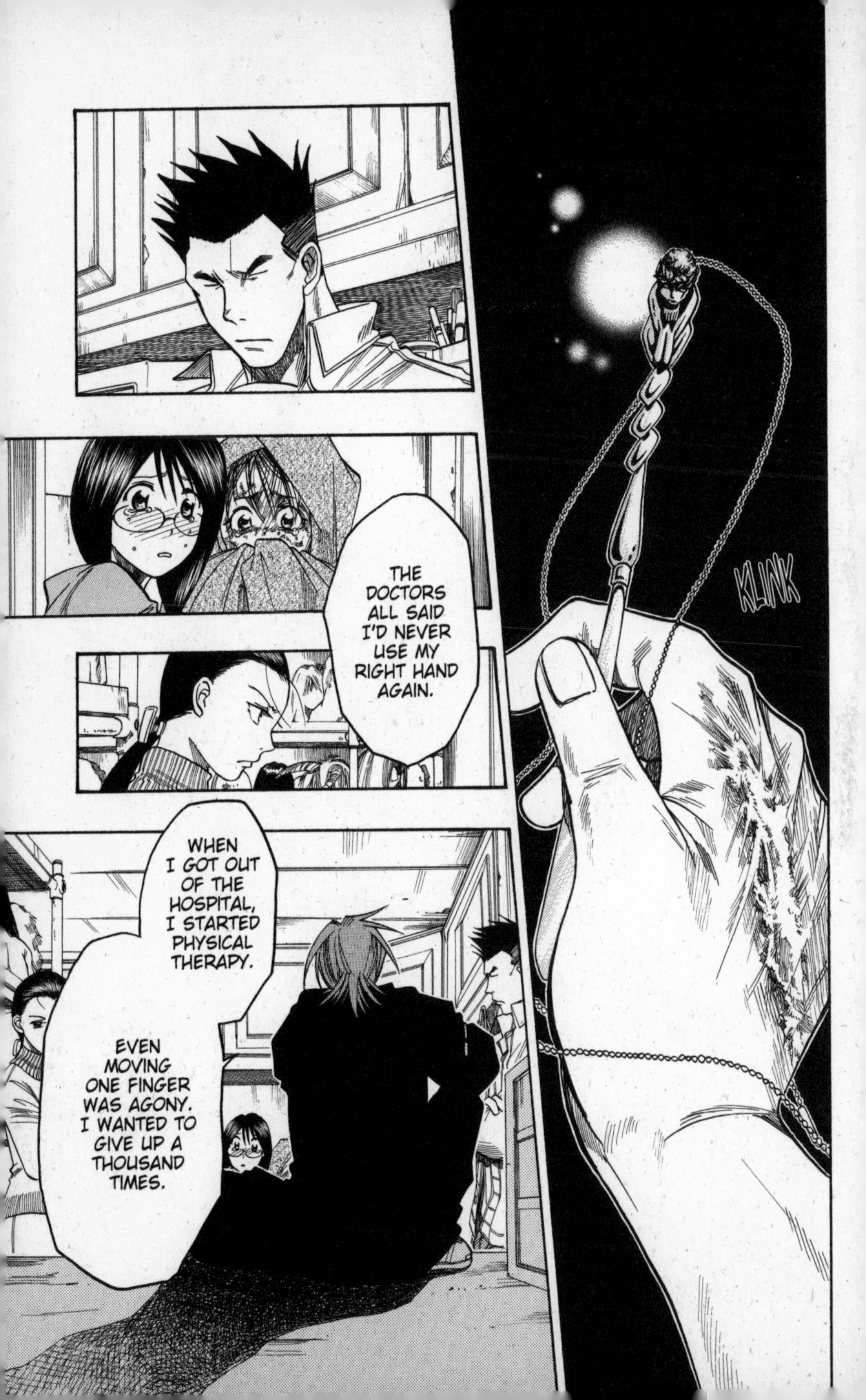
KLINK
THE DOCTORS ALL SAID I'D NEVER USE MY RIGHT HAND AGAIN.
WHEN I GOT OUT OF THE HOSPITAL, I STARTED PHYSICAL THERAPY.
EVEN MOVING ONE FINGER WAS AGONY. I WANTED TO GIVE UP A THOUSAND TIMES.

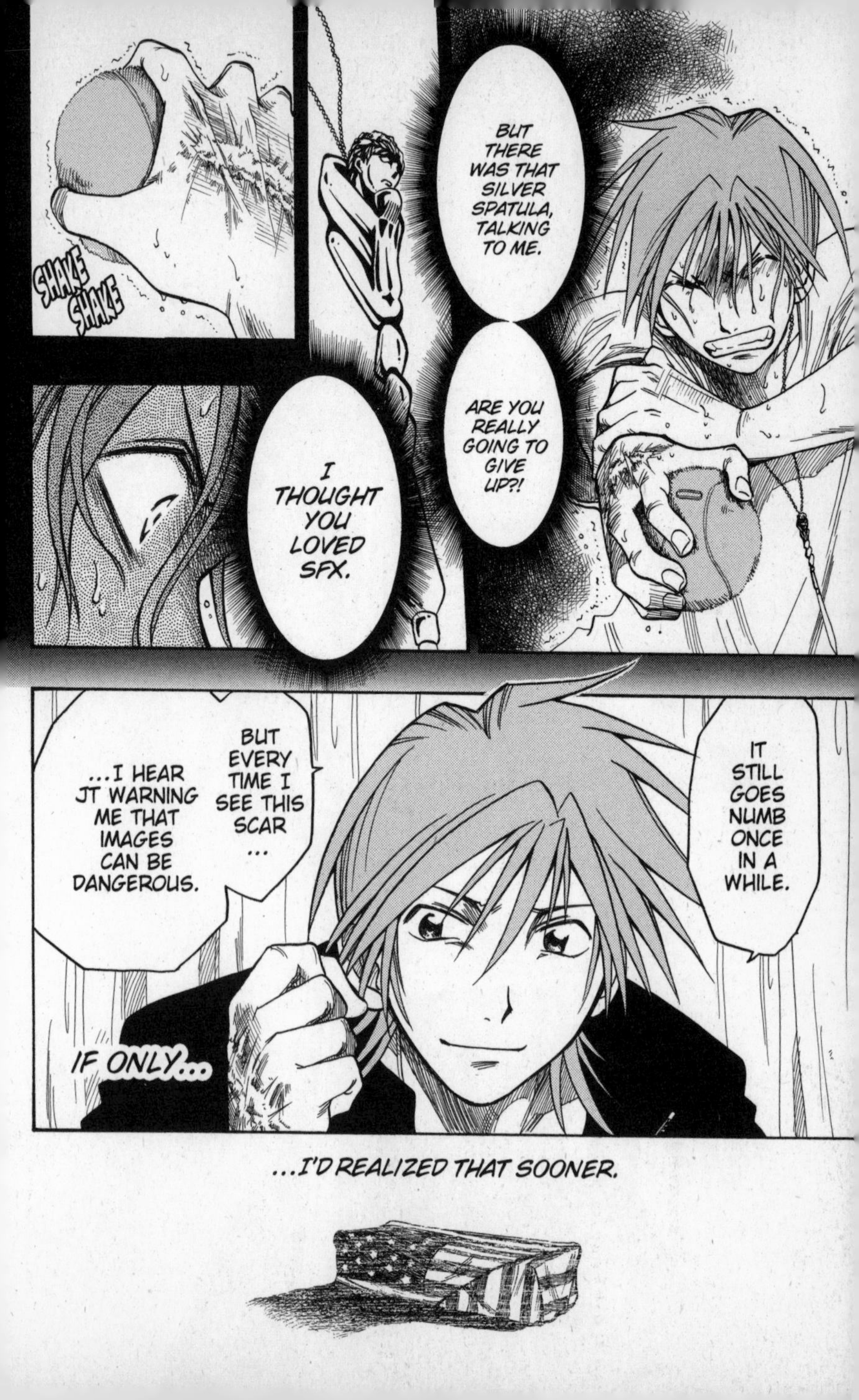
BUT THERE WAS THAT SILVER SPATULA, TALKING TO ME.
ARE YOU REALLY GOING TO GIVE UP?!
I THOUGHT YOU LOVED SFX.
SHAKE SHAKE
IT STILL GOES NUMB ONCE IN A WHILE.
BUT EVERY TIME I SEE THIS SCAR...
...I HEAR JT WARNING ME THAT IMAGES CAN BE DANGEROUS.
IF ONLY...
...I'D REALIZED THAT SOONER.

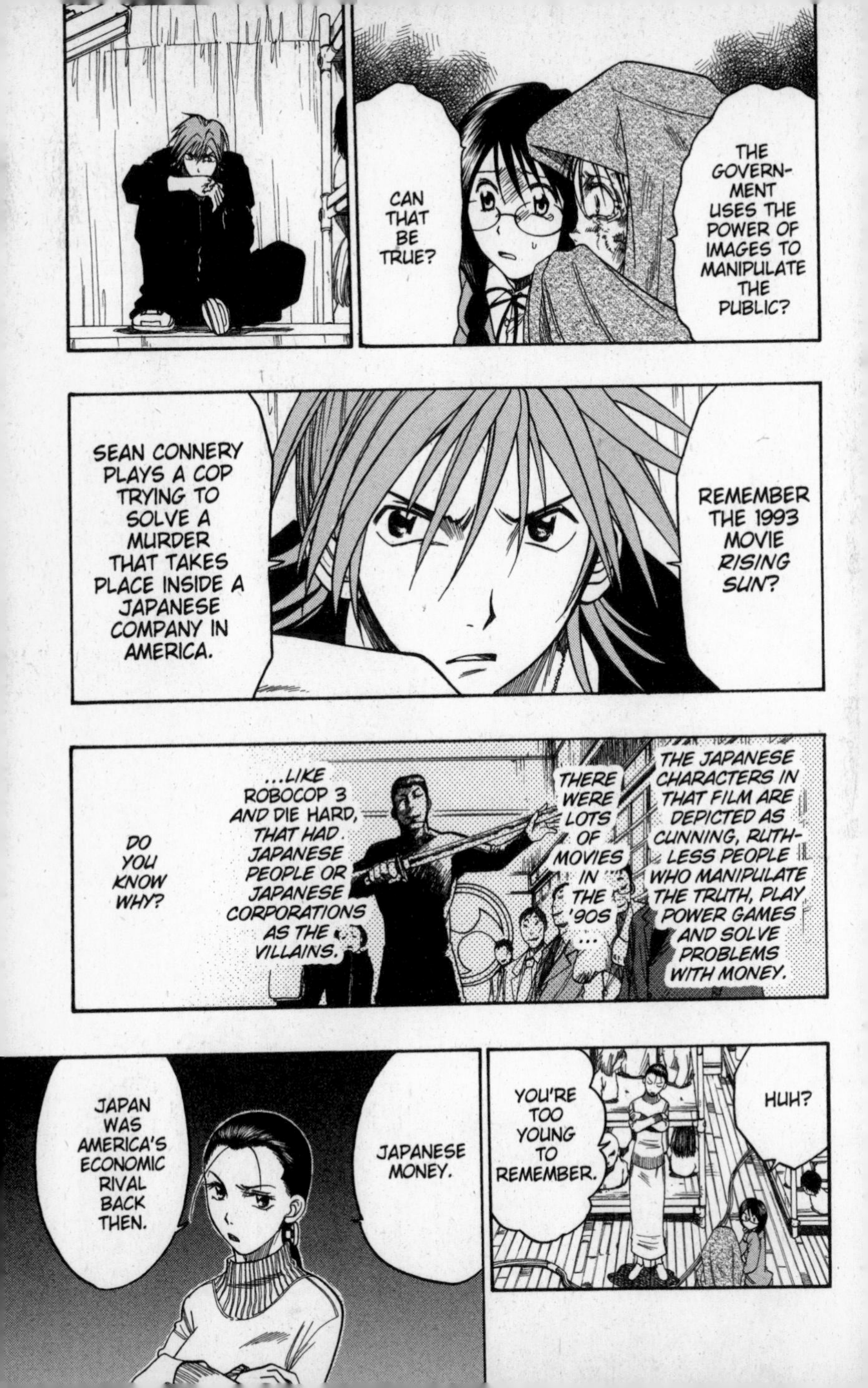
THE GOVERNMENT USES THE POWER OF IMAGES TO MANIPULATE THE PUBLIC?
CAN THAT BE TRUE?
REMEMBER THE 1993 MOVIE *RISING SUN*?
SEAN CONNERY PLAYS A COP TRYING TO SOLVE A MURDER THAT TAKES PLACE INSIDE A JAPANESE COMPANY IN AMERICA.
THE JAPANESE CHARACTERS IN THAT FILM ARE DEPICTED AS CUNNING, RUTHLESS PEOPLE WHO MANIPULATE THE TRUTH, PLAY POWER GAMES AND SOLVE PROBLEMS WITH MONEY.
THERE WERE LOTS OF MOVIES IN THE '90S...
...LIKE ROBOCOP 3 AND DIE HARD, THAT HAD JAPANESE PEOPLE OR JAPANESE CORPORATIONS AS THE VILLAINS.
DO YOU KNOW WHY?
HUH?
YOU'RE TOO YOUNG TO REMEMBER.
JAPANESE MONEY.
JAPAN WAS AMERICA'S ECONOMIC RIVAL BACK THEN.

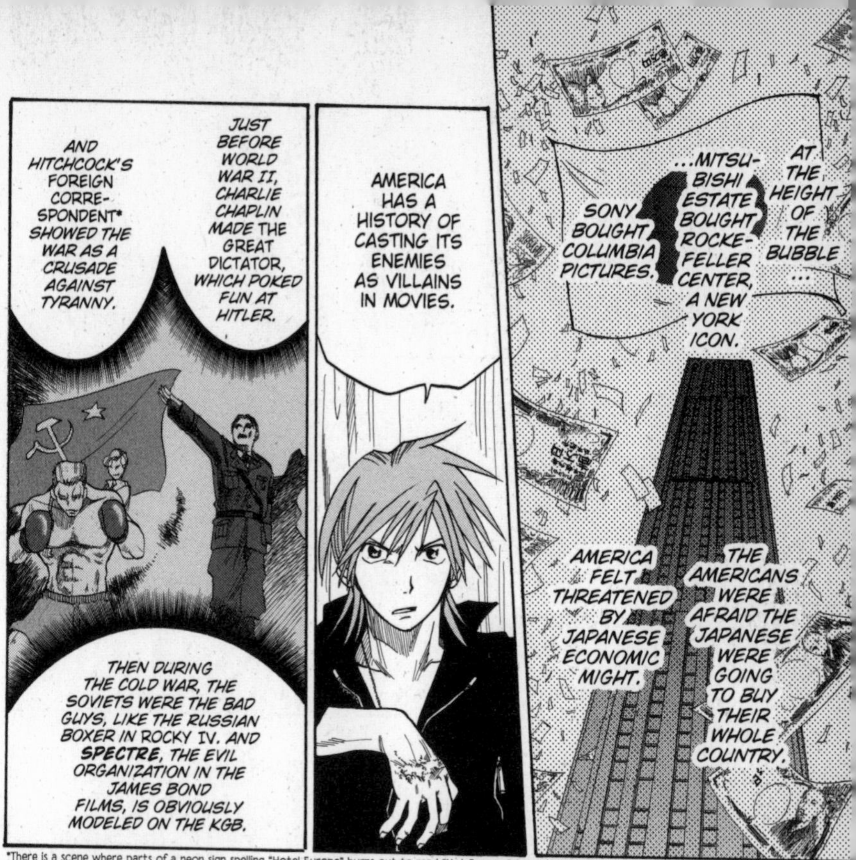
AT THE HEIGHT OF THE BUBBLE...
...MITSUBISHI ESTATE BOUGHT ROCKEFELLER CENTER, A NEW YORK ICON.
SONY BOUGHT COLUMBIA PICTURES.
THE AMERICANS WERE AFRAID THE JAPANESE WERE GOING TO BUY THEIR WHOLE COUNTRY.
AMERICA FELT THREATENED BY JAPANESE ECONOMIC MIGHT.
AMERICA HAS A HISTORY OF CASTING ITS ENEMIES AS VILLAINS IN MOVIES.
JUST BEFORE WORLD WAR II, CHARLIE CHAPLIN MADE THE GREAT DICTATOR, WHICH POKED FUN AT HITLER.
AND HITCHCOCK'S FOREIGN CORRESPONDENT* SHOWED THE WAR AS A CRUSADE AGAINST TYRANNY.
THEN DURING THE COLD WAR, THE SOVIETS WERE THE BAD GUYS, LIKE THE RUSSIAN BOXER IN ROCKY IV. AND SPECTRE, THE EVIL ORGANIZATION IN THE JAMES BOND FILMS, IS OBVIOUSLY MODELED ON THE KGB.

*There is a scene where parts of a neon sign spelling "Hotel Europe" burns out to read "Hot Europe." Some think that this was a message from the English director Hitchcock urging the United States to join the war to free Europe from the Nazi threat. At the end of the movie, the main character says, "Hello, America, hang on to your lights: they're the only lights left in the world." The year following the release of the movie, the United States officially entered World War II.

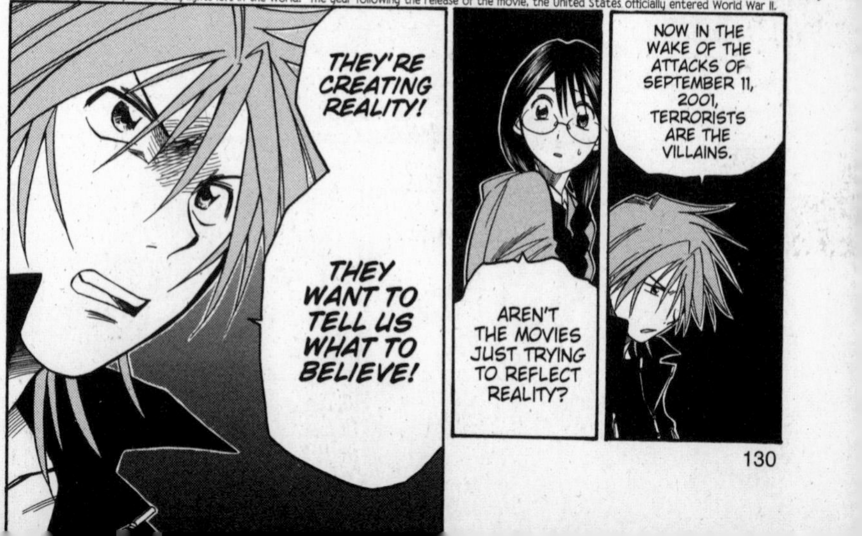
NOW IN THE WAKE OF THE ATTACKS OF SEPTEMBER 11, 2001, TERRORISTS ARE THE VILLAINS.
AREN'T THE MOVIES JUST TRYING TO REFLECT REALITY?
THEY'RE CREATING REALITY!
THEY WANT TO TELL US WHAT TO BELIEVE!

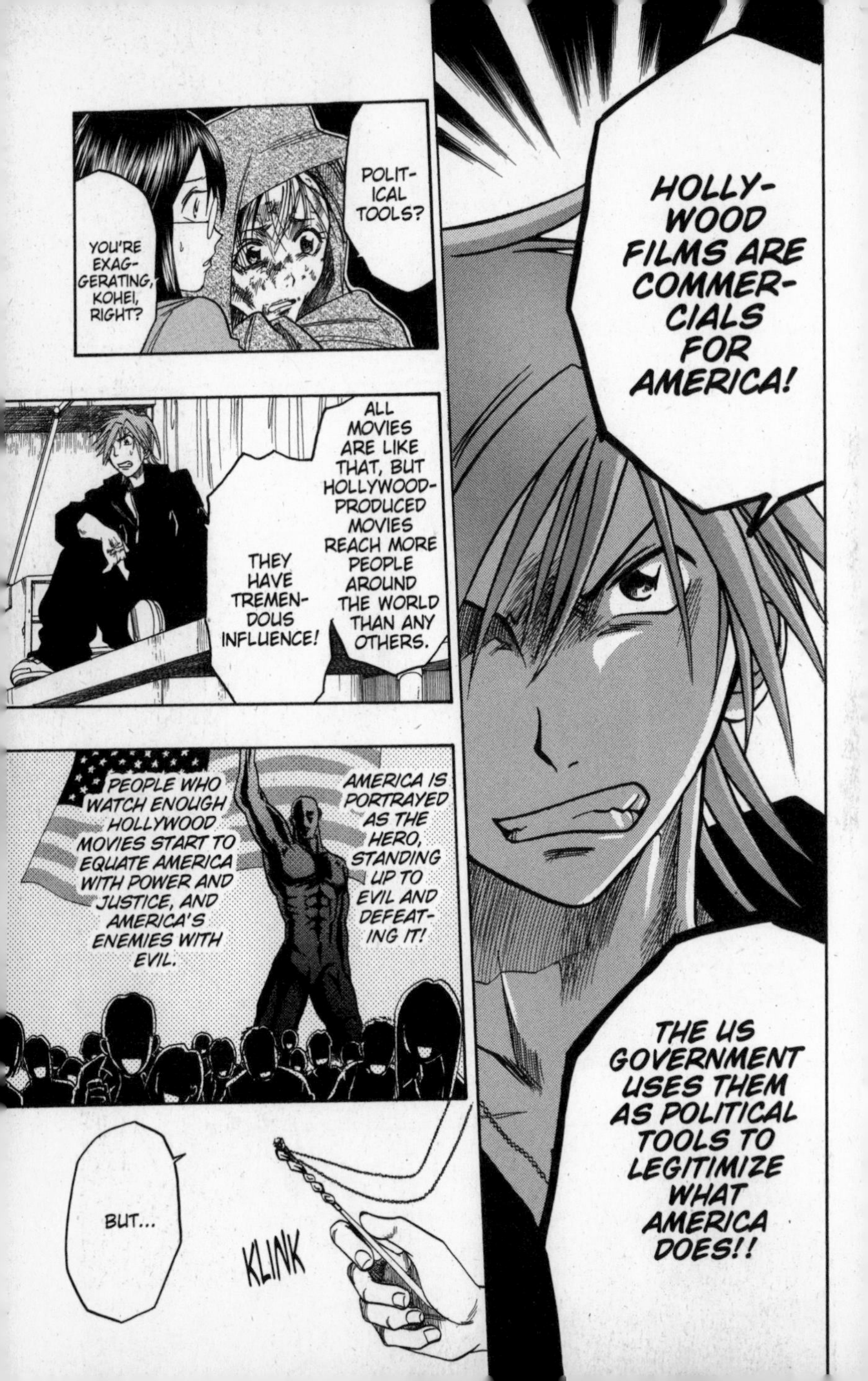
HOLLYWOOD FILMS ARE COMMERCIALS FOR AMERICA!
THE US GOVERNMENT USES THEM AS POLITICAL TOOLS TO LEGITIMIZE WHAT AMERICA DOES!!
POLITICAL TOOLS?
YOU'RE EXAGGERATING, KOHEI, RIGHT?
ALL MOVIES ARE LIKE THAT, BUT HOLLYWOOD-PRODUCED MOVIES REACH MORE PEOPLE AROUND THE WORLD THAN ANY OTHERS.
THEY HAVE TREMENDOUS INFLUENCE!
AMERICA IS PORTRAYED AS THE HERO, STANDING UP TO EVIL AND DEFEATING IT!
PEOPLE WHO WATCH ENOUGH HOLLYWOOD MOVIES START TO EQUATE AMERICA WITH POWER AND JUSTICE, AND AMERICA'S ENEMIES WITH EVIL.
KLINK
BUT...

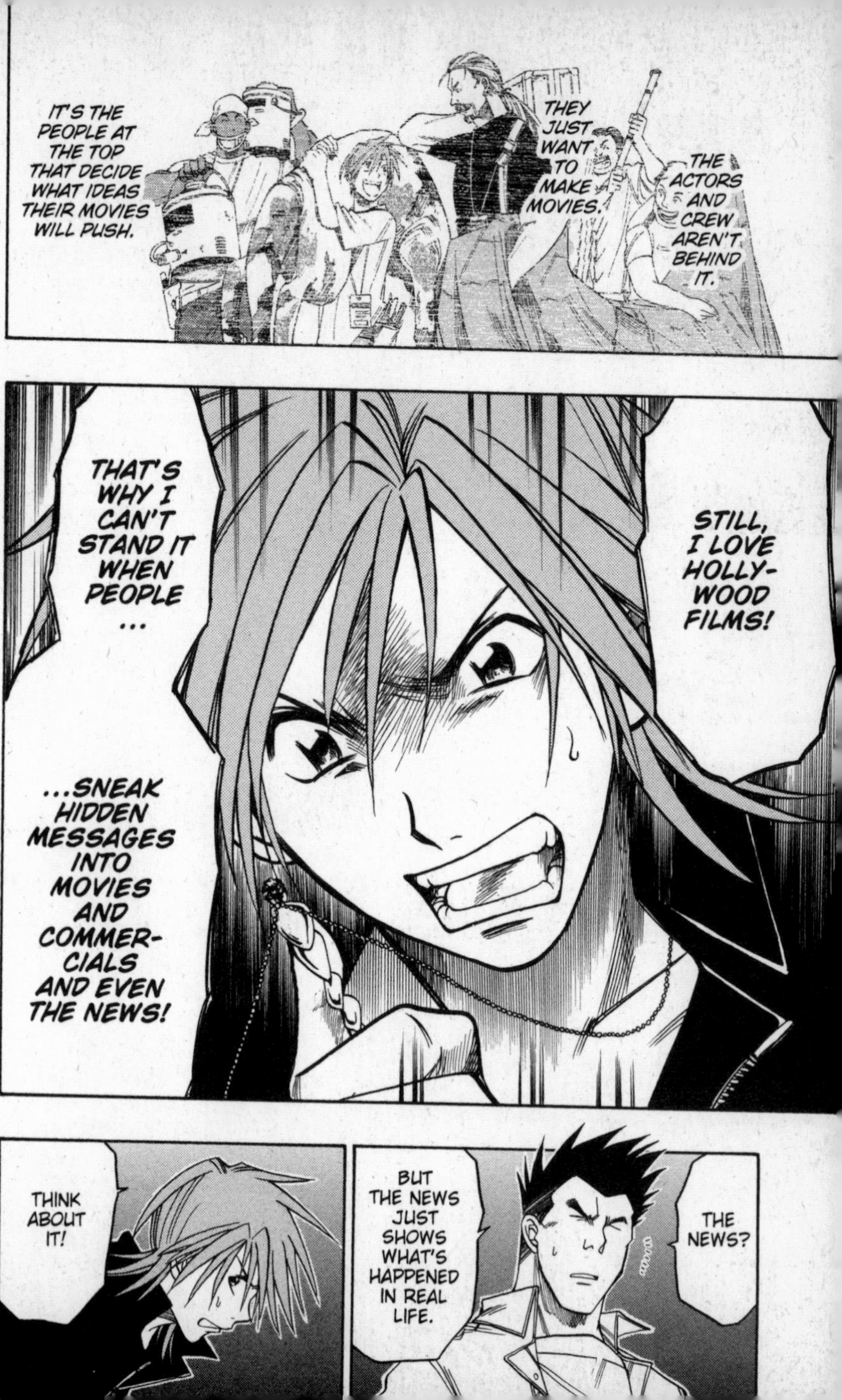
THE ACTORS AND CREW AREN'T BEHIND IT.
THEY JUST WANT TO MAKE MOVIES.
IT'S THE PEOPLE AT THE TOP THAT DECIDE WHAT IDEAS THEIR MOVIES WILL PUSH.
STILL, I LOVE HOLLY-WOOD FILMS!
THAT'S WHY I CAN'T STAND IT WHEN PEOPLE ...
...SNEAK HIDDEN MESSAGES INTO MOVIES AND COMMER-CIALS AND EVEN THE NEWS!
THE NEWS?
BUT THE NEWS JUST SHOWS WHAT'S HAPPENED IN REAL LIFE.
THINK ABOUT IT!

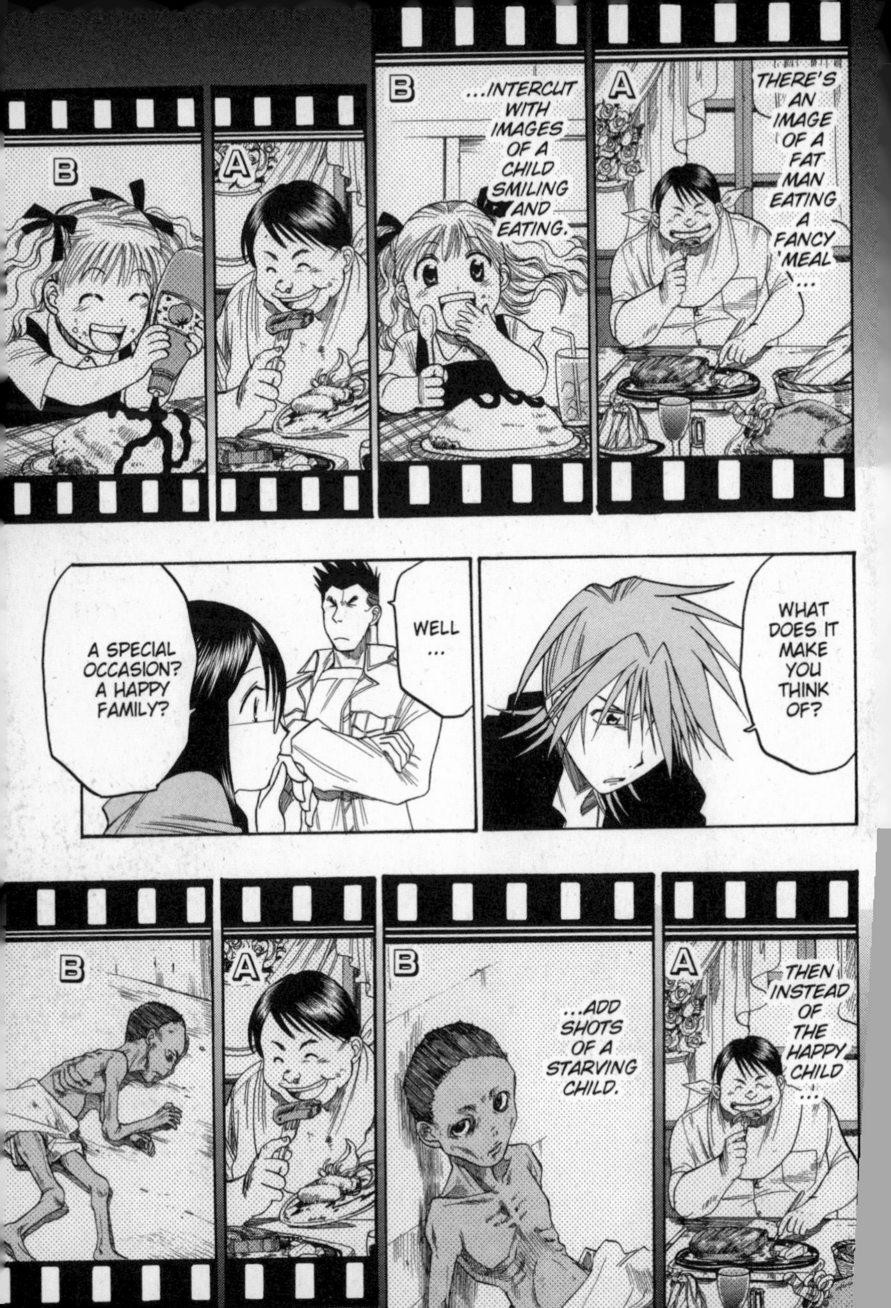
A
THERE'S AN IMAGE OF A FAT MAN EATING A FANCY MEAL...
B
...INTERCUT WITH IMAGES OF A CHILD SMILING AND EATING.
A
B
WHAT DOES IT MAKE YOU THINK OF?
WELL...
A SPECIAL OCCASION? A HAPPY FAMILY?
A
THEN INSTEAD OF THE HAPPY CHILD...
B
...ADD SHOTS OF A STARVING CHILD.
A
B

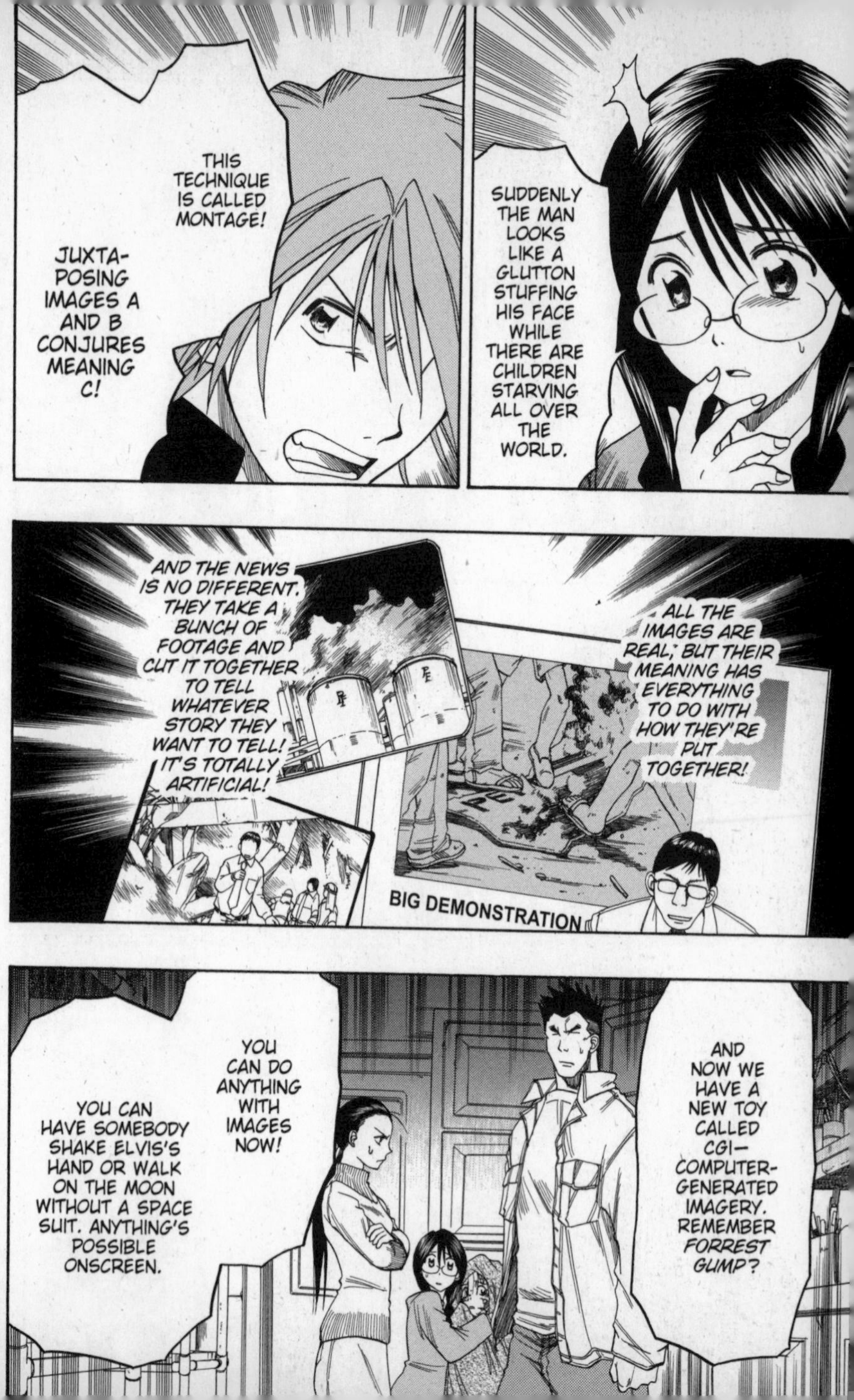
SUDDENLY THE MAN LOOKS LIKE A GLUTTON STUFFING HIS FACE WHILE THERE ARE CHILDREN STARVING ALL OVER THE WORLD.
THIS TECHNIQUE IS CALLED MONTAGE!
JUXTA-POSING IMAGES A AND B CONJURES MEANING C!
ALL THE IMAGES ARE REAL, BUT THEIR MEANING HAS EVERYTHING TO DO WITH HOW THEY'RE PUT TOGETHER!
AND THE NEWS IS NO DIFFERENT. THEY TAKE A BUNCH OF FOOTAGE AND CUT IT TOGETHER TO TELL WHATEVER STORY THEY WANT TO TELL! IT'S TOTALLY ARTIFICIAL!
BIG DEMONSTRATION
AND NOW WE HAVE A NEW TOY CALLED CGI—COMPUTER-GENERATED IMAGERY. REMEMBER FORREST GUMP?
YOU CAN DO ANYTHING WITH IMAGES NOW!
YOU CAN HAVE SOMEBODY SHAKE ELVIS'S HAND OR WALK ON THE MOON WITHOUT A SPACE SUIT. ANYTHING'S POSSIBLE ONSCREEN.

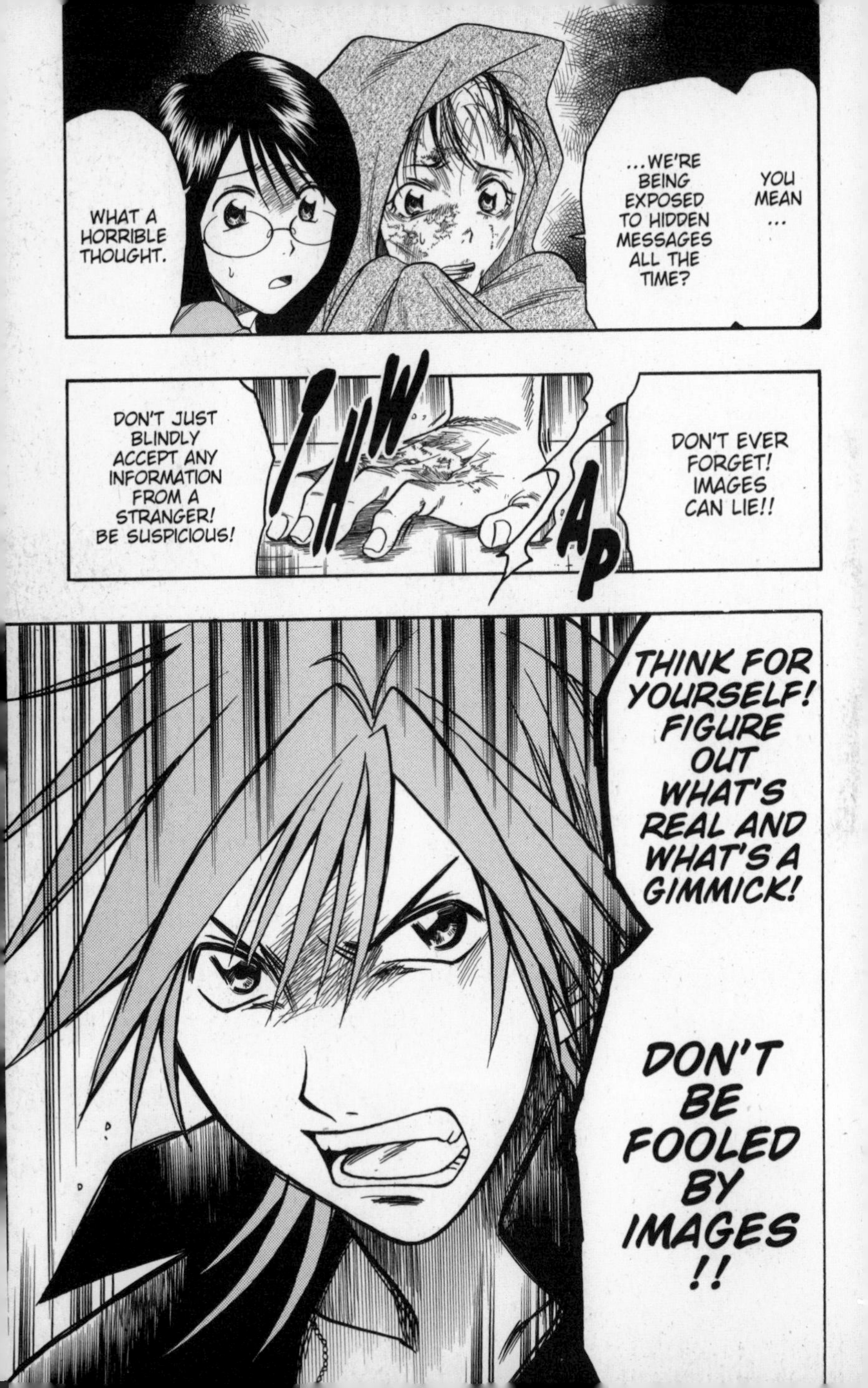
YOU MEAN ...
...WE'RE BEING EXPOSED TO HIDDEN MESSAGES ALL THE TIME?
WHAT A HORRIBLE THOUGHT.
DON'T EVER FORGET! IMAGES CAN LIE!!
WHAP
DON'T JUST BLINDLY ACCEPT ANY INFORMATION FROM A STRANGER! BE SUSPICIOUS!
THINK FOR YOURSELF! FIGURE OUT WHAT'S REAL AND WHAT'S A GIMMICK!
DON'T BE FOOLED BY IMAGES!!

GIMMICK!

Scene 44: Field of Dreams (Part 6)

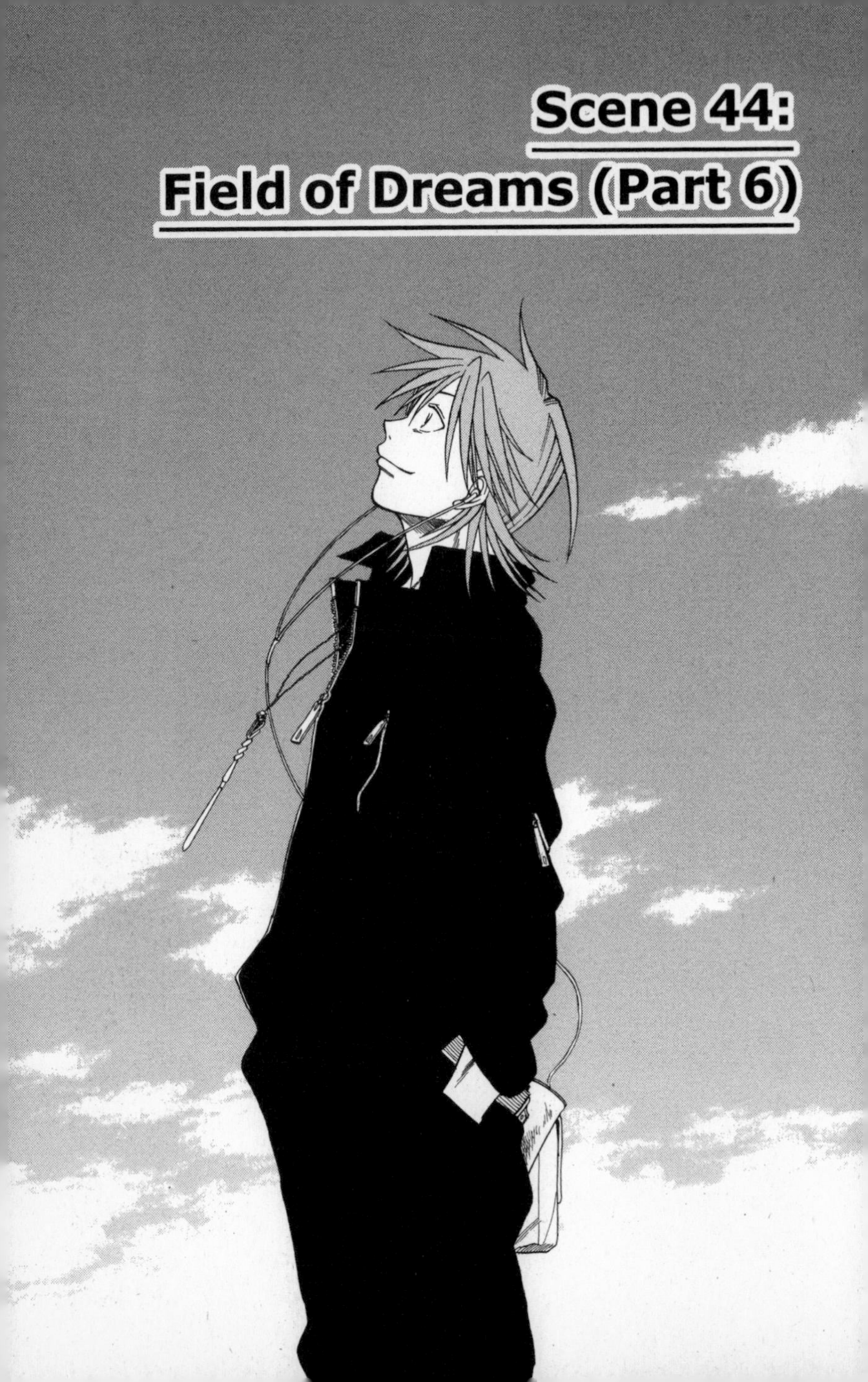

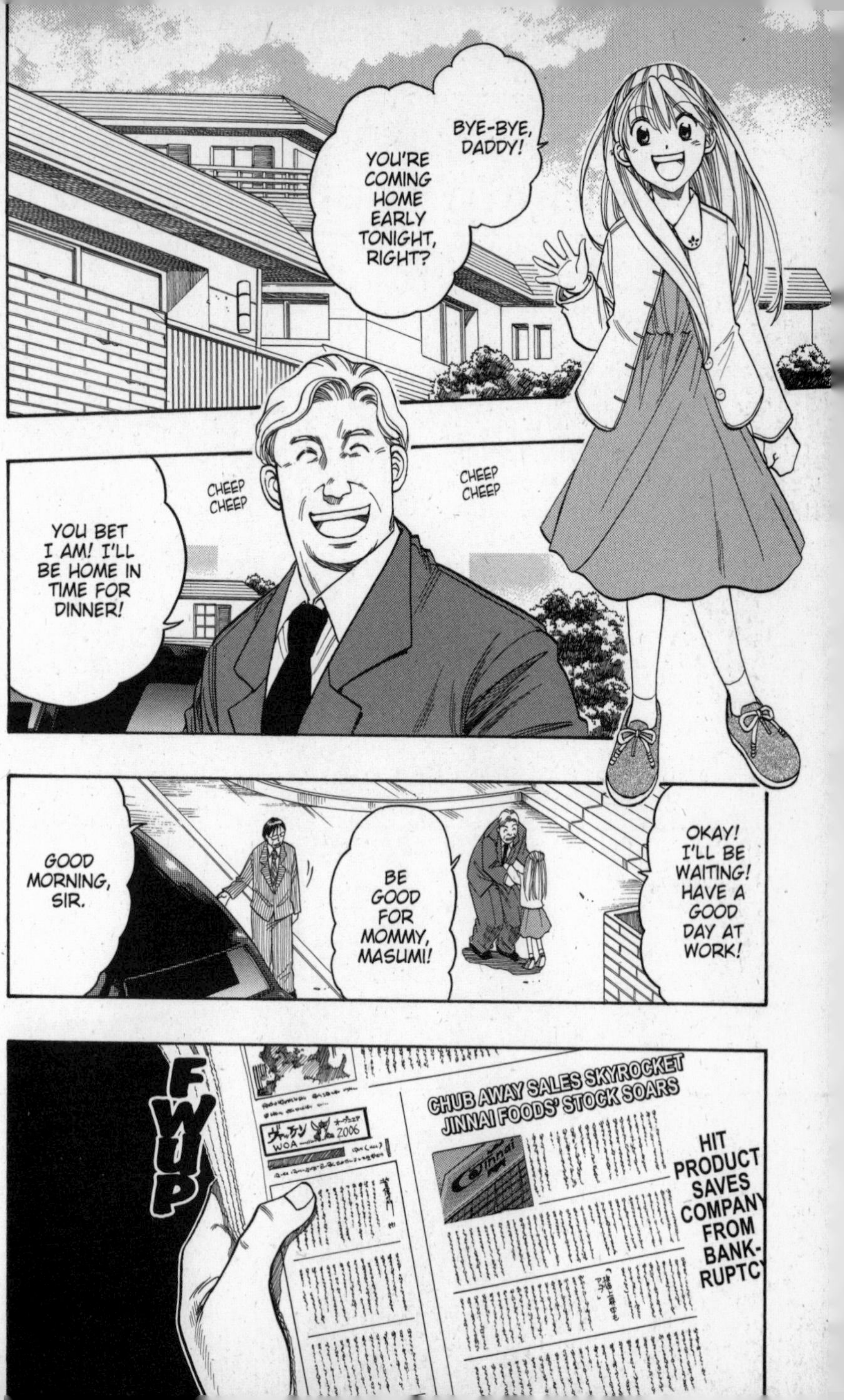
BYE-BYE, DADDY!
YOU'RE COMING HOME EARLY TONIGHT, RIGHT?
CHEEP CHEEP
CHEEP CHEEP
YOU BET I AM! I'LL BE HOME IN TIME FOR DINNER!
OKAY! I'LL BE WAITING! HAVE A GOOD DAY AT WORK!
BE GOOD FOR MOMMY, MASUMI!
GOOD MORNING, SIR.
CHUB AWAY SALES SKYROCKET
JINNAI FOODS' STOCK SOARS
HIT PRODUCT SAVES COMPANY FROM BANK-RUPTCY
FWUP

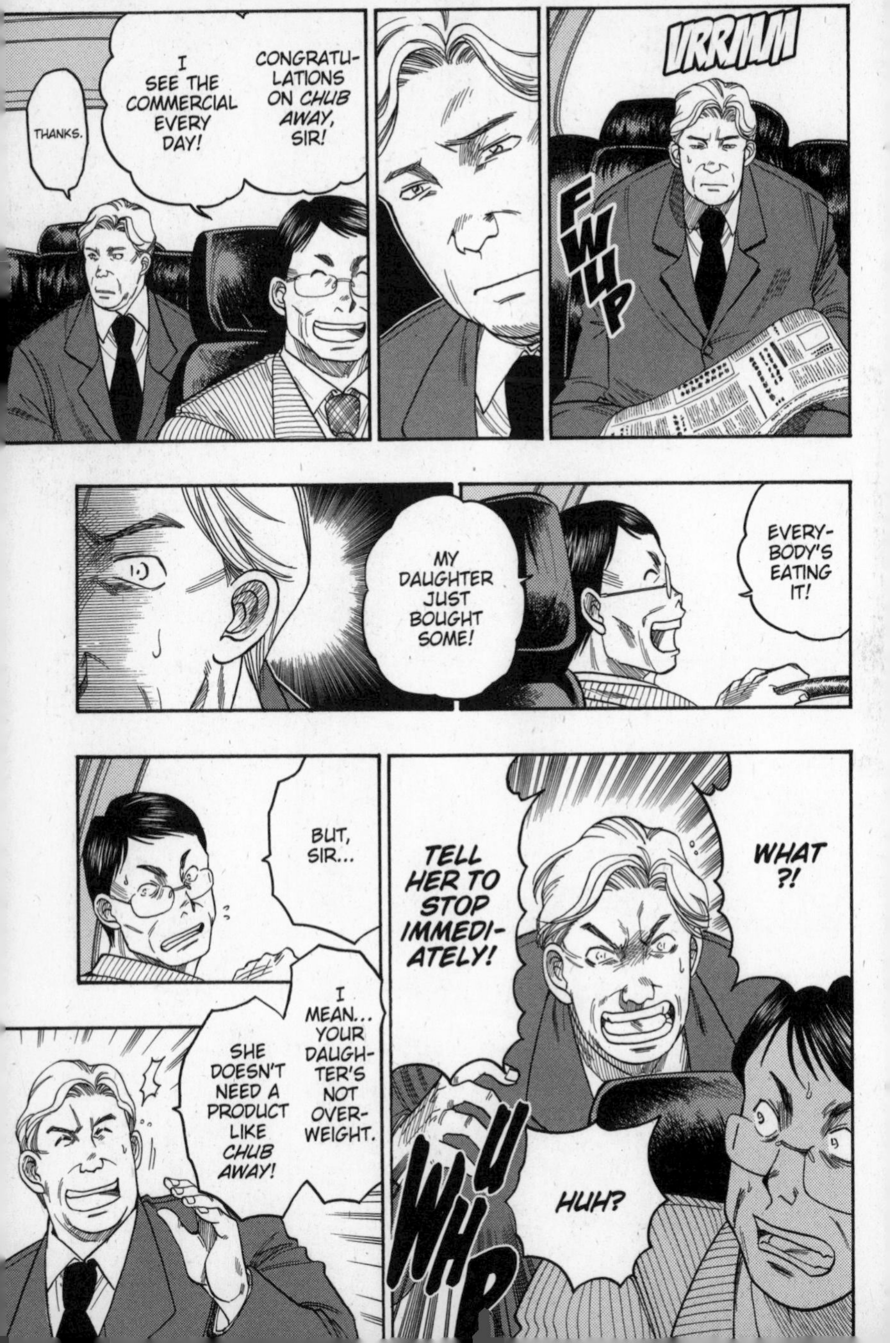
VRRMM
FWUP
CONGRATULATIONS ON CHUB AWAY, SIR!
I SEE THE COMMERCIAL EVERY DAY!
THANKS.
EVERYBODY'S EATING IT!
MY DAUGHTER JUST BOUGHT SOME!
WHAT?!
TELL HER TO STOP IMMEDIATELY!
HUH?
WHUP
BUT, SIR...
I MEAN... YOUR DAUGHTER'S NOT OVERWEIGHT.
SHE DOESN'T NEED A PRODUCT LIKE CHUB AWAY!

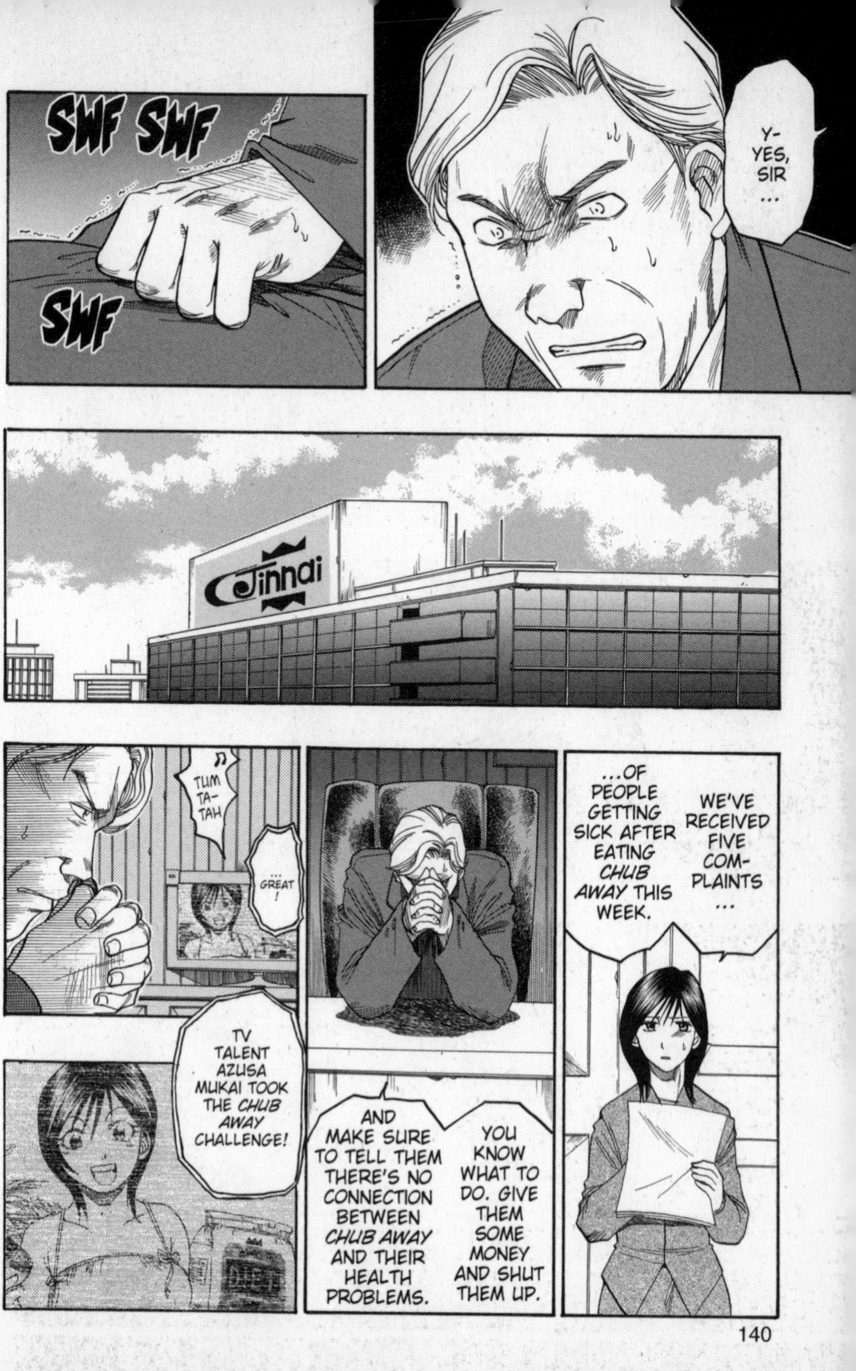
Y-YES, SIR ...
SWF SWF
SWF
Jinnai
WE'VE RECEIVED FIVE COMPLAINTS ...
...OF PEOPLE GETTING SICK AFTER EATING *CHUB AWAY* THIS WEEK.
YOU KNOW WHAT TO DO. GIVE THEM SOME MONEY AND SHUT THEM UP.
AND MAKE SURE TO TELL THEM THERE'S NO CONNECTION BETWEEN *CHUB AWAY* AND THEIR HEALTH PROBLEMS.
TUM TA-TAH
... GREAT!
TV TALENT AZUSA MUKAI TOOK THE *CHUB AWAY* CHALLENGE!

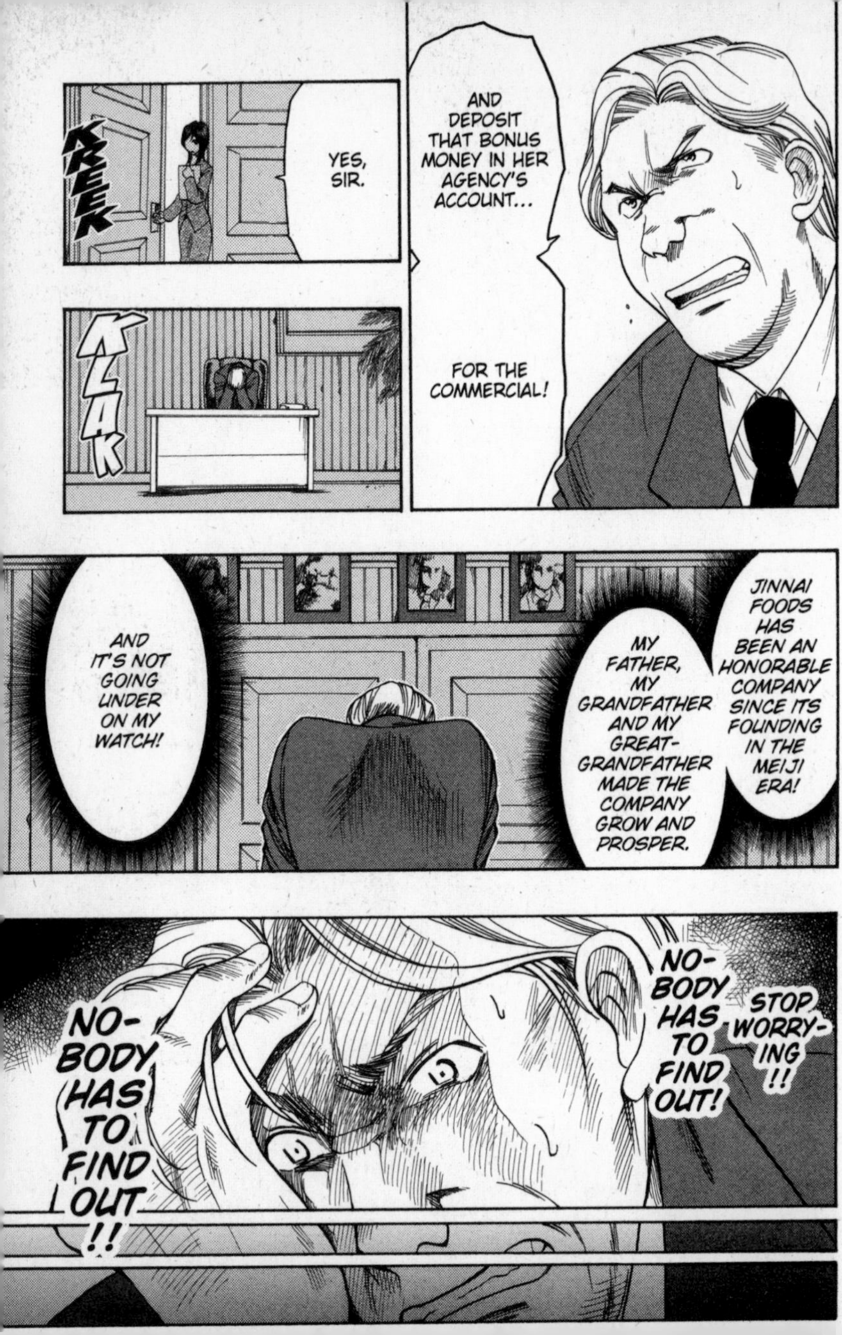
AND DEPOSIT THAT BONUS MONEY IN HER AGENCY'S ACCOUNT...
FOR THE COMMERCIAL!
YES, SIR.
KREEK
KLAK
JINNAI FOODS HAS BEEN AN HONORABLE COMPANY SINCE ITS FOUNDING IN THE MEIJI ERA!
MY FATHER, MY GRANDFATHER AND MY GREAT-GRANDFATHER MADE THE COMPANY GROW AND PROSPER.
AND IT'S NOT GOING UNDER ON MY WATCH!
STOP WORRY-ING!!
NO-BODY HAS TO FIND OUT!
NO-BODY HAS TO FIND OUT!!

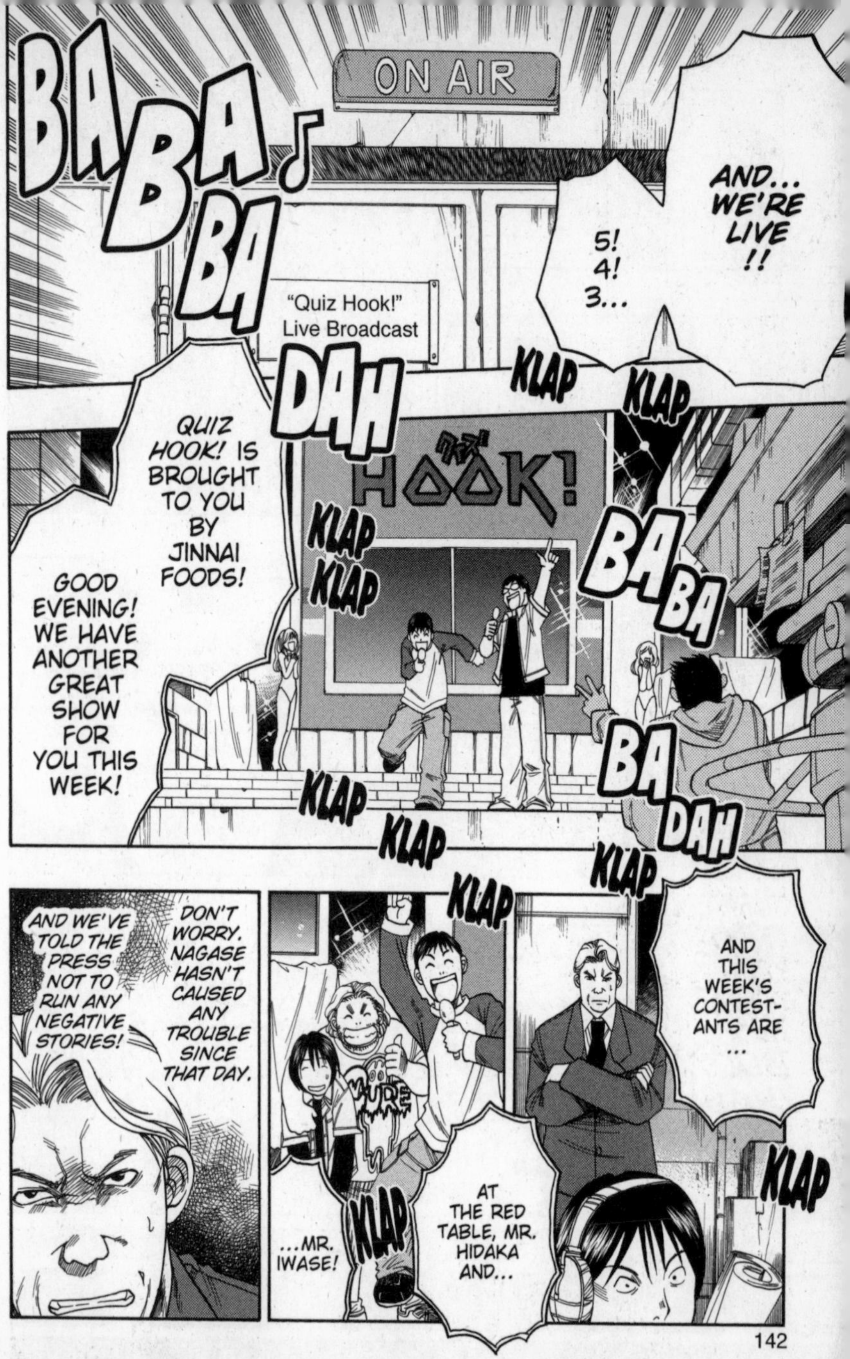
AND... WE'RE LIVE !!
5! 4! 3...
ON AIR
BA BA BA BA ♪
"Quiz Hook!" Live Broadcast
DAH
KLAP KLAP
HOOK!
BA BA BA BA DAH
QUIZ HOOK! IS BROUGHT TO YOU BY JINNAI FOODS!
GOOD EVENING! WE HAVE ANOTHER GREAT SHOW FOR YOU THIS WEEK!
KLAP KLAP KLAP KLAP KLAP
KLAP KLAP
AND THIS WEEK'S CONTEST-ANTS ARE ...
KLAP
AT THE RED TABLE, MR. HIDAKA AND...
KLAP
...MR. IWASE!
DON'T WORRY. NAGASE HASN'T CAUSED ANY TROUBLE SINCE THAT DAY.
AND WE'VE TOLD THE PRESS NOT TO RUN ANY NEGATIVE STORIES!

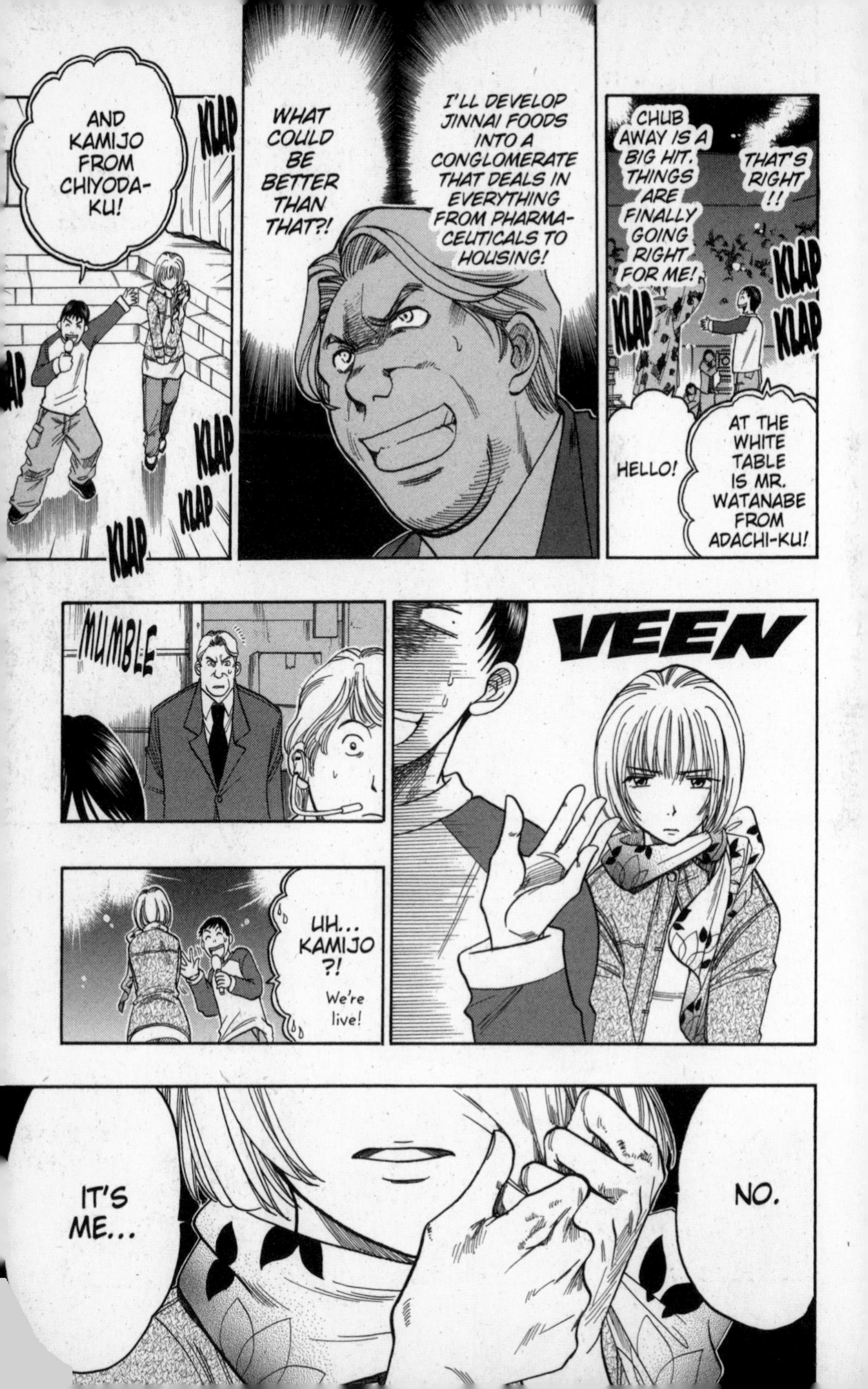
CHUB AWAY IS A BIG HIT. THINGS ARE FINALLY GOING RIGHT FOR ME!
THAT'S RIGHT!!
KLAP
KLAP
KLAP
AT THE WHITE TABLE IS MR. WATANABE FROM ADACHI-KU!
HELLO!
I'LL DEVELOP JINNAI FOODS INTO A CONGLOMERATE THAT DEALS IN EVERYTHING FROM PHARMACEUTICALS TO HOUSING!
WHAT COULD BE BETTER THAN THAT?!
KLAP
AND KAMIJO FROM CHIYODA-KU!
KLAP
KLAP
KLAP
KLAP
VEEN
MUMBLE
UH... KAMIJO?!
We're live!
NO.
IT'S ME...

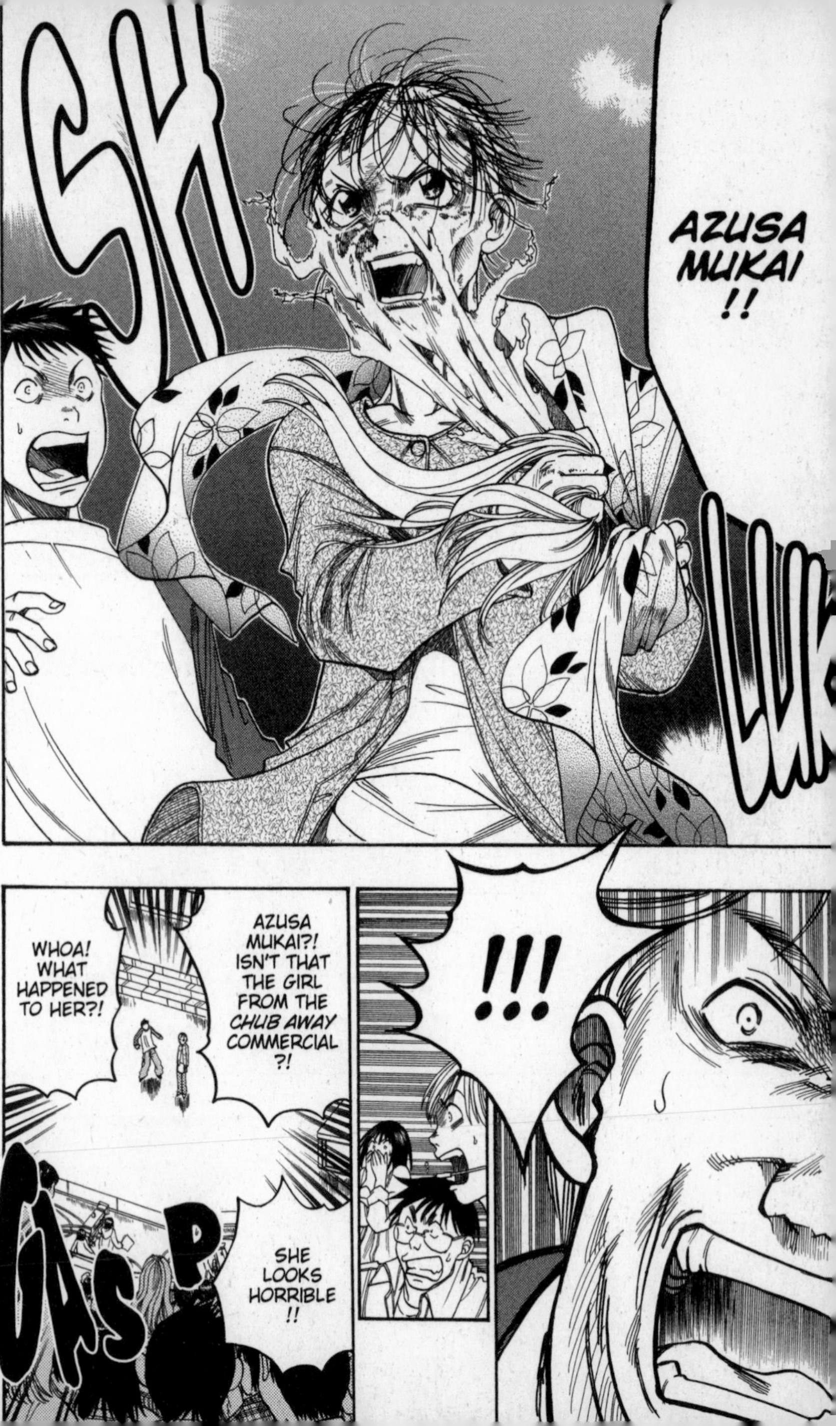
AZUSA MUKAI !!
SH
LUK
!!!
AZUSA MUKAI?! ISN'T THAT THE GIRL FROM THE CHUB AWAY COMMERCIAL ?!
WHOA! WHAT HAPPENED TO HER?!
SHE LOOKS HORRIBLE !!
GASP

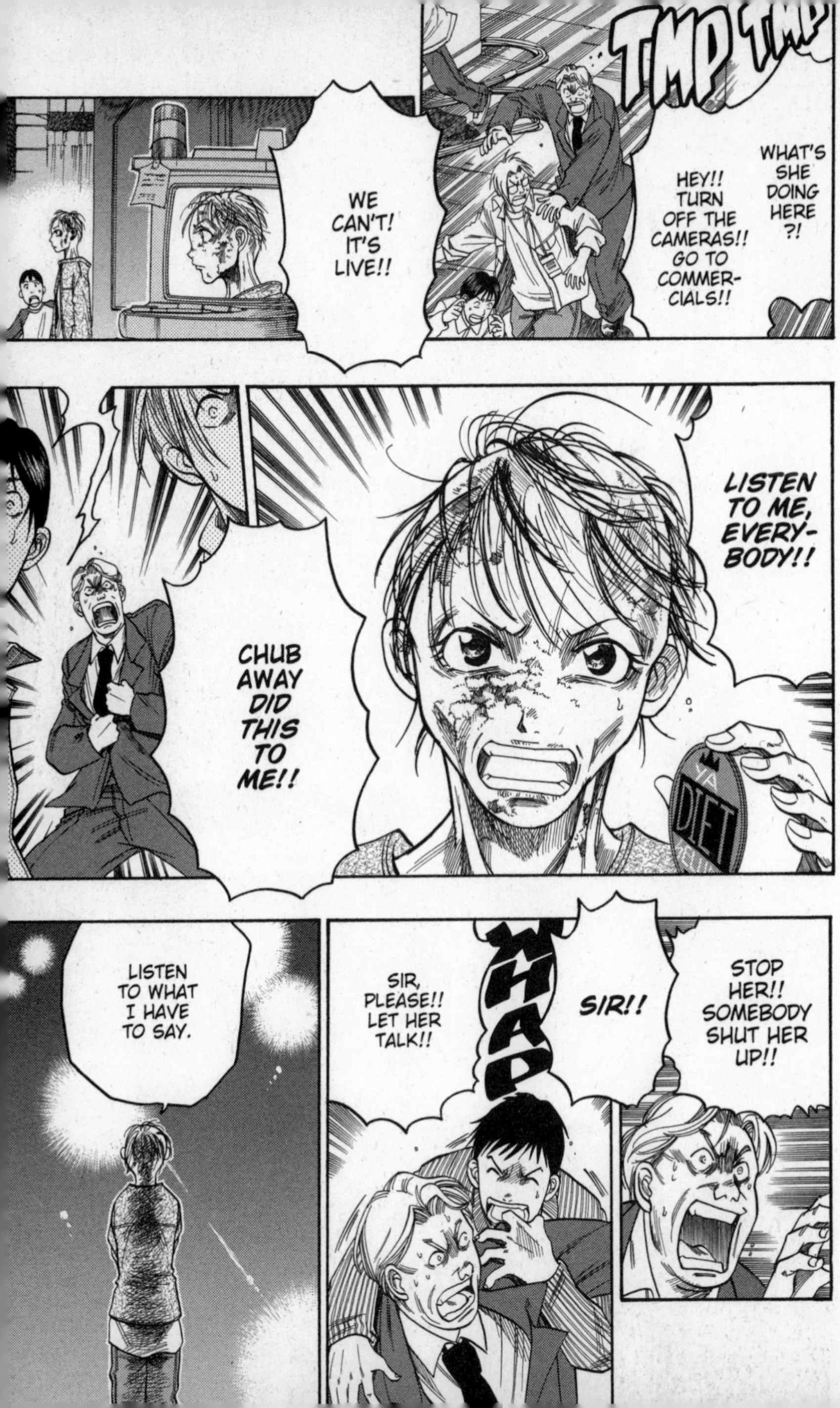
TMP TMP
WHAT'S SHE DOING HERE?!
HEY!! TURN OFF THE CAMERAS!! GO TO COMMERCIALS!!
WE CAN'T! IT'S LIVE!!
LISTEN TO ME, EVERYBODY!!
CHUB AWAY DID THIS TO ME!!
DIET
STOP HER!! SOMEBODY SHUT HER UP!!
SIR!!
WHAP
SIR, PLEASE!! LET HER TALK!!
LISTEN TO WHAT I HAVE TO SAY.

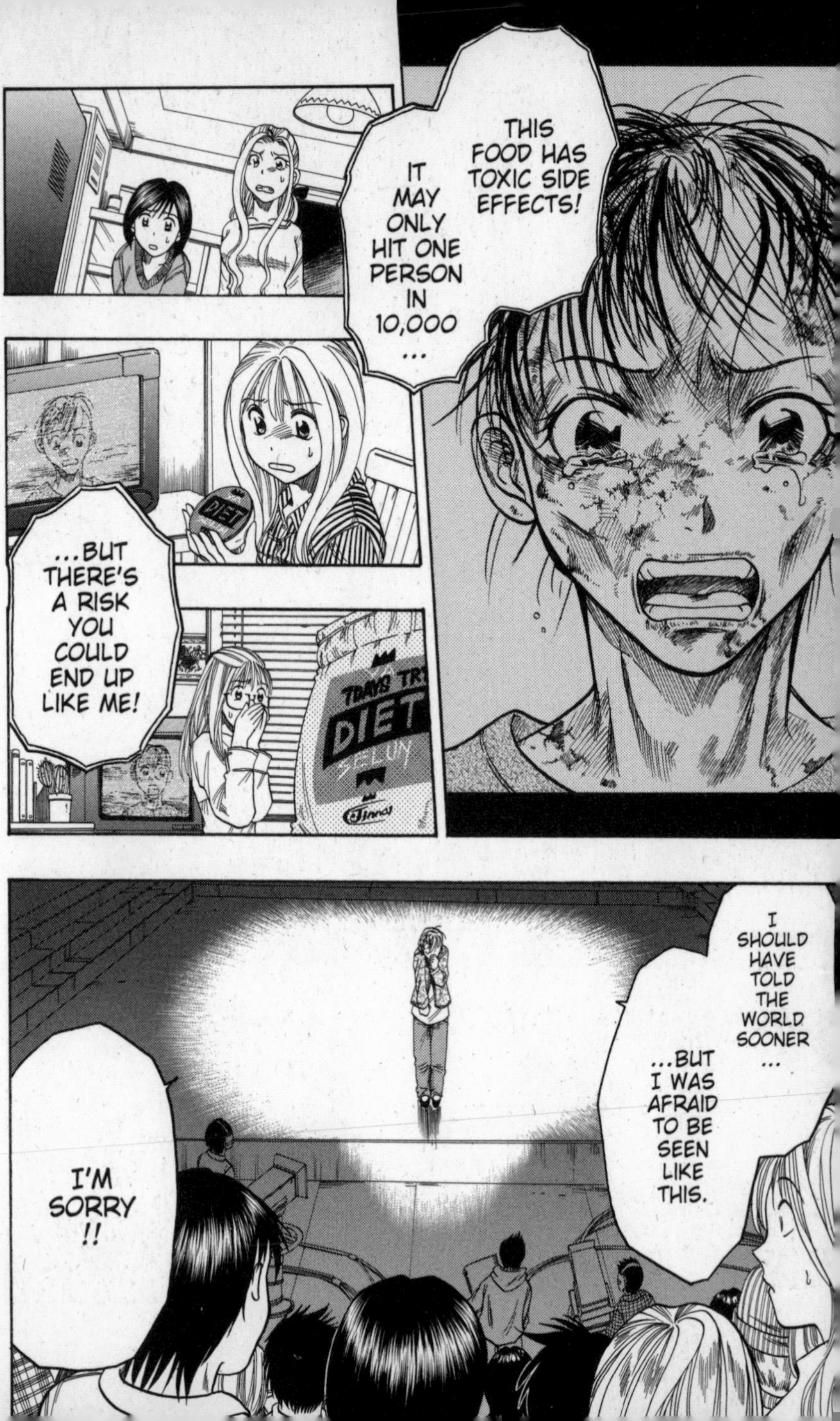
THIS FOOD HAS TOXIC SIDE EFFECTS!
IT MAY ONLY HIT ONE PERSON IN 10,000...
...BUT THERE'S A RISK YOU COULD END UP LIKE ME!
I SHOULD HAVE TOLD THE WORLD SOONER...
...BUT I WAS AFRAID TO BE SEEN LIKE THIS.
I'M SORRY!!

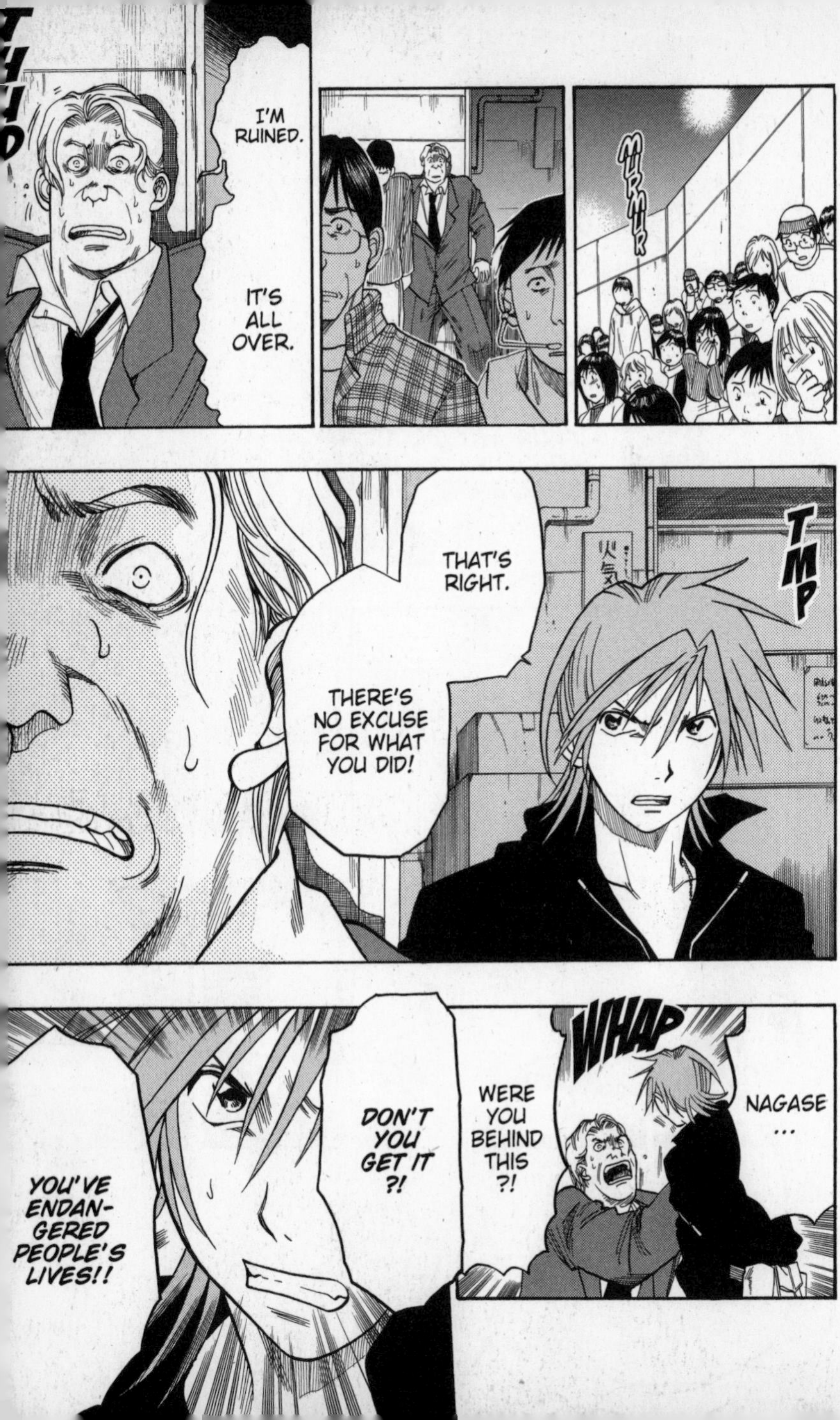
MURMUR
THUD
I'M RUINED.
IT'S ALL OVER.
TMP
THAT'S RIGHT.
THERE'S NO EXCUSE FOR WHAT YOU DID!
WHAP
NAGASE ...
WERE YOU BEHIND THIS ?!
DON'T YOU GET IT ?!
YOU'VE ENDANGERED PEOPLE'S LIVES!!

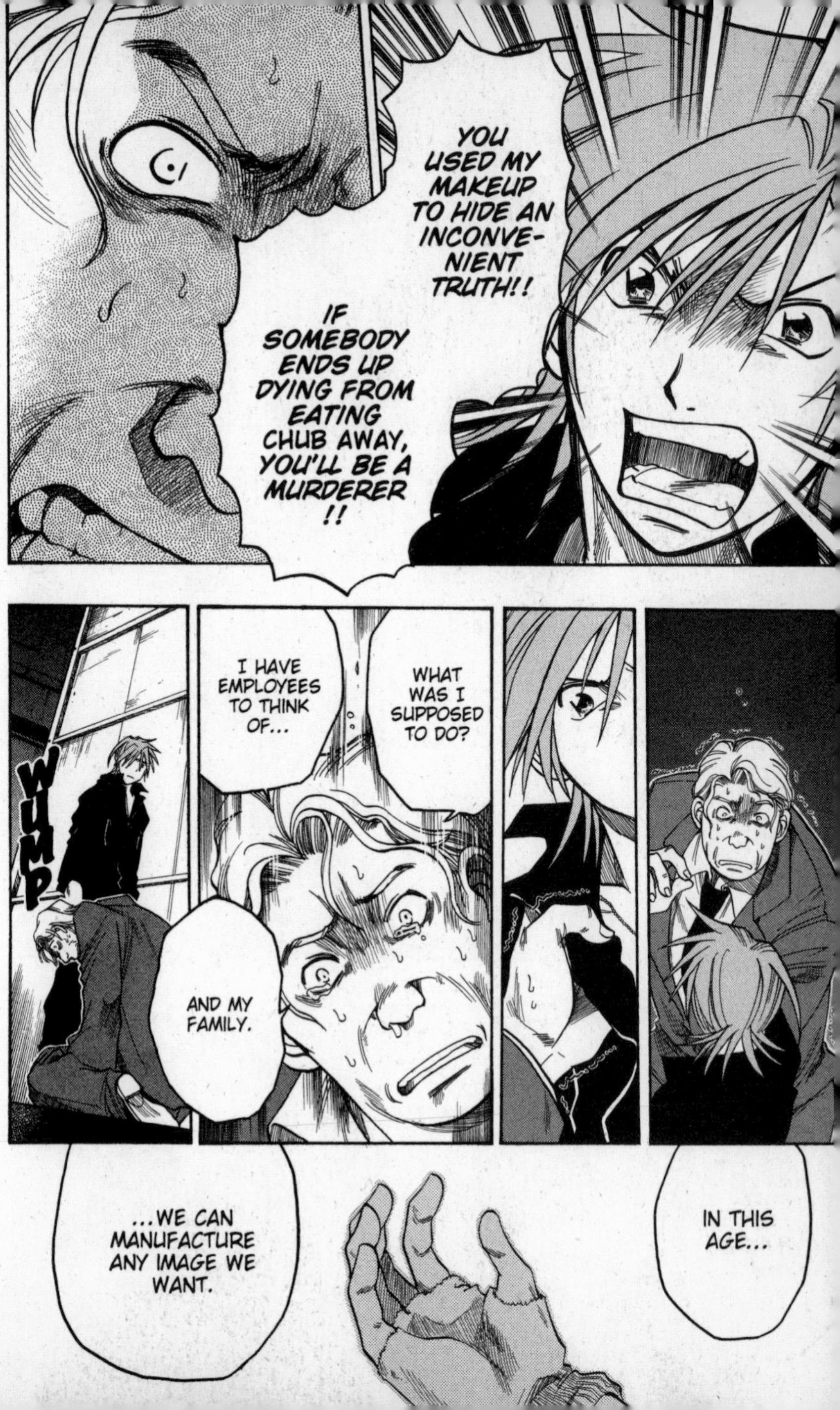
YOU USED MY MAKEUP TO HIDE AN INCONVENIENT TRUTH!!
IF SOMEBODY ENDS UP DYING FROM EATING CHUB AWAY, YOU'LL BE A MURDERER!!
WHAT WAS I SUPPOSED TO DO?
I HAVE EMPLOYEES TO THINK OF...
AND MY FAMILY.
WUMP
IN THIS AGE...
...WE CAN MANUFACTURE ANY IMAGE WE WANT.

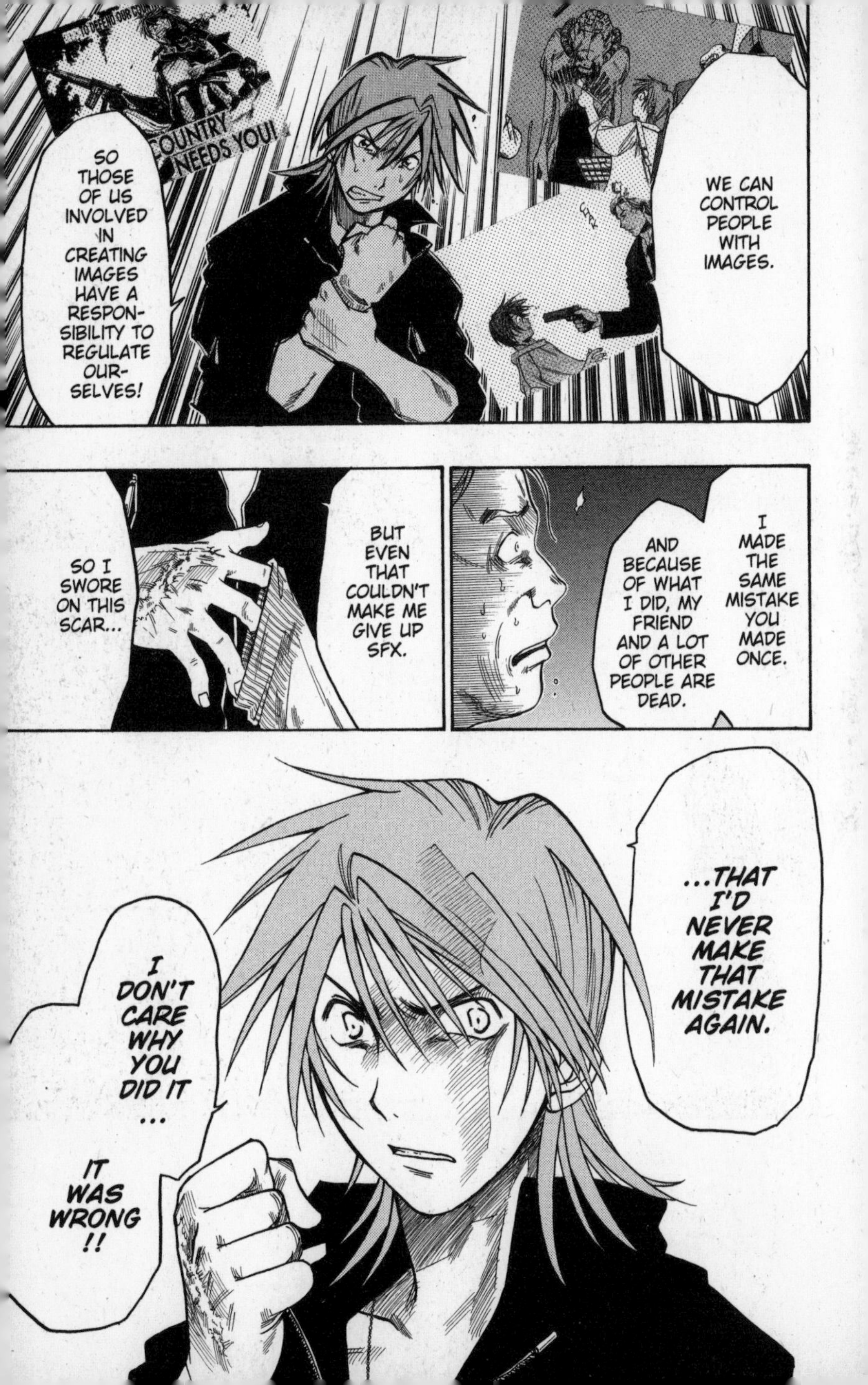
WE CAN CONTROL PEOPLE WITH IMAGES.
COUNTRY NEEDS YOU!
SO THOSE OF US INVOLVED IN CREATING IMAGES HAVE A RESPONSIBILITY TO REGULATE OURSELVES!
I MADE THE SAME MISTAKE YOU MADE ONCE.
AND BECAUSE OF WHAT I DID, MY FRIEND AND A LOT OF OTHER PEOPLE ARE DEAD.
BUT EVEN THAT COULDN'T MAKE ME GIVE UP SFX.
SO I SWORE ON THIS SCAR...
...THAT I'D NEVER MAKE THAT MISTAKE AGAIN.
I DON'T CARE WHY YOU DID IT...
IT WAS WRONG!!

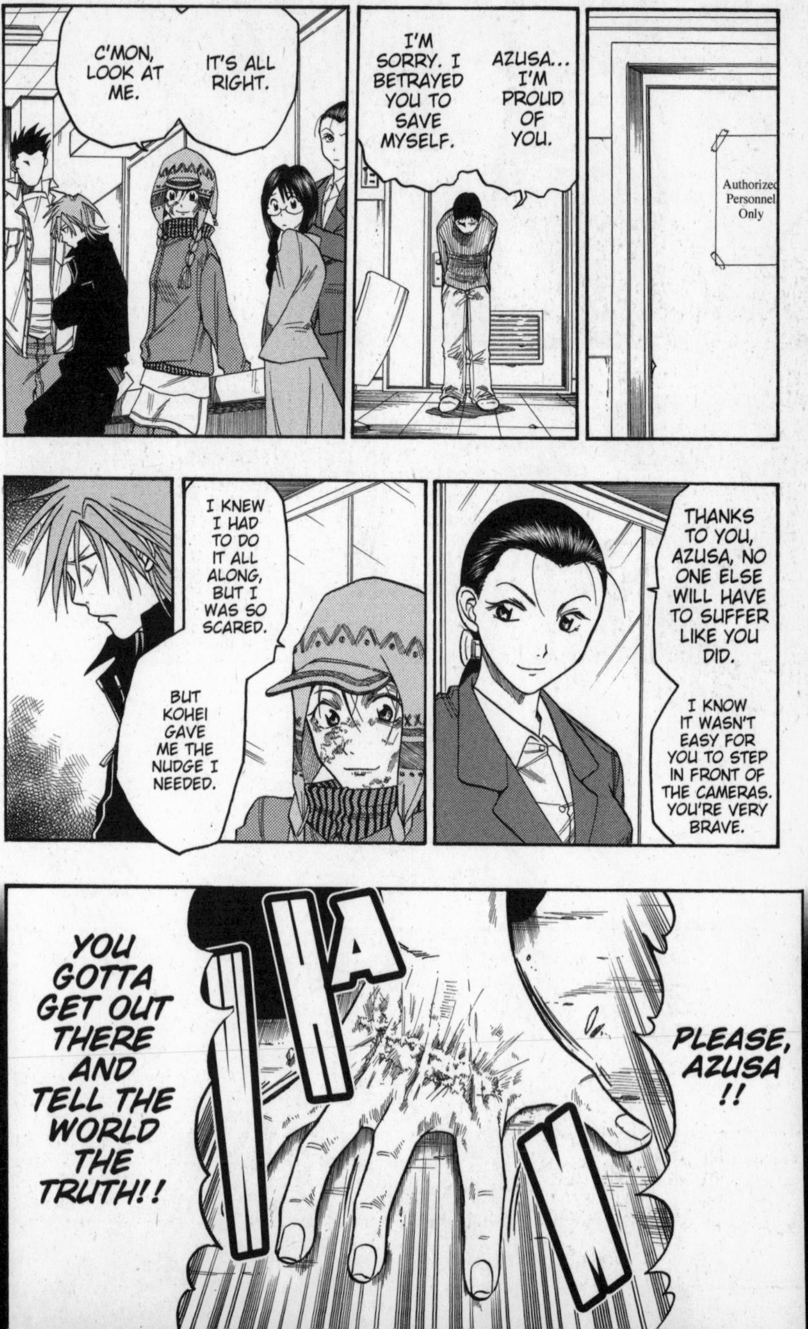
Authorized Personnel Only
AZUSA... I'M PROUD OF YOU.
I'M SORRY. I BETRAYED YOU TO SAVE MYSELF.
IT'S ALL RIGHT.
C'MON, LOOK AT ME.
THANKS TO YOU, AZUSA, NO ONE ELSE WILL HAVE TO SUFFER LIKE YOU DID.
I KNOW IT WASN'T EASY FOR YOU TO STEP IN FRONT OF THE CAMERAS. YOU'RE VERY BRAVE.
I KNEW I HAD TO DO IT ALL ALONG, BUT I WAS SO SCARED.
BUT KOHEI GAVE ME THE NUDGE I NEEDED.
PLEASE, AZUSA!!
YOU GOTTA GET OUT THERE AND TELL THE WORLD THE TRUTH!!
WHAM

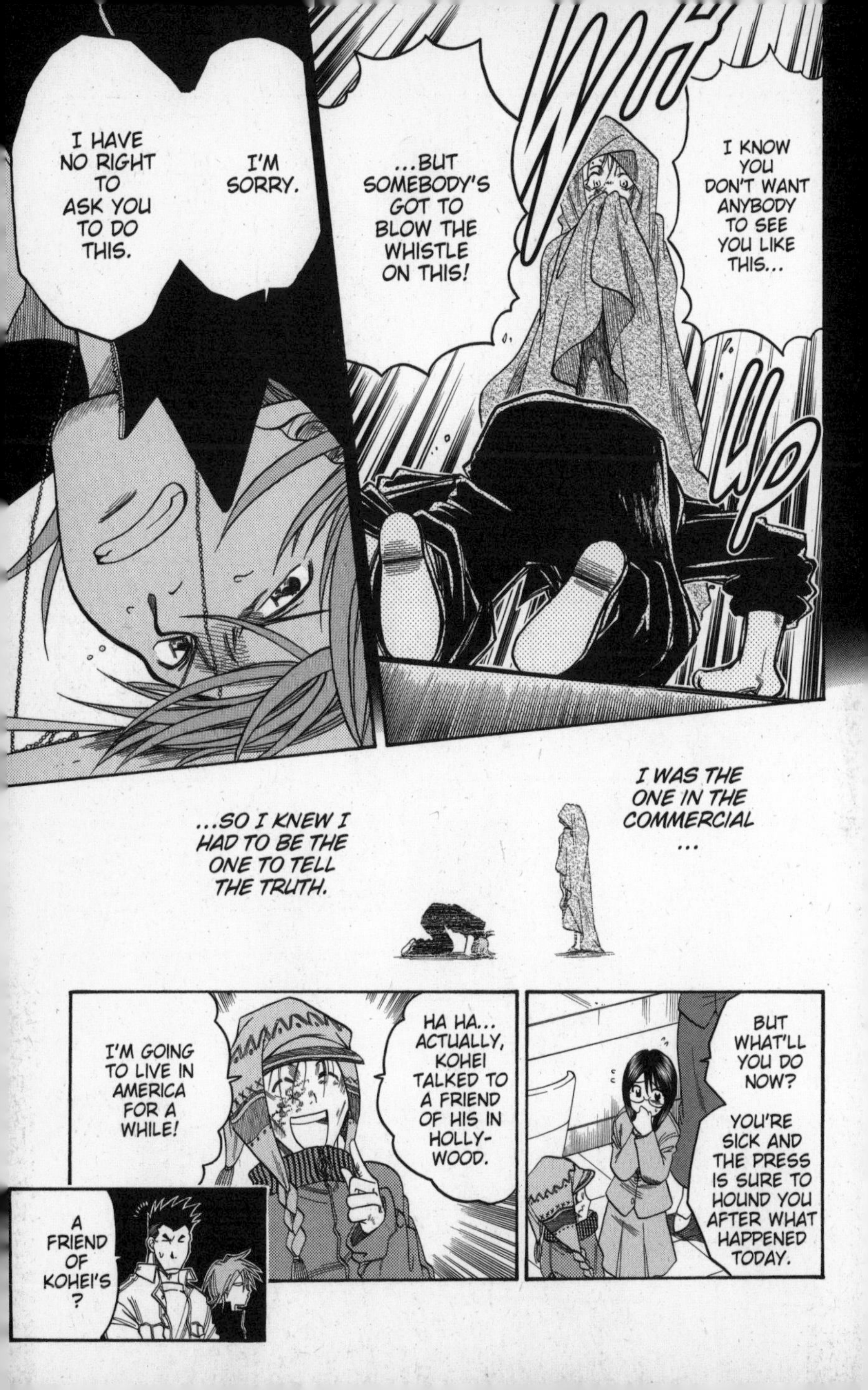
I KNOW YOU DON'T WANT ANYBODY TO SEE YOU LIKE THIS...
...BUT SOMEBODY'S GOT TO BLOW THE WHISTLE ON THIS!
UP
I'M SORRY.
I HAVE NO RIGHT TO ASK YOU TO DO THIS.
I WAS THE ONE IN THE COMMERCIAL...
...SO I KNEW I HAD TO BE THE ONE TO TELL THE TRUTH.
BUT WHAT'LL YOU DO NOW?
YOU'RE SICK AND THE PRESS IS SURE TO HOUND YOU AFTER WHAT HAPPENED TODAY.
HA HA... ACTUALLY, KOHEI TALKED TO A FRIEND OF HIS IN HOLLY-WOOD.
I'M GOING TO LIVE IN AMERICA FOR A WHILE!
A FRIEND OF KOHEI'S?

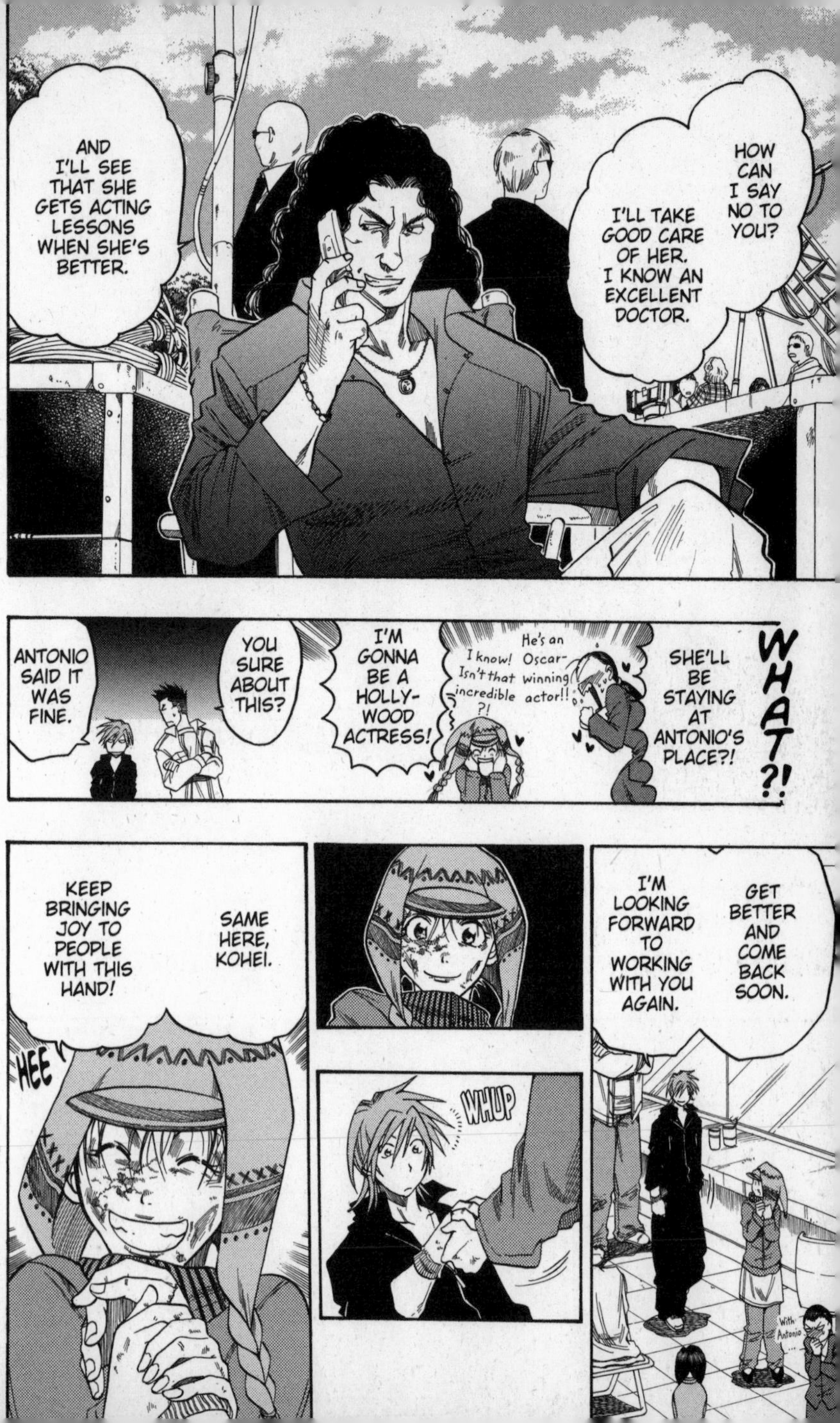
HOW CAN I SAY NO TO YOU?
I'LL TAKE GOOD CARE OF HER. I KNOW AN EXCELLENT DOCTOR.
AND I'LL SEE THAT SHE GETS ACTING LESSONS WHEN SHE'S BETTER.
WHAT?!
SHE'LL BE STAYING AT ANTONIO'S PLACE?!
He's an Oscar-winning actor!!
I know! Isn't that incredible ?!
I'M GONNA BE A HOLLY-WOOD ACTRESS!
YOU SURE ABOUT THIS?
ANTONIO SAID IT WAS FINE.
GET BETTER AND COME BACK SOON.
I'M LOOKING FORWARD TO WORKING WITH YOU AGAIN.
With Antonio ...
WHUP
SAME HERE, KOHEI.
KEEP BRINGING JOY TO PEOPLE WITH THIS HAND!
HEE

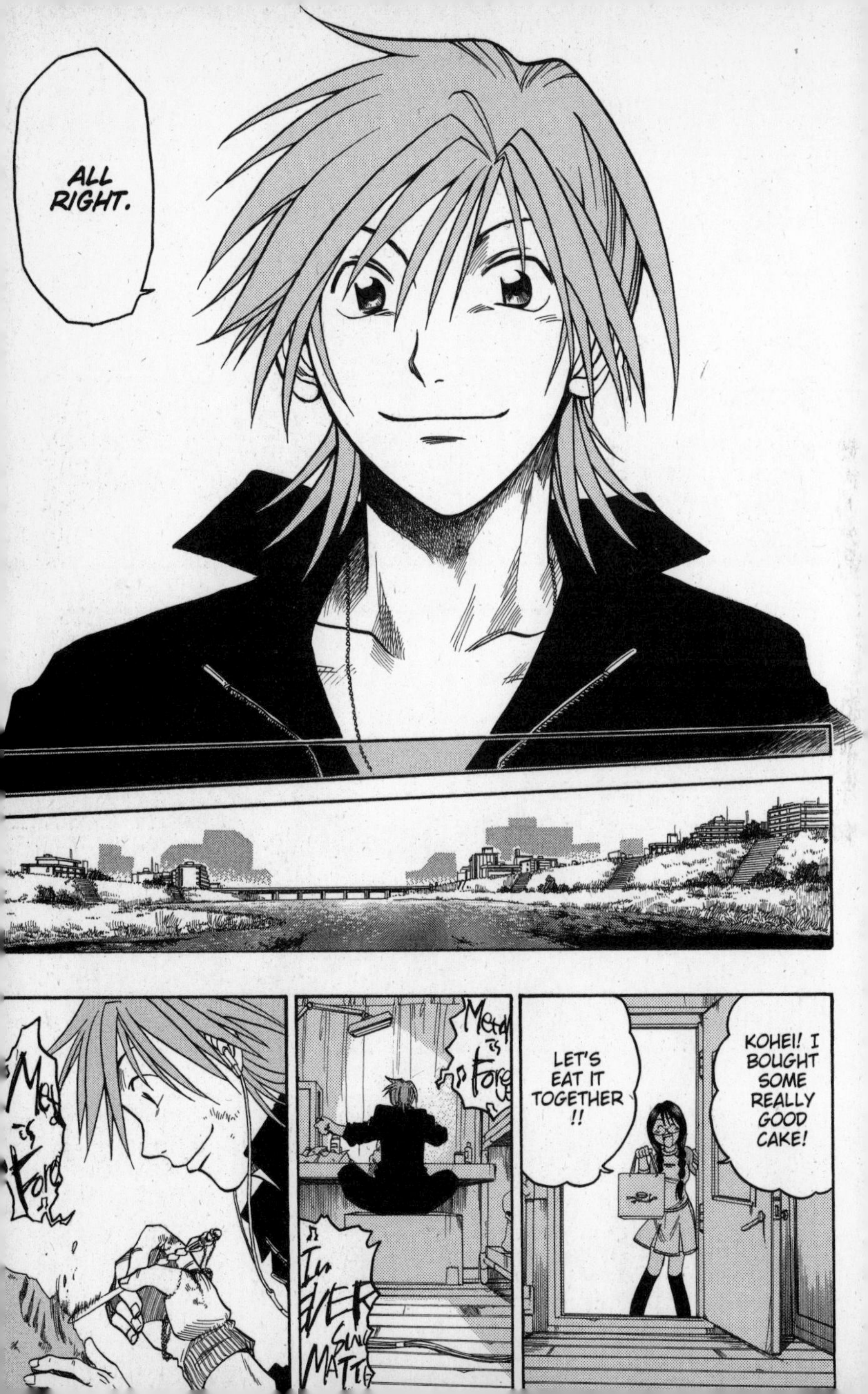
ALL RIGHT.
KOHEI! I BOUGHT SOME REALLY GOOD CAKE!
LET'S EAT IT TOGETHER!!

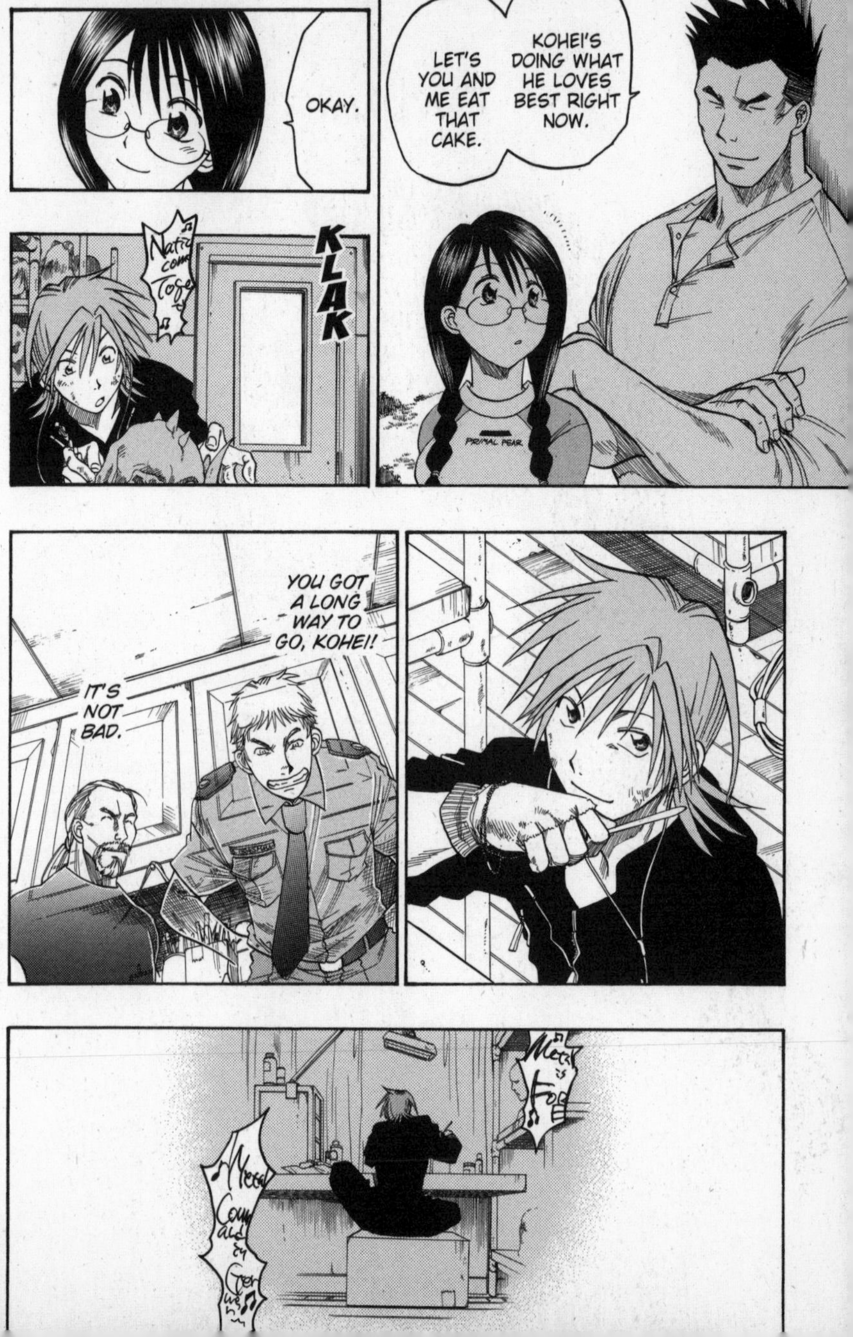
KOHEI'S DOING WHAT HE LOVES BEST RIGHT NOW.
LET'S YOU AND ME EAT THAT CAKE.
OKAY.
KLAK
YOU GOT A LONG WAY TO GO, KOHEI!!
IT'S NOT BAD.

Scene EX: Old Lady Mach!!!

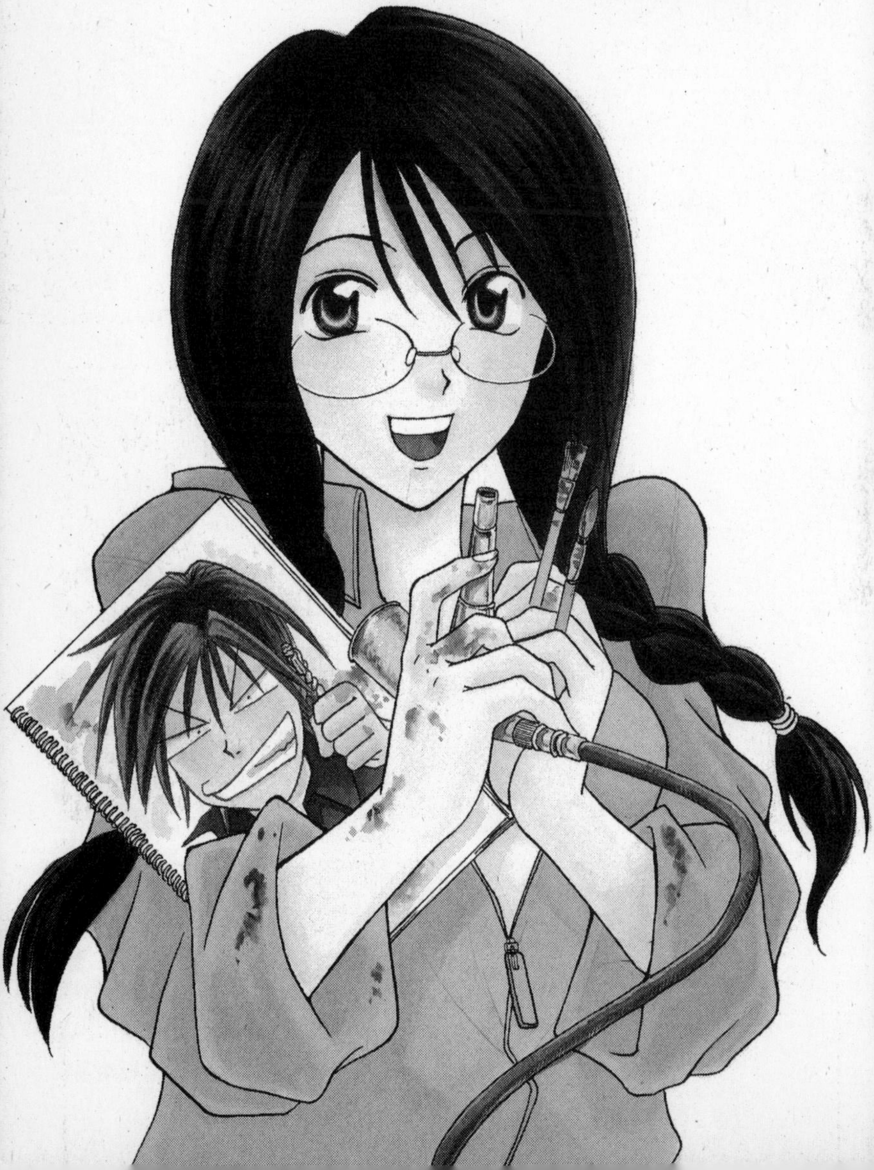

GIMMICK!

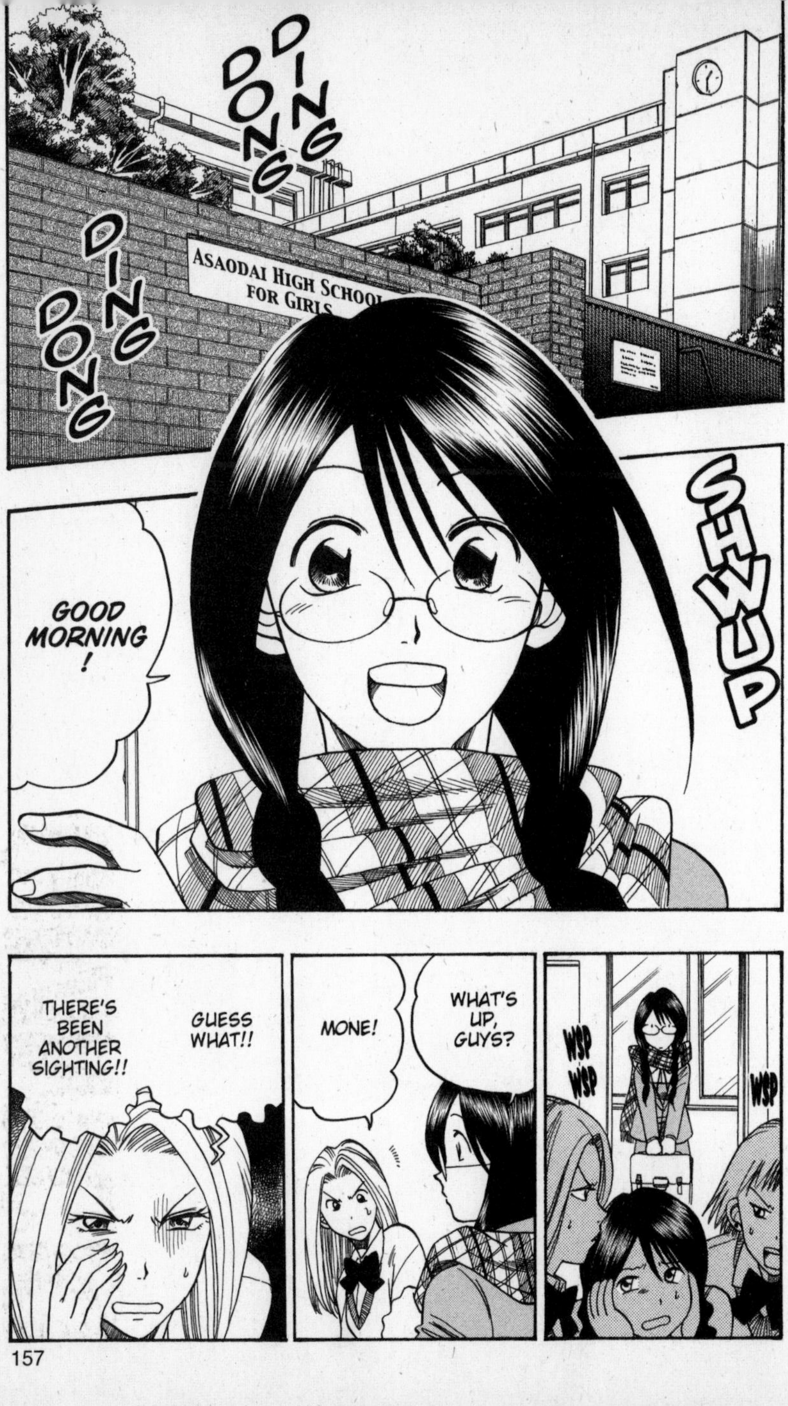
DING DONG
ASAODAI HIGH SCHOOL FOR GIRLS
DING DONG
SHWUP
GOOD MORNING!
WSP WSP
WSP
WHAT'S UP, GUYS?
MONE!
GUESS WHAT!!
THERE'S BEEN ANOTHER SIGHTING!!

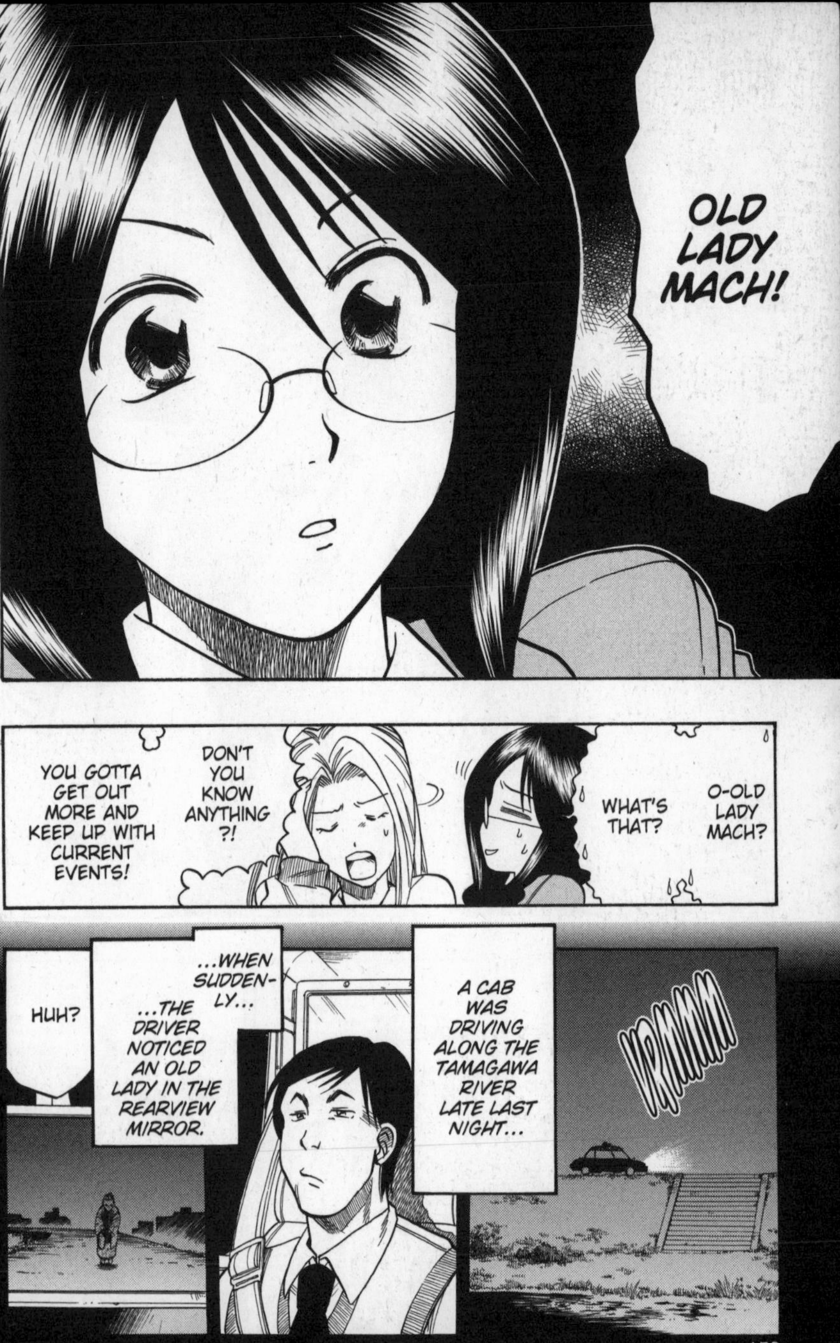
OLD LADY MACH!
O-OLD LADY MACH?
WHAT'S THAT?
DON'T YOU KNOW ANYTHING?!
YOU GOTTA GET OUT MORE AND KEEP UP WITH CURRENT EVENTS!
A CAB WAS DRIVING ALONG THE TAMAGAWA RIVER LATE LAST NIGHT...
...WHEN SUDDEN-LY...
...THE DRIVER NOTICED AN OLD LADY IN THE REARVIEW MIRROR.
HUH?

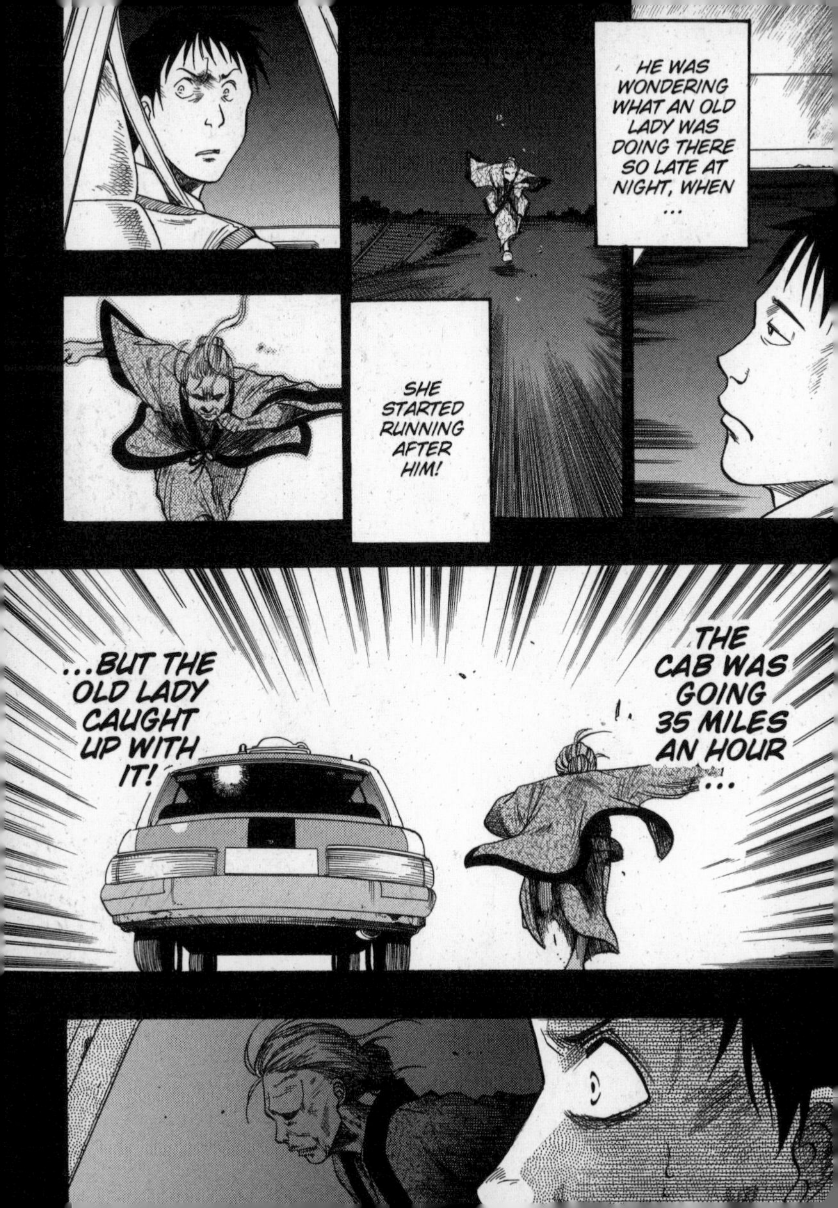
HE WAS WONDERING WHAT AN OLD LADY WAS DOING THERE SO LATE AT NIGHT, WHEN ...
SHE STARTED RUNNING AFTER HIM!
THE CAB WAS GOING 35 MILES AN HOUR ...
...BUT THE OLD LADY CAUGHT UP WITH IT!

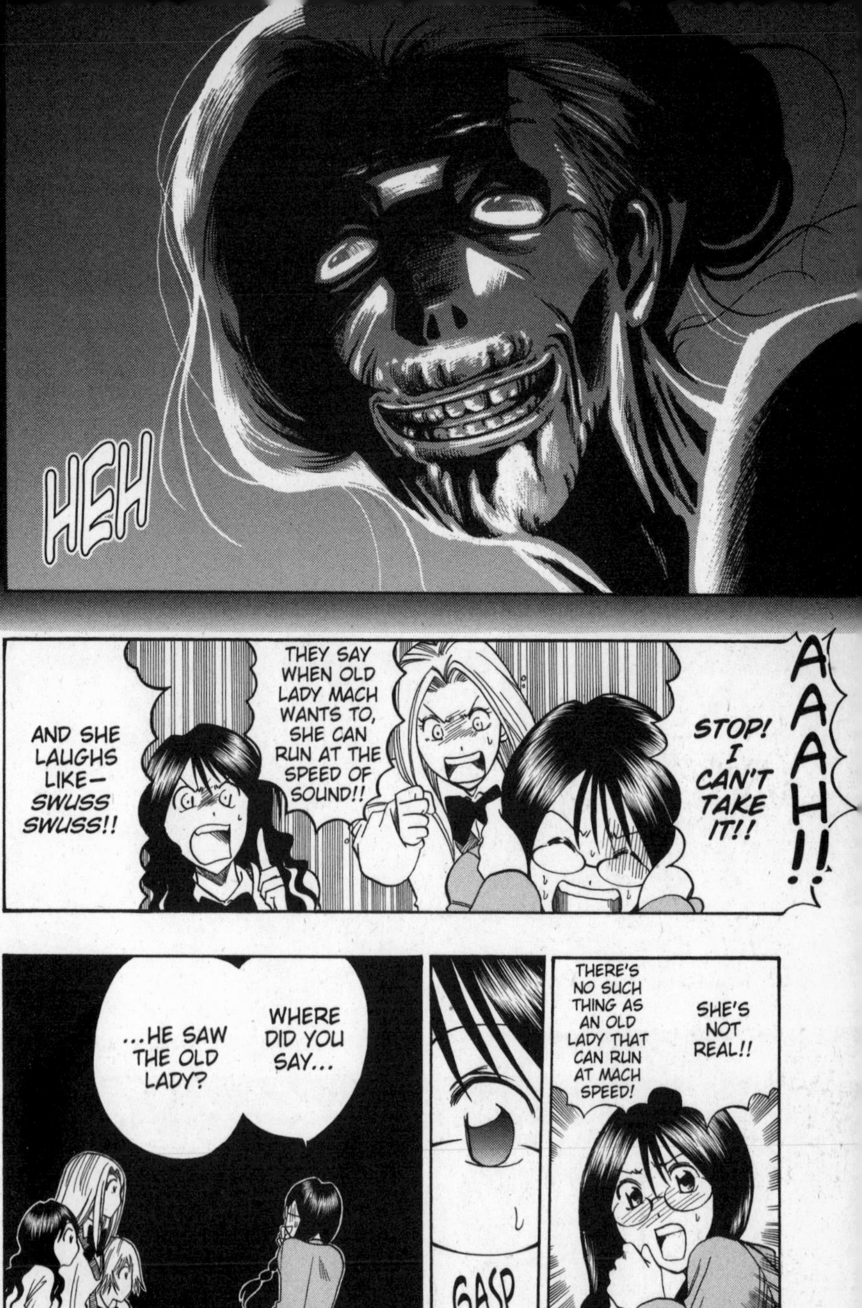
HEH
AAAH!!
STOP! I CAN'T TAKE IT!!
THEY SAY WHEN OLD LADY MACH WANTS TO, SHE CAN RUN AT THE SPEED OF SOUND!!
AND SHE LAUGHS LIKE— SWUSS SWUSS!!
SHE'S NOT REAL!!
THERE'S NO SUCH THING AS AN OLD LADY THAT CAN RUN AT MACH SPEED!
GASP
WHERE DID YOU SAY...
...HE SAW THE OLD LADY?

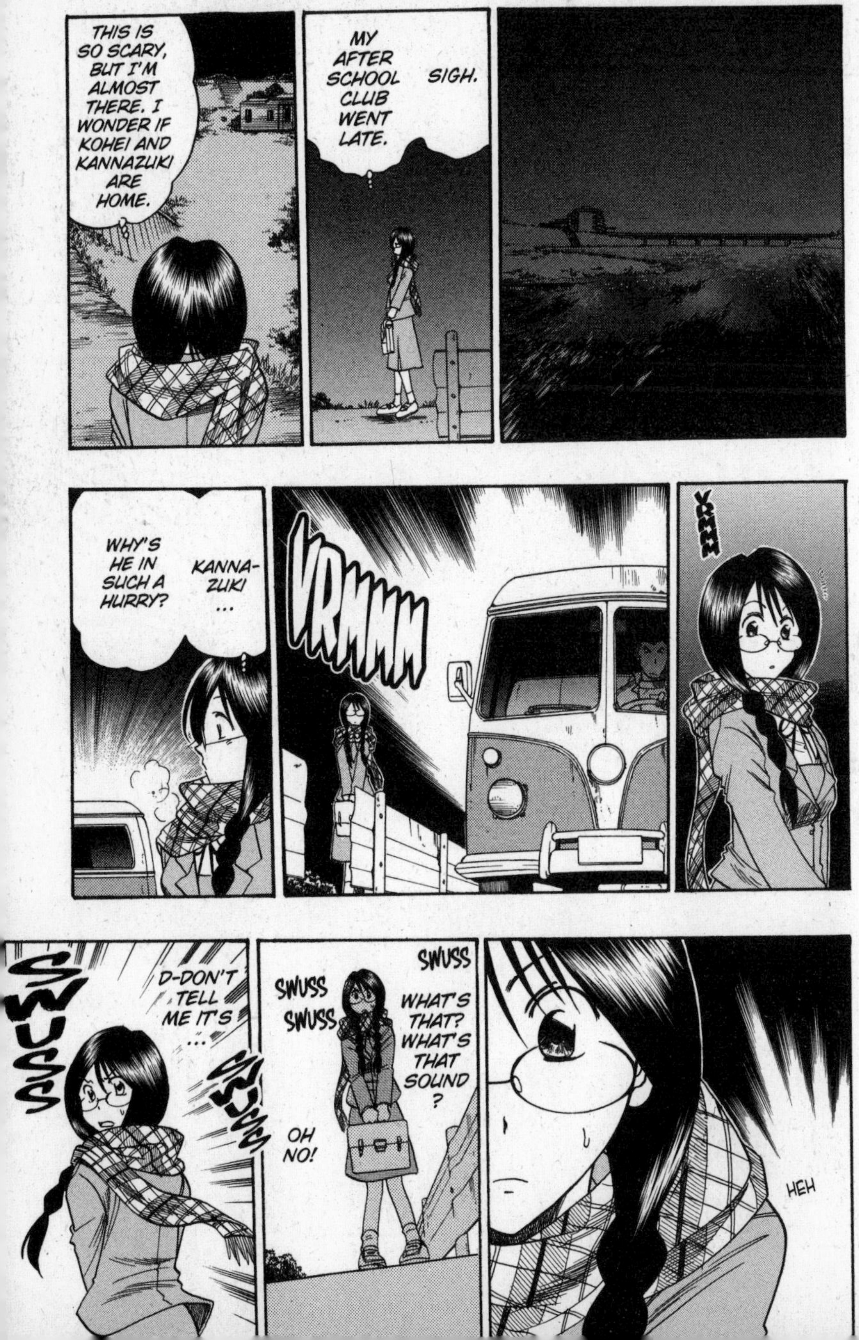
SIGH.
MY AFTER SCHOOL CLUB WENT LATE.
THIS IS SO SCARY, BUT I'M ALMOST THERE. I WONDER IF KOHEI AND KANNAZUKI ARE HOME.
VRMMM
VRMMMM
KANNAZUKI ...
WHY'S HE IN SUCH A HURRY?
HEH
SWUSS
WHAT'S THAT? WHAT'S THAT SOUND?
SWUSS
SWUSS
OH NO!
D-DON'T TELL ME IT'S ...
SWUSS
SWUSS

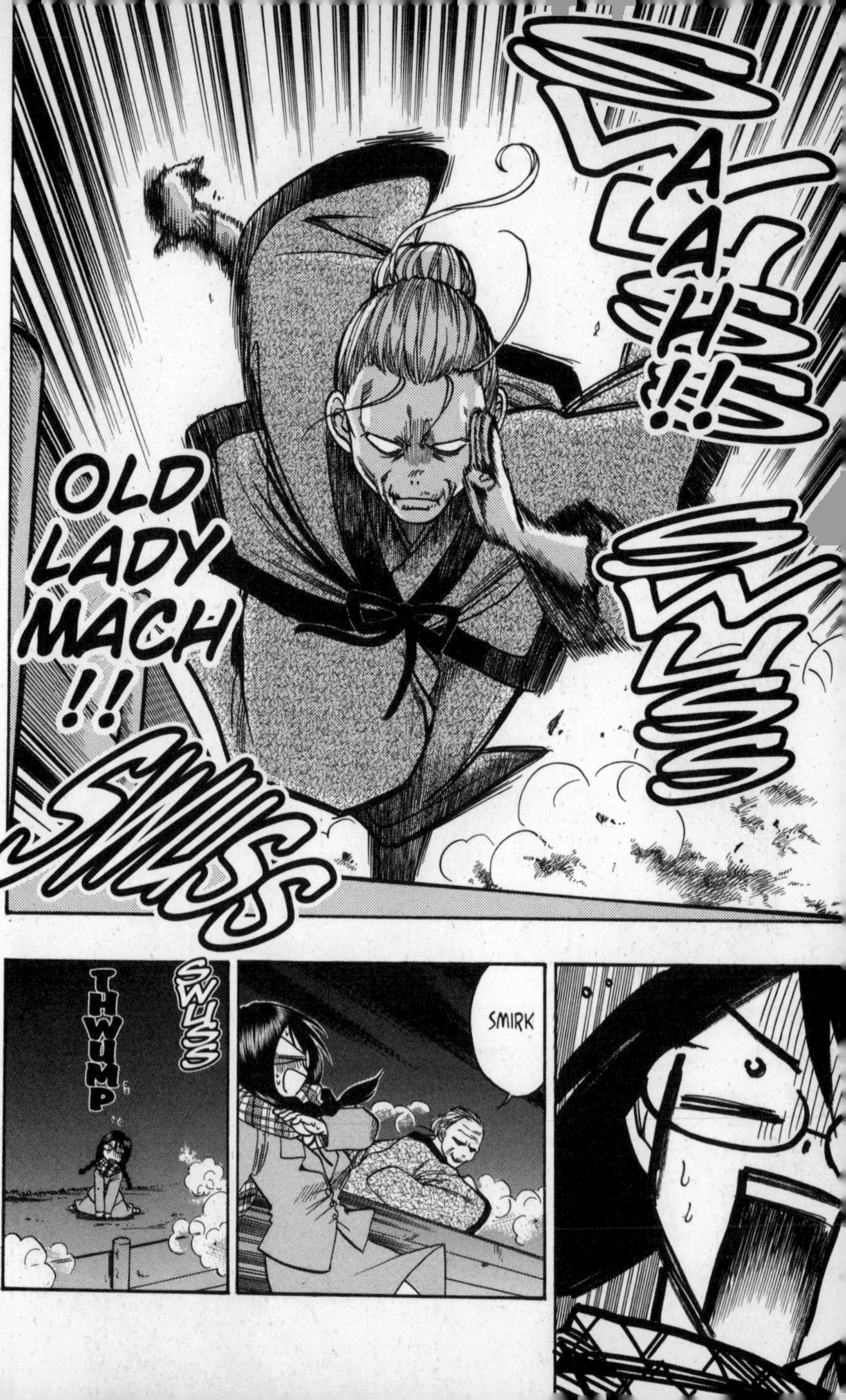
AAH!!
SWUSS
OLD LADY MACH!!
SWUSS
SMIRK
SWUSS
THWUMP

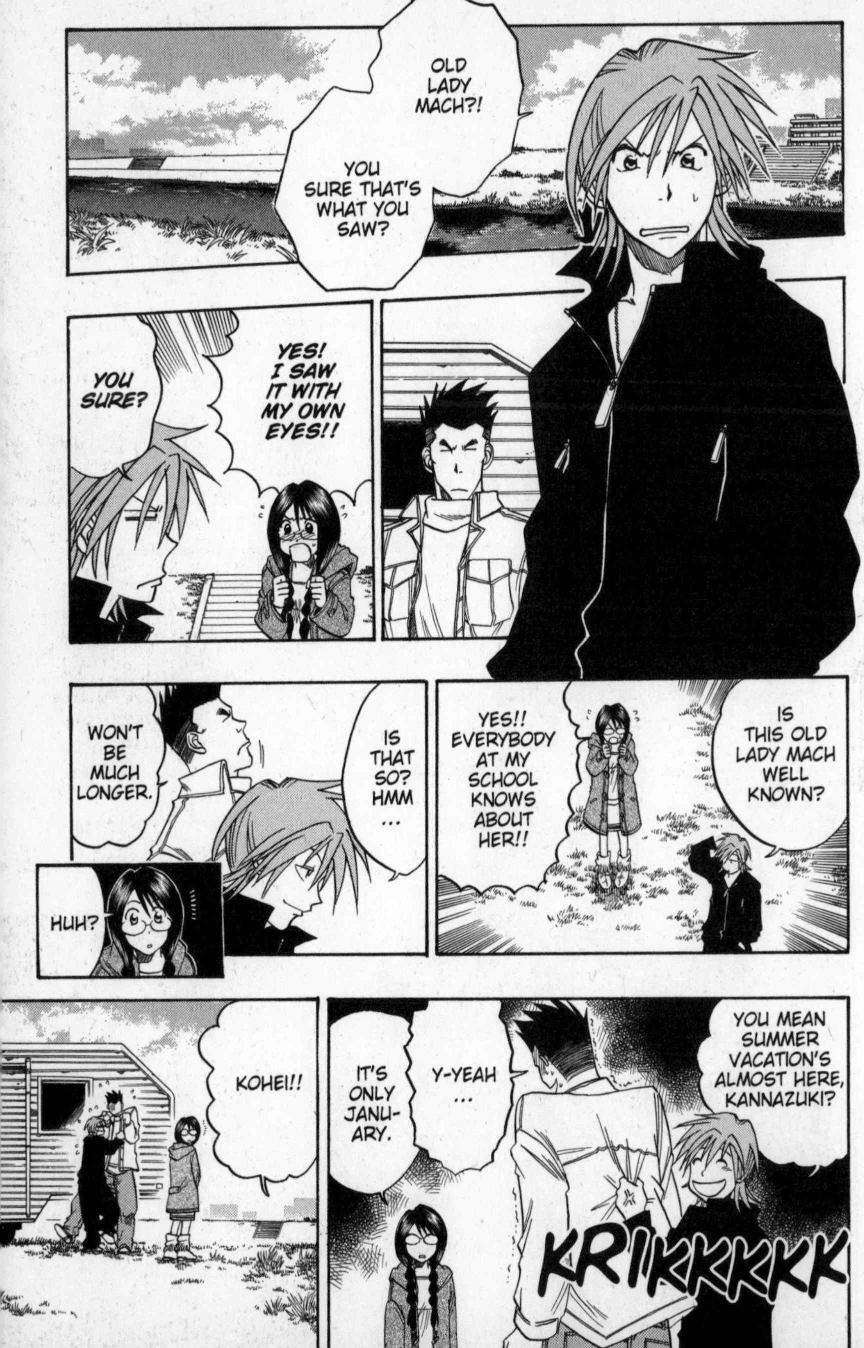
OLD LADY MACH?!
YOU SURE THAT'S WHAT YOU SAW?
YES! I SAW IT WITH MY OWN EYES!!
YOU SURE?
IS THIS OLD LADY MACH WELL KNOWN?
YES!! EVERYBODY AT MY SCHOOL KNOWS ABOUT HER!!
IS THAT SO? HMM ...
WON'T BE MUCH LONGER.
HUH?
YOU MEAN SUMMER VACATION'S ALMOST HERE, KANNAZUKI?
Y-YEAH ...
IT'S ONLY JANUARY.
KRIKKKKKK
KOHEI!!

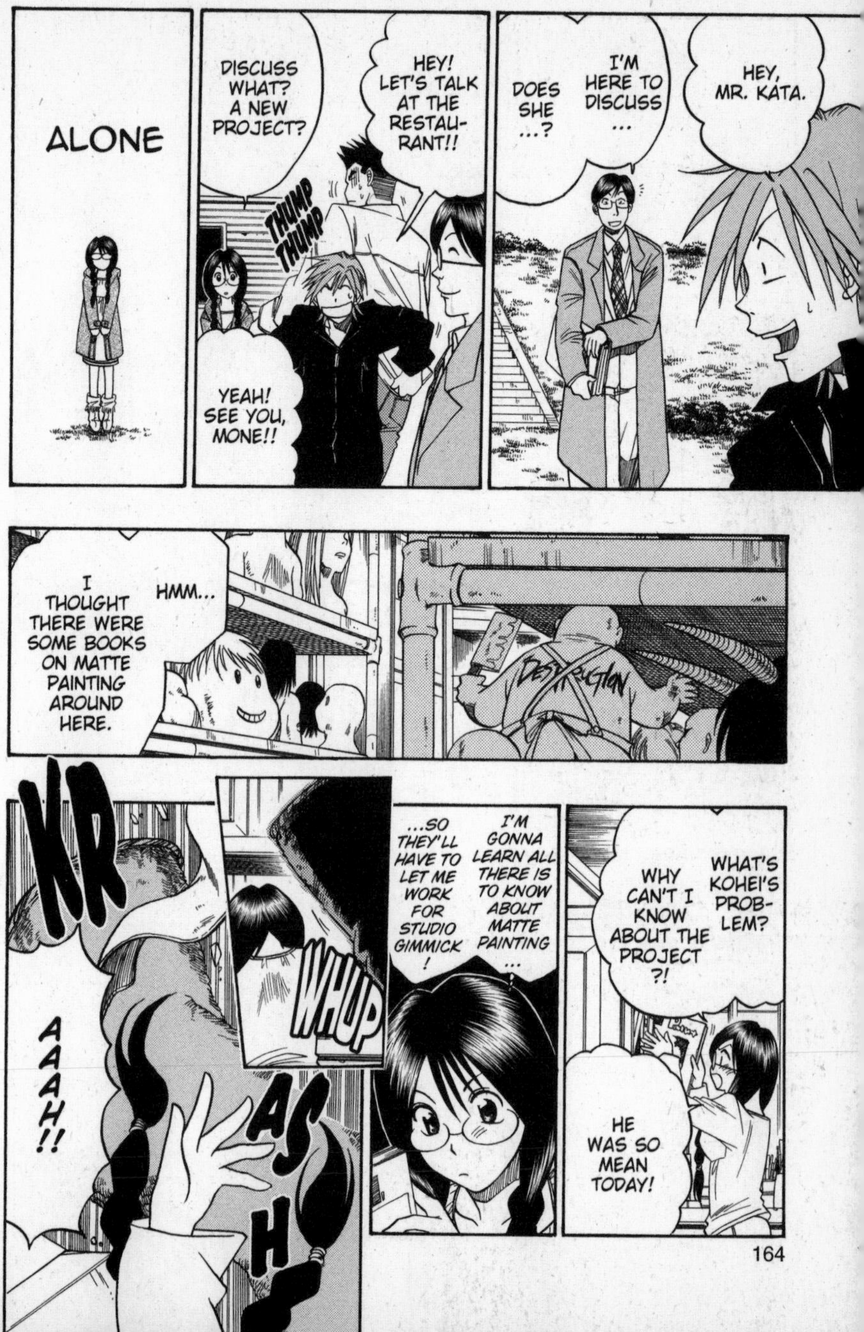
HEY, MR. KATA.
I'M HERE TO DISCUSS ...
DOES SHE ...?
HEY! LET'S TALK AT THE RESTAU-RANT!!
DISCUSS WHAT? A NEW PROJECT?
THUMP THUMP
YEAH! SEE YOU, MONE!!
ALONE
HMM...
I THOUGHT THERE WERE SOME BOOKS ON MATTE PAINTING AROUND HERE.
WHAT'S KOHEI'S PROB-LEM?
WHY CAN'T I KNOW ABOUT THE PROJECT?!
HE WAS SO MEAN TODAY!
I'M GONNA LEARN ALL THERE IS TO KNOW ABOUT MATTE PAINTING...
...SO THEY'LL HAVE TO LET ME WORK FOR STUDIO GIMMICK!
WHUP
KRASH
AAAAH!!

OUCH!!
WHAT'S
THIS?!

A
RUG?!

IT'S A
SAFETY
HAZARD!

WHUP

IT'S
...

DON'T
TELL
ME
...

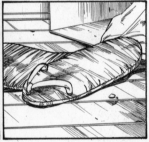

GASP

WHUP

IT
CAN'T
BE
!!

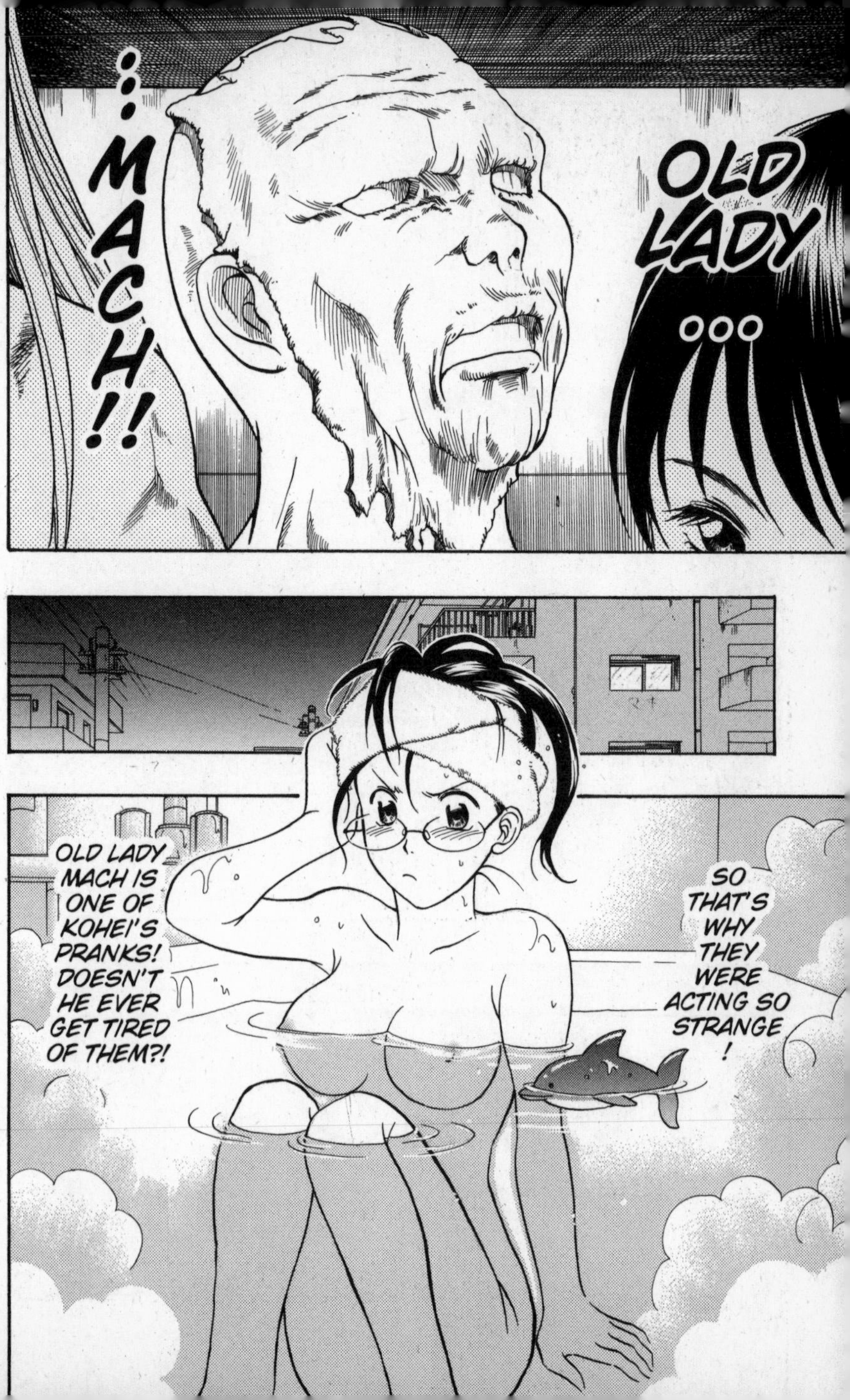
OLD LADY...
...MACH!!
SO THAT'S WHY THEY WERE ACTING SO STRANGE!
OLD LADY MACH IS ONE OF KOHEI'S PRANKS! DOESN'T HE EVER GET TIRED OF THEM?!

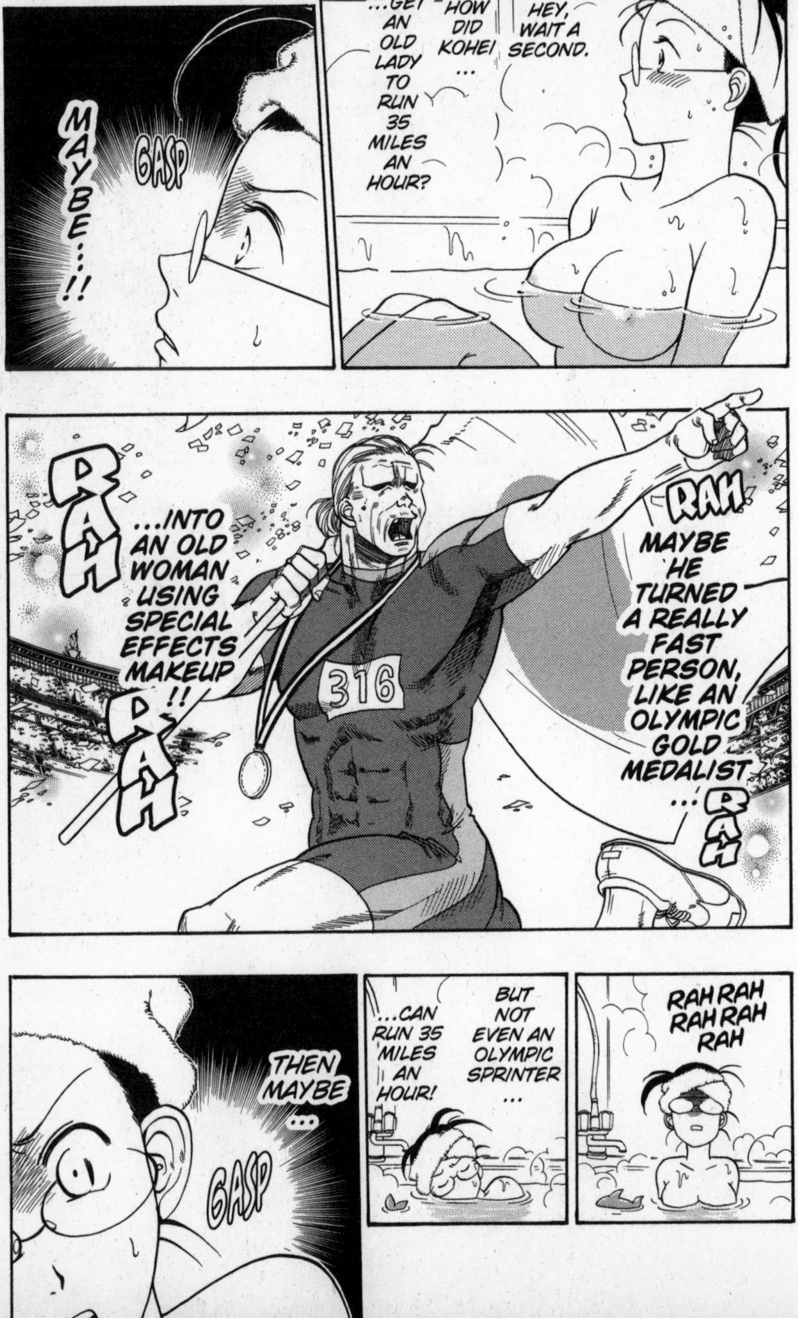
HEY, WAIT A SECOND.
HOW DID KOHEI...
...GET AN OLD LADY TO RUN 35 MILES AN HOUR?
GASP
MAYBE...!!
RAH
MAYBE HE TURNED A REALLY FAST PERSON, LIKE AN OLYMPIC GOLD MEDALIST...
RAH
316
RAH
...INTO AN OLD WOMAN USING SPECIAL EFFECTS MAKEUP!!
RAH
RAH RAH RAH RAH RAH
BUT NOT EVEN AN OLYMPIC SPRINTER...
...CAN RUN 35 MILES AN HOUR!
THEN MAYBE...
GASP

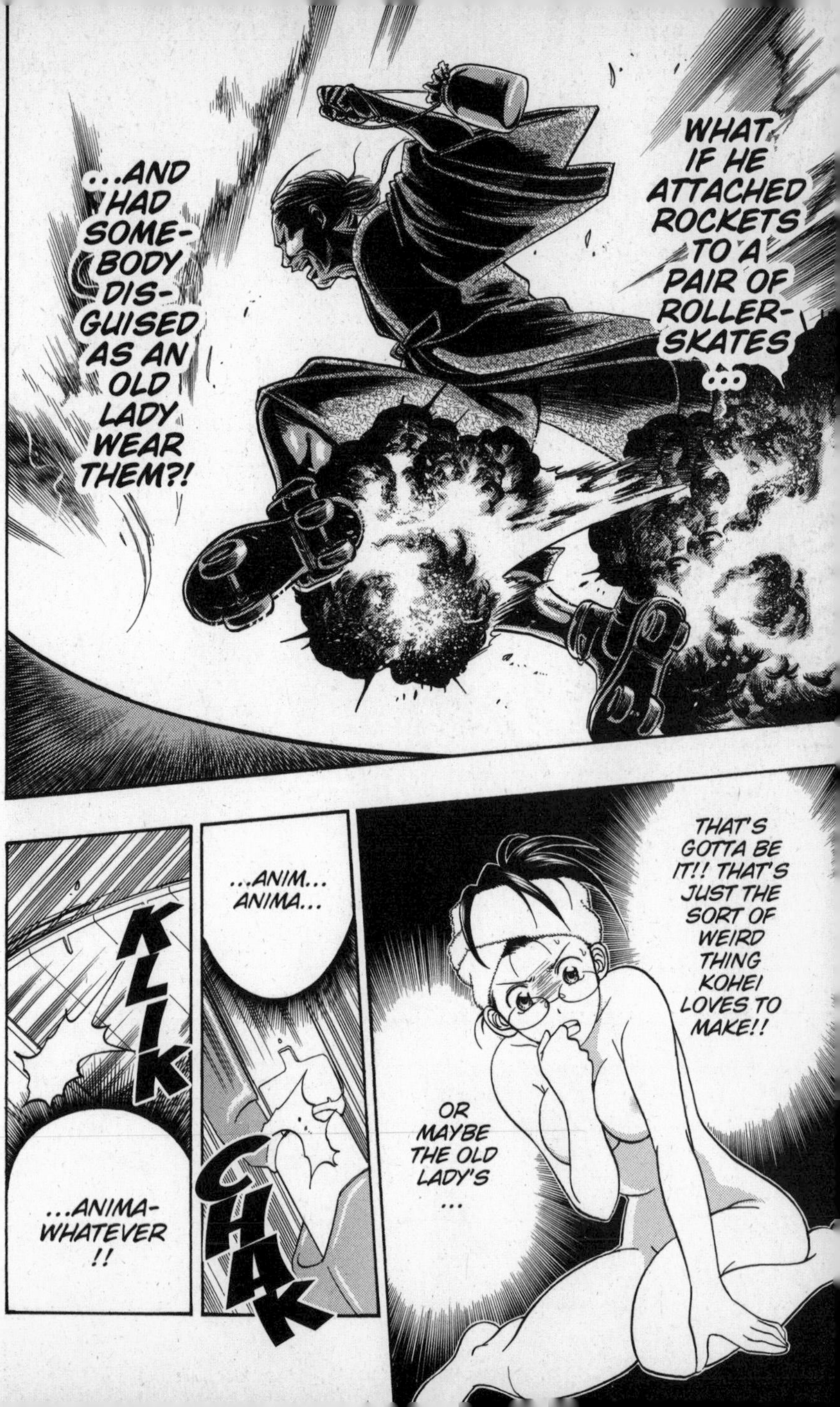

WHAT IF HE ATTACHED ROCKETS TO A PAIR OF ROLLER-SKATES...
...AND HAD SOME-BODY DIS-GUISED AS AN OLD LADY WEAR THEM?!
THAT'S GOTTA BE IT!! THAT'S JUST THE SORT OF WEIRD THING KOHEI LOVES TO MAKE!!
OR MAYBE THE OLD LADY'S...
...ANIM... ANIMA...
CHAK
KLIK
...ANIMA-WHATEVER!!

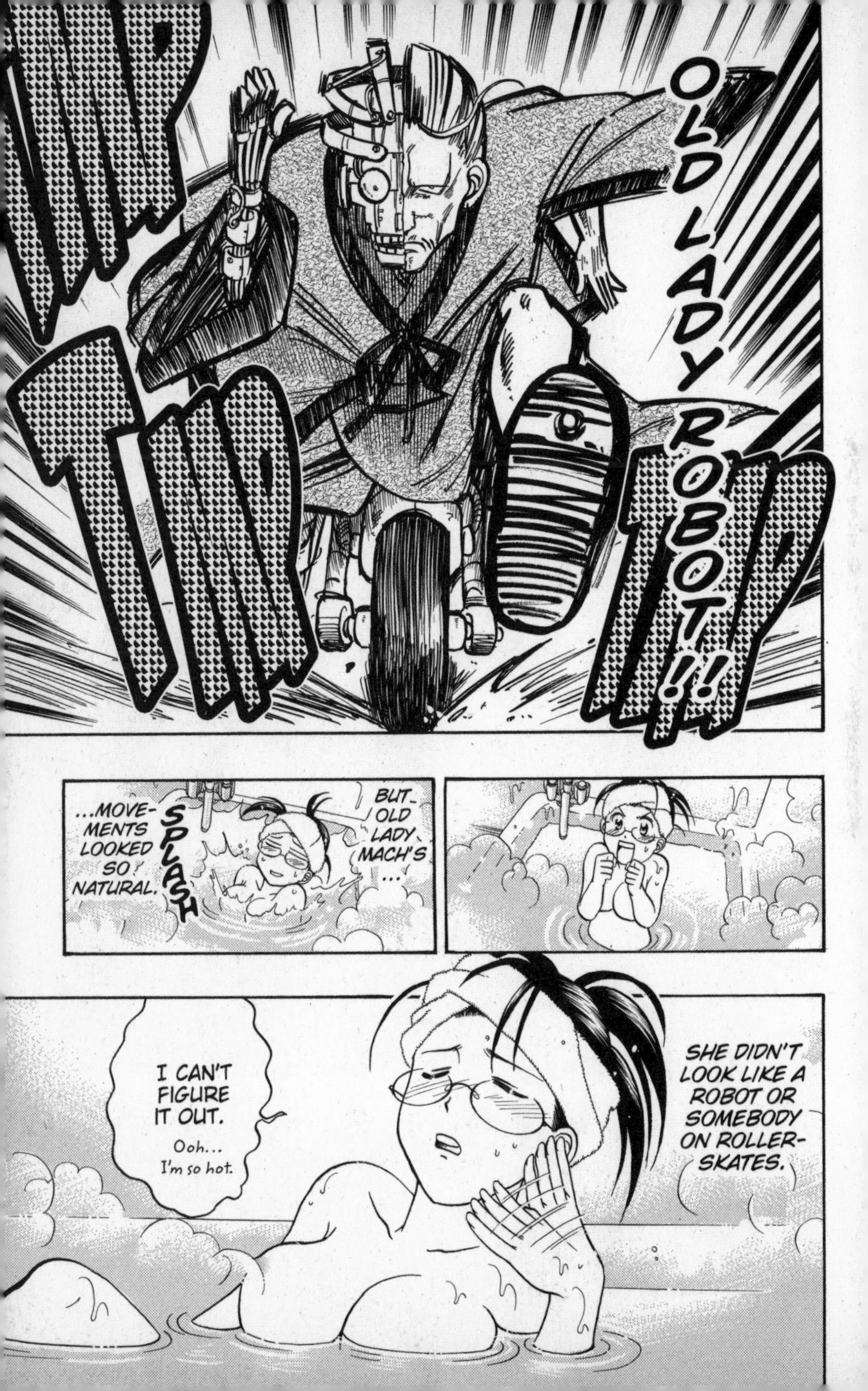
OLD LADY ROBOT!!
BUT OLD LADY MACH'S ...
SPLASH
...MOVE-MENTS LOOKED SO NATURAL.
SHE DIDN'T LOOK LIKE A ROBOT OR SOMEBODY ON ROLLER-SKATES.
I CAN'T FIGURE IT OUT.
Ooh... I'm so hot.

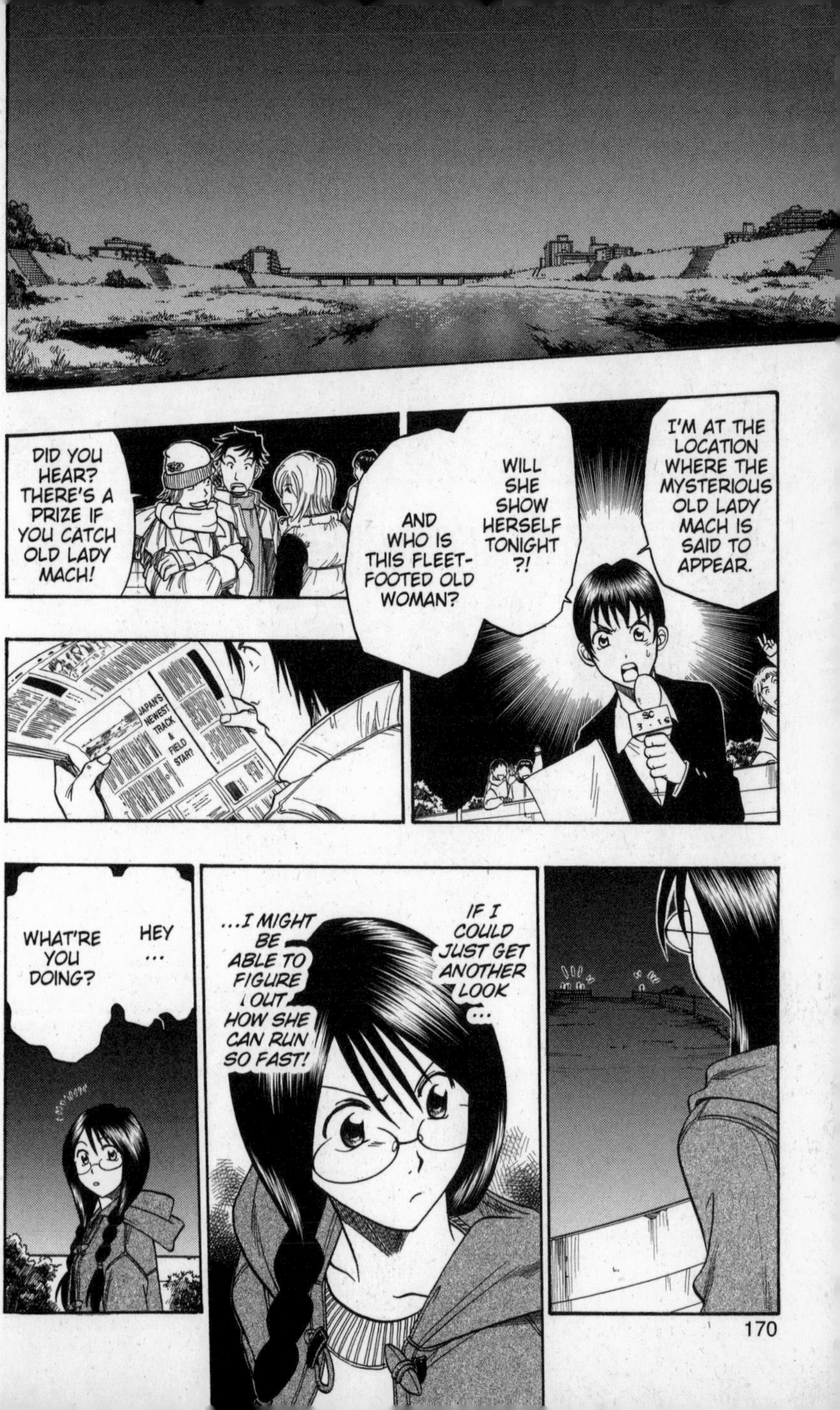
I'M AT THE LOCATION WHERE THE MYSTERIOUS OLD LADY MACH IS SAID TO APPEAR.
WILL SHE SHOW HERSELF TONIGHT?!
AND WHO IS THIS FLEET-FOOTED OLD WOMAN?
DID YOU HEAR? THERE'S A PRIZE IF YOU CATCH OLD LADY MACH!
JAPAN'S NEWEST TRACK & FIELD STAR?
IF I COULD JUST GET ANOTHER LOOK...
...I MIGHT BE ABLE TO FIGURE OUT HOW SHE CAN RUN SO FAST!
HEY...
WHAT'RE YOU DOING?

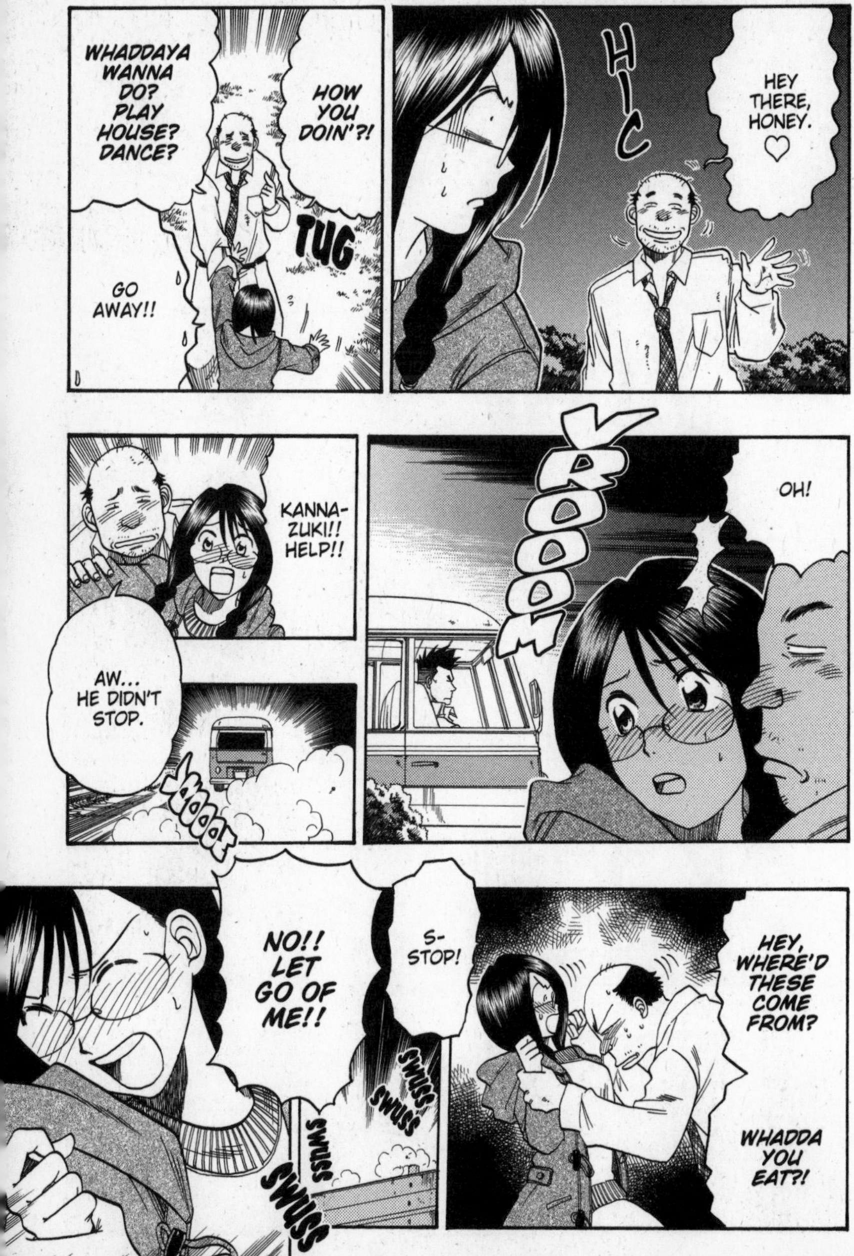
HEY THERE, HONEY. ♡
HIC
HOW YOU DOIN'?!
WHADDAYA WANNA DO? PLAY HOUSE? DANCE?
TUG
GO AWAY!!
OH!
VROOOM
KANNA-ZUKI!! HELP!!
AW... HE DIDN'T STOP.
HEY, WHERE'D THESE COME FROM?
S-STOP!
WHADDA YOU EAT?!
NO!! LET GO OF ME!!
SWUSS
SWUSS
SWUSS
SWUSS

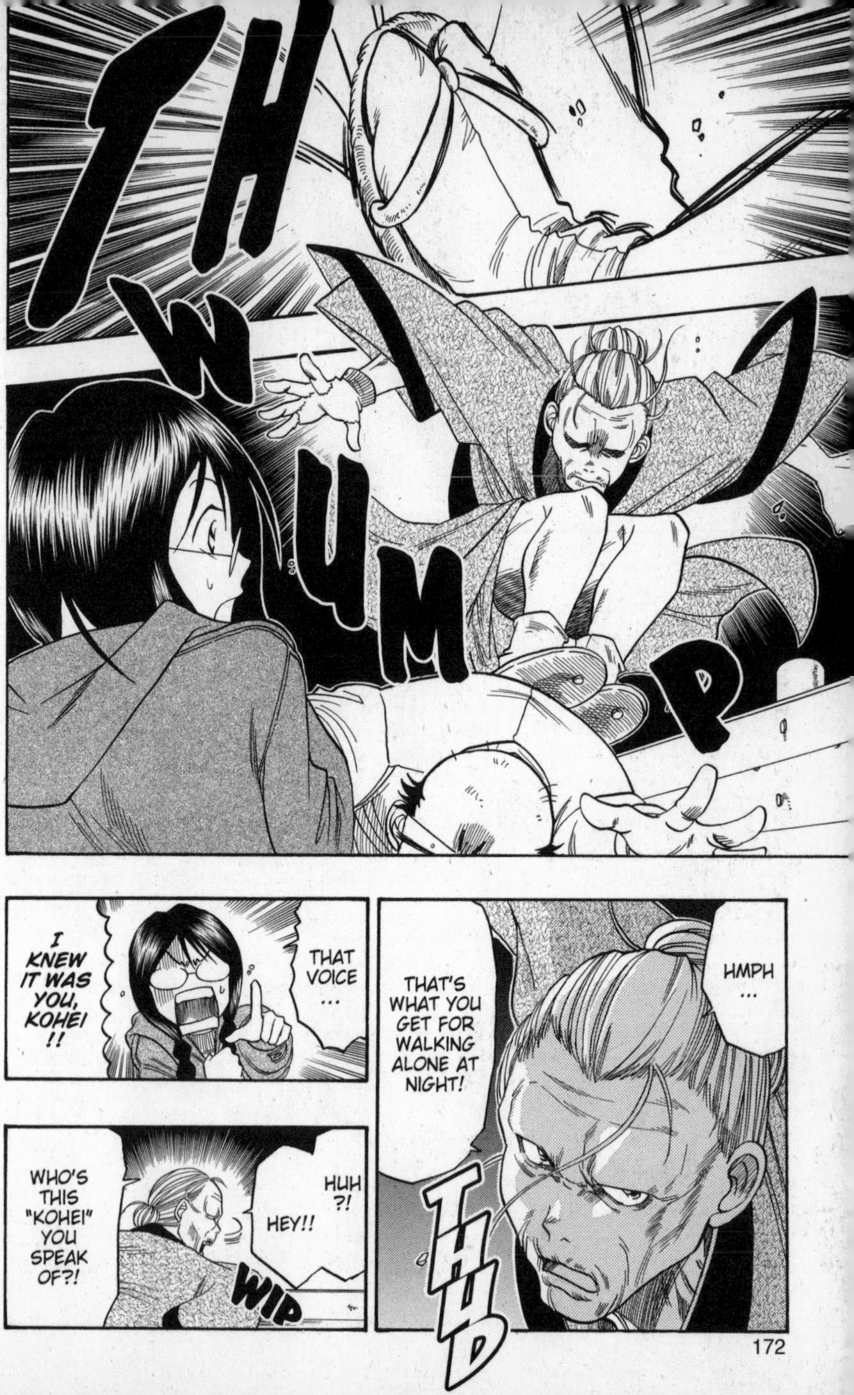
THWUMP
HMPH ...
THAT'S WHAT YOU GET FOR WALKING ALONE AT NIGHT!
THUD
THAT VOICE ...
I KNEW IT WAS YOU, KOHEI !!
HUH ?!
HEY!!
WHO'S THIS "KOHEI" YOU SPEAK OF?!
WIP

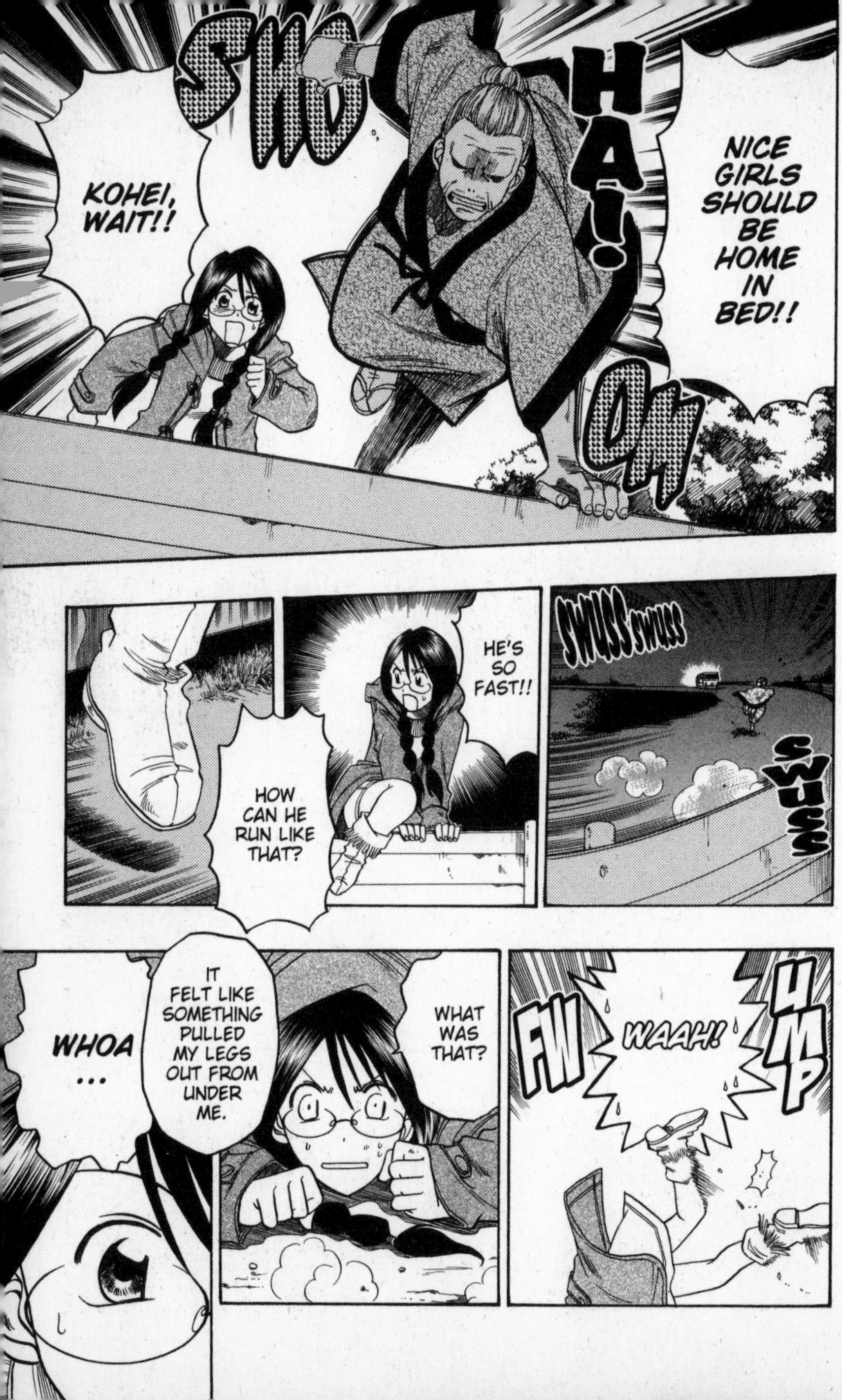
NICE GIRLS SHOULD BE HOME IN BED!!
SHO
HA!
OM
KOHEI, WAIT!!
SWUSS SWUSS
SWUSS
HE'S SO FAST!!
HOW CAN HE RUN LIKE THAT?
FW
UMP
WAAH!
WHAT WAS THAT?
IT FELT LIKE SOMETHING PULLED MY LEGS OUT FROM UNDER ME.
WHOA ...

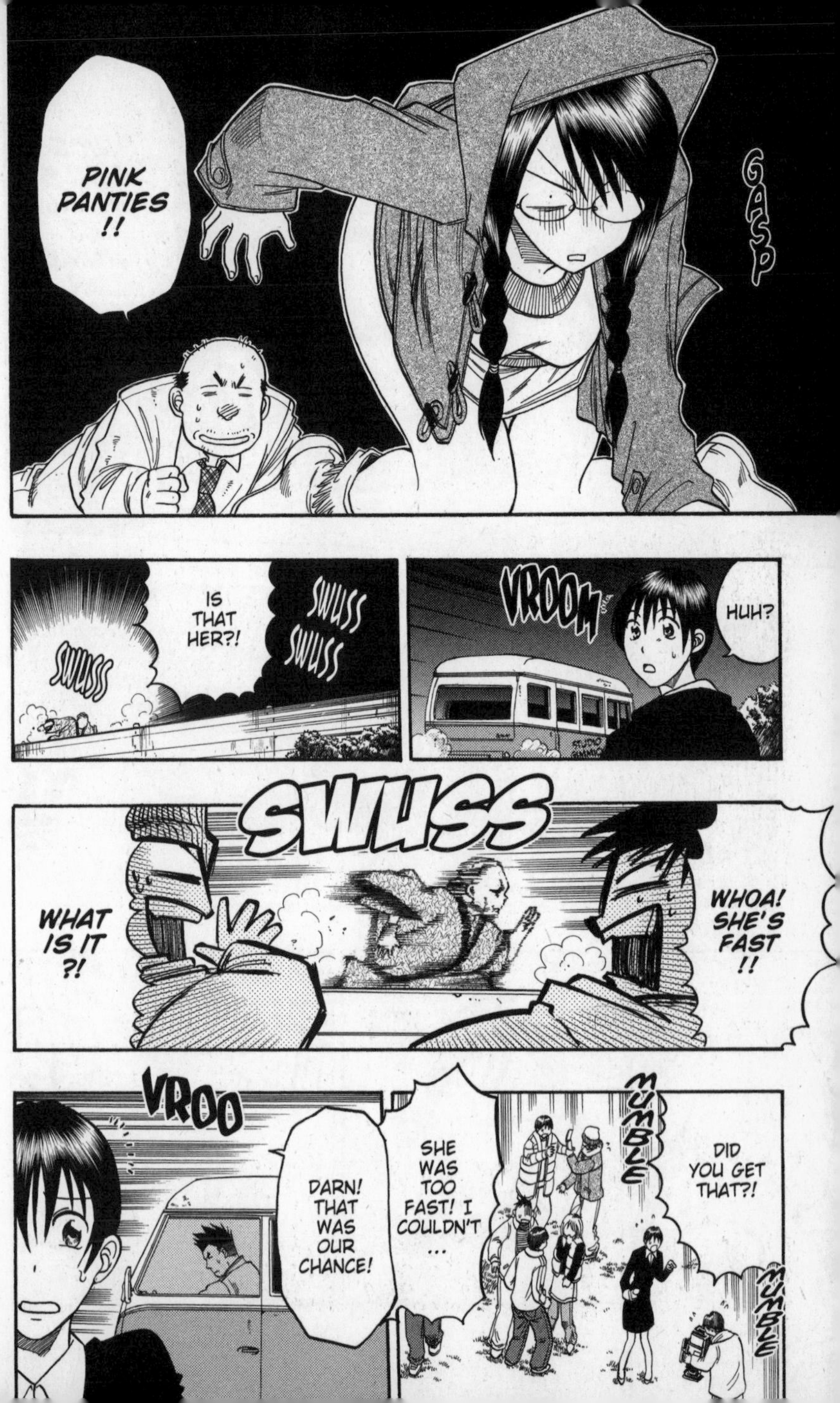
GASP
PINK PANTIES !!
HUH?
VROOM
IS THAT HER?!
SWUSS SWUSS
SWUSS
SWUSS
WHOA! SHE'S FAST !!
WHAT IS IT ?!
MUMBLE
MUMBLE
DID YOU GET THAT?!
SHE WAS TOO FAST! I COULDN'T ...
DARN! THAT WAS OUR CHANCE!
VROO

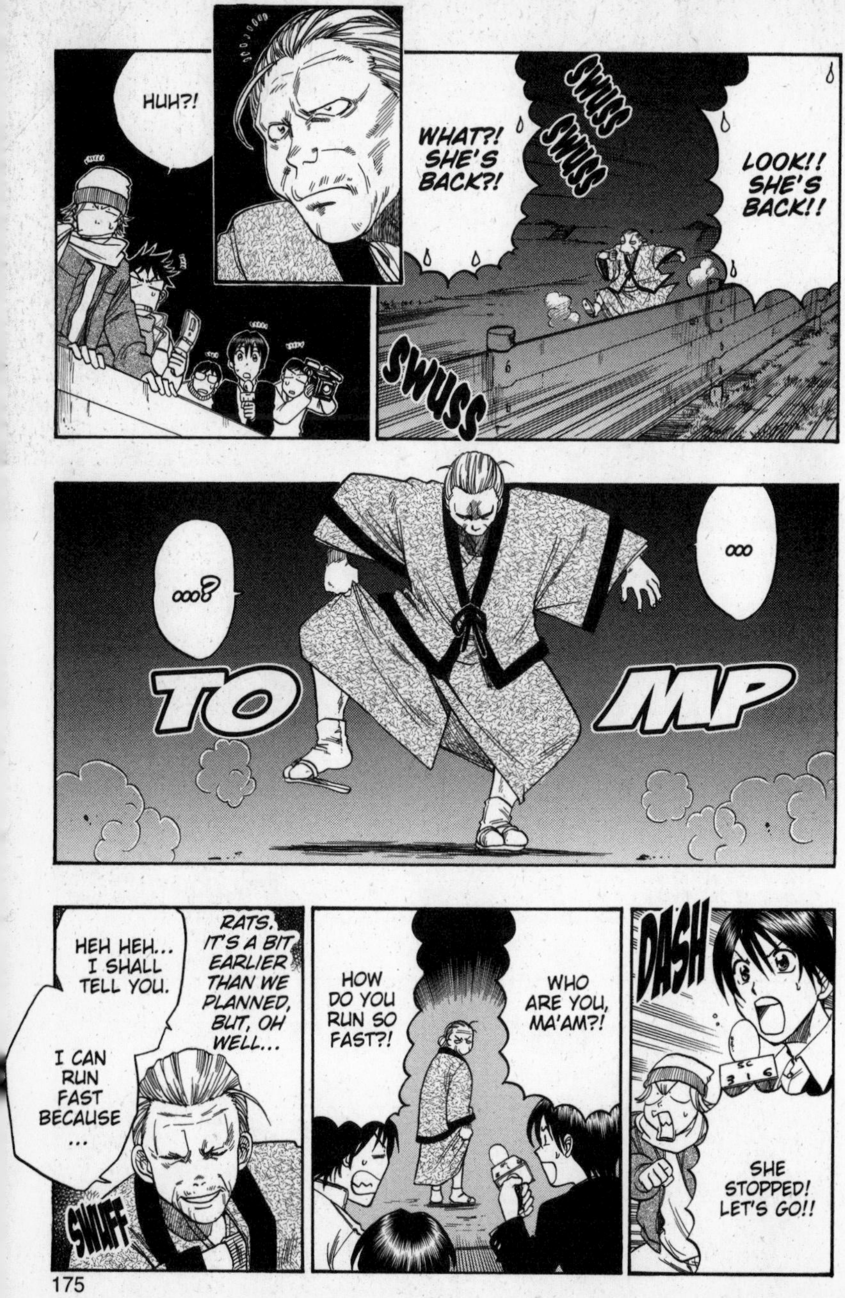
LOOK!! SHE'S BACK!!
SWUSS
SWUSS
WHAT?! SHE'S BACK?!
SWUSS
HUH?!
...
...?
TOMP
DASH
SC 316
SHE STOPPED! LET'S GO!!
WHO ARE YOU, MA'AM?!
HOW DO YOU RUN SO FAST?!
RATS. IT'S A BIT EARLIER THAN WE PLANNED, BUT, OH WELL...
HEH HEH... I SHALL TELL YOU.
I CAN RUN FAST BECAUSE ...
SWUFF

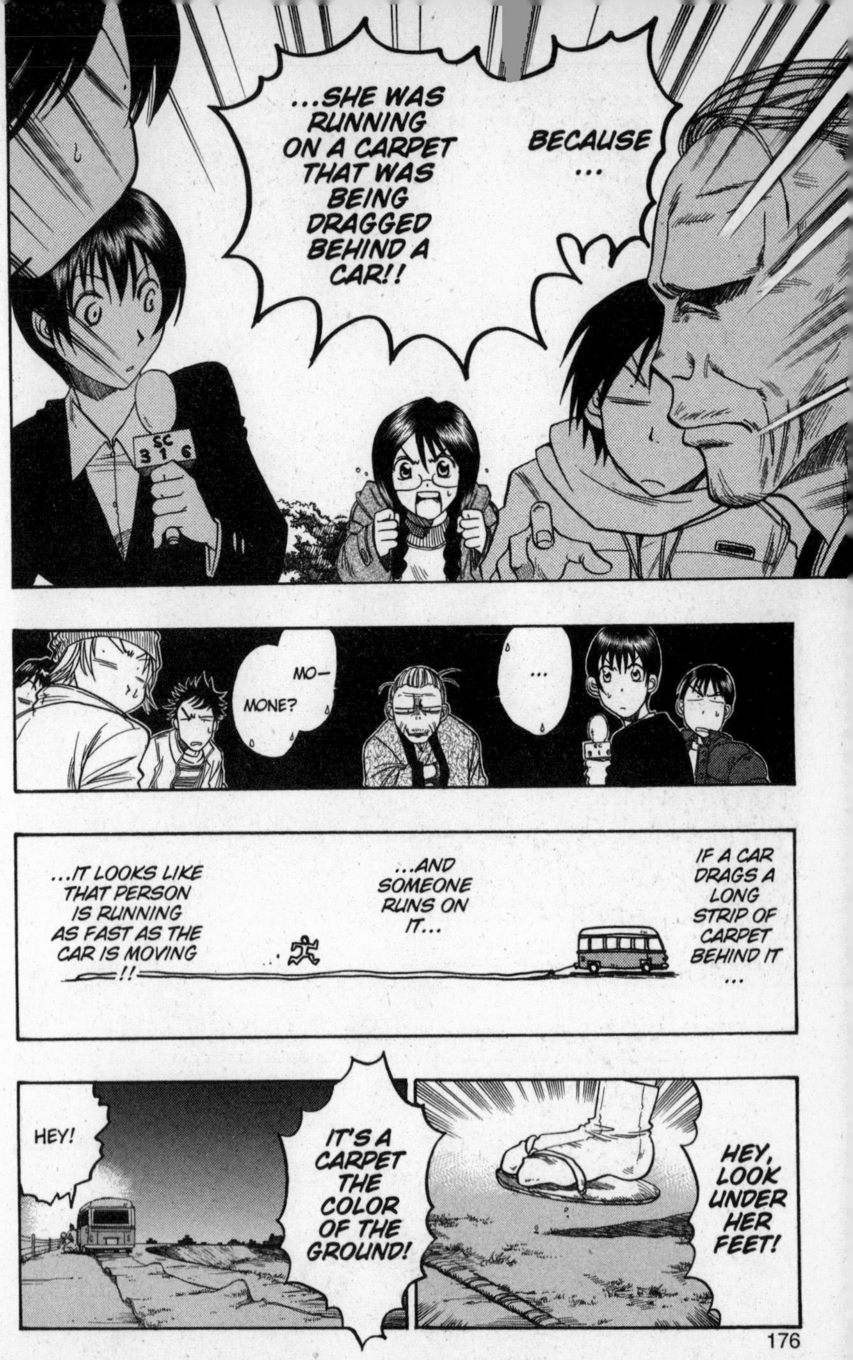
BECAUSE ...
...SHE WAS RUNNING ON A CARPET THAT WAS BEING DRAGGED BEHIND A CAR!!
...
MO-MONE?
IF A CAR DRAGS A LONG STRIP OF CARPET BEHIND IT ...
...AND SOMEONE RUNS ON IT...
...IT LOOKS LIKE THAT PERSON IS RUNNING AS FAST AS THE CAR IS MOVING!!
HEY, LOOK UNDER HER FEET!
IT'S A CARPET THE COLOR OF THE GROUND!
HEY!

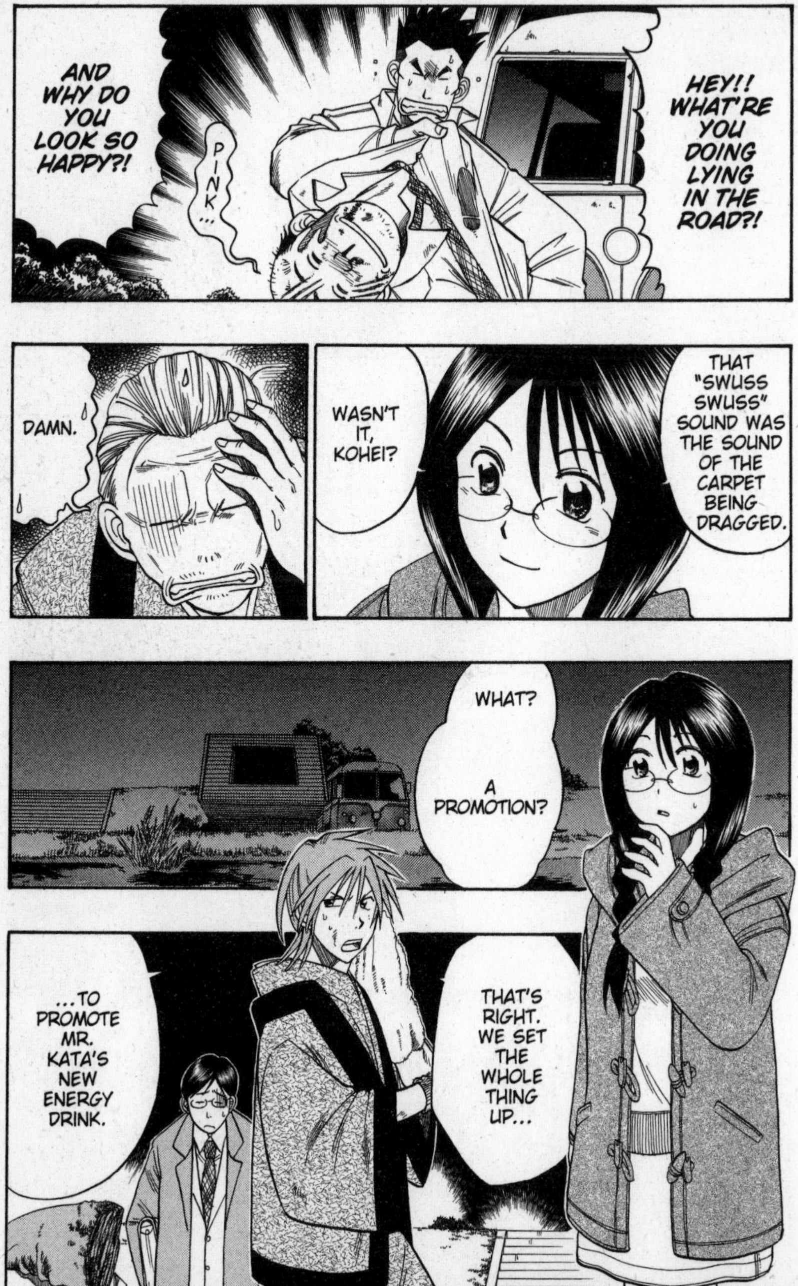
HEY!! WHAT'RE YOU DOING LYING IN THE ROAD?!
PINK...
AND WHY DO YOU LOOK SO HAPPY?!
THAT "SWUSS SWUSS" SOUND WAS THE SOUND OF THE CARPET BEING DRAGGED.
WASN'T IT, KOHEI?
DAMN.
WHAT?
A PROMOTION?
THAT'S RIGHT. WE SET THE WHOLE THING UP...
...TO PROMOTE MR. KATA'S NEW ENERGY DRINK.

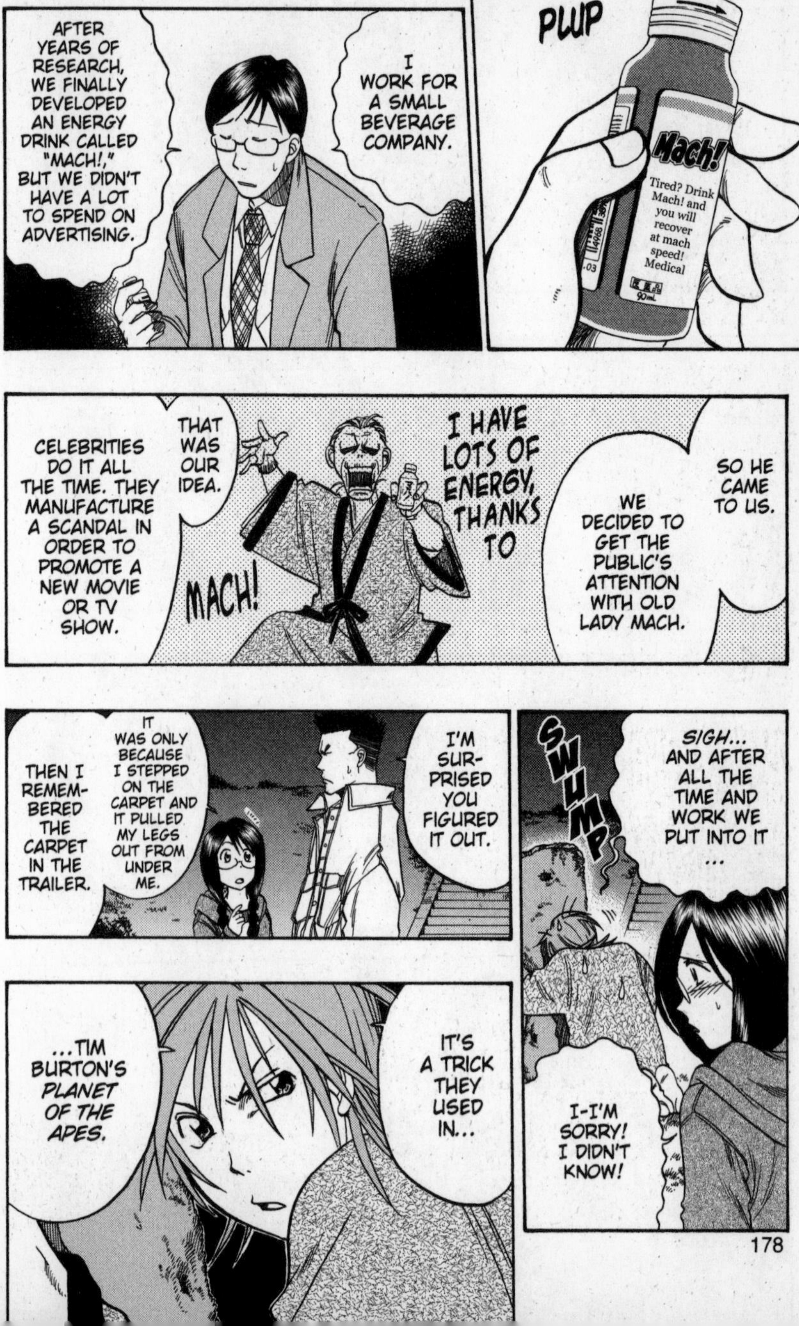
PLUP
Mach!
Tired? Drink Mach! and you will recover at mach speed! Medical
90mL
I WORK FOR A SMALL BEVERAGE COMPANY.
AFTER YEARS OF RESEARCH, WE FINALLY DEVELOPED AN ENERGY DRINK CALLED "MACH!," BUT WE DIDN'T HAVE A LOT TO SPEND ON ADVERTISING.
SO HE CAME TO US.
WE DECIDED TO GET THE PUBLIC'S ATTENTION WITH OLD LADY MACH.
I HAVE LOTS OF ENERGY, THANKS TO MACH!
THAT WAS OUR IDEA.
CELEBRITIES DO IT ALL THE TIME. THEY MANUFACTURE A SCANDAL IN ORDER TO PROMOTE A NEW MOVIE OR TV SHOW.
SWUMP
SIGH... AND AFTER ALL THE TIME AND WORK WE PUT INTO IT...
I-I'M SORRY! I DIDN'T KNOW!
I'M SURPRISED YOU FIGURED IT OUT.
IT WAS ONLY BECAUSE I STEPPED ON THE CARPET AND IT PULLED MY LEGS OUT FROM UNDER ME.
THEN I REMEMBERED THE CARPET IN THE TRAILER.
IT'S A TRICK THEY USED IN...
...TIM BURTON'S *PLANET OF THE APES*.

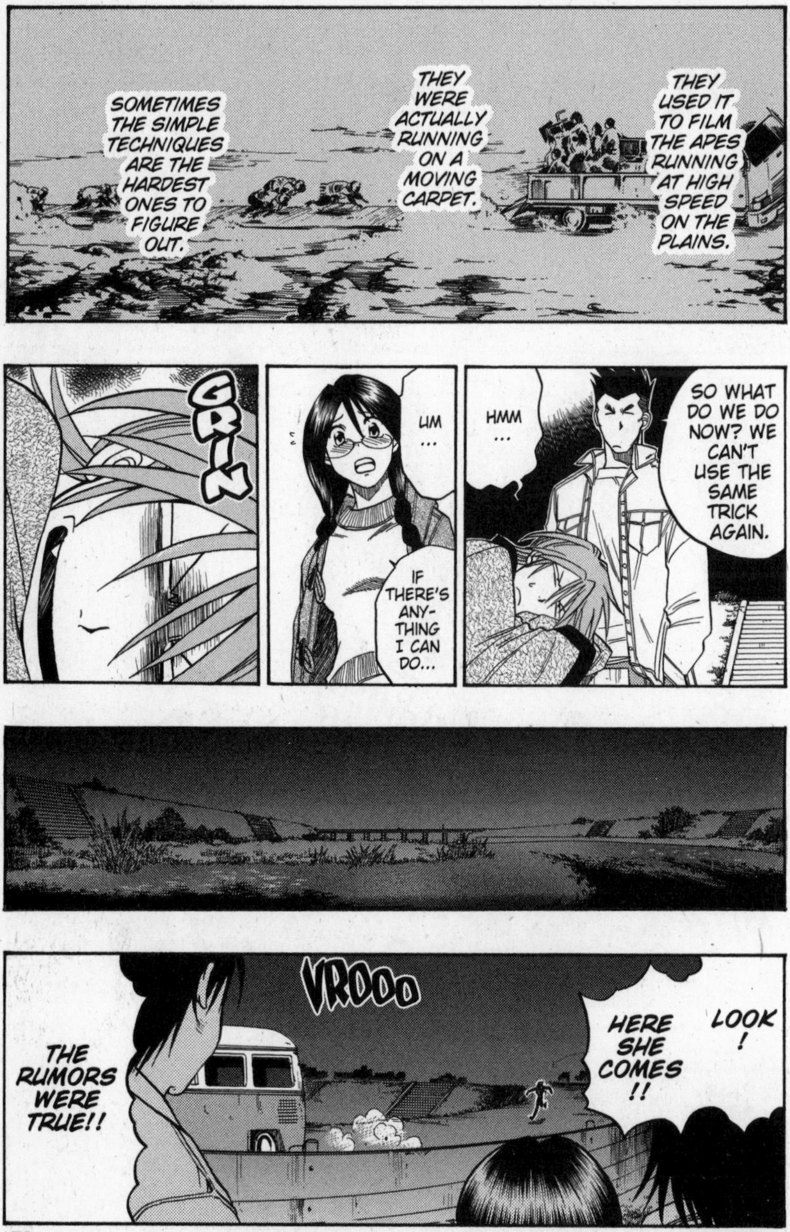
THEY USED IT TO FILM THE APES RUNNING AT HIGH SPEED ON THE PLAINS.
THEY WERE ACTUALLY RUNNING ON A MOVING CARPET.
SOMETIMES THE SIMPLE TECHNIQUES ARE THE HARDEST ONES TO FIGURE OUT.
SO WHAT DO WE DO NOW? WE CAN'T USE THE SAME TRICK AGAIN.
HMM ...
UM ...
IF THERE'S ANYTHING I CAN DO...
GRIN
LOOK!
HERE SHE COMES!!
VROOO
THE RUMORS WERE TRUE!!

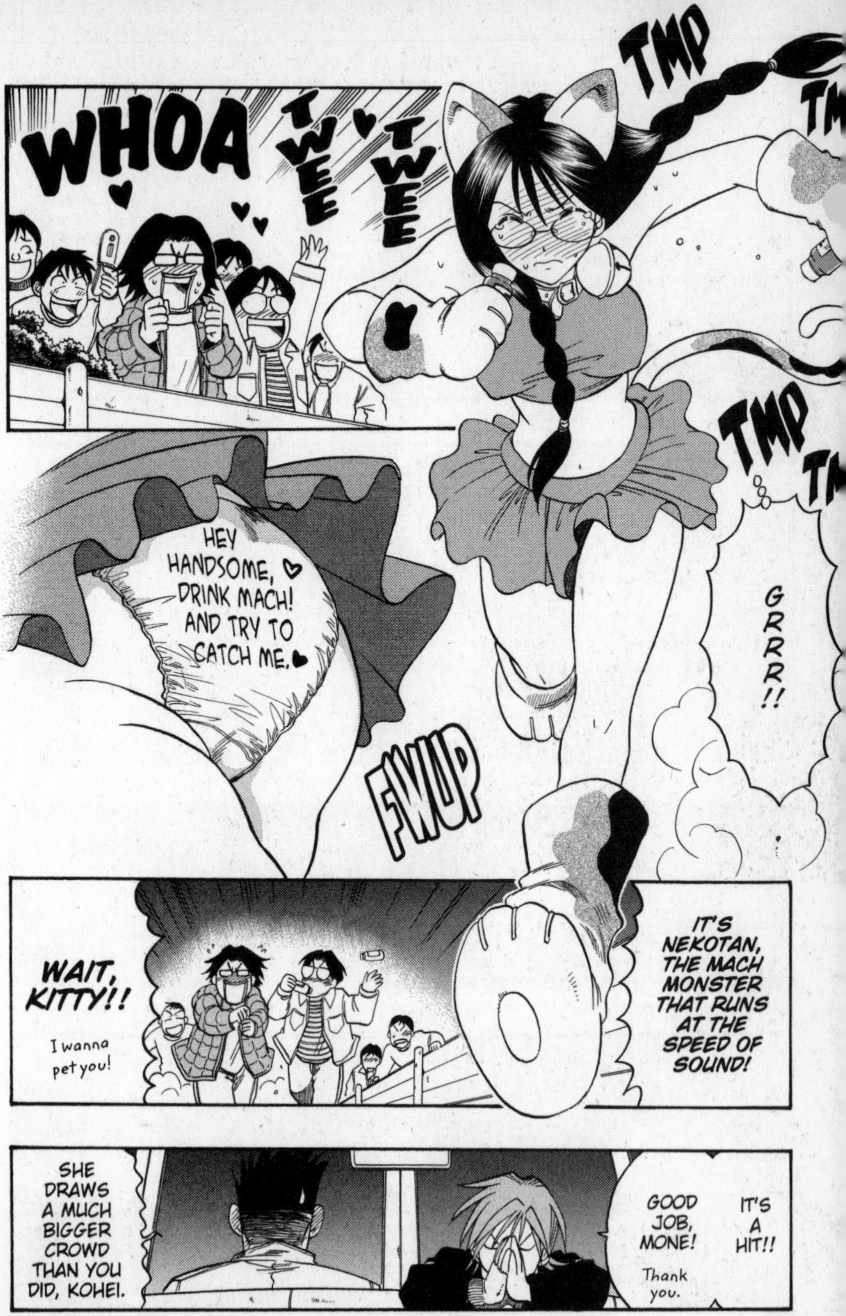
TMP
TM
TMP
TM
GRRR!!
WHOA
TWEE TWEE
HEY HANDSOME, ♡ DRINK MACH! AND TRY TO CATCH ME. ♥
FWUP
IT'S NEKOTAN, THE MACH MONSTER THAT RUNS AT THE SPEED OF SOUND!
WAIT, KITTY!!
I wanna pet you!
IT'S A HIT!!
GOOD JOB, MONE!
Thank you.
SHE DRAWS A MUCH BIGGER CROWD THAN YOU DID, KOHEI.

Scene 45: My Favorite Things (Part 1)

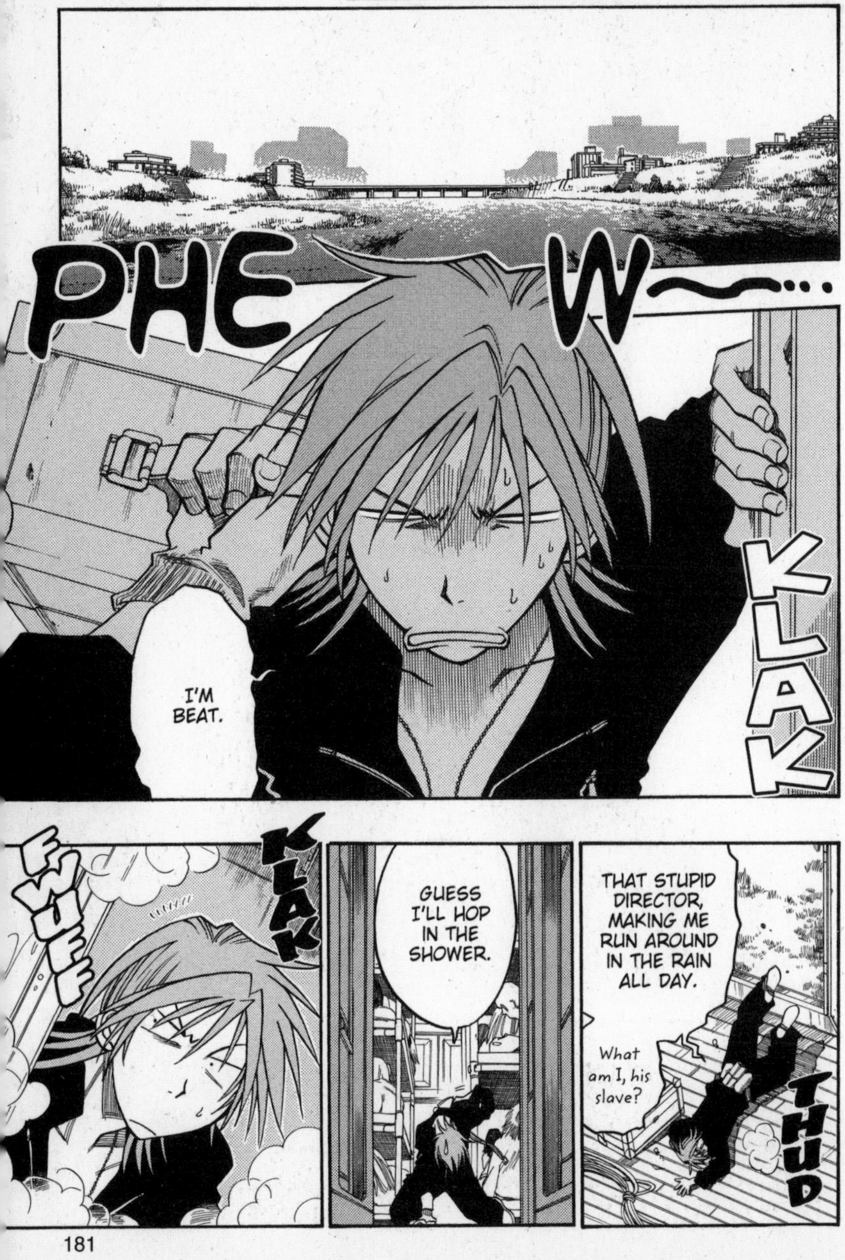
PHEW~~...
I'M BEAT.
KLLAK
THAT STUPID DIRECTOR, MAKING ME RUN AROUND IN THE RAIN ALL DAY.
What am I, his slave?
THUD
GUESS I'LL HOP IN THE SHOWER.
KLAK
FWUFF

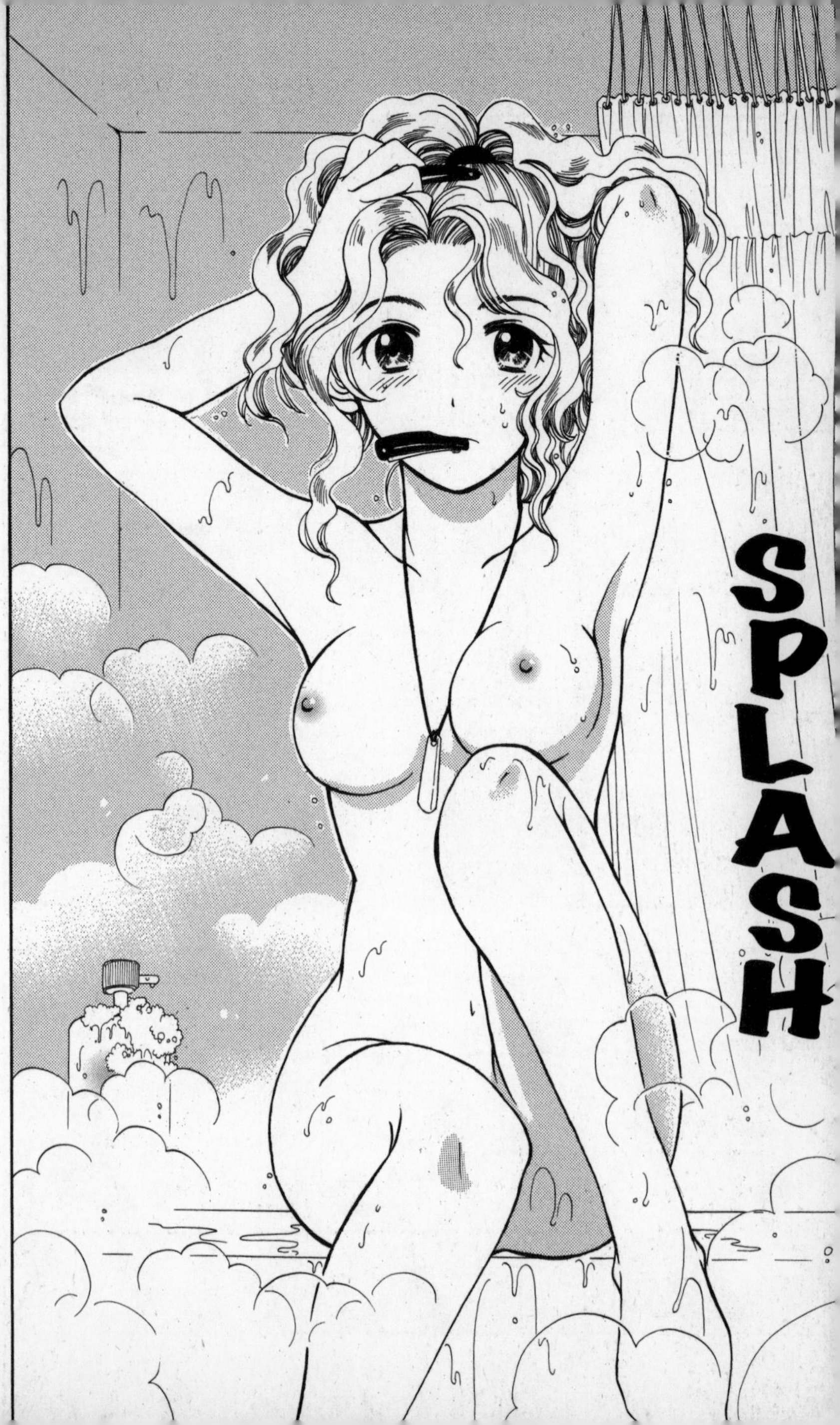
SPLASH

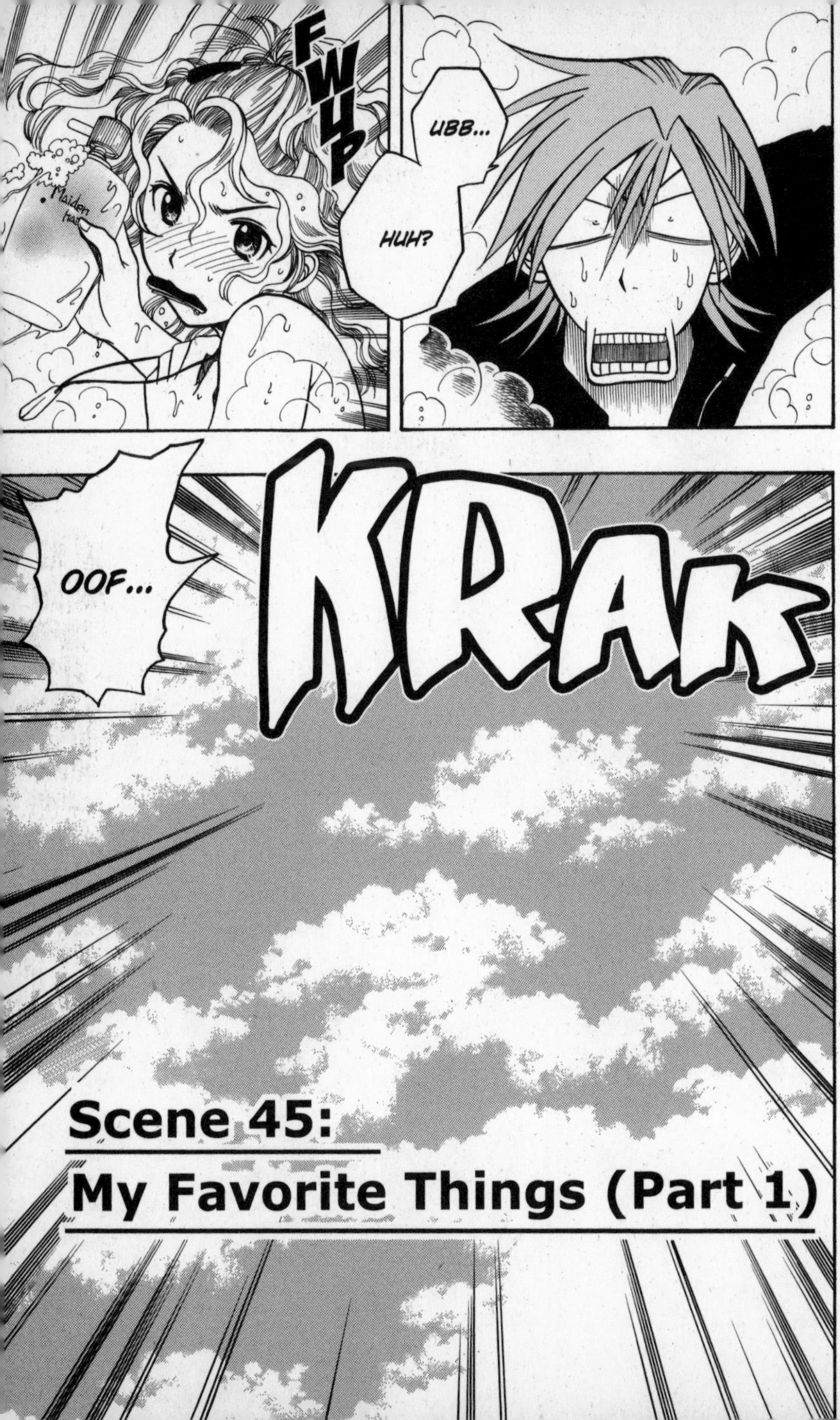
UBB...
HUH?
FWUP
KRAK
OOF...

Scene 45: My Favorite Things (Part 1)

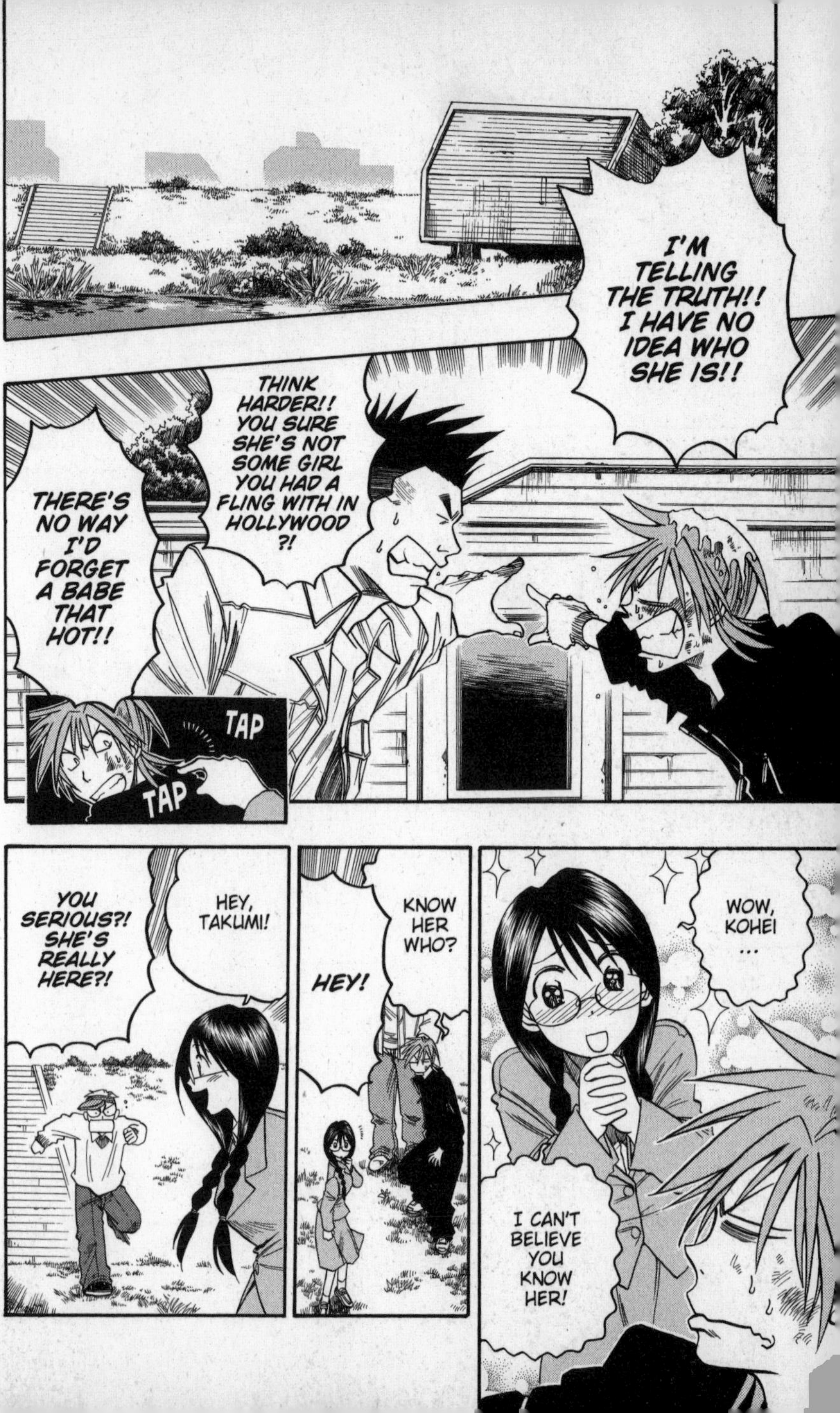
I'M TELLING THE TRUTH!! I HAVE NO IDEA WHO SHE IS!!
THINK HARDER!! YOU SURE SHE'S NOT SOME GIRL YOU HAD A FLING WITH IN HOLLYWOOD ?!
THERE'S NO WAY I'D FORGET A BABE THAT HOT!!
TAP
TAP
WOW, KOHEI ...
I CAN'T BELIEVE YOU KNOW HER!
KNOW HER WHO?
HEY!
HEY, TAKUMI!
YOU SERIOUS?! SHE'S REALLY HERE?!

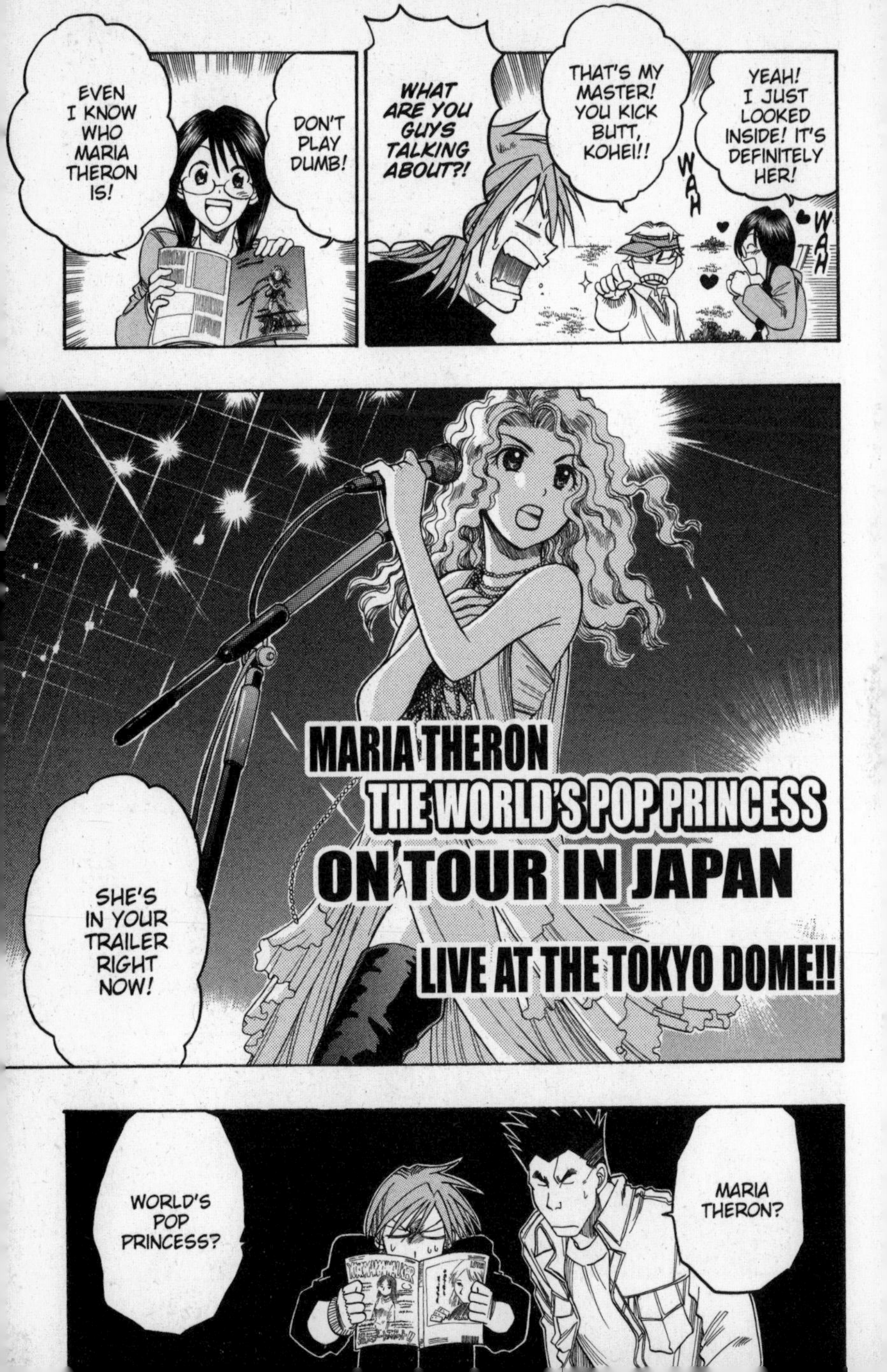
YEAH! I JUST LOOKED INSIDE! IT'S DEFINITELY HER!
WAH
WAH
THAT'S MY MASTER! YOU KICK BUTT, KOHEI!!
WHAT ARE YOU GUYS TALKING ABOUT?!
DON'T PLAY DUMB!
EVEN I KNOW WHO MARIA THERON IS!
MARIA THERON
THE WORLD'S POP PRINCESS
ON TOUR IN JAPAN
LIVE AT THE TOKYO DOME!!
SHE'S IN YOUR TRAILER RIGHT NOW!
MARIA THERON?
WORLD'S POP PRINCESS?

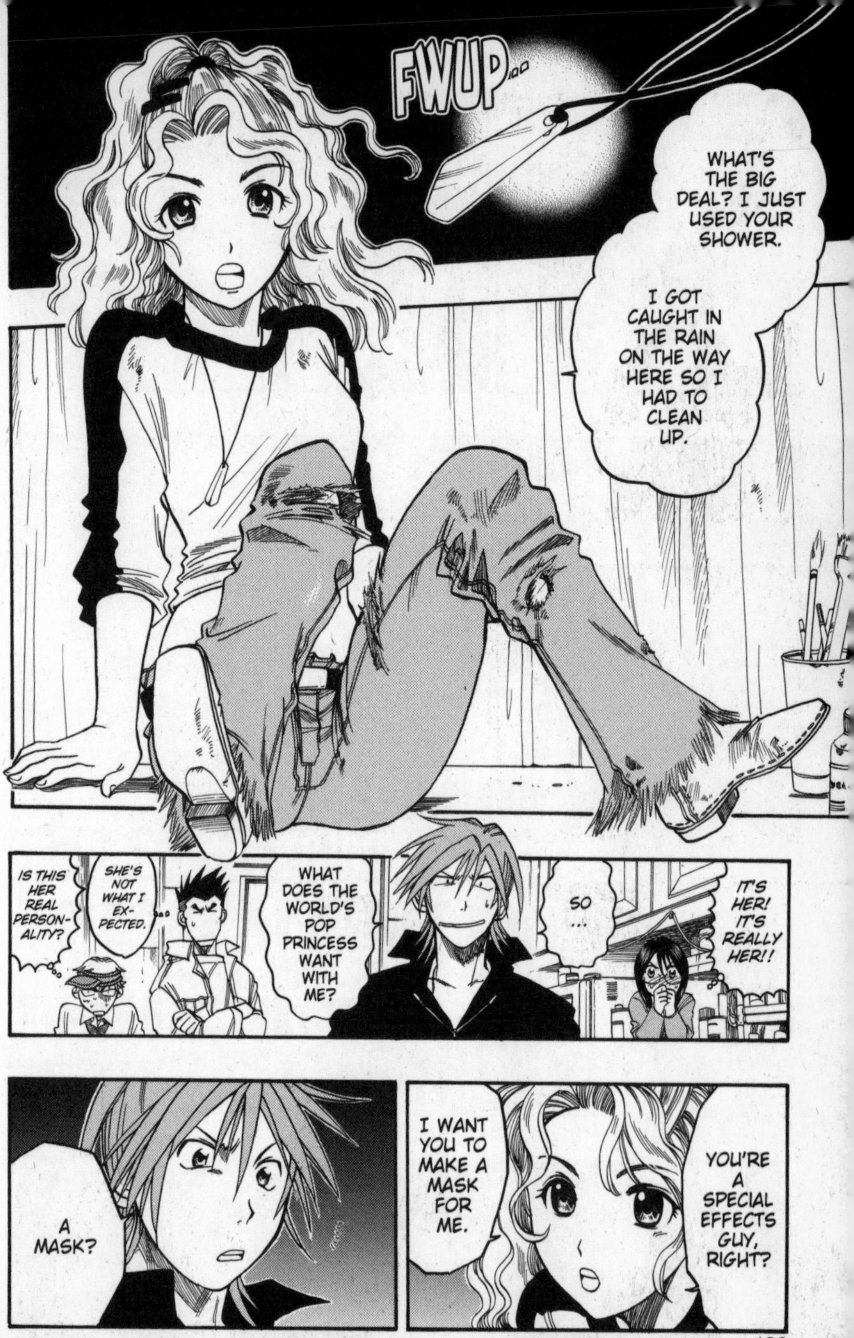
FWUP
WHAT'S THE BIG DEAL? I JUST USED YOUR SHOWER.
I GOT CAUGHT IN THE RAIN ON THE WAY HERE SO I HAD TO CLEAN UP.
IT'S HER! IT'S REALLY HER!!
SO ...
WHAT DOES THE WORLD'S POP PRINCESS WANT WITH ME?
SHE'S NOT WHAT I EX-PECTED.
IS THIS HER REAL PERSON-ALITY?
YOU'RE A SPECIAL EFFECTS GUY, RIGHT?
I WANT YOU TO MAKE A MASK FOR ME.
A MASK?

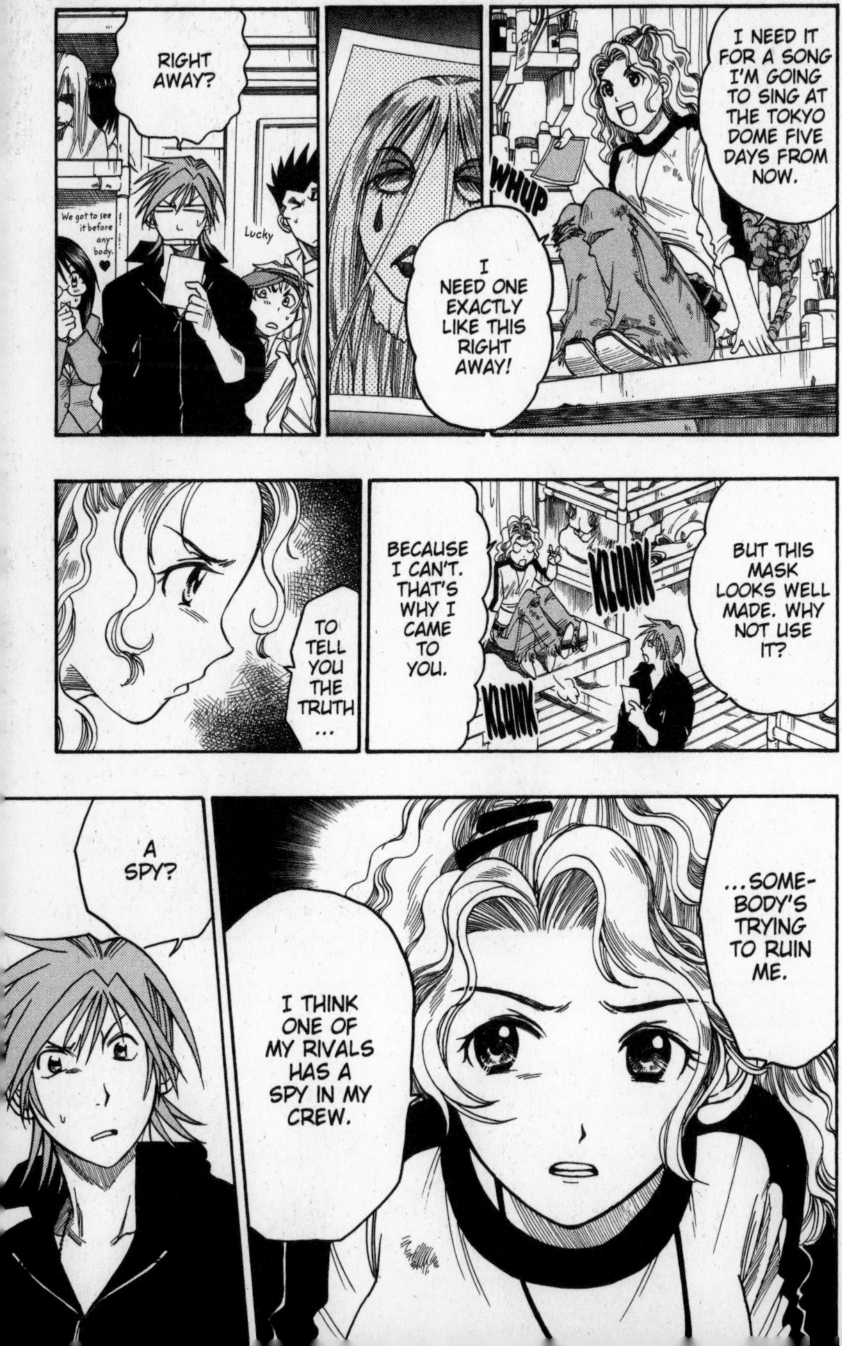
I NEED IT FOR A SONG I'M GOING TO SING AT THE TOKYO DOME FIVE DAYS FROM NOW.
WHUP
I NEED ONE EXACTLY LIKE THIS RIGHT AWAY!
RIGHT AWAY?
Lucky
We got to see it before anybody. ♥
BUT THIS MASK LOOKS WELL MADE. WHY NOT USE IT?
KLUNK
KLUNK
BECAUSE I CAN'T. THAT'S WHY I CAME TO YOU.
TO TELL YOU THE TRUTH ...
...SOMEBODY'S TRYING TO RUIN ME.
I THINK ONE OF MY RIVALS HAS A SPY IN MY CREW.
A SPY?

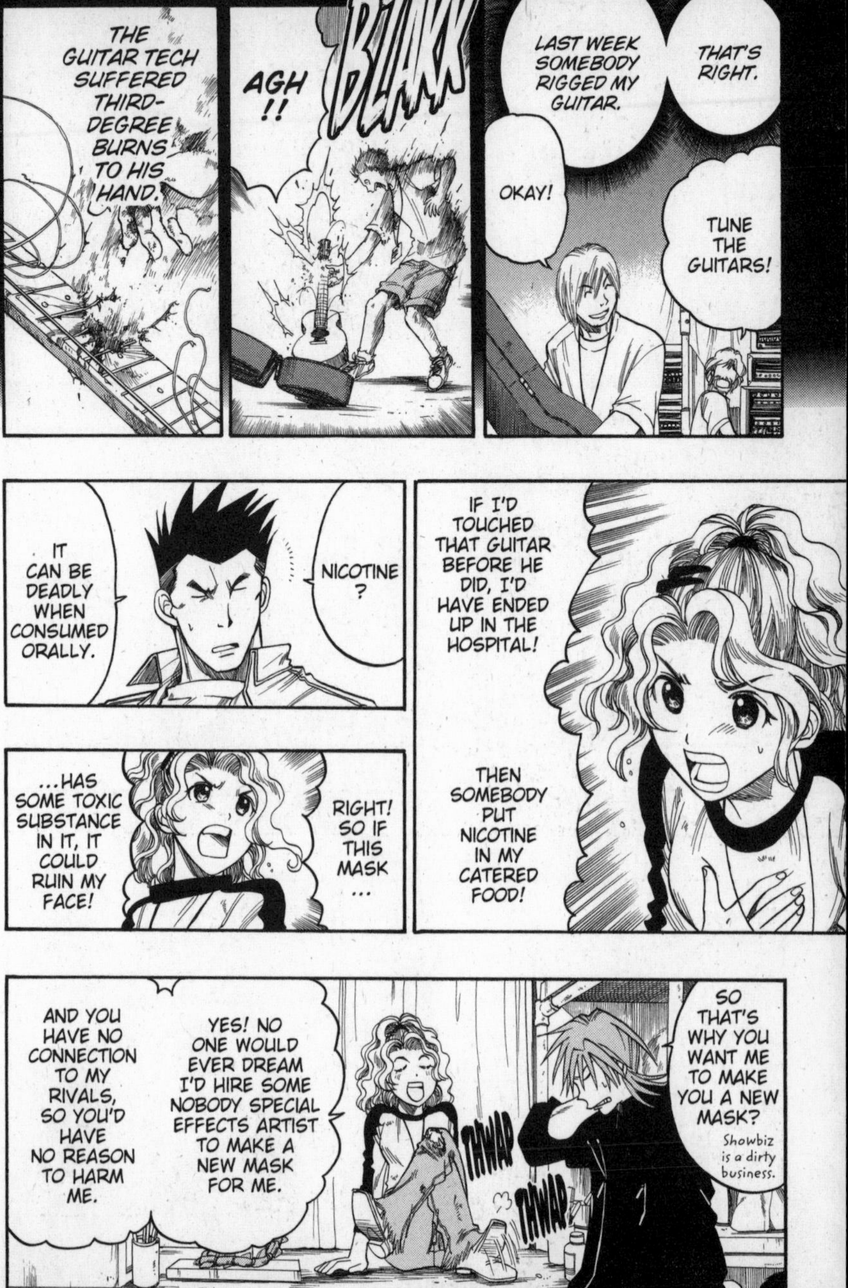
THAT'S RIGHT.
LAST WEEK SOMEBODY RIGGED MY GUITAR.
TUNE THE GUITARS!
OKAY!
BZAKK
AGH!!
THE GUITAR TECH SUFFERED THIRD-DEGREE BURNS TO HIS HAND.
IF I'D TOUCHED THAT GUITAR BEFORE HE DID, I'D HAVE ENDED UP IN THE HOSPITAL!
THEN SOMEBODY PUT NICOTINE IN MY CATERED FOOD!
NICOTINE?
IT CAN BE DEADLY WHEN CONSUMED ORALLY.
RIGHT! SO IF THIS MASK...
...HAS SOME TOXIC SUBSTANCE IN IT, IT COULD RUIN MY FACE!
SO THAT'S WHY YOU WANT ME TO MAKE YOU A NEW MASK?
Showbiz is a dirty business.
THWAP
THWAP
YES! NO ONE WOULD EVER DREAM I'D HIRE SOME NOBODY SPECIAL EFFECTS ARTIST TO MAKE A NEW MASK FOR ME.
AND YOU HAVE NO CONNECTION TO MY RIVALS, SO YOU'D HAVE NO REASON TO HARM ME.

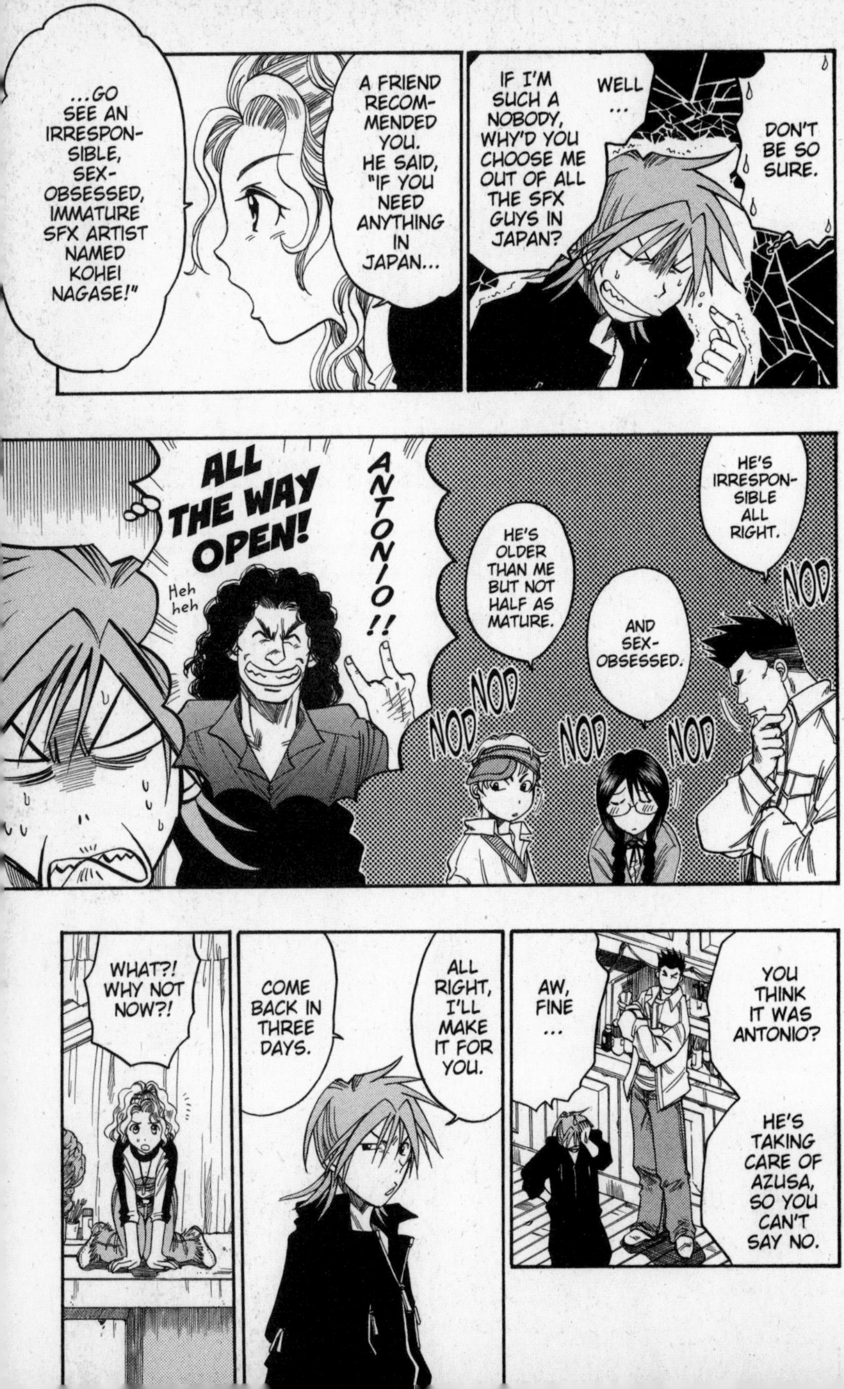
DON'T BE SO SURE.
WELL ...
IF I'M SUCH A NOBODY, WHY'D YOU CHOOSE ME OUT OF ALL THE SFX GUYS IN JAPAN?
A FRIEND RECOMMENDED YOU. HE SAID, "IF YOU NEED ANYTHING IN JAPAN...
...GO SEE AN IRRESPONSIBLE, SEX-OBSESSED, IMMATURE SFX ARTIST NAMED KOHEI NAGASE!"
HE'S IRRESPONSIBLE ALL RIGHT.
NOD
HE'S OLDER THAN ME BUT NOT HALF AS MATURE.
AND SEX-OBSESSED.
NOD
NOD
NOD NOD
ANTONIO!!
ALL THE WAY OPEN!
Heh heh
YOU THINK IT WAS ANTONIO?
HE'S TAKING CARE OF AZUSA, SO YOU CAN'T SAY NO.
AW, FINE ...
ALL RIGHT, I'LL MAKE IT FOR YOU.
COME BACK IN THREE DAYS.
WHAT?! WHY NOT NOW?!

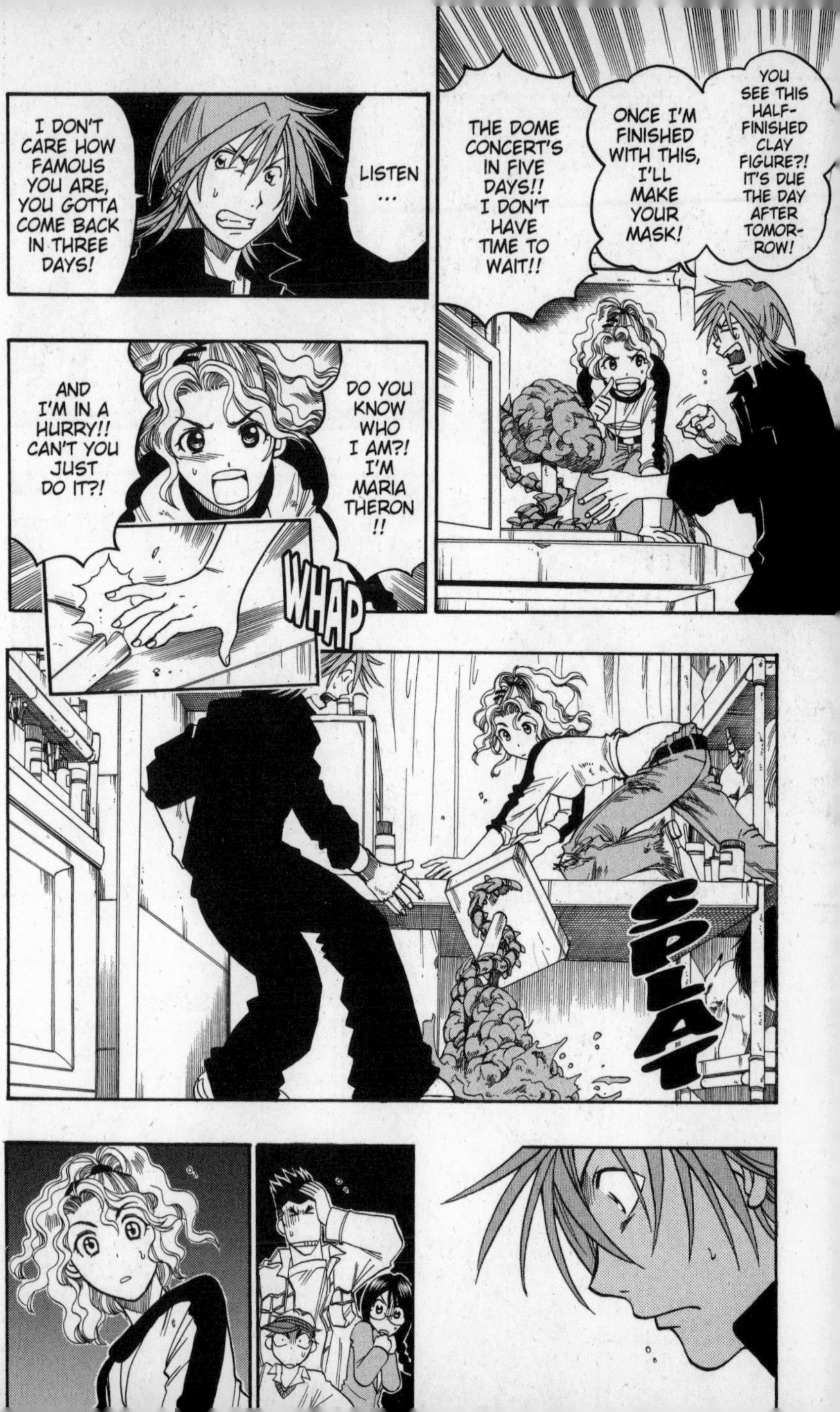
YOU SEE THIS HALF-FINISHED CLAY FIGURE?! IT'S DUE THE DAY AFTER TOMORROW!
ONCE I'M FINISHED WITH THIS, I'LL MAKE YOUR MASK!
THE DOME CONCERT'S IN FIVE DAYS!! I DON'T HAVE TIME TO WAIT!!
LISTEN ...
I DON'T CARE HOW FAMOUS YOU ARE, YOU GOTTA COME BACK IN THREE DAYS!
DO YOU KNOW WHO I AM?! I'M MARIA THERON!!
AND I'M IN A HURRY!! CAN'T YOU JUST DO IT?!
WHAP
SPLAT

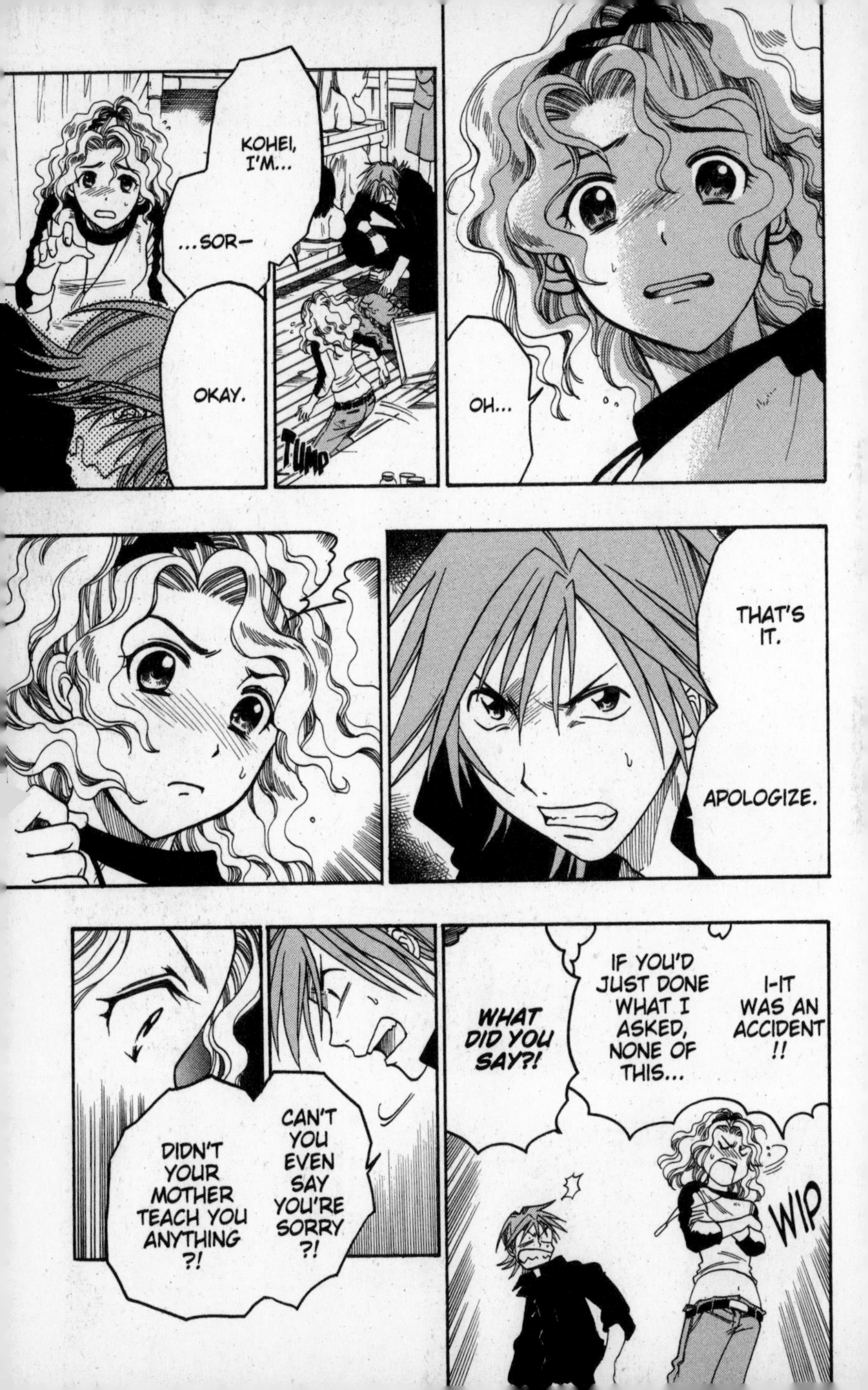

OH...
TUMP
KOHEI, I'M...
...SOR—
OKAY.
THAT'S IT.
APOLOGIZE.
I-IT WAS AN ACCIDENT !!
IF YOU'D JUST DONE WHAT I ASKED, NONE OF THIS...
WHAT DID YOU SAY?!
WIP
CAN'T YOU EVEN SAY YOU'RE SORRY ?!
DIDN'T YOUR MOTHER TEACH YOU ANYTHING ?!

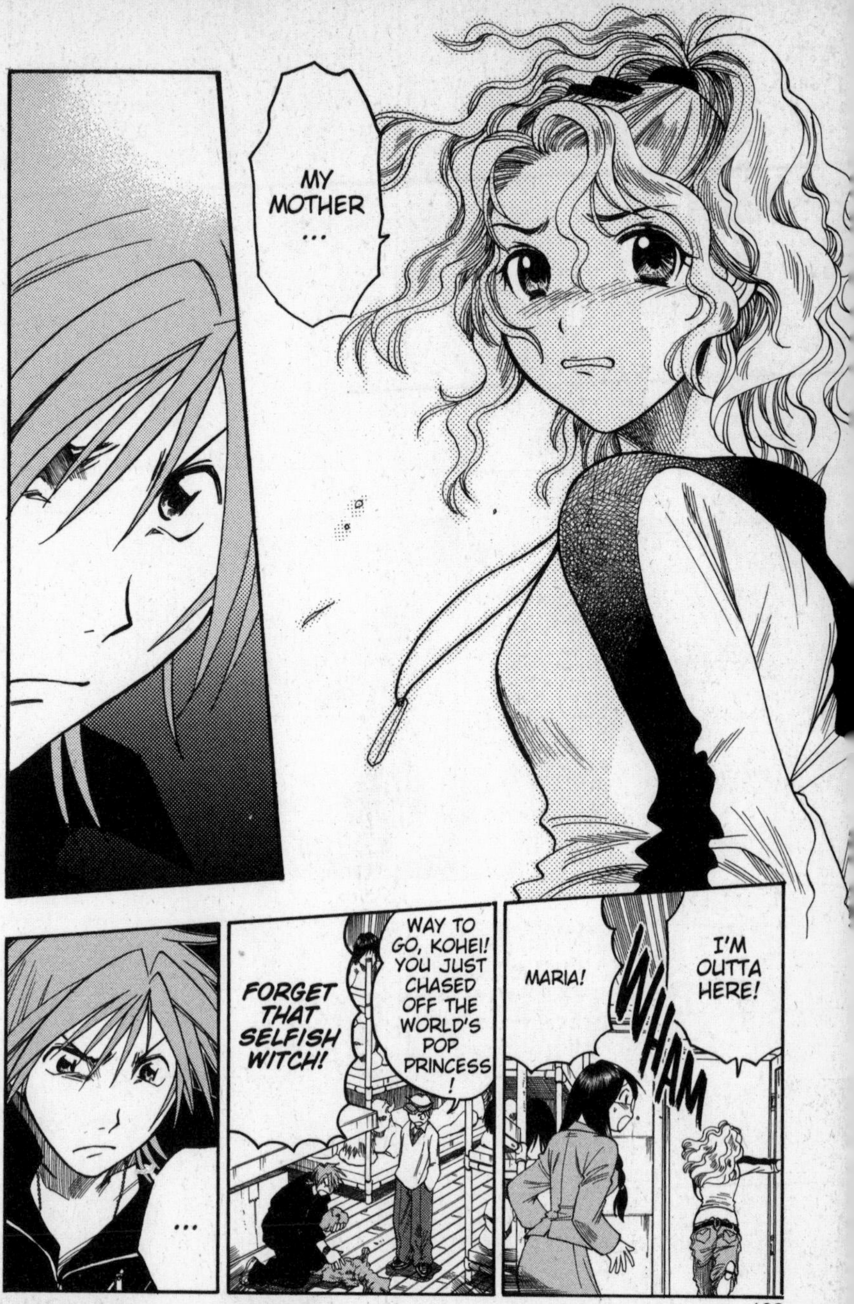
MY MOTHER ...
I'M OUTTA HERE!
WHAM
MARIA!
WAY TO GO, KOHEI! YOU JUST CHASED OFF THE WORLD'S POP PRINCESS!
FORGET THAT SELFISH WITCH!
...

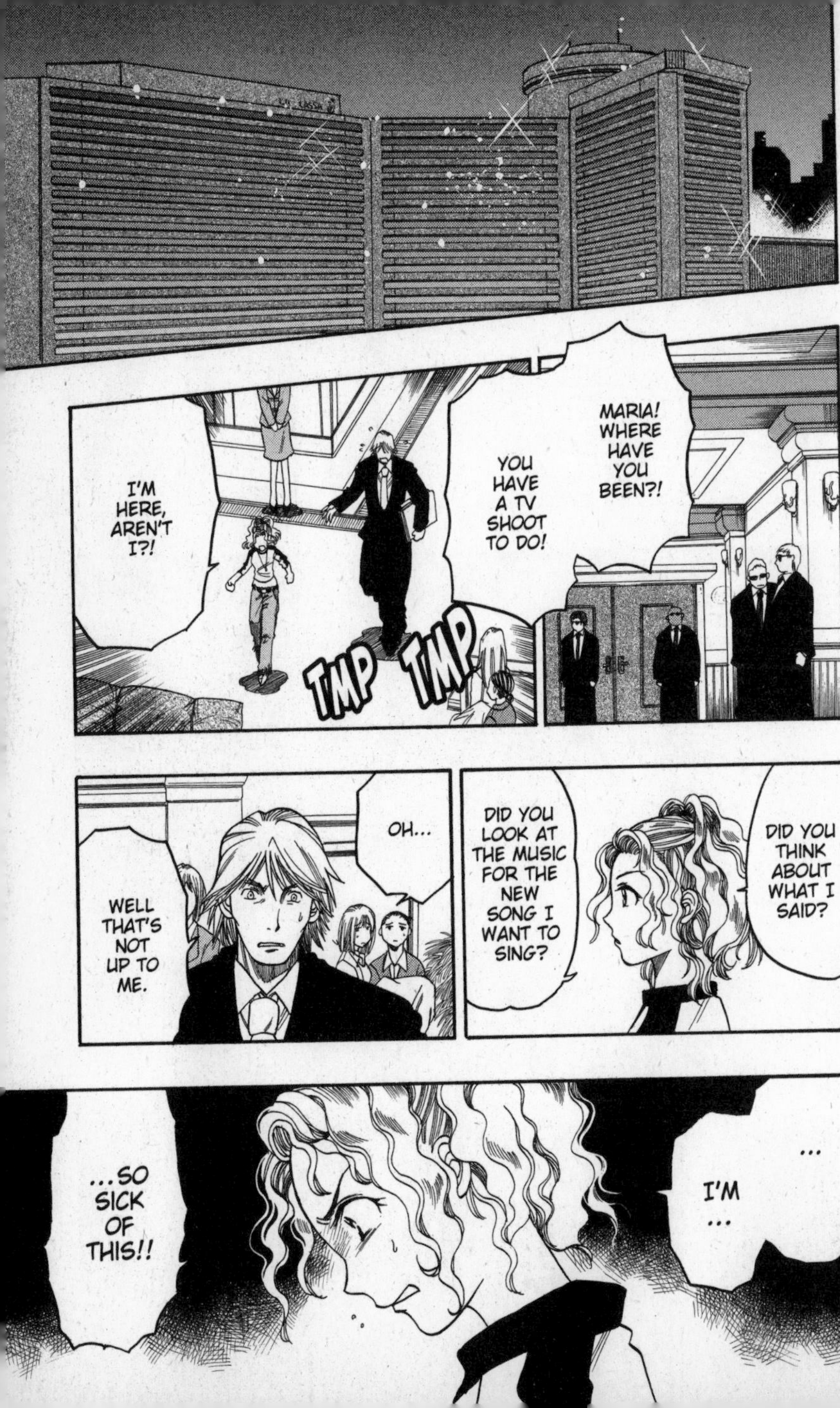
MARIA! WHERE HAVE YOU BEEN?!
YOU HAVE A TV SHOOT TO DO!
TMP TMP
I'M HERE, AREN'T I?!
DID YOU THINK ABOUT WHAT I SAID?
DID YOU LOOK AT THE MUSIC FOR THE NEW SONG I WANT TO SING?
OH...
WELL THAT'S NOT UP TO ME.
... I'M ...
...SO SICK OF THIS!!

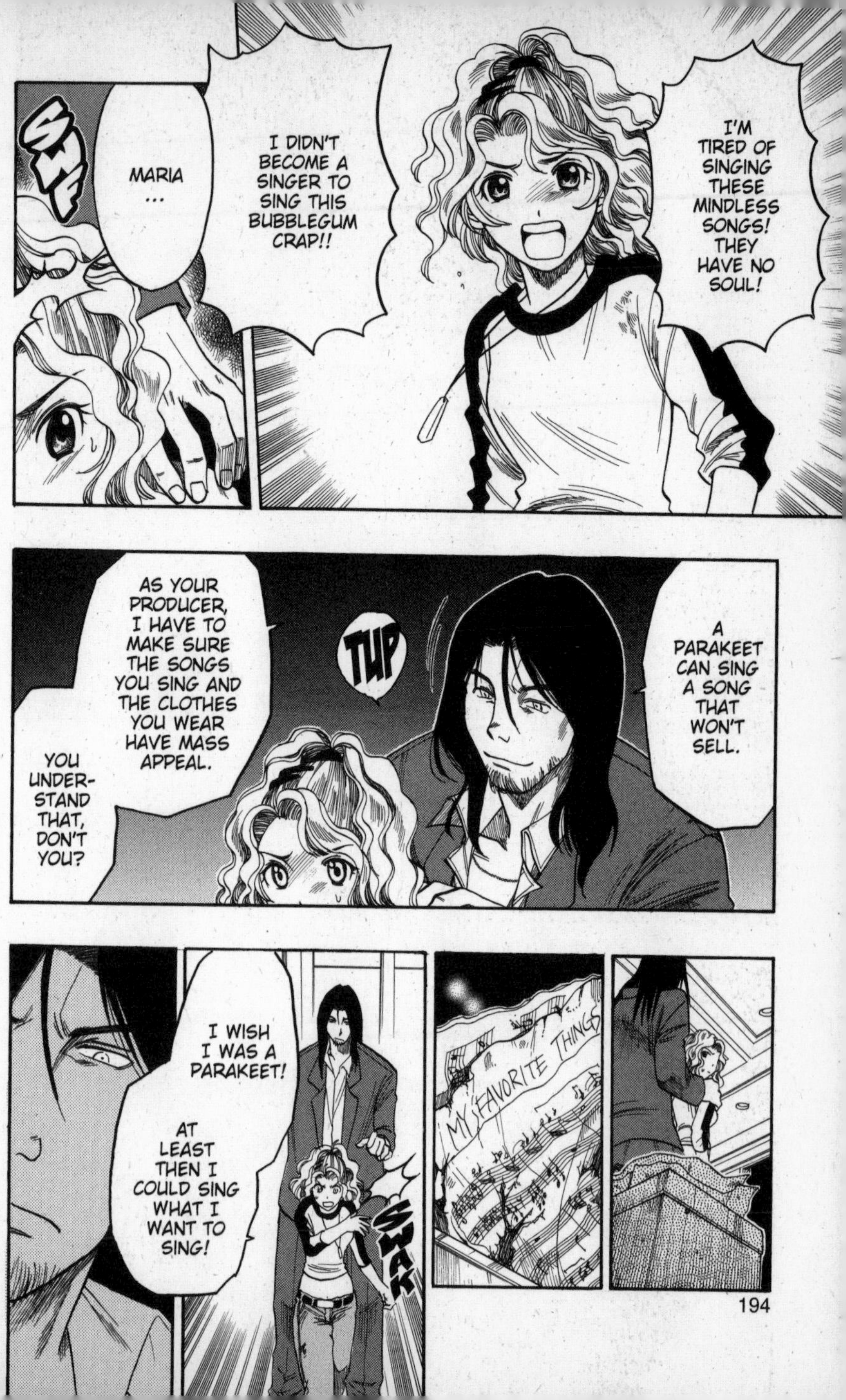
I'M TIRED OF SINGING THESE MINDLESS SONGS! THEY HAVE NO SOUL!
I DIDN'T BECOME A SINGER TO SING THIS BUBBLEGUM CRAP!!
SWF
MARIA ...
A PARAKEET CAN SING A SONG THAT WON'T SELL.
TUP
AS YOUR PRODUCER, I HAVE TO MAKE SURE THE SONGS YOU SING AND THE CLOTHES YOU WEAR HAVE MASS APPEAL.
YOU UNDERSTAND THAT, DON'T YOU?
MY FAVORITE THINGS
SWAK
I WISH I WAS A PARAKEET!
AT LEAST THEN I COULD SING WHAT I WANT TO SING!

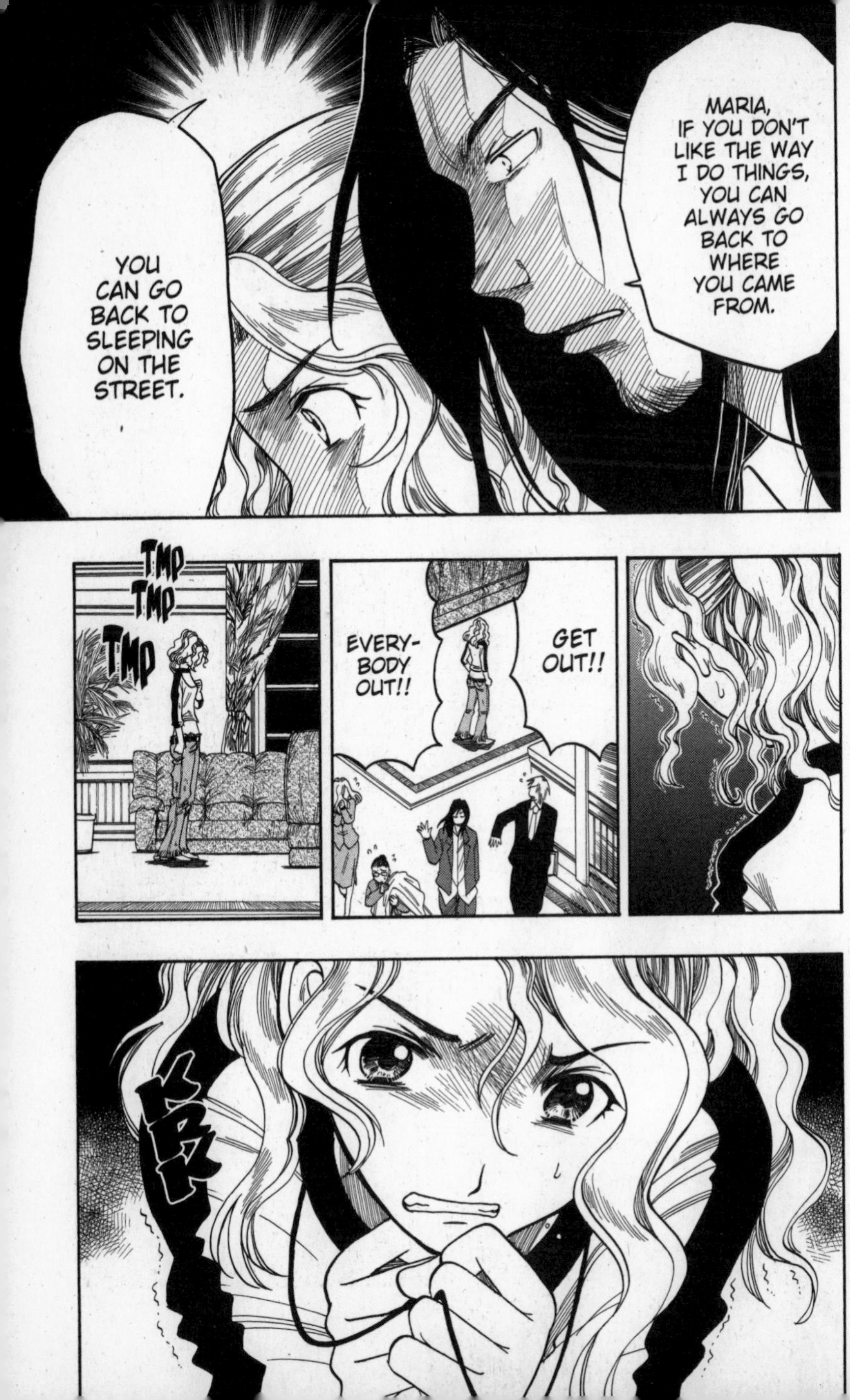
MARIA, IF YOU DON'T LIKE THE WAY I DO THINGS, YOU CAN ALWAYS GO BACK TO WHERE YOU CAME FROM.
YOU CAN GO BACK TO SLEEPING ON THE STREET.
GET OUT!!
EVERY-BODY OUT!!
TMP TMP TMP

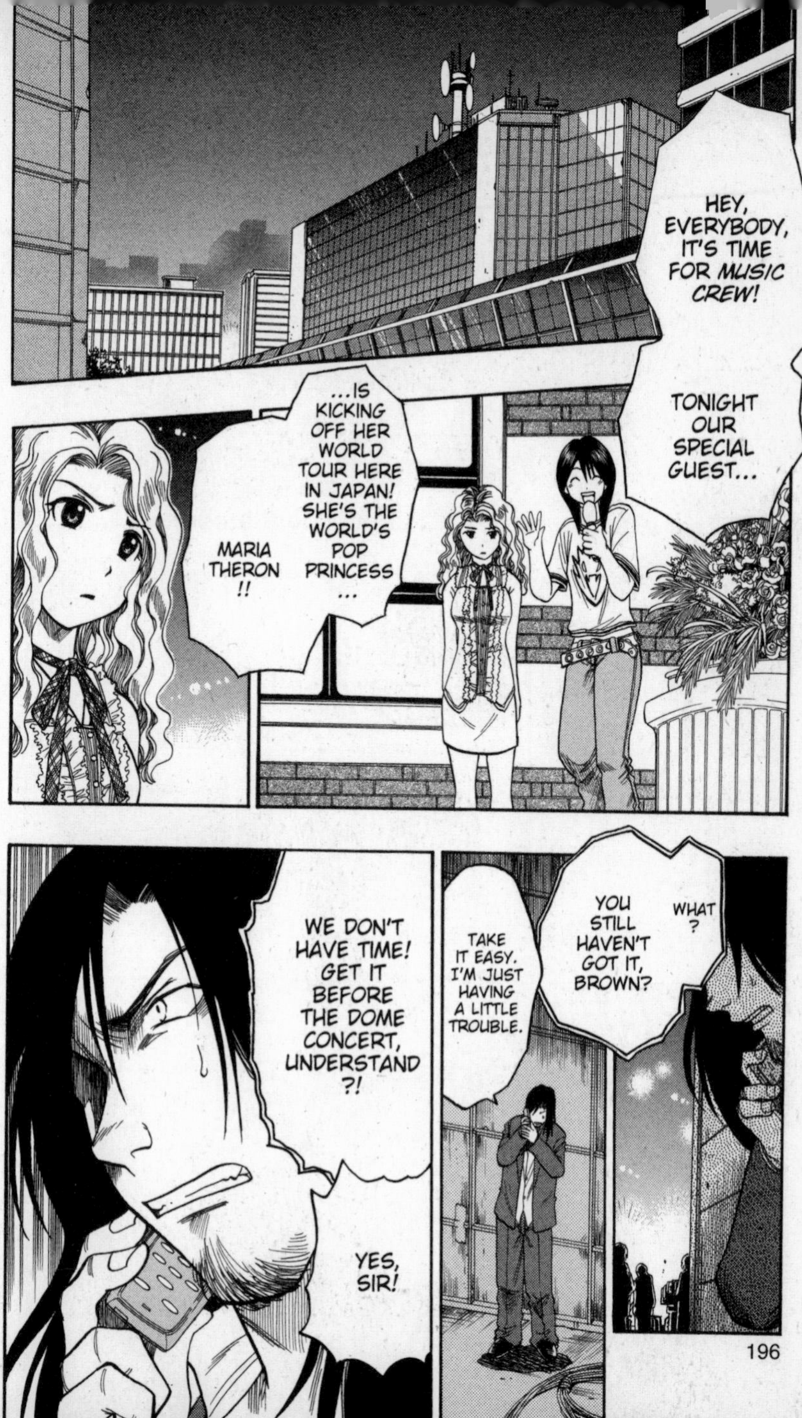
HEY, EVERYBODY, IT'S TIME FOR *MUSIC CREW!*
TONIGHT OUR SPECIAL GUEST...
...IS KICKING OFF HER WORLD TOUR HERE IN JAPAN! SHE'S THE WORLD'S POP PRINCESS...
MARIA THERON!!
WHAT?
YOU STILL HAVEN'T GOT IT, BROWN?
TAKE IT EASY. I'M JUST HAVING A LITTLE TROUBLE.
WE DON'T HAVE TIME! GET IT BEFORE THE DOME CONCERT, UNDERSTAND?!
YES, SIR!

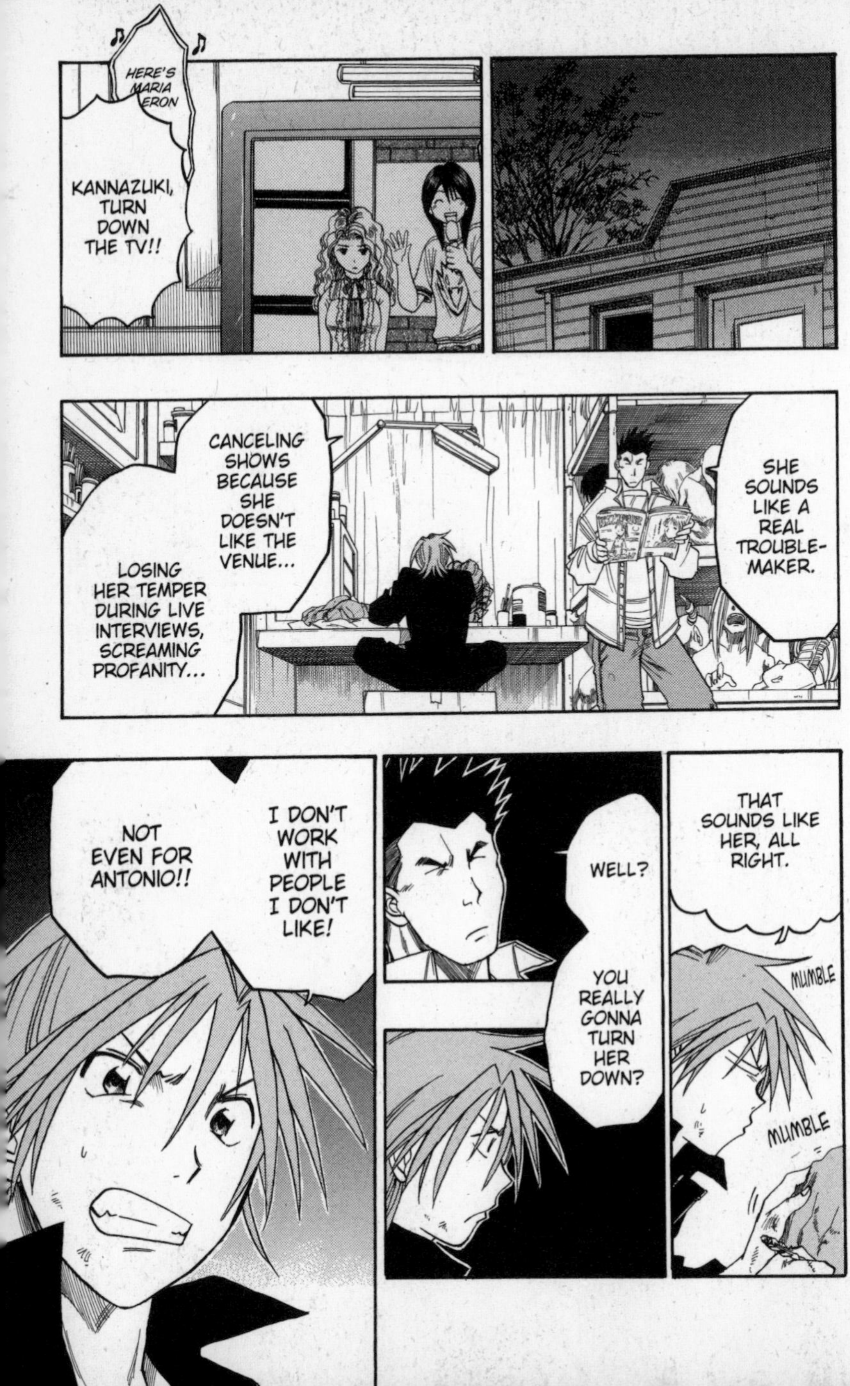
HERE'S MARIA ERON
KANNAZUKI, TURN DOWN THE TV!!
SHE SOUNDS LIKE A REAL TROUBLE-MAKER.
CANCELING SHOWS BECAUSE SHE DOESN'T LIKE THE VENUE...
LOSING HER TEMPER DURING LIVE INTERVIEWS, SCREAMING PROFANITY...
THAT SOUNDS LIKE HER, ALL RIGHT.
MUMBLE
MUMBLE
WELL?
YOU REALLY GONNA TURN HER DOWN?
I DON'T WORK WITH PEOPLE I DON'T LIKE!
NOT EVEN FOR ANTONIO!!

SWIP

SWF

Scene 46: My Favorite Things (Part 2)

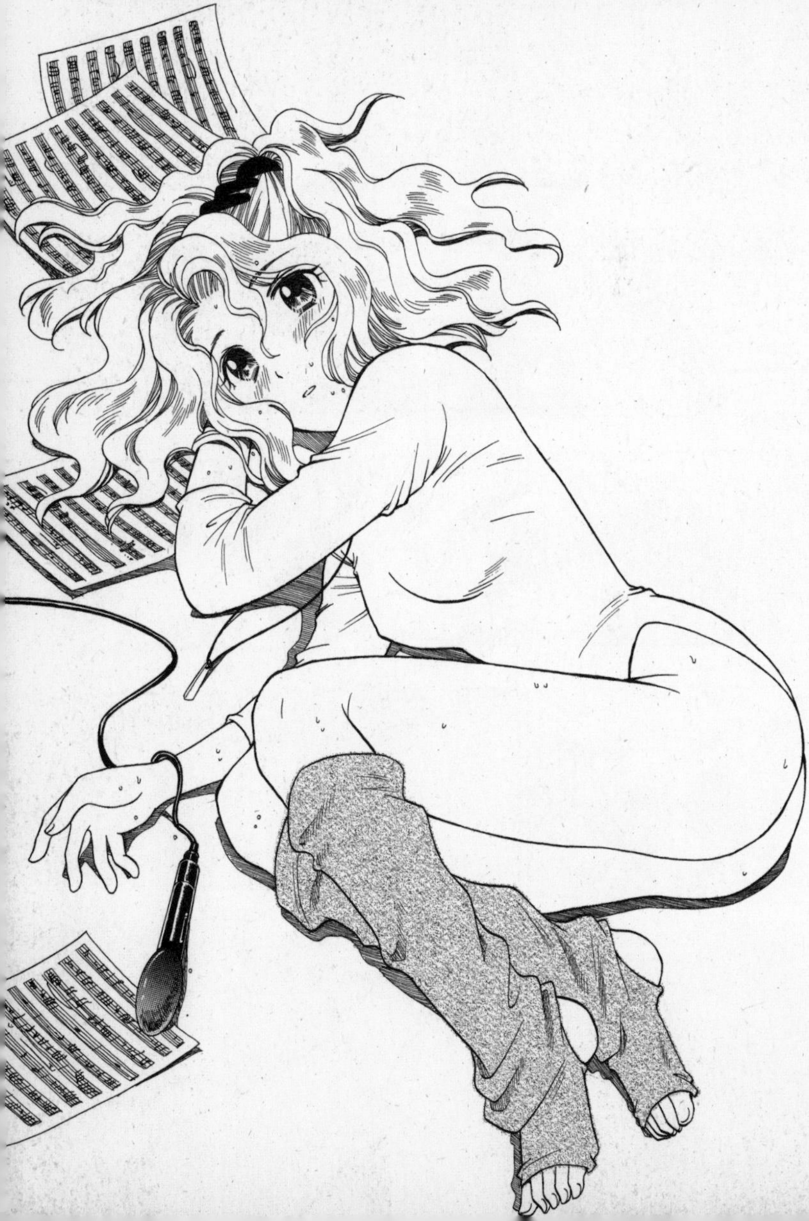

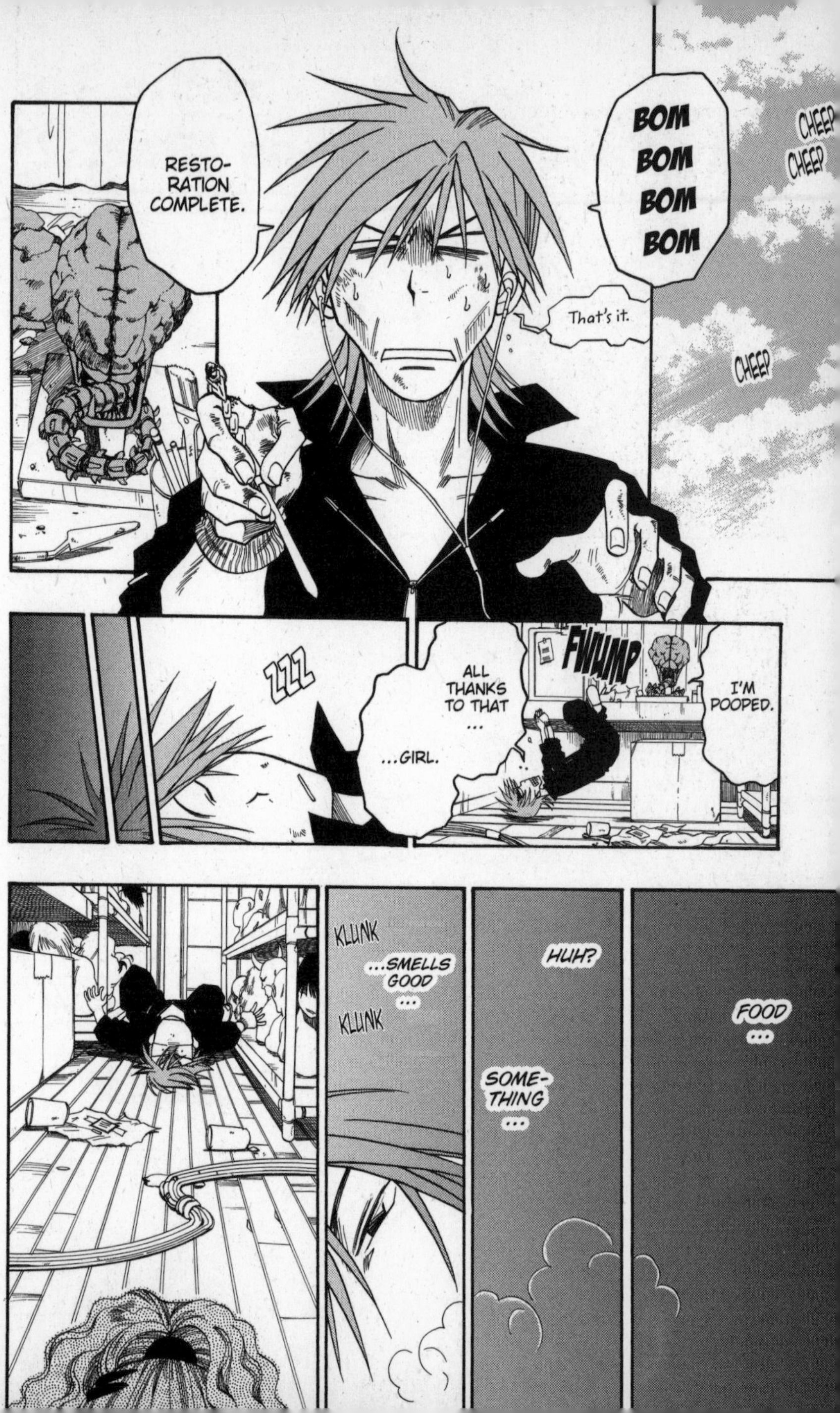
CHEEP
CHEEP
CHEEP
BOM BOM BOM BOM
That's it.
RESTO-RATION COMPLETE.
I'M POOPED.
FWUMP
ALL THANKS TO THAT ...
...GIRL.
ZZZ
FOOD ...
HUH?
SOME-THING ...
KLUNK
...SMELLS GOOD ...
KLUNK

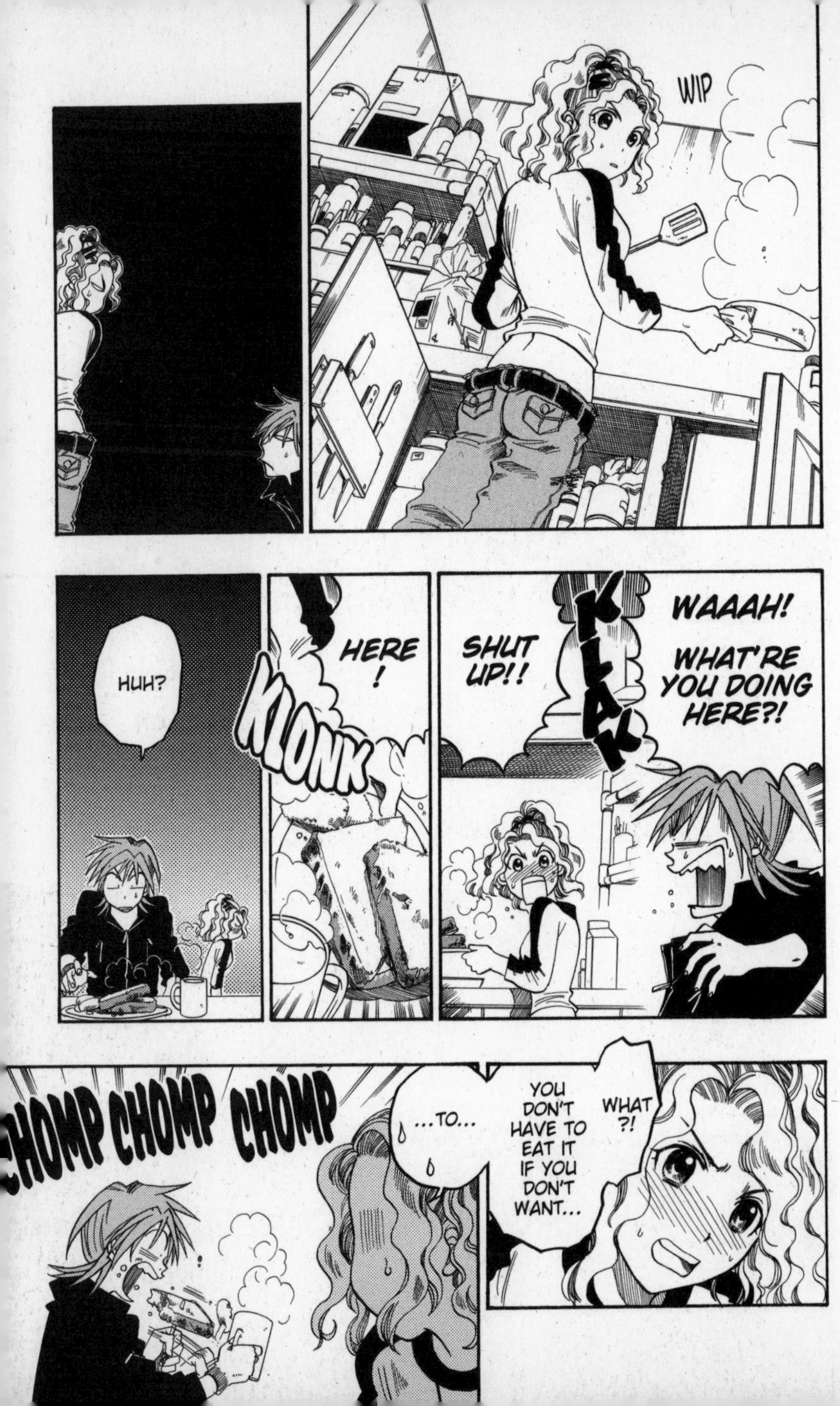
WIP
WAAAH!
WHAT'RE YOU DOING HERE?!
SHUT UP!!
KLAK
HERE!
KLONK
HUH?
WHAT?!
YOU DON'T HAVE TO EAT IT IF YOU DON'T WANT...
...TO...
CHOMP CHOMP CHOMP

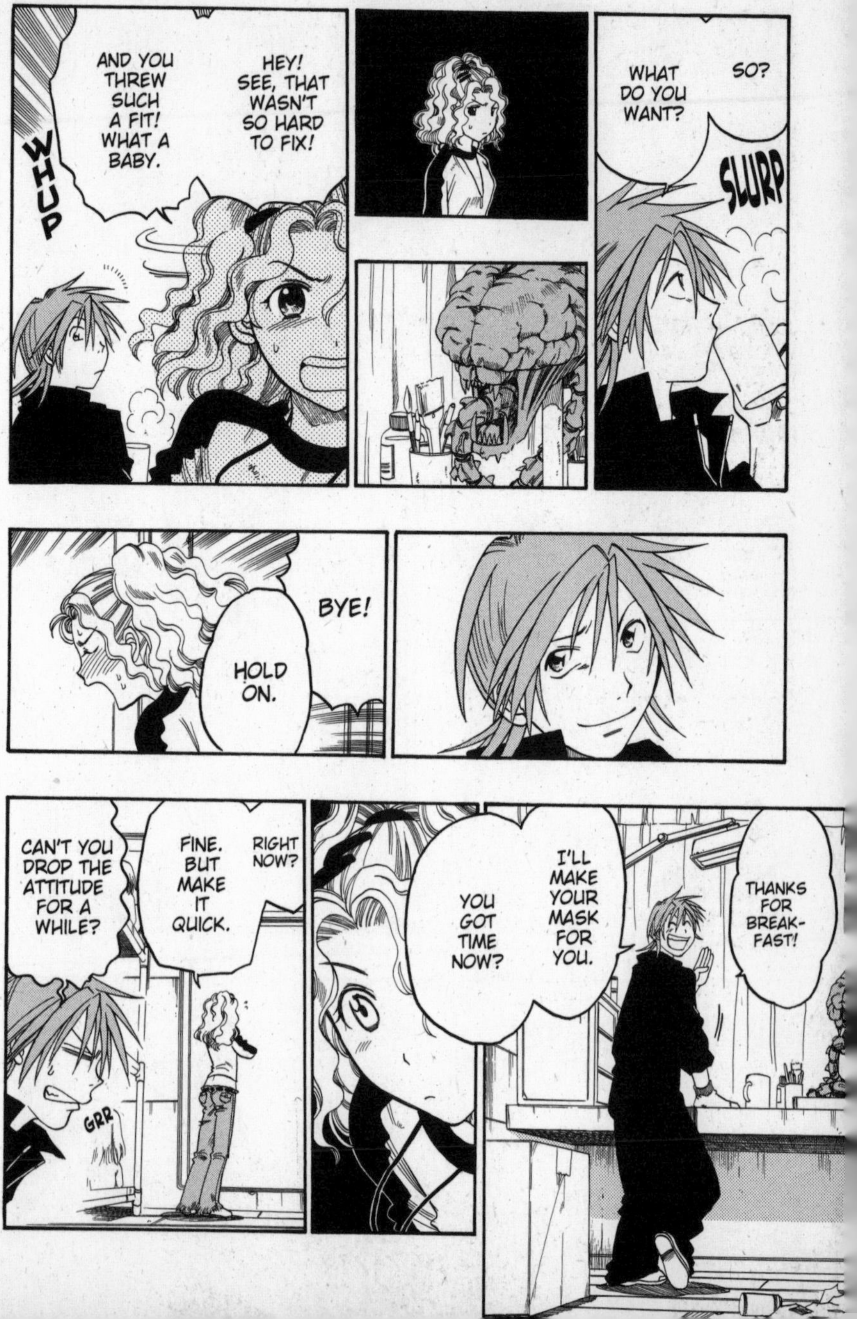
SO?
WHAT DO YOU WANT?
SLURP
HEY! SEE, THAT WASN'T SO HARD TO FIX!
AND YOU THREW SUCH A FIT! WHAT A BABY.
WHUP
BYE!
HOLD ON.
THANKS FOR BREAK-FAST!
I'LL MAKE YOUR MASK FOR YOU.
YOU GOT TIME NOW?
RIGHT NOW?
FINE. BUT MAKE IT QUICK.
CAN'T YOU DROP THE ATTITUDE FOR A WHILE?
GRR

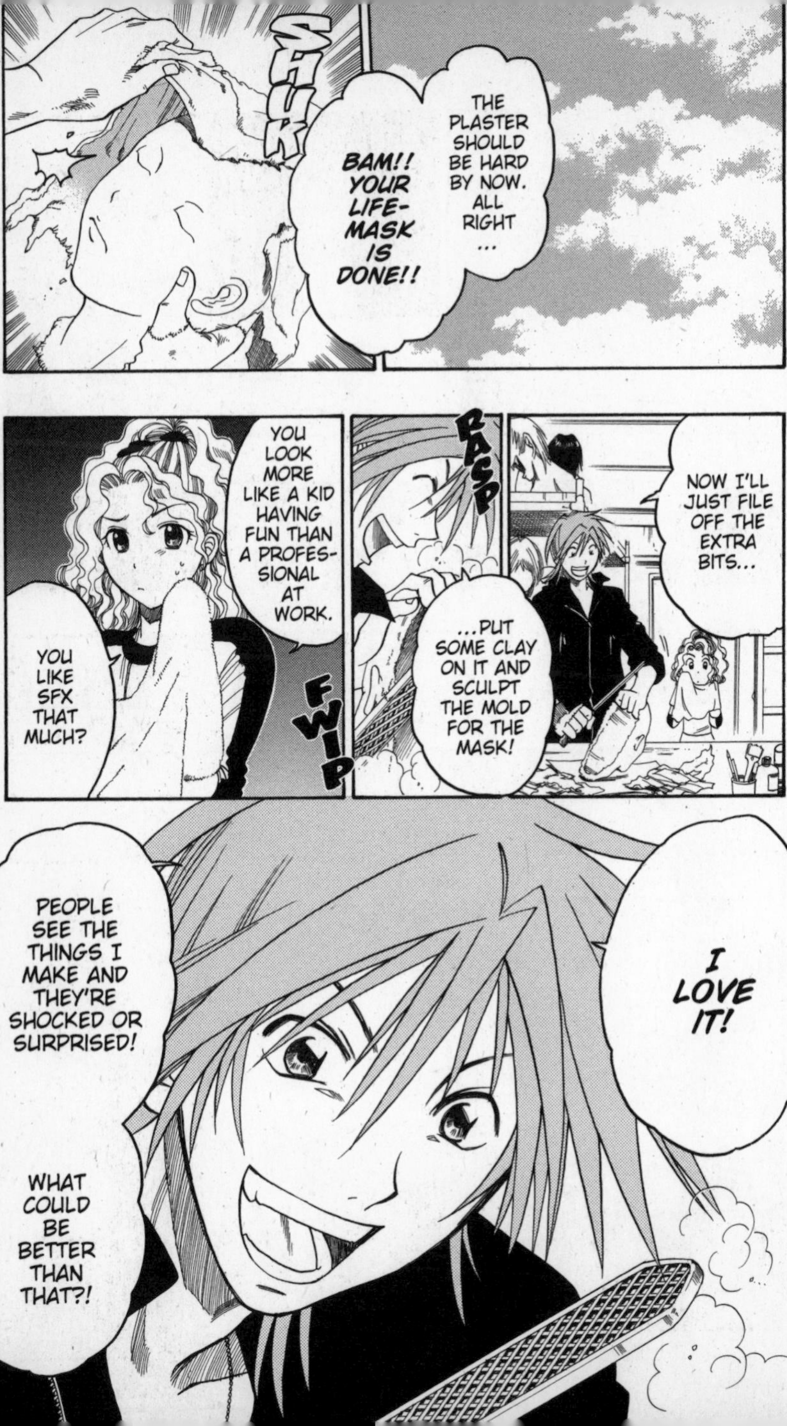
THE PLASTER SHOULD BE HARD BY NOW. ALL RIGHT...
BAM!! YOUR LIFE-MASK IS DONE!!
SHUK
NOW I'LL JUST FILE OFF THE EXTRA BITS...
RASP
...PUT SOME CLAY ON IT AND SCULPT THE MOLD FOR THE MASK!
YOU LOOK MORE LIKE A KID HAVING FUN THAN A PROFES-SIONAL AT WORK.
FWIP
YOU LIKE SFX THAT MUCH?
I LOVE IT!
PEOPLE SEE THE THINGS I MAKE AND THEY'RE SHOCKED OR SURPRISED!
WHAT COULD BE BETTER THAN THAT?!

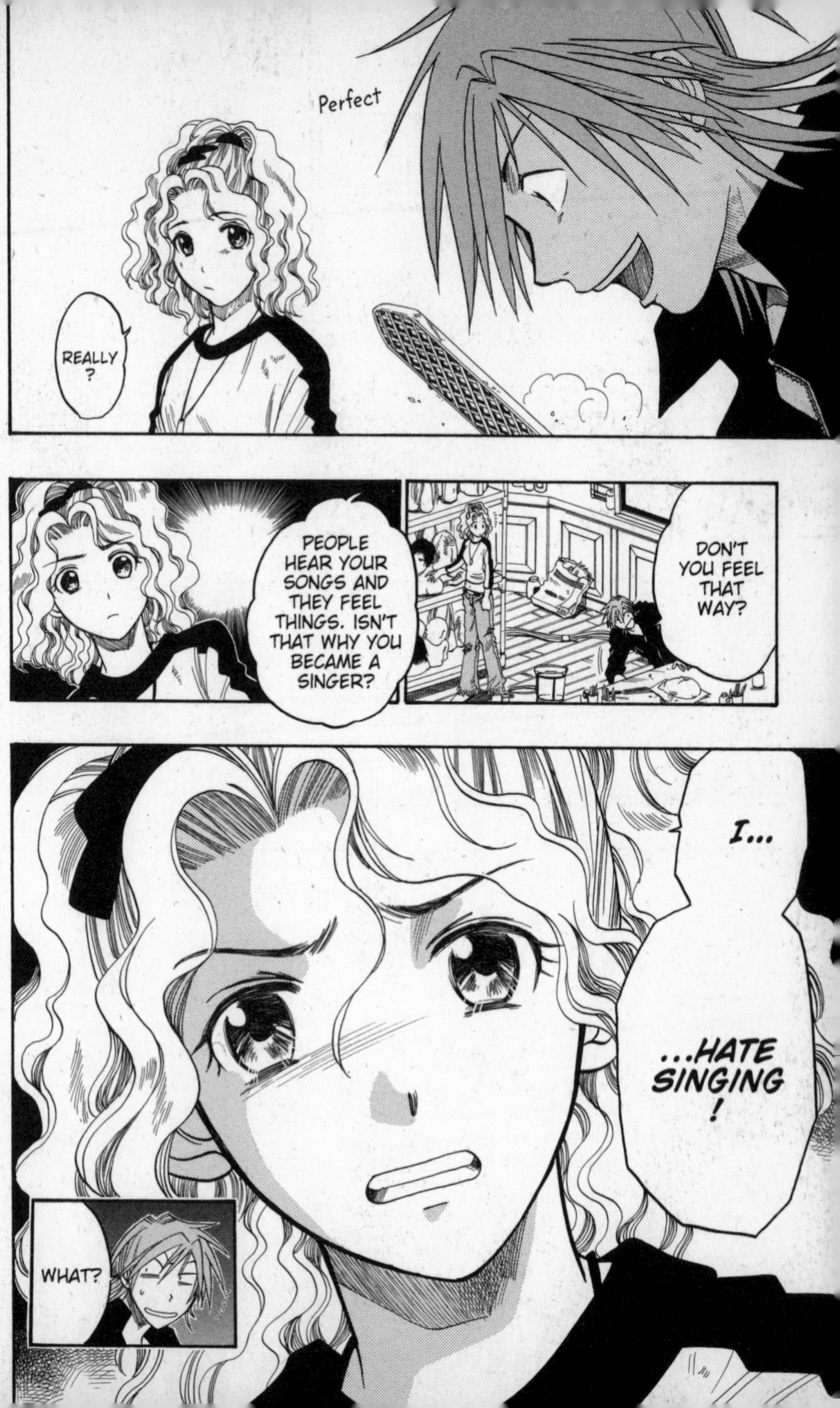
Perfect
REALLY?
DON'T YOU FEEL THAT WAY?
PEOPLE HEAR YOUR SONGS AND THEY FEEL THINGS. ISN'T THAT WHY YOU BECAME A SINGER?
I...
...HATE SINGING!
WHAT?

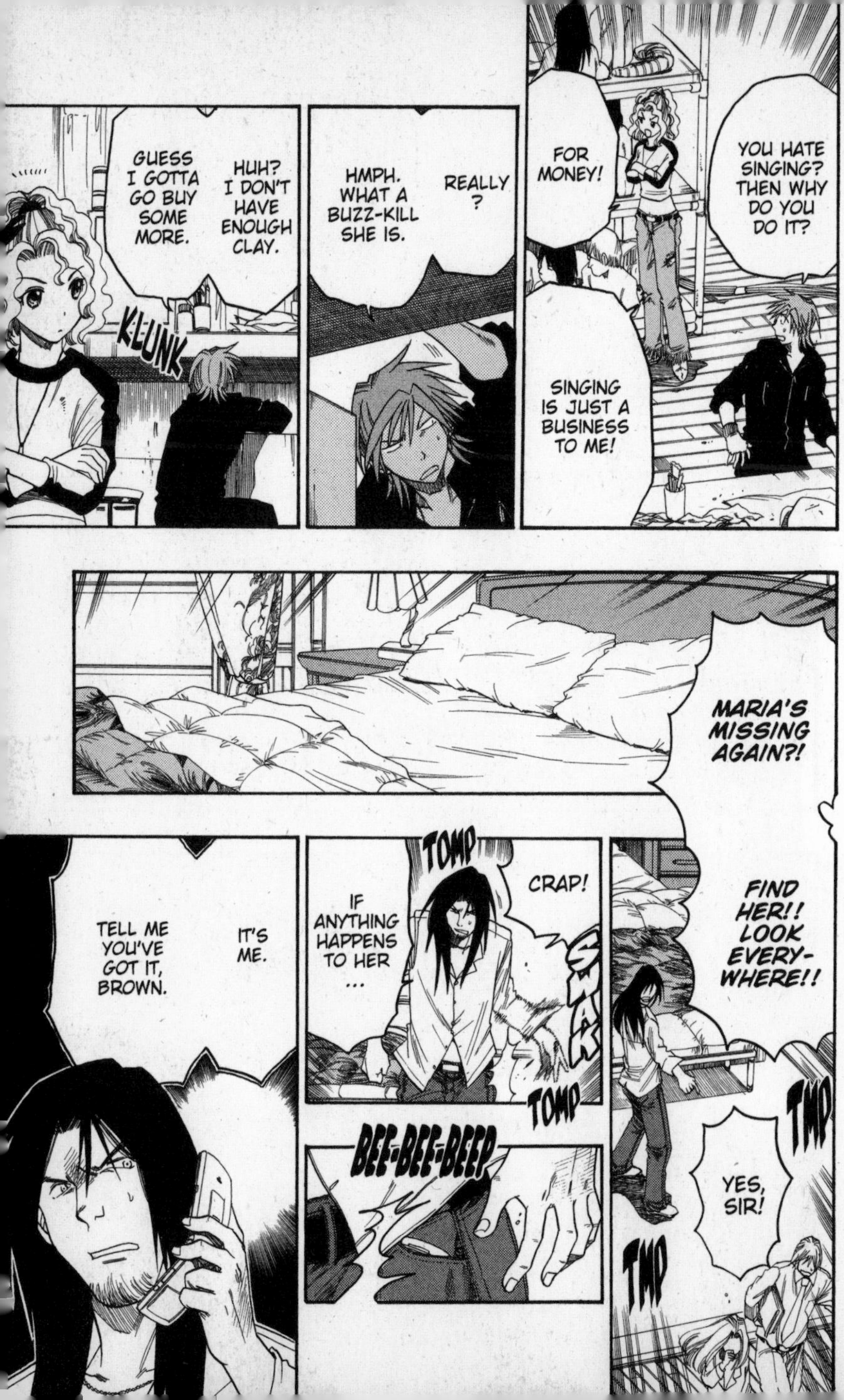
YOU HATE SINGING? THEN WHY DO YOU DO IT?
FOR MONEY!
SINGING IS JUST A BUSINESS TO ME!
REALLY?
HMPH. WHAT A BUZZ-KILL SHE IS.
HUH? I DON'T HAVE ENOUGH CLAY.
GUESS I GOTTA GO BUY SOME MORE.
KLUNK
MARIA'S MISSING AGAIN?!
FIND HER!! LOOK EVERY-WHERE!!
YES, SIR!
TMP
TMP
TOMP
CRAP!
IF ANYTHING HAPPENS TO HER ...
SWAK
TOMP
BEE-BEE-BEEP
IT'S ME.
TELL ME YOU'VE GOT IT, BROWN.

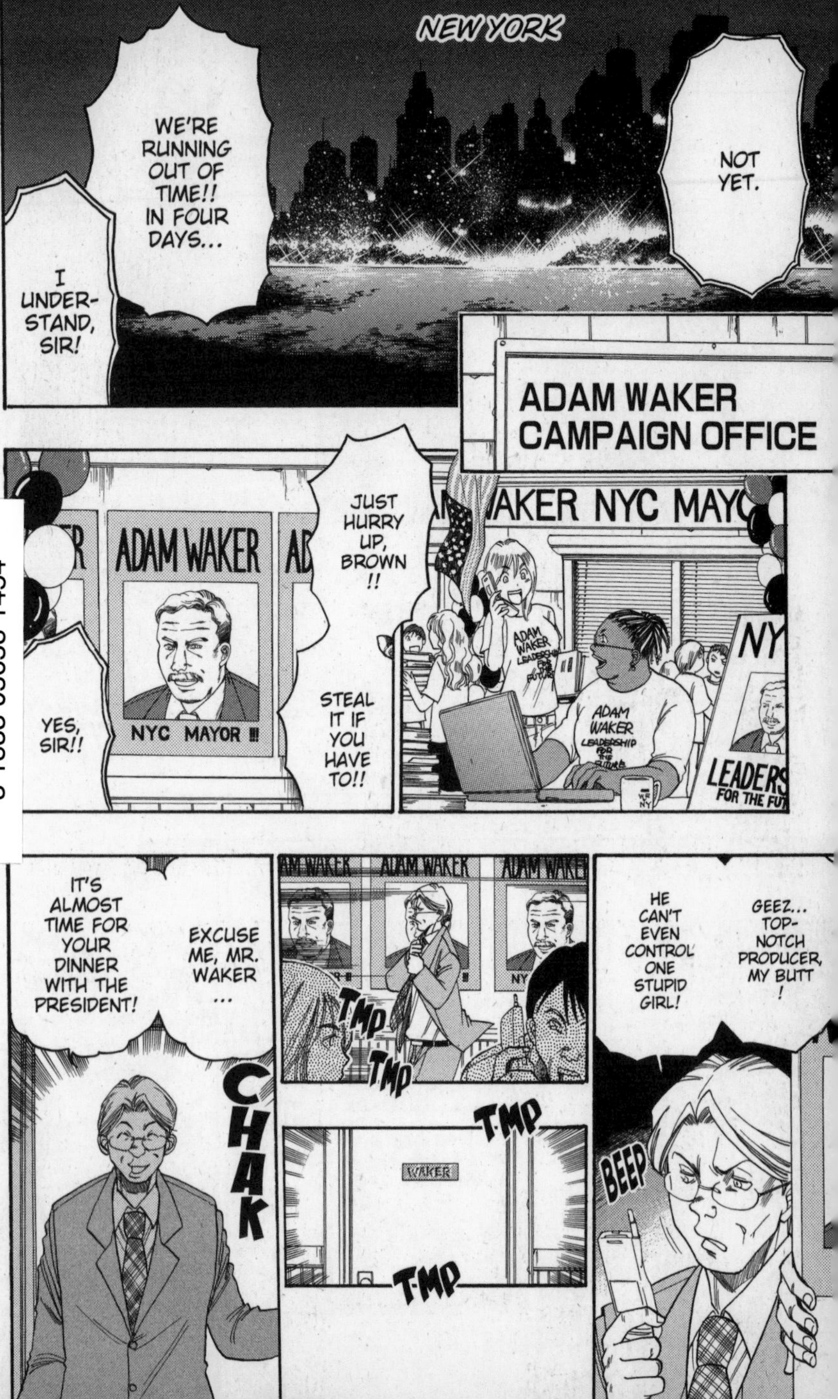
NEW YORK
NOT YET.
WE'RE RUNNING OUT OF TIME!! IN FOUR DAYS...
I UNDERSTAND, SIR!
ADAM WAKER CAMPAIGN OFFICE
ADAM WAKER NYC MAYO
ADAM WAKER LEADERSHIP FOR THE FUTURE
NY
LEADERS FOR THE FU
JUST HURRY UP, BROWN!!
STEAL IT IF YOU HAVE TO!!
ADAM WAKER
NYC MAYOR !!!
YES, SIR!!
GEEZ... TOP-NOTCH PRODUCER, MY BUTT!
HE CAN'T EVEN CONTROL ONE STUPID GIRL!
BEEP
ADAM WAKER
TMP
TMP
T-MP
WAKER
T-MP
EXCUSE ME, MR. WAKER...
IT'S ALMOST TIME FOR YOUR DINNER WITH THE PRESIDENT!
CHAK

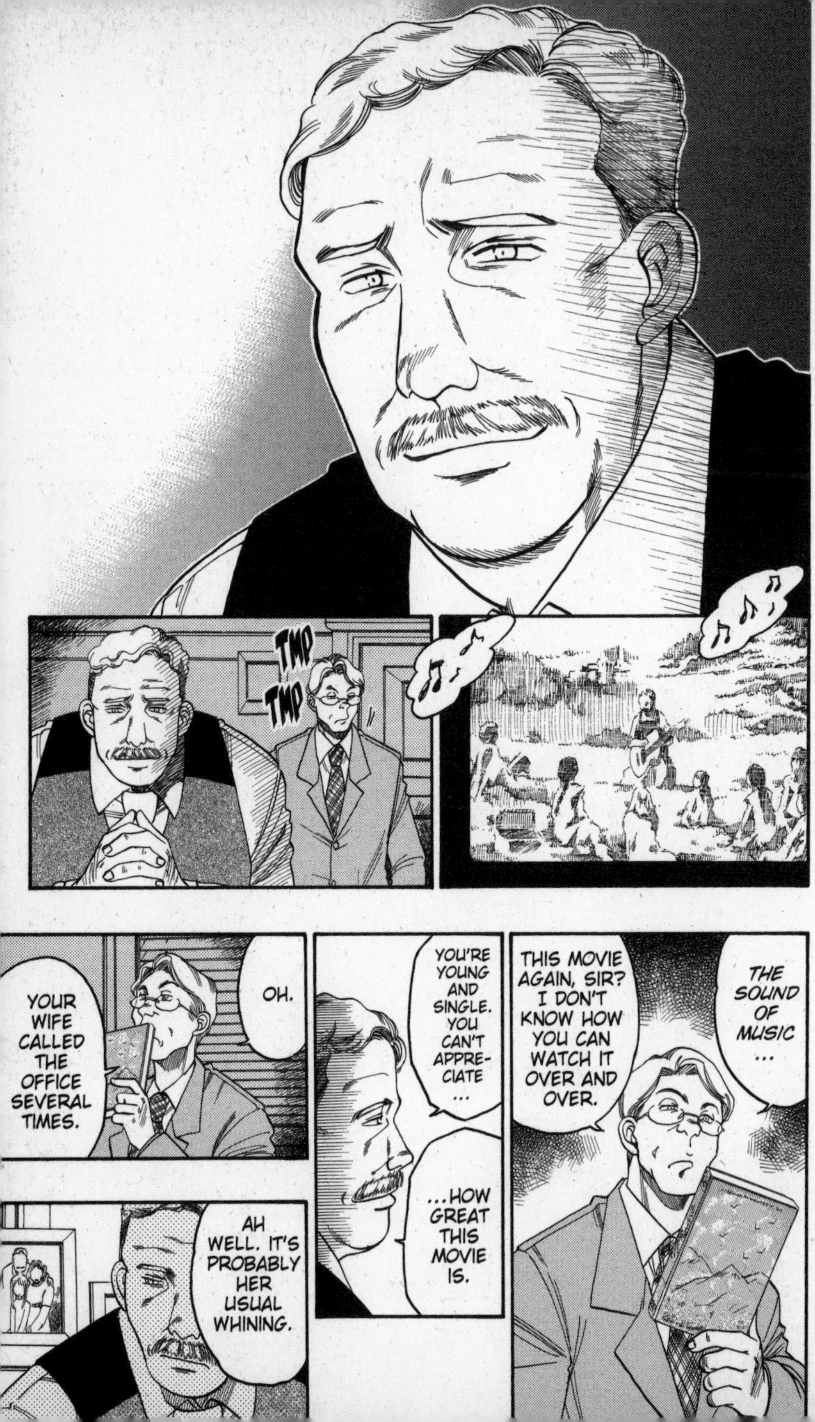
TMP
TMP
THE SOUND OF MUSIC...
THIS MOVIE AGAIN, SIR? I DON'T KNOW HOW YOU CAN WATCH IT OVER AND OVER.
YOU'RE YOUNG AND SINGLE. YOU CAN'T APPRECIATE...
...HOW GREAT THIS MOVIE IS.
OH.
YOUR WIFE CALLED THE OFFICE SEVERAL TIMES.
AH WELL. IT'S PROBABLY HER USUAL WHINING.

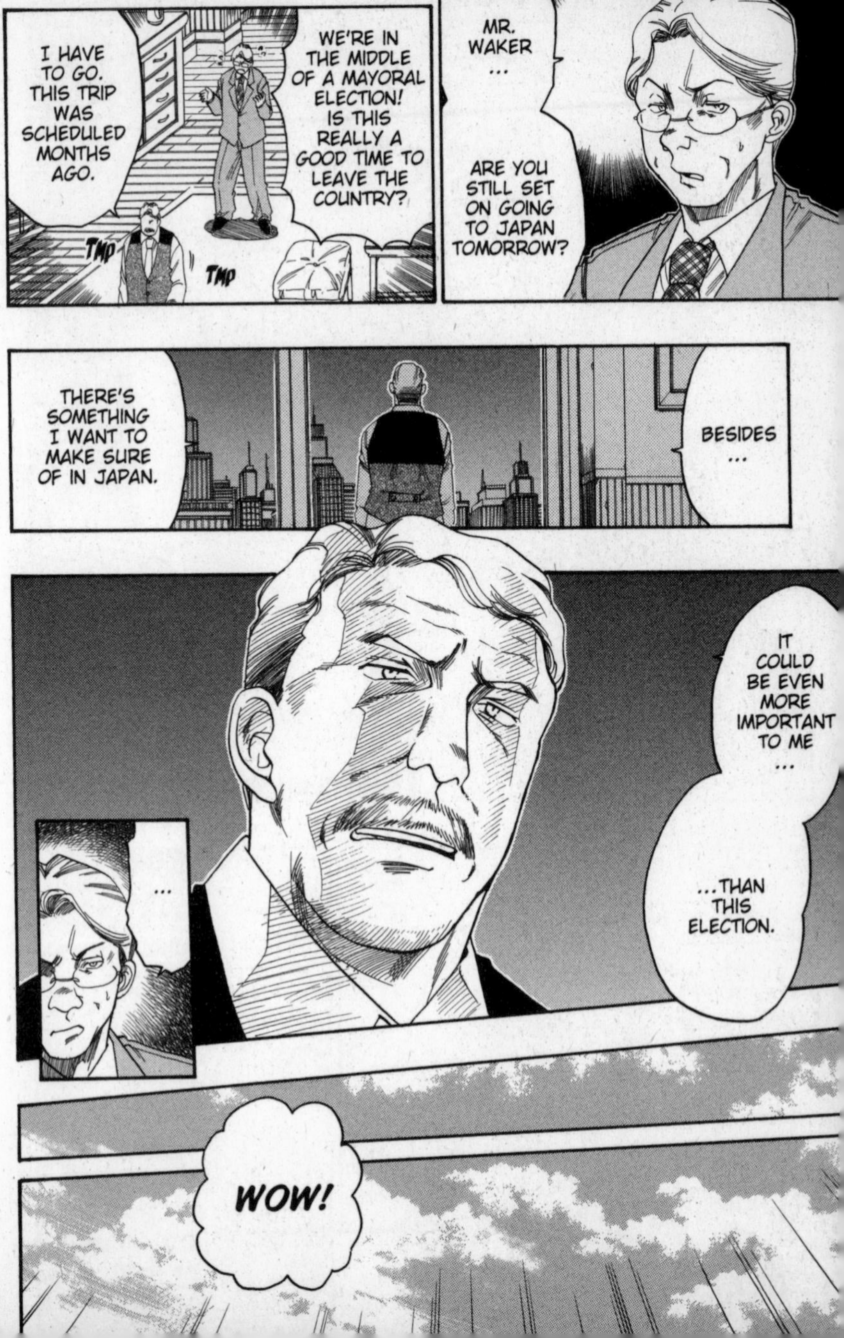
MR. WAKER ...
ARE YOU STILL SET ON GOING TO JAPAN TOMORROW?
WE'RE IN THE MIDDLE OF A MAYORAL ELECTION! IS THIS REALLY A GOOD TIME TO LEAVE THE COUNTRY?
I HAVE TO GO. THIS TRIP WAS SCHEDULED MONTHS AGO.
TMP
TMP
BESIDES ...
THERE'S SOMETHING I WANT TO MAKE SURE OF IN JAPAN.
IT COULD BE EVEN MORE IMPORTANT TO ME ...
...THAN THIS ELECTION.
...
WOW!

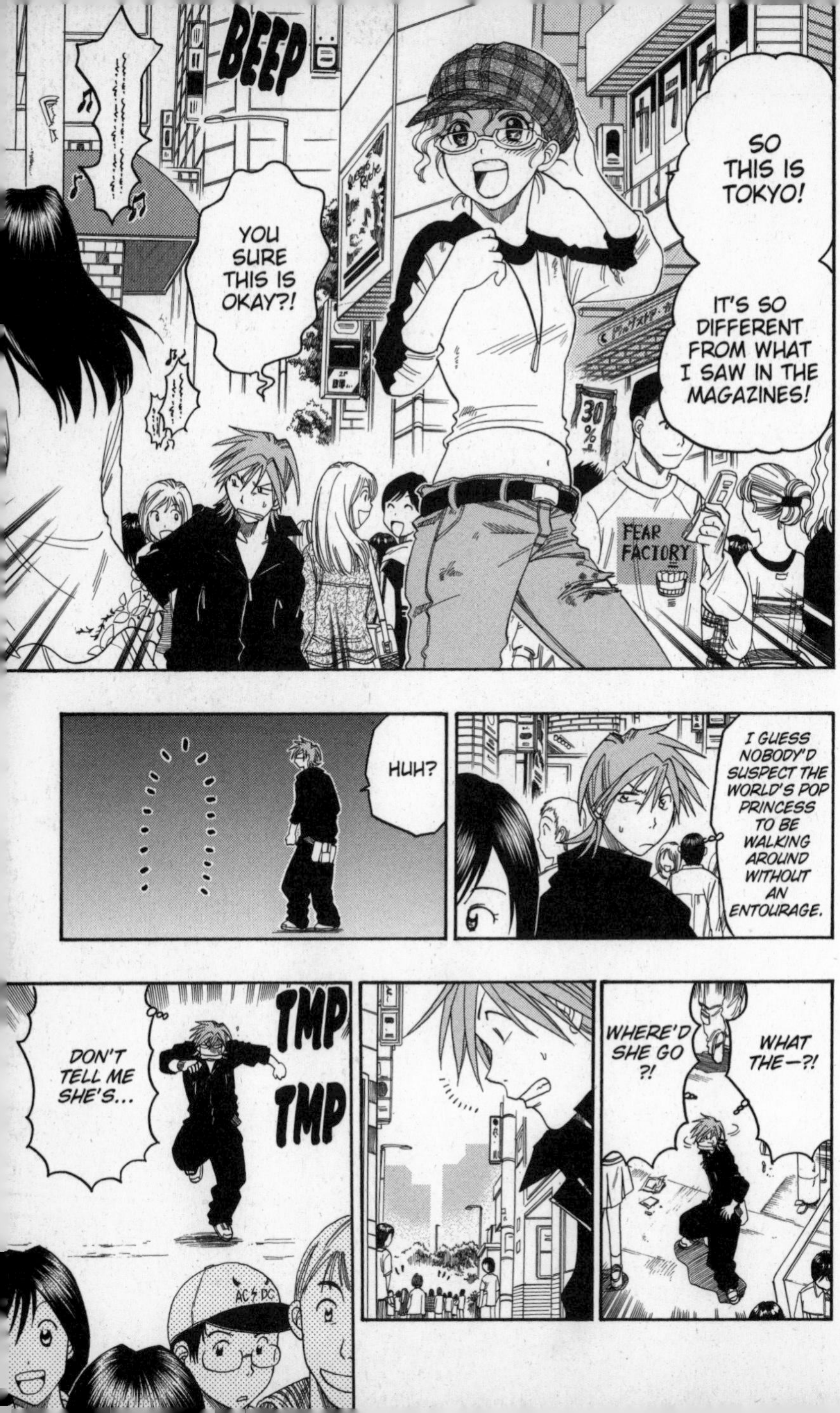
SO THIS IS TOKYO!
IT'S SO DIFFERENT FROM WHAT I SAW IN THE MAGAZINES!
BEEP
YOU SURE THIS IS OKAY?!
30%
FEAR FACTORY
I GUESS NOBODY'D SUSPECT THE WORLD'S POP PRINCESS TO BE WALKING AROUND WITHOUT AN ENTOURAGE.
HUH?
WHAT THE—?!
WHERE'D SHE GO ?!
TMP
TMP
DON'T TELL ME SHE'S...
AC/DC

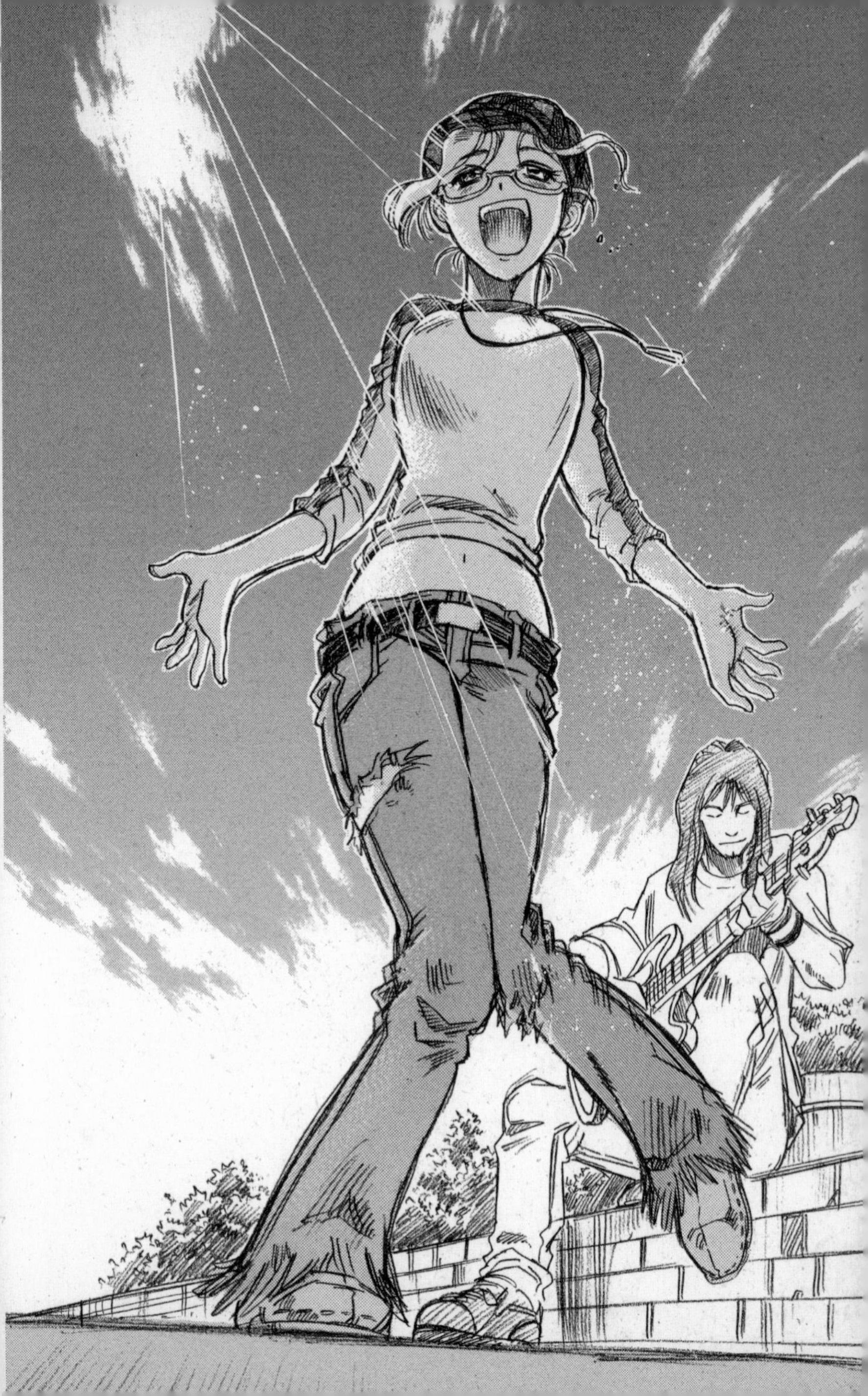

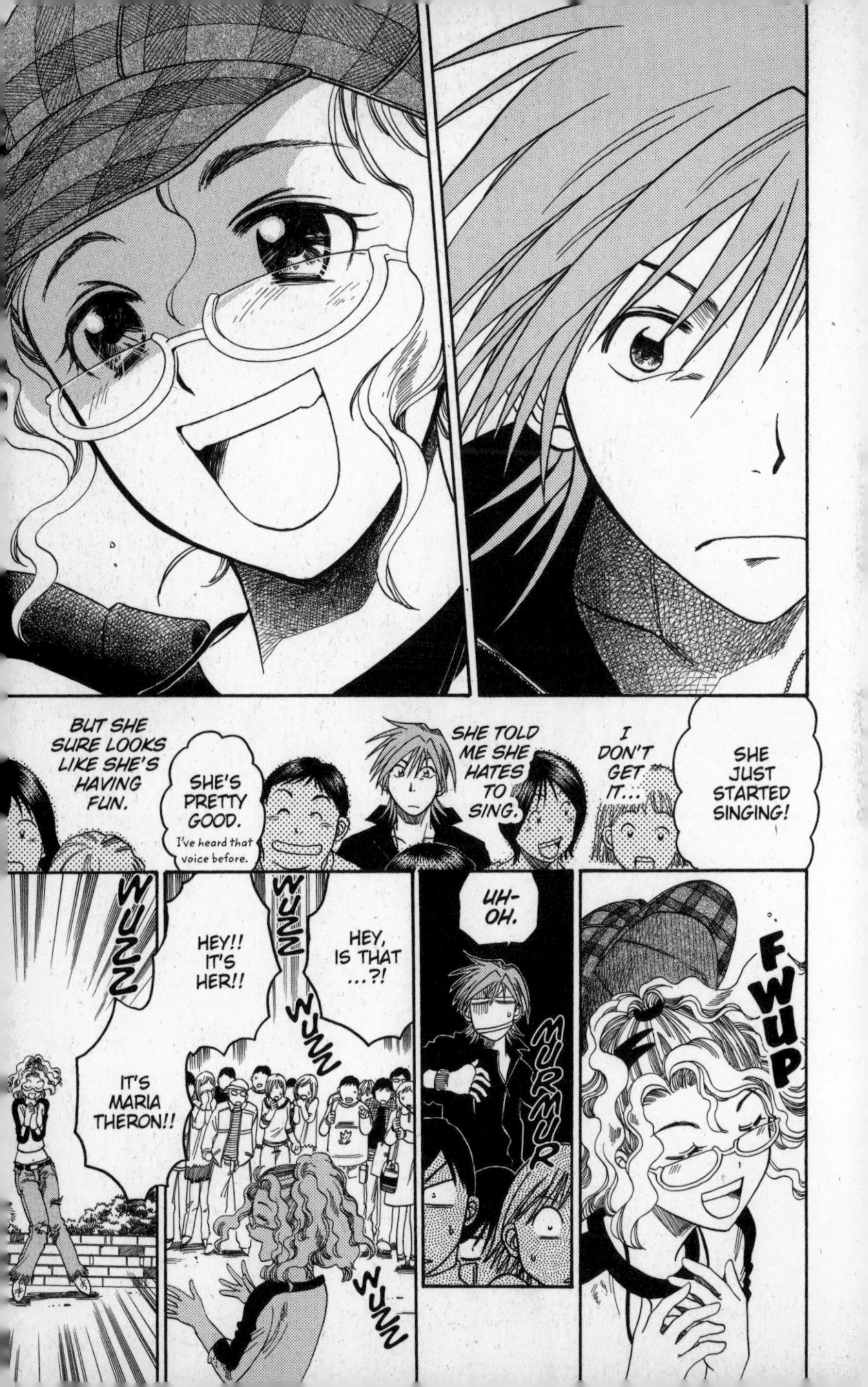
SHE JUST STARTED SINGING!
I DON'T GET IT...
SHE TOLD ME SHE HATES TO SING.
SHE'S PRETTY GOOD.
I've heard that voice before.
BUT SHE SURE LOOKS LIKE SHE'S HAVING FUN.
FWUP
UH-OH.
MURMUR
HEY, IS THAT ...?!
WUZZ
HEY!! IT'S HER!!
WUZZ
WJNN
IT'S MARIA THERON!!
WJNN

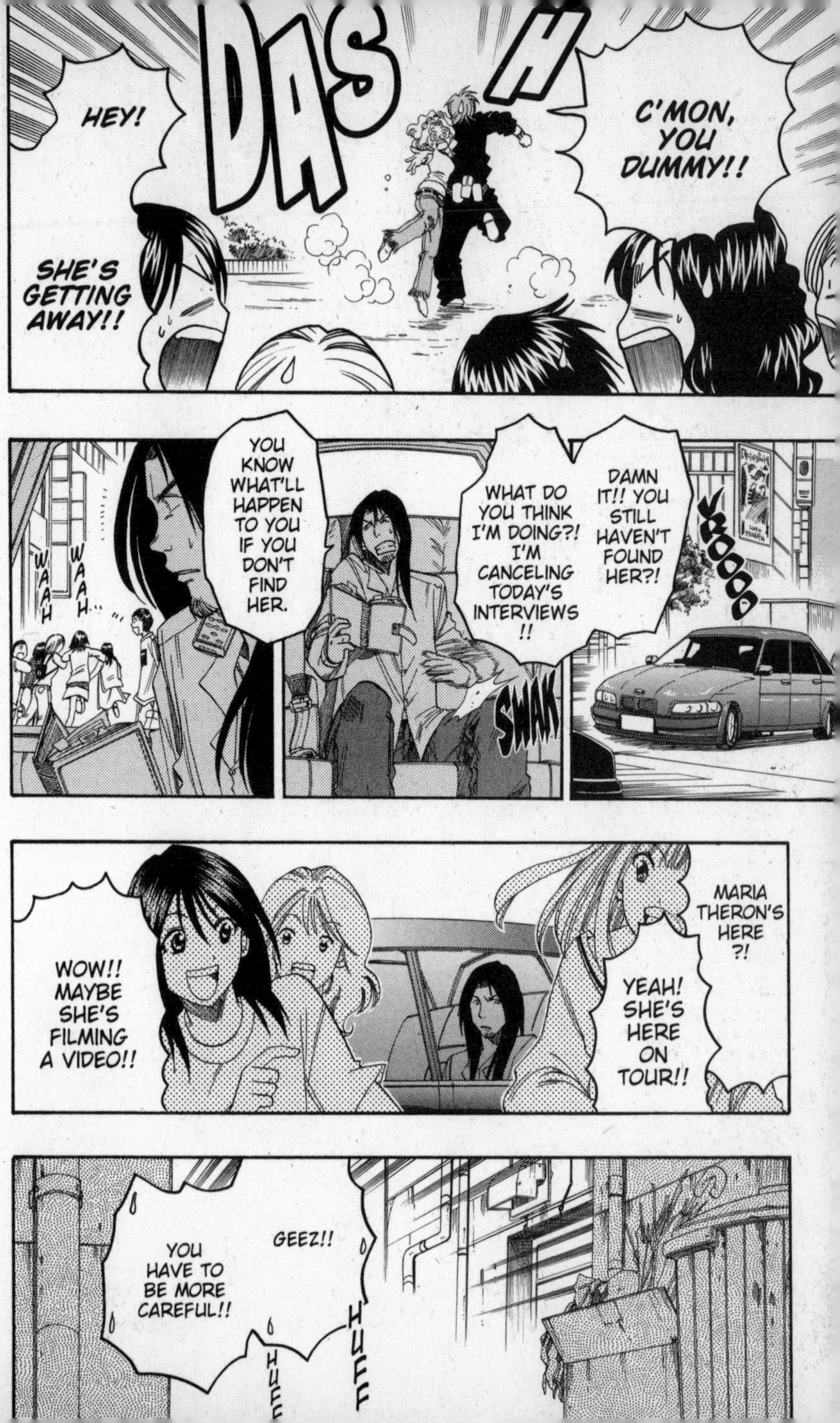
C'MON, YOU DUMMY!!
DASH
HEY!
SHE'S GETTING AWAY!!
VROOOOO
DAMN IT!! YOU STILL HAVEN'T FOUND HER?!
WHAT DO YOU THINK I'M DOING?! I'M CANCELING TODAY'S INTERVIEWS!!
SWAK
YOU KNOW WHAT'LL HAPPEN TO YOU IF YOU DON'T FIND HER.
WAAH
WAAH...
MARIA THERON'S HERE?!
YEAH! SHE'S HERE ON TOUR!!
WOW!! MAYBE SHE'S FILMING A VIDEO!!
HUFF
HUFF
GEEZ!!
YOU HAVE TO BE MORE CAREFUL!!

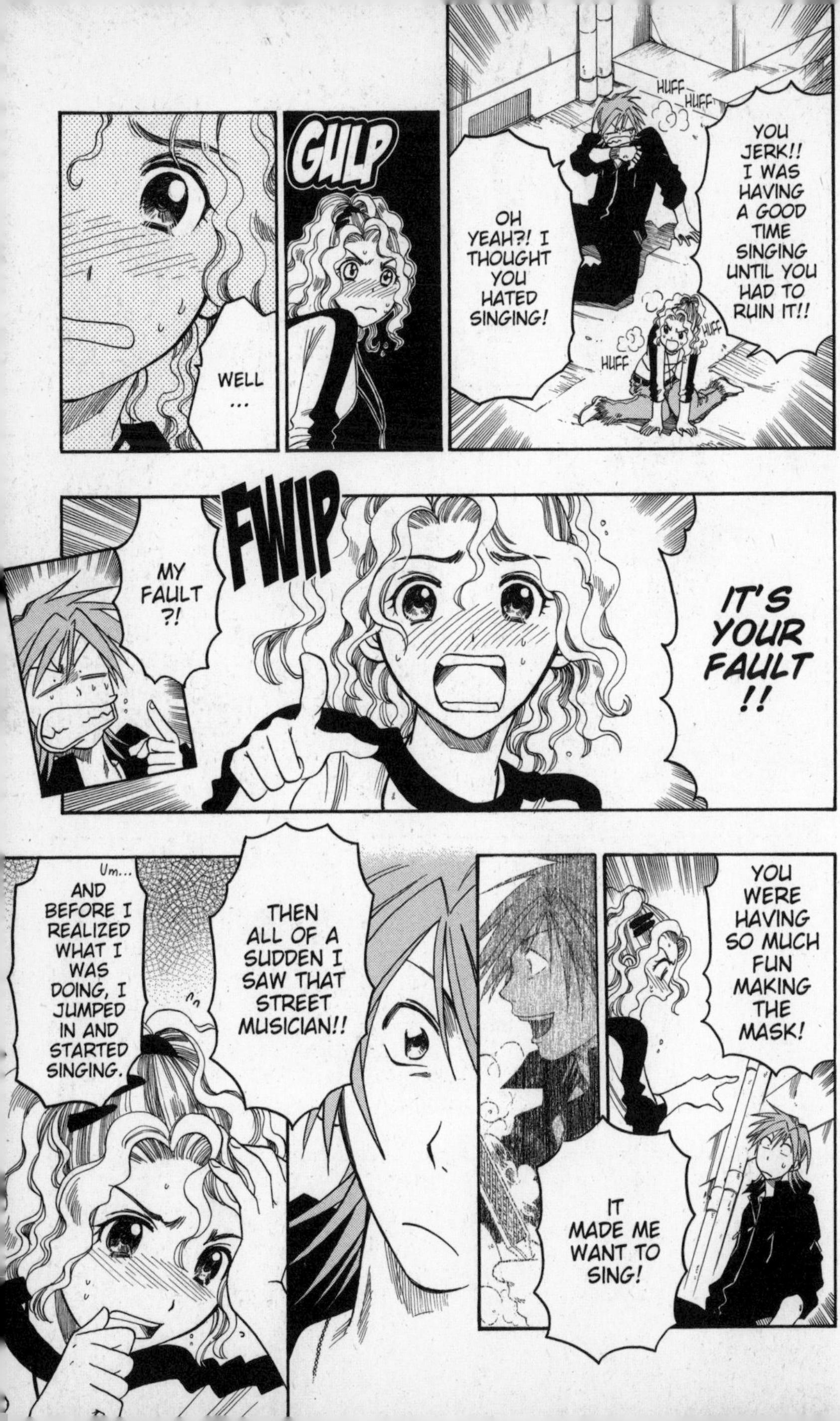
HUFF HUFF
YOU JERK!! I WAS HAVING A GOOD TIME SINGING UNTIL YOU HAD TO RUIN IT!!
OH YEAH?! I THOUGHT YOU HATED SINGING!
HUFF
HUFF
GULP
WELL ...
IT'S YOUR FAULT!!
FWIP
MY FAULT?!
YOU WERE HAVING SO MUCH FUN MAKING THE MASK!
IT MADE ME WANT TO SING!
THEN ALL OF A SUDDEN I SAW THAT STREET MUSICIAN!!
Um...
AND BEFORE I REALIZED WHAT I WAS DOING, I JUMPED IN AND STARTED SINGING.

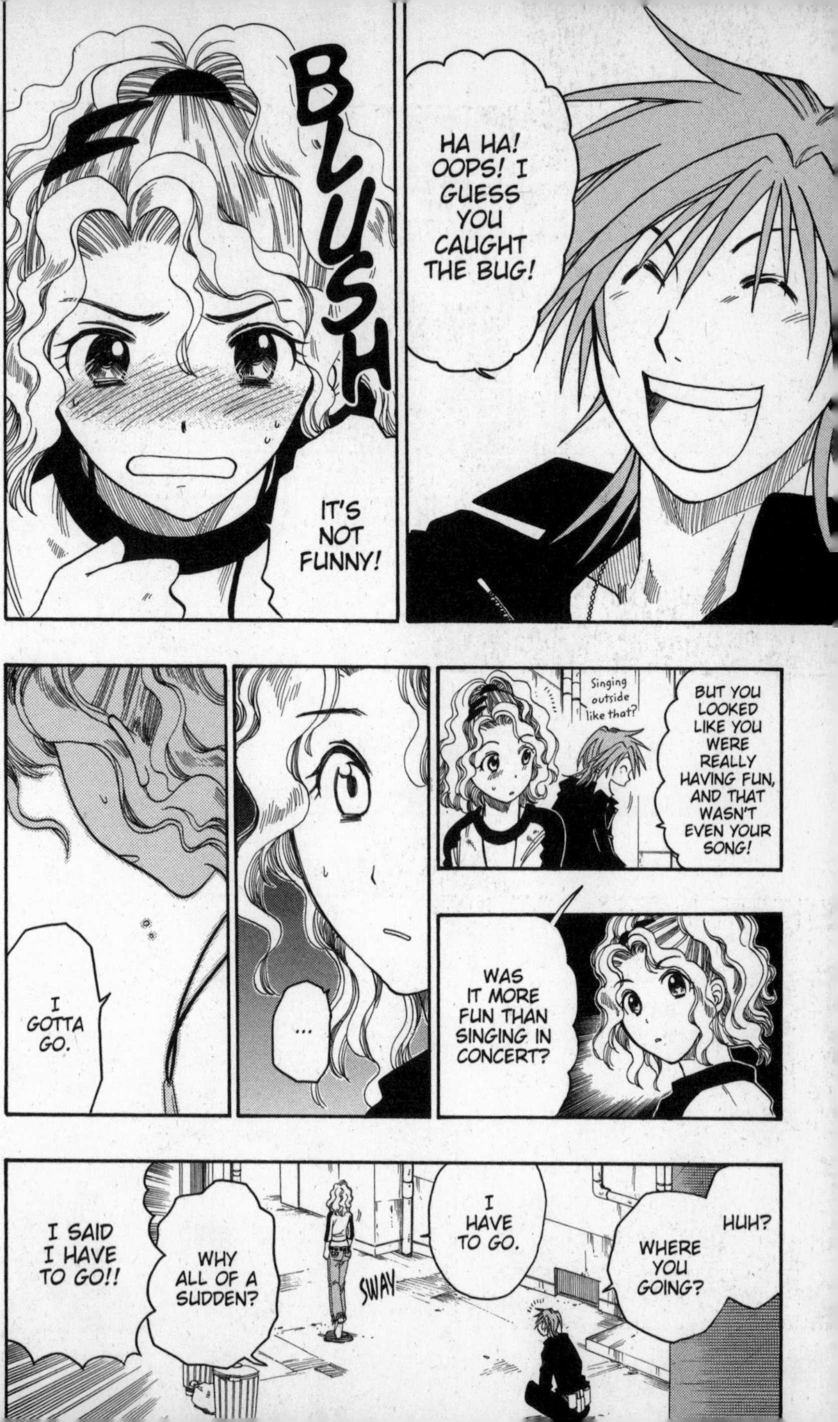
HA HA! OOPS! I GUESS YOU CAUGHT THE BUG!
BLUSH
IT'S NOT FUNNY!
BUT YOU LOOKED LIKE YOU WERE REALLY HAVING FUN, AND THAT WASN'T EVEN YOUR SONG!
Singing outside like that?
WAS IT MORE FUN THAN SINGING IN CONCERT?
...
I GOTTA GO.
HUH?
WHERE YOU GOING?
I HAVE TO GO.
SWAY
WHY ALL OF A SUDDEN?
I SAID I HAVE TO GO!!

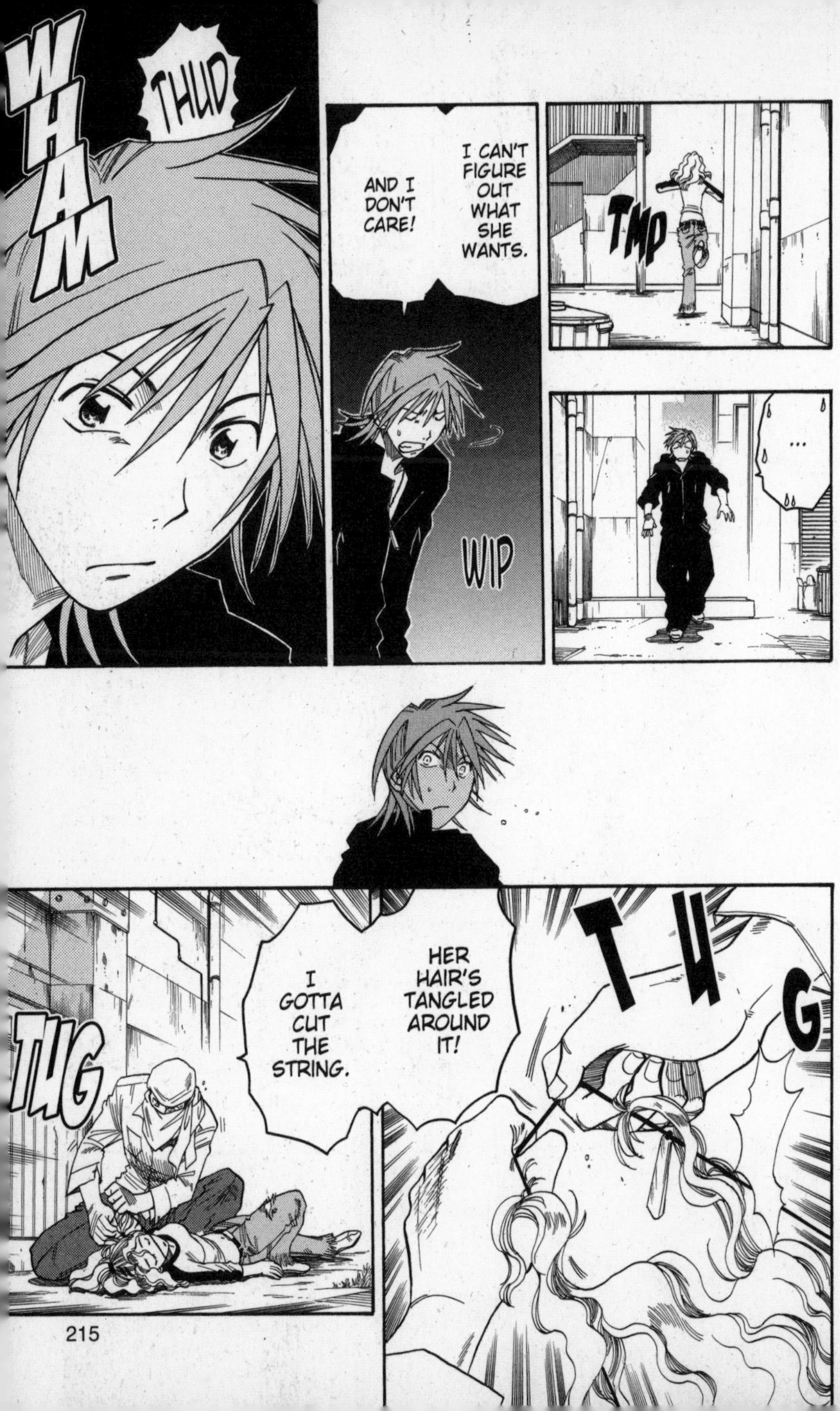
TMP
...
I CAN'T FIGURE OUT WHAT SHE WANTS.
AND I DON'T CARE!
WIP
THUD
WHAM
TUG
HER HAIR'S TANGLED AROUND IT!
I GOTTA CUT THE STRING.
TUG

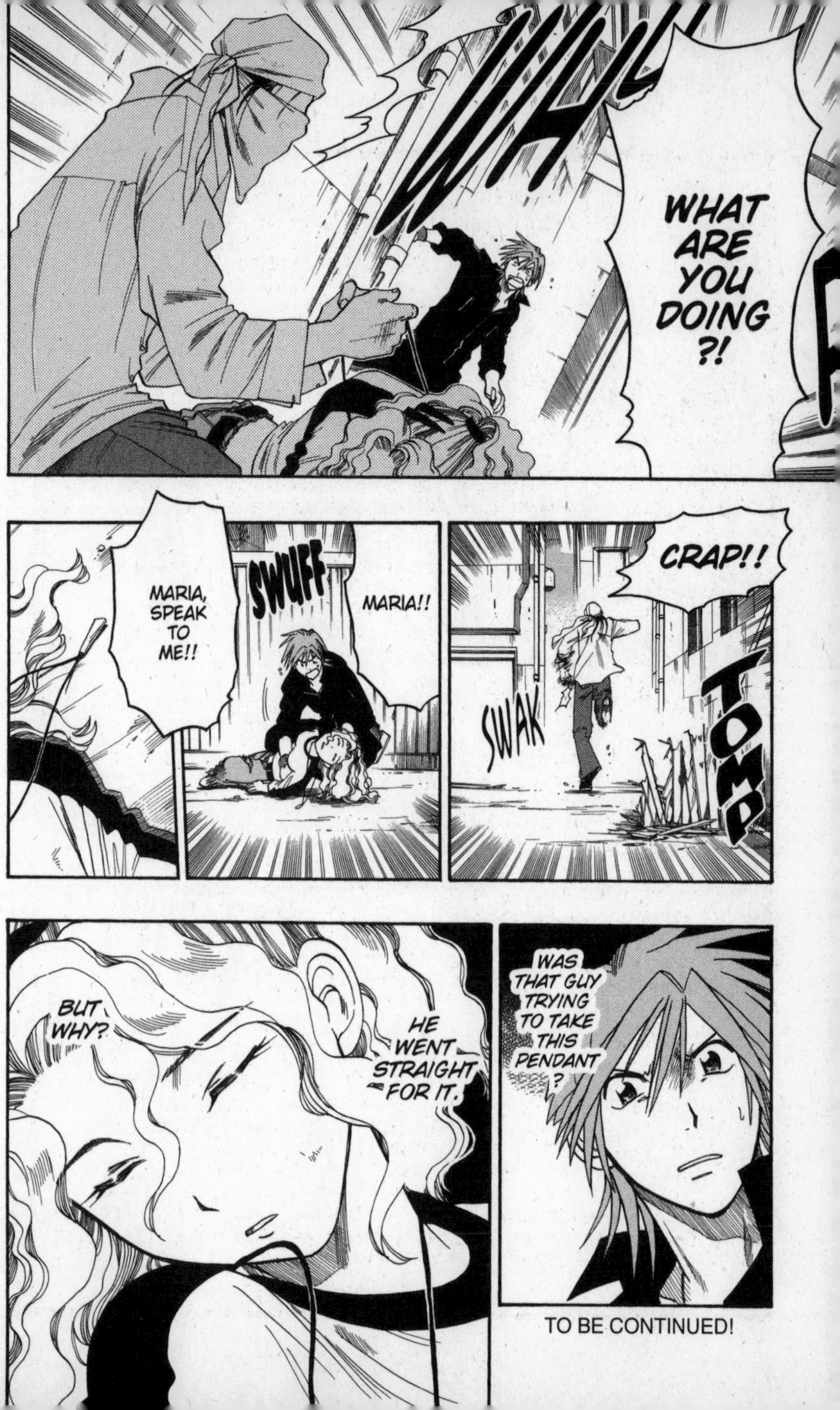
WHAT ARE YOU DOING?!
CRAP!!
TOMP
SWAK
MARIA!!
SWUFF
MARIA, SPEAK TO ME!!
WAS THAT GUY TRYING TO TAKE THIS PENDANT?
HE WENT STRAIGHT FOR IT.
BUT WHY?

TO BE CONTINUED!

THE MAKING OF GIMMICK!
Episode 5   By Youzaburou Kanari

"ALIEN PANIC"
THIS WAS ABOUT THE TIME WE VISITED RICK BAKER IN
AMERICA BEFORE THE COMIC WAS PUBLISHED. HE SHOWED
US ONE OF THE ACTUAL ANIMATRONIC CREATURES USED IN
MEN IN BLACK. IT LOOKED LIKE IT COULD COME TO LIFE
ANY SECOND, AND I THOUGHT ABOUT HOW MUCH FUN IT
WOULD BE IF WE COULD TAKE IT OUT INTO THE STREET. WE
COULD THROW THE WHOLE CITY INTO A PANIC WITH IT. AND
THAT WAS THE SEED OF THE STORY. ANTARO HAS BEEN AN
IMPORTANT MEMBER OF STUDIO GIMMICK EVER SINCE.

"THE MASK OF DEL FUEGO"
MR. KAZUHIRO TSUJI, WHO IS RICK BAKER'S RIGHT-HAND
MAN IN HOLLYWOOD, ACTUALLY MADE A MASK FOR A
FAMOUS HOLLYWOOD STAR TO WEAR WHEN HE WENT OUT.
HE SHOWED US A PHOTO OF THE ACTOR IN DISGUISE.
MR. TSUJI SAID HE'S AN ACTOR THAT EVERYBODY KNOWS,
BUT NO MATTER HOW CLOSELY I LOOKED, I COULDN'T
FIGURE IT OUT. MR. TSUJI, PLEASE TELL ME WHO HE IS!!

"OVER THE RAINBOW"
THIS WAS MONE SHIMAKURA'S DEBUT STORY! OUR EDITOR,
MR. I-TANI, WAS DEEPLY INVOLVED IN THE CREATION
OF THIS CHARACTER, FROM HER FACE TO THE SIZE OF
HER BREASTS AND HER HAIRSTYLE. SHE IS A REFLECTION
OF HIS TASTES.
WHILE WRITING THIS STORY, WE MET MR. FUCHIMU SHIMAKURA,
A MATTE PAINTER WHO'S REVERED IN THE INDUSTRY. THEY SAY
NO ONE IN JAPAN PAINTS BETTER CLOUDS THAN HE DOES.
HE MENTIONED SOME SCENES HE HAD PAINTED THE BACK-
GROUNDS FOR AND I WAS SPEECHLESS. I HAD NO IDEA I'D
BEEN LOOKING AT MATTE PAINTINGS IN THOSE MOVIES!

"TB CONFIDENTIAL"
NOBODY FIGURED IT OUT SO I'M GOING TO REVEAL IT MY-
SELF! THE TB IN THE TITLE STANDS FOR TOKYO BAY. THAT'S
RIGHT, THIS TITLE IS A PARODY OF **L.A. CONFIDENTIAL!**
THIS STORY HAD ITS ORIGIN WHEN I WAS SPEAKING TO
MR. USUI OF A.T. ILLUSION ABOUT CREATING SPECIAL
MAKEUP EFFECTS USING HOUSEHOLD ITEMS. HE TAUGHT US
A LOT OF OTHERS TRICKS THAT DIDN'T MAKE IT INTO THIS
STORY. BUT YOU'LL GET TO SEE THEM EVENTUALLY. THE
STORY TAKES PLACE ON A CRUISE SHIP. THE SENSE OF
CONFINEMENT AND OF BEING CUT OFF FROM THE REST OF
THE WORLD HEIGHTENS THE TENSION.

CONTINUED IN VOLUME 6

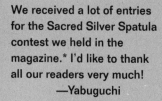

We received a lot of entries for the Sacred Silver Spatula contest we held in the magazine.* I'd like to thank all our readers very much!
—Yabuguchi

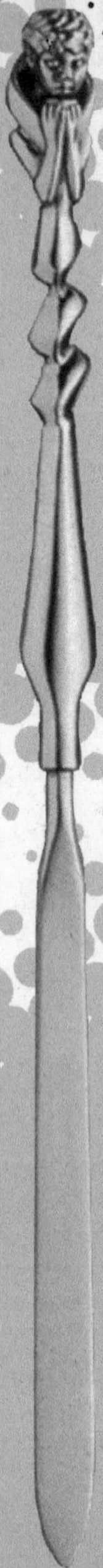

This silver spatula is actually being used by a professional. Who knows? Maybe it will show up in a bonus feature of a certain DVD!
—Kanari

* Contest was held in *Young Jump*, the Japanese manga magazine *Gimmick!* was serialized in.

GIMMICK!
Vol. 5

Story by Youzaburou Kanari
Art by Kuroko Yabuguchi

English Adaptation/Lance Caselman
Translation/Joe Yamazaki
Touch-up Art & Lettering/Rina Mapa
Design/Amy Martin
Editor/Megan Bates

Editor in Chief, Books/Alvin Lu
Editor in Chief, Magazines/Marc Weidenbaum
VP, Publishing Licensing/Rika Inouye
VP, Sales & Product Marketing/Gonzalo Ferreyra
VP, Creative/Linda Espinosa
Publisher/Hyoe Narita

Printed in the U.S.A.

Published by VIZ Media, LLC
P.O. Box 77010
San Francisco, CA 94107

10 9 8 7 6 5 4 3 2 1
First printing, February 2009

www.viz.com

store.viz.com

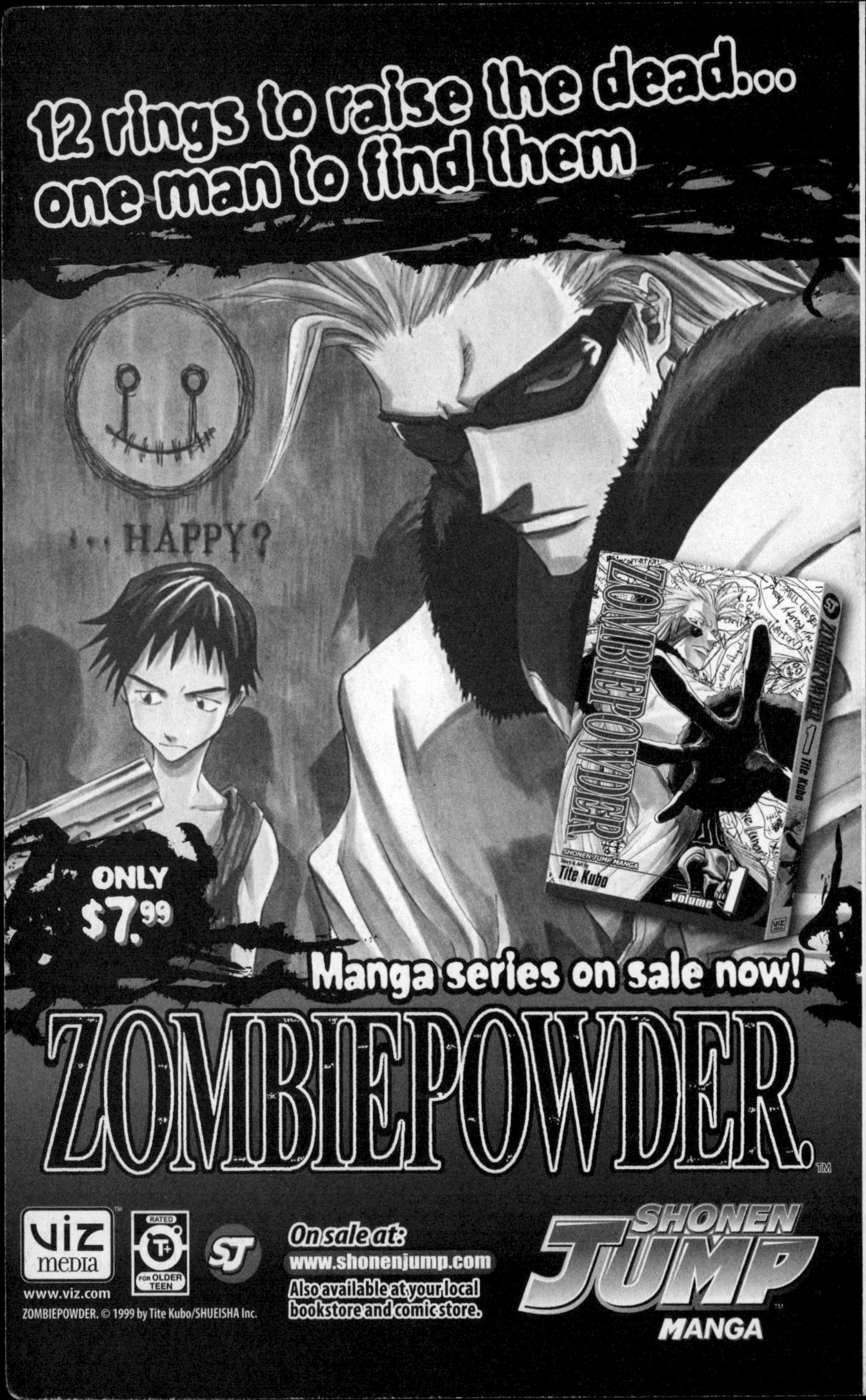
12 rings to raise the dead...
one man to find them
...HAPPY?
ONLY $7.99
Manga series on sale now!
ZOMBIEPOWDER.™
viz media
www.viz.com
ZOMBIEPOWDER. © 1999 by Tite Kubo/SHUEISHA Inc.
RATED T+ FOR OLDER TEEN
On sale at:
www.shonenjump.com
Also available at your local bookstore and comic store.
SHONEN JUMP MANGA

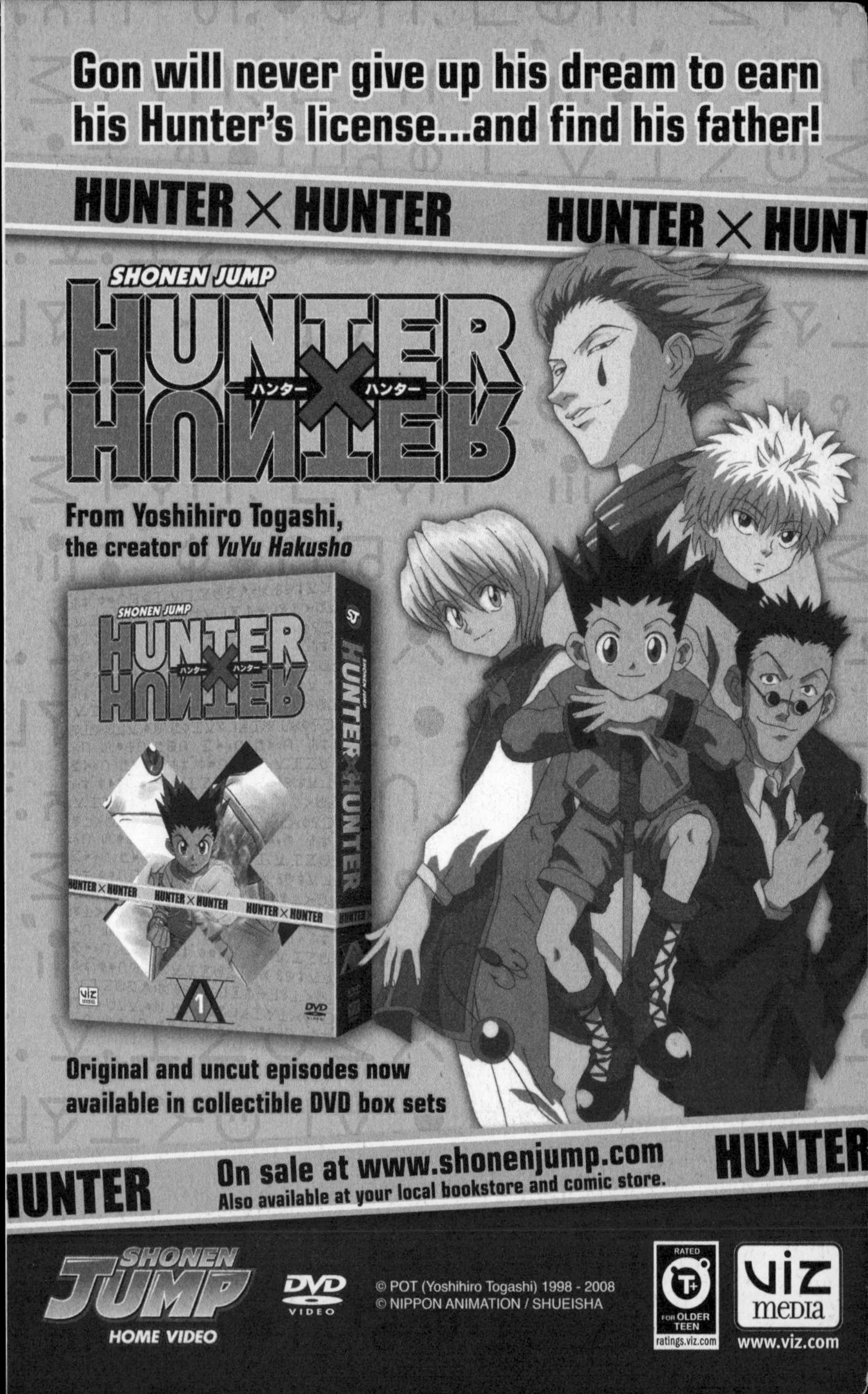
Gon will never give up his dream to earn his Hunter's license...and find his father!
HUNTER × HUNTER
HUNTER × HUNT
SHONEN JUMP
HUNTER × HUNTER
ハンター ハンター
From Yoshihiro Togashi, the creator of YuYu Hakusho
SHONEN JUMP
HUNTER × HUNTER
HUNTER × HUNTER
1
DVD
Original and uncut episodes now available in collectible DVD box sets
HUNTER
On sale at www.shonenjump.com
Also available at your local bookstore and comic store.
HUNTER
SHONEN JUMP HOME VIDEO
DVD VIDEO
© POT (Yoshihiro Togashi) 1998 - 2008
© NIPPON ANIMATION / SHUEISHA
RATED T+ FOR OLDER TEEN
ratings.viz.com
viz media
www.viz.com

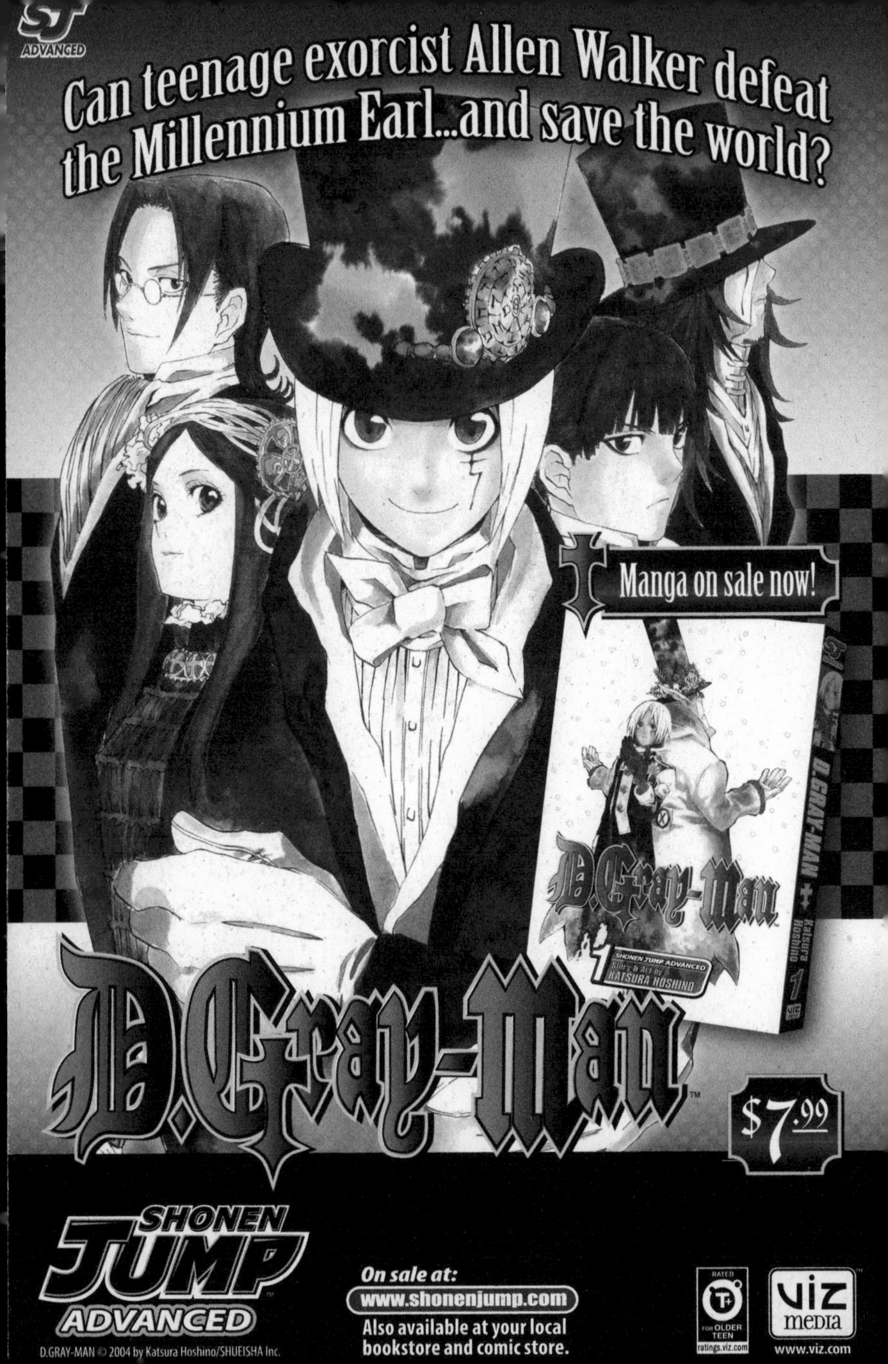
SJ ADVANCED
Can teenage exorcist Allen Walker defeat the Millennium Earl...and save the world?
Manga on sale now!
D.Gray-man
1
SHONEN JUMP ADVANCED
Story & Art by KATSURA HOSHINO
D.Gray-man™
$7.99
SHONEN JUMP ADVANCED
On sale at:
www.shonenjump.com
Also available at your local bookstore and comic store.
D.GRAY-MAN © 2004 by Katsura Hoshino/SHUEISHA Inc.
RATED T+ FOR OLDER TEEN
ratings.viz.com
VIZ media
www.viz.com